THE
GREAT AWAKENINGS
AND THE
RESTORATION MOVEMENT

The Bible Study Textbook Series

NEW TESTAMENT

The Bible Study New Testament Ed. By Rhoderick Ice	**The Gospel of Matthew** In Four Volumes By Harold Fowler (Vol. IV not yet available)	**The Gospel of Mark** By B. W. Johnson and Don DeWelt
The Gospel of Luke By T. R. Applebury	**The Gospel of John** By Paul T. Butler	**Acts Made Actual** By Don DeWelt
Romans Realized By Don DeWelt	**Studies in Corinthians** By T. R. Applebury	**Guidance From Galatians** By Don Earl Boatman
The Glorious Church (Ephesians) By Wilbur Fields	**Philippians - Colossians Philemon** By Wilbur Fields	**Thinking Through Thessalonians** By Wilbur Fields
Paul's Letters To Timothy & Titus By Don DeWelt	**Helps From Hebrews** By Don Earl Boatman	**James & Jude** By Don Fream
Letters From Peter By Bruce Oberst	**Hereby We Know (I-II-III John)** By Clinton Gill	**The Seer, The Saviour, and The Saved (Revelation)** By James Strauss

OLD TESTAMENT

O.T. History By William Smith and Wilbur Fields	**Genesis** In Four Volumes By C. C. Crawford	**Exploring Exodus** By Wilbur Fields	**Leviticus** By Don DeWelt
Numbers By Brant Lee Doty	**Deuteronomy** By Bruce Oberst	**Joshua - Judges Ruth** By W. W. Winter	**I & II Samuel** By W. W. Winter
I & II Kings By James E. Smith	**I & II Chronicles** By Robert E. Black	**Ezra, Nehemiah & Esther** By Ruben Ratzlaff & Paul T. Butler	**The Shattering of Silence (Job)** By James Strauss
Psalms In Two Volumes By J. B. Rotherham	**Proverbs** By Donald Hunt	**Ecclesiastes and Song of Solomon** — By R. J. Kidwell and Don DeWelt	
Isaiah In Three Volumes By Paul T. Butler	**Jeremiah and Lamentations** By James E. Smith	**Ezekiel** By James E. Smith	
Daniel By Paul T. Butler	**Hosea - Joel - Amos Obadiah - Jonah** By Paul T. Butler	**Micah - Nahum - Habakkuk Zephaniah - Haggai - Zechariah Malachi** — By Clinton Gill	

SPECIAL STUDIES

The Church In The Bible By Don DeWelt	**The Eternal Spirit** By C. C. Crawford	**World & Literature of the Old Testament** Ed. By John Willis	**Survey Course In Christian Doctrine** Two Bks. of Four Vols. By C. C. Crawford
New Testament History — Acts By Gareth Reese	**Learning From Jesus** By Seth Wilson	**You Can Understand The Bible** By Grayson H. Ensign	

THE GREAT AWAKENINGS AND THE RESTORATION MOVEMENT

A Study
of the 1790 - 1860 History of the Awakenings and
their impact upon the formation and early
development and growth of the Christian
Churches-Churches of Christ.

by

Max Ward Randall

College Press Publishing Company, Joplin, Missouri

iii

Library of Congress Catalog Card Number: 82-74537
International Standard Book Number: 0-89900-229-3

To his three sons, all ministers of the Lord Jesus Christ, the author is most grateful. For years, as often as they were with him, the conversation has focused on the sovereignty of God, upon His grace, love and mercy, upon the lostness of man without God, and his need for a Savior. Their conversations often held their attention on the merciful way God has worked through His servants and through His Church across the world, from the beginning until now.

Most important of all, for her patience, understanding, encouragement and love, the author wishes to thank his wife, Gladys. Across six continents and traversing three oceans, involving years of unsettlement, living in dozens of hotels and traveling tens of thousands of miles, she has never complained, and without her this volume would not have happened.

Introductions

Max Ward Randall — I first heard his name when I was a young college student on the West Coast. In those days he was a daring pioneer missionary opening up a section of dark Africa to the Gospel, an inspired lonely hunter whose quarry was souls, a dare-devil pilot whose adventures and near-misses were legendary. In all his escapades, he took orders only from the Lord he served.

Through the years, Dr. Randall's careers have changed but his influence has steadily grown. He returned from Africa to reflect and research; he was not satisfied with what he had accomplished in Zambia nor was he content with the practices of modern missions in general. There must be a better way. His studies in church growth led to his appointment as a professor of missions and church growth, a position which enabled him to multiply his effectiveness. Whatever his job, he has never abandoned his true calling in missions as an inspired gadfly. He pesters complacent Christians, he torments Pharisaical religious leaders, he marshalls every resource in his power to prod a reluctant Church into action. Yet all along he has retained the respect and even affection of the very ones whose consciences he has pricked.

Dr. Randall is a rare individual who has grown better as he has grown older. He no longer moves with the incredible energy that once was his trademark; his arthritis has forced him to slow down. No, I didn't say that right. It has slowed his body, but the man keeps forging ahead. What he can no longer do himself, he inspires and teaches others to do. Restricted by his reluctant physique, he relies more than ever on the power of prayer and the dynamic of the Holy Spirit. Even in repose his restless spirit groans over the persons who remain outside the saving embrace of his Lord.

I haven't asked him, but I suspect the same drive that propelled him to Africa to rescue the perishing has driven him to research and write *The Great Awakenings and the Restoration Movement.* Dissatisfied with the minimal accomplishments of the Christian Churches and Churches of Christ in the twentieth century, Randall has turned back to the expansive years of this Movement to find out what was different then. Why are today's churches, churches that claim the same doctrine and principles as their nineteenth century precursors, not experiencing growth? Why do so many of today's leaders seem content with holding their own? Why has The Restoration Movement sometimes been called 'a movement without movement'?

It was not always so. The nineteenth century Reformation enjoyed a heady success, the statistics of which Randall carefully records in this volume. The Reform benefited from the two Great Awakenings which turned young America back to God in an amazing way. As a unity effort, the Reform did not withdraw from but rather participated in the Awakenings. Randall traces this involvement so intently that the reader can almost hear him asking, Why is this not happening in our time? Have we become too rationalistic? Have we proscribed the activity of the Holy Spirit to the point of denying His independence of our doctrines and practices? Have we isolated ourselves from evangelical Christianity, preferring to go it alone rather than have fellowship with others whose experience in the Spirit or whose definition of revival differs from ours? If the Spirit were to inspire another Great Awakening today, would we attend?

Randall strains to point out that the early leaders of the movement were products of their time, just as we are.

Further, they gladly let themselves be influenced by Christian leaders of stature and godliness among Christian denominations. They did not hesitate to borrow from others when they spoke the truth. I especially appreciate the author's regard for the diversity that has characterized the Restoration Movement from the beginning. Because Alexander Campbell's strong intellect and prolific pen quickly propelled him into leadership, some latter-day restorationists think of him as the only voice of the nineteenth century movement. We still hear of Campbellites, for example, but never, or hardly ever, does anyone speak of Stoneites. Yet Stone and his followers, who differed frequently and sometimes vigorously with Campbell, made major contributions to the Reform effort.

Unfortunately, some disciples of Campbell have adopted not only his theological stance but also his less attractive dogmatism. Unity would have been impossible without Stone's humility and generosity. We can praise God that from the beginning there has been room for Campbell *and* Stone, for the person whose faith must be intellectually consistent and for the one who rather prefers to be "led by the Spirit." Even in names there has always been diversity, with some Reformers being called "disciples" and others desiring to be "Christians."

For a movement whose members have protested that they are "Christians only and not the only Christians," *The Great Awakenings and the Restoration Movement* places the nineteenth century reformation right where it belongs, in the heart of a wider Christward movement on the American frontier. Never intended as a separatist effort, the Movement sought to call all persons to oneness in the Lord Jesus Christ. Its genius could only be expressed as its devotees pushed themselves forward into the heart of divided Christendom. So Stone gave himself fully to the revivals of Kentucky and Campbell spent himself in debates with leaders of the denominational world—and did not even back away from an encounter with the famous atheist Robert Owens, and Scott preached tirelessly to frontiersmen of every persuasion.

In those days, the Movement moved. Its priorities were clear: the unity of all Christians and the salvation of all sinners. Using the principle of restoring the church of Christ as revealed in the scriptures as a means to accomplish unity (and not as an end in itself), the movement made good sense to Christians tired of the infighting of denominations within themselves and against one another. It still makes sense.

Leroy Lawson
Central Christian Church
North Hobson Street
Mesa, Arizona 85203

In a day when our high mobility increases our rootlessness, it is good to read a history that forces us back into our heritage.

In his book, Max Ward Randall has not only dealt with people, places, and dates but also issues that contributed to the emergence of the Restoration Movement.

More specifically, Randall has shown us that the Restoration Movement did not arise in a vacuum. The emergence and the rapid growth of the Restoration Movement owes much more to the kind of influences that the Great Awakening was pouring into the American environment than many of us have acknowledged.

In a real sense, the Restoration Movement needed the Great Awakening. If we can honestly admit that, then we may be able to progress better in acknowledging our need of our brothers and sisters around us who are not identified with the historical Restoration Movement. The willingness to associate with others and learn from others without being totally absorbed by them may be a major factor in the rapid growth of the Restoration Movement in its earlier days that needs to be recaptued in our day.

Randall's history is both refreshing and incisive. But more important than that it has in it the inherent ability to call us to a commitment to be willing to learn from our other brothers and sisters in Christ from whom we have traditionally avoided. In a real sense, Randall reminds us that if we take our history seriously, we must take our unwillingness to learn from others less seriously. That is not easy, but it is essential for growth today as it was then.

So in a real sense there is woven into this history, an important factor for church growth. I commend it to those who want to get on with being a part of a movement that is willing to really move.

Knofel Staton
Pacific Christian College
2500 E. Nutwood Ave.
Fullerton, California 92631

Dr. Randall has performed a distinct service to all the heirs of the "Reformation of the Nineteenth Century," and to those who are interested in reformation in our own times. The results of his careful research have been placed within the larger context of early American Awakenings, with the result that both the Awakenings and the Reformation of the Nineteenth Century may be more adquately understood.

Robert O. Fife
Westwood Christian Foundation
10808 Le Conte Ave.
Los Angeles, California 90024

Max Ward Randall's book is historical, but it has powerful contemporary implications. Dr. Randall details how the early movers of the Restoration Movement, with all their magnificent concepts, linked their message to the converging of many historical, social, intellectual, cultural and spiritual dynamics. These men set their sails to catch the winds that were then blowing; they caught the tides that were then moving and used them to implement their grand dream of New Testament Christianity restored. Thus Restoration became "an idea whose time had come."

The challenge to our generation is to learn from that generation in order to take advantage of today's convergence of the historical, social, cultural, intellectual, and spiritual dynamics which, in many ways, provides us an even more promising moment of opportunity.

It is my hope that the heirs of the Restoration Movement may learn Dr. Randall's lessons from history in order to propagate in our moment in history the great idea of Restoration, an idea whose time may well have come — again.

Joe S. Ellis
Cincinnati Christian Seminary
2700 Glenway
Cincinnati, Ohio 45204

xii

Dr. Max Ward Randall's stated purpose, ". . . to show the impact of the Great Awakenings upon the Restoration Movement," has been, in this reviewer's judgment, admirably and faithfully accomplished.

The writing shows the meticulous care of responsible scholarship, painstakingly ferreting out sources both well-known and little-known.

Dr. Randall shows conclusively that it had been grossly misleading to "write off" all of the evangelism and revivalism of the era with the genre of Cane Ridge, with all its "barking" and convulsing; that actually the Nineteenth Century Reformation (or Restoration) was itself a very sane and orderly part of the Awakening.

As retrospect frequently enjoys more objectivity and wisdom than on-site immediacy, it might well be wished that the progenitors of the "movement to restore the ancient order of things" might have grasped the opportunity to identify with the prevailing mood of revival and have infiltrated it with the Biblical insights which the restorers had received.

In their defense it may be observed that, as the Reformers ploughed their way through the entanglements of false doctrinal accretions, they moved cautiously, no doubt with understandable insecurity, not to say with no little exclusive isolationism — much of which we, their spiritual heirs, have imbibed and perpetuated.

Truth will defend itself, but truth isolated by legalistic separatism, is helpless to enlighten. We who have had the great good fortune to have been led back to the sources of the stream where the water flows sparkling clear, should not hoard this among fellows of our conformity, but "speaking the *truth* in *love*," mingle with good faith, balancing sweetness of spirit with careful adherence to truth, that all of God's children may constitute the "one flock" under the One Shepherd.

Dr. Randall has done us a great service by more accurately placing the exciting explosion of the Restoration in the context of its day.

Wilford F. Lown
Central Christian Church
2900 North Rock Road
Wichita, KS 67226

In the record of God's dealings with His people, there have been several occasions where an outpouring of the Holy Spirit in revival and awakening have produced a restoration movement to carry on the impetus of the work of God. The Restoration Movement, variously known as the Disciples of Christ, the Christian Church or the Church of Christ, is no exception to this, having arisen out of the Awakenings of 1800 and 1830. To my knowledge, there has been no study made of the continuing effect of awakenings upon the Restoration Movement, or of the attitude of the Restoration Movement to such awakenings. Professor Max Ward Randall has performed a service to the whole body of Christians in researching this subject. His work is well documented, and the facts that he has collated are well put together. In the Psalms, we are urged to tell our children's children the works of God, that they may put their trust in God and forget not His Commandments. Likewise, the Acts of the Apostles have rehearsed the works of God. A blessing will follow the ministry of this book, *The Great Awakenings and the Restoration Movement.*

> J. Edwin Orr
> Oxford Association for Research
>   in Revival
> 11451 Berwick Street
> Los Angeles, CA 90049

This book is essential reading for Restoration Movement men and women. Dr. Randall, an ardent advocate of restoration, here sets forth several almost unknown factors which caused our churches to multiply amazingly for the first seven decades. Readers will finish the book with a far deeper understanding of what really happened. As our churches seek to recapture the verve and power of those early years and begin to harvest the ripened fields which stretch away on every side, they will find these currently neglected secrets of dynamic Christian life stimulating and still very effective.

While the book discusses what the Christian Churches/Churches of Christ did many decades ago, its message is immensely germane today. The secrets of our past power will IF PUT INTO OPERATION, prove to be the secrets of effective evangelism today and tomorrow. Buy it. Read it. Have all your elders read it. Put it into operation.

> Donald McGavran
> Fuller Theological Seminary
> Pasadena California
> October 1, 1982

Preface

I make no claim to being a historian and must admit from the outset that, before I began the extensive research required for this effort, there was a question as to whether I could, from the sources, establish the desired thesis for the book. So far as existing histories of the Restoration Movement dealt with the subject, there was little to encourage me, and I was told by several brethren that there was no need for another Restoration history.

This self-imposed assignment was done because of a deep conviction that out of the historical context from which the Restoration Movement grew there was more to the beginnings and development of the Movement than existing Restoration Histories revealed. This study was first of all undertaken as a doctoral dissertation at The School of World Mission at Fuller Theological Seminary. In a real sense it provided the motivation for pursuing the degree and the degree provided the disciplinary incentive to hold me to the exhaustive task of travel and research necessary for an acceptable piece of writing.

It was written through the inspiration and encouragement of my friend and former professor, Dr. J. Edwin Orr. Through him I had acquired a growing interest in the Great Awakenings and Revival and, though Restoration Histories had little to say about the impact of the Awakenings upon the Restoration Movement, I was convinced, though with little proof, that the Restoration Churches were touched by the Awakenings and accompanying Revivals as well.

As the following chapters boldly indicate, little did I know what my research and writing would reveal, but I am happily convinced that all who read this work will agree that my travel, labor and time spent were worth while and that the information, some never before made available, will be a blessing to all who have been influenced and claim a part of the Restoration Heritage.

I am grateful to a number of dear friends who have read the book, giving it high commendation: brethren like Dr. Robert O. Fife of Westwood Christian Foundation, Los Angeles, CA, Mr. Carl Ketcherside, St. Louis, MO, Dr. Lynn Hieronymus, Lincoln Christian College, Lincoln, IL, Dr. Joe S. Ellis, Cincinnati Christian Seminary, Cincinnati, OH, Dr. Leroy Lawson, Central Christian Church, Mesa, AZ, Dr. Don DeWelt, College Press Publishing Company, Joplin, MO, Dr. Myron Taylor, Westwood Christian Church, Los Angeles, CA, Dr. Wilford F. Lown, Central Christian Church, Wichita, KS, and Dr. Knofel Staton, Pacific Christian College, Fullerton, CA. I also appreciate deeply the critical reading of brethren like Dr. Enos Dowling of Lincoln Christian Seminary, Lincoln, IL, Dr. James North, Cincinnati Christian Seminary, Cincinnati, OH, Dr. Donald A. McGavran, Fuller Theological Seminary, Pasadena, CA, and Dr. J. Edwin Orr, also of Fuller Theological Seminary in Pasadena. These brethren enabled me to sharpen the manuscript in numerous ways I would have missed without their help.

I am also appreciative of the support given by Lincoln Christian College and Seminary for continued encouragement and help in bringing this project to its successful conclusion. Without it, this volume would never have become a reality.

Max Ward Randall
Lincoln Christian College
and Seminary
Lincoln, IL 62656

Table of Contents

TABLE OF CONTENTS

INTRODUCTION

The Purpose of This Study.

The object of this volume is to show the impact of the Great Awakenings upon the Restoration Movement. That impact has been most extra-ordinary, in spite of the ambivalence of Alexander Campbell and his contemporaries, and in spite of the low view of many contemporary Restoration Movement adherents to the Awakenings or Revivals as well.

The Disciples of Christ, Christian Churches or Churches of Christ, have long known the Campbells, father and son, Walter Scott, Barton Warren Stone, Raccoon John Smith and John T. Johnson. Many have been acquainted with men like Rice Haggard and James O'Kelly. Some will also be aware of such men as John Glas, Robert Sandeman, James and Robert Haldane and others.

Historians have been faithful in revealing the relationships between these good men, but they have too often ignored any influences of the Great Awakenings upon these worthies, or the dynamics at work between them in bringing the Restoration Movement into existence.

Restoration Movement historians have too often ignored any relationship between the Awakenings and the growth of the churches. The "Christian" Churches of Barton Warren Stone started at the crest of the 1790-1830 Evangelical Awakenings and grew at a phenomenal pace during those years. The "Reformers" following the Campbells had their beginnings in 1809, also at the peak of the same Awakenings, and their first surge of growth, through the preaching of Walter Scott, took place at that time.

After the post-1832 union of the Campbell and Stone streams, an explosive growth within the churches took place,

1

and tens of thousands were added, all this at a time when Baptists, Methodists and Presbyterians were enjoying the same ingatherings in greater or lesser degree.

In twelve months of 1858-1859, the churches of the Restoration Movement enjoyed their most outstanding growth for any year to that time. These were the same years of the world-wide Evangelical Awakenings, and denominational churches of the United States and Europe and churches of many foreign mission fields were adding millions to their memberships.

Adherents of the Restoration Movement too often have equated the Awakenings or Revivals with the unusual phenomena associated with Logan County, Kentucky and Cane Ridge of 1800 and 1801 and similar events in the United States, Britain, and elsewhere. This evaluation has to be modified. Circumstances surrounding the Revivals among many denominations were quiet and orderly in the same way as were the ingatherings within churches of the Restoration Movement.

The Use of the Word, Revival

The normal use of the word "revival" is generally understood. Webster defines it as "an act or instance of being revived; a renewed attention or interest in something." This is the general meaning of the word in every context except religion. The word "revival" was first used in a religious context in 1702 to refer to a dynamic spiritual awakening claiming attention at the beginning of the eighteenth century (Orr 1975b).

One century later, in the period covered by this study, and during the Second Great Awakening, the word "revivalism" appeared. From 1815 it was defined as "the spirit or

2

methods characteristic of religious revivals." J. Edwin Orr says that by 1820 the word "revivalist" was used to designate "one who promotes, produces or participates in a religious revival" (1975b). It soon referred to one who promotes religious revivals; specifically an evangelist. The above definitions are contemporary in both American and British dictionaries.

The British, however, have not used the American term "revival meeting" to apply to an evangelistic mission or meeting, but illogical as it is, the term is widely used in American churches and churches of the Restoration Movement.

This author met with American, British and European historians, authors, professors and missionaries at Regent's Park College of Oxford, England, during the summers of 1974 and 1975. All reject the American use of the term "revival." At each session, the papers read and the discussions shared underscored that revival and spiritual awakening are the work of God.

Revival in Scripture

The Scriptures emphasize that God gives revival. David asked, "wilt thou not revive us again; that thy people may rejoice in thee?" (Ps. 85:6). Isaiah wrote,

> For thus saith the high and lofty one that inhabiteth eternity whose name is holy; I dwell in the high and holy place, with him also that is of a contrite and humble spirit, to revive the spirit of the humble, and to revive the heart of the contrite ones (Isa. 57:15).

Revival is Distinctly the Work of God

Habakkuk cried out to God for revival. "O Lord, revive thy work in the midst of the years, in the midst of the years

3

make known; in wrath remember mercy" (Hab. 3:2). Often the people of God, in both Israel and Judah, illustrated this principle, crying out to God in prayer and repentence, and God revived them.

Some insist that revival or spiritual awakening is not spoken of or inferred, in the New Testament. They are mistaken.

Those chapters of the acts of the apostles that speak of the coming of the Jews into the Christian faith, are a description of a massive spiritual awakening. God was at work reviving his people, and through the preaching of the crucified and risen Messiah and through repentance and conversion, "times of refreshing" were coming "from the presence of the Lord" (Acts 3:19).

The book of Acts begins with revival on the day of Pentecost. The promise of the Holy Spirit in John 14, 15 and 16 was fulfilled on that day. God kept His word. Disciples of Jesus, weak and vacillating, became advocates of power. God revived them, and the Acts, the entire New Testament, and the acts of the people of God from Pentecost until now, are the result.

The positive influence of the Great Awakenings has seldom been given within the Restoration Movement. One of the larger religious movements in America, it would never have begun nor grown so phenomenally except for the revival factor.

Many Notable Historians Agree that the Restoration Movement Is a Product of Revival

Dr. J. Edwin Orr, well known authority on revival and the Awakenings, has written of the Restoration Movement as one of the results of the late eighteenth, early nineteenth

4

century revivals in America (1965:55). "The Second Great Awakening brought about a new major denomination, the Disciples of Christ." Again he has said (1975a:64), referring to the 1801 Kentucky Revival and Barton Warren Stone, "He and his presbytery seceded to form the Christian Church, one of the components of the Restoration Movement known as the Disciples of Christ, Churches of Christ, or Christian Churches." In the same volume, speaking of the 1830 Awakening, Orr writes (p. 40),

> Several small groups committed to a restoration of New Testament simplicity in doctrine and practice came together to form the Disciples of Christ denomination, also known as the Christian Churches or Churches of Christ. These restoration fellowships were thriving during the earlier decades of revival, encouraged by denominational reaction and resistance to change.

William Warren Sweet (1973:226-238) also associates the Restoration Movement through Stone and the Campbells with the revivals of the late eighteenth, early nineteenth century, as does Kenneth Scott Latourette (1964: 1040-1042; 1971: Vol. 4, 196-200).

Few Restoration Movement Historians Have Much to Say About the Awakenings.

Historians of the Restoration Movement give limited credit to the influence of the Awakenings. James DeForest Murch (1961:83), after describing the days of spiritual decline following the revolution, wrote that in the midst of these discouraging days came the great revival. He speaks of "a tremendous moving of the Spirit of God"; who "in His providence was moving in America to infuse the Church with new life . . ." He affirms that "this major phenomenon

5

in American church history prepared the way for the Restoration Movement."

Enos Dowling has three paragraphs on Religious Awakening (1964:10) as he discusses the background to the Movement. David Edwin Harrell (1966:2-3) does little more than mention the Awakenings. Winfred Ernest Garrison (1931: 52-53; 1946:49) has as little to say, and Walter Wilson Jennings (1919:26-27) all but ignores the Awakenings as well. Errett Gates (1905:72) speaks only of the religious excitement of the latter eighteenth, early nineteenth century, and M. M. Davis (1915:20) speaks of the leaven at work. B. A. Abbott (1924:11) is content to refer to the Cane Ridge Revival as ". . . one of the most remarkable spiritual manifestations in the history of Christianity." Oliver Read Whitley (1959:39-46) devotes only a few pages to the Kentucky Revival of the early nineteenth century.

James DeForest Murch (1961:22) is correct in pointing out that "previous volumes have taken too slight note of the great revival."

God's approbation was on the Awakenings of the eighteenth and early nineteenth centuries. In spite of some of their physical excesses, even the frontier revivals were blessed of God. The Reformation or Restoration Movement was so touched by the Awakenings, that it is unlikely it would have been founded, and likely it would have foundered, except for the revival factor. There are examples where both the gentle, quiet influences, as well as the earthshaking impact of the Great Awakenings, impinged upon the founders of the Restoration Movement.

Personalities Behind the Restoration Movement

This study of the Restoration Movement must focus upon a number of outstanding men, some of them familiar

6

names, such as Thomas and Alexander Campbell, Walter Scott and Barton Warren Stone. It will also focus on little known men as Benjamin Grosvenor, Samuel Davies, James O'Kelly, Rice Haggard, James Madison and others.

Influences of the Times

This history was affected, not only by unusual men, but also by circumstances of the times, both in the British Isles and in America. The sectarianism of Scotland, Ireland, England and Wales, exported to the American Colonies, influenced the thinking and theology of religious leaders of the day, and the spirit of the revolutionary age provided the kind of soil in which the new Reformation could take root and grow.

The impact of the First and Second Great Awakenings in the eighteenth and early nineteenth centuries demands careful research to determine the dynamics at work in the development of the Restoration Movement. There are lessons in this record for churches of the movement in this last quarter of the twentieth century.

Underlying Purpose of This Work

There is no intent to minimize the importance of the doctrinal uniqueness of churches of the Restoration Movement. Those truths need to be preached and taught with fervor. Nor is there any wish to denigrate the movement's emphasis upon Christian unity, a doctrine taught by the Lord Himself.

However, at this time in the Restoration Movement, many are filled with the very denominational pride their beginnings taught them to abhor. Sectarian barriers have been erected, divisions have been multiplied between the churches, so powerful that a once great brotherhood has been rent into three or more parts, and doctrinal exclusiveness often leaves the impression that only Restoration churches are true to the Scriptures and all others are apostate and their adherents damned.

Should one suggest that many adherents preach, teach and practice salvation by works, the charge would be denied and the one making the suggestion marked as suspect. If one were to give too much emphasis to God's sovereignty, His grace, mercy and love, winsomely taught by a number of denominations condemned by Restoration Movement advocates, he might be branded a Calvinist, to be feared more than Satan himself.

This narrow bigotry often evident, resulting in denominational exclusiveness, must be seen for what it is. The tendency to denigrate and to look down upon those who are Bible-believing, God-fearing members of other churches must be corrected. Without sacrificing one truth or the emphasis upon Christian unity, it can be done, and if it is possible to be done, every effort should be made to do it.

The threads of influence, woven into the tapestry that became the Restoration Movement, came out of the eighteenth, early nineteenth century Awakenings, and were tinted and colored by them. Men out of such backgrounds as the Reformed Presbyterian churches, the Church of England, the Baptist churches, Methodist churches and Independent movements enunciated biblical truths that found expression in the new Reformation. Contemporary adherents of the Movement need to see this and praise God for it, and thank Him, too, for those denominational brethren (there is no other kind) who enunciated truths that our forefathers heard and that we need to heed today.

Chapter One

THE CHURCH IN THE MIDST OF TURMOIL, REVOLUTION AND UNBELIEF: 1750-1800

The Church in the Context of the Times

Efforts to count the churches of each denomination at the close of the colonial era reveal a total of 3,105 congregations, equally divided between the colonies of New England and the middle and southern colonies (Sweet 1973:172-173). The Congregationalists with 658 churches had their greatest strength in New England. The larger part of 543 congregations of the Presbyterians was concentrated in the middle colonies. The Baptists had 498 churches, slightly more than the Anglicans with 480. There were 295 assemblies of Quakers, 251 congregations of German and Dutch Reformed, 151 Lutheran churches and fifty Catholic, and the Methodists with thirty-seven circuits, all these located primarily in Maryland and Virginia. Established churches, underwritten by taxation and protected by law, were located in nine of the Puritan colonies. The Congregational Church was supported by three colonies and the Anglican by six.

The Churches Were Essentially American

All the churches in colonial America had direct ties with the churches of the British Isles and Europe, but they must not be considered foreign or imported (Qualben 1942:441-442). Particularly in the later colonial period, the revolutionary years and the early years of the Republic, these churches became charter members of the young nation by right of creation. The American Revolution was unique. Unlike other revolutions, it was more than political. It was also a religious revolution. Churches from north to

9

south, were centers of revolutionary activity, arousing public opinion and spreading information, urging the people to stand together, and when the conflict started, the churches gave their young men and their resources.

The Anglican Church The Anglican Church suffered several handicaps at the beginning of the war. Particularly in New England, and to a degree in the middle colonies as well, the established churches were looked upon as oppressors of the fathers of the colonists.

The Anglican Church had been pro-royalist and colonial, under the ecclesiastical oversight of the Bishop of London, never more than partially staffed by *The British Society for the Propagation of the Gospel* and powerless to educate and ordain its own clergy or administer the spiritual needs of its own members (Garrison and DeGroot 1948:71-72). At the close of the war, nearly all the missionaries of the SPG were forced to return to England, and the society withdrew. Many Anglican priests left and did not return. Their loyalties had been with the king (Latourette 1964:1035-1036). To compound the problem, there was a major theological difference. The Anglicans of the north were generally "high" church, emphasizing the characteristics of the Catholic tradition. The Anglicans of the south were primarily "low" church, stressing their Protestant inheritance.

In the southern colonies, the Anglican Church was primarily pro-American with men such as George Washington, Alexander Hamilton, Patrick Henry, John Marshall and James Madison members. Likely two-thirds of the signers of the Declaration of Independence were Anglican. Until after the war, the established churches had little influence upon the colonists. Three-fourths of the people of Virginia were outside the Establishment (The Church of England).

10

Its concern for its political association and its failure to satisfy the spiritual needs of the people forced it to near extinction by the end of the war. When a specially called convention was convened in Virginia in 1813 to choose a successor to the late bishop who had died, only seven clergymen and eighteen laymen were there to participate. Only by radical readjustment, initiated by two of its prominent men, was it reorganized in 1789, independent of both state and English hierarchical control with representatives made up of both clergymen and laymen. The new organization was named the Protestant Episcopal Church in the United States.

The Congregational and Presbyterian Churches The Congregational and Presbyterian clergy, essentially Puritan, wielded more influence than any other denomination, and after 1750, it was not uncommon for Puritan sermons to be used for political instruction (Qualben 1942:442). Puritan clergymen shared more than those of any other profession in developing the political philosophy of the American Revolution as set forth in the Preamble of the Declaration of Independence. The democracy of the young nation came from Christian foundations. "The way had been prepared . . . by the Reformed faith and the sermons of the clergy, especially in New England" (Latourette 1964: 1006). However, the Unitarian Movement within the Congregational Church was gaining considerable strength, and its influence was increasingly formidable (Sweet 1973: 241-242).

The Presbyterians, including the colonists of Presbyterian descent such as the Huguenots, the Dutch Reformed and the Scotch-Irish, like the Congregationalists, were strong friends of the colonies. Presbyterians of Scotch-Irish descent from Virginia and North Carolina drafted, as early as January, 1775, a declaration of independence. Many of their leaders assumed major roles in the war and in politics.

With the conclusion of hostilities, however, the Presbyterians had cause for alarm. In 1792 the General Assembly described the religious conditions in the Church across the land as

> a general dereliction of religious principles and practice among our fellow citizens, a visible and prevailing impiety and contempt for the laws and institutions of religions, and an abounding infidelity which in many instances tends to atheism itself (1973:224).

The Lutheran Church The American Lutherans gave near unanimous support to the struggle. Their men fought in the war and served in the political arena, and yet, following the war, the Lutherans were so weakened that, for a time they discussed union with the Anglicans who appeared also to be dying.

The Roman Catholics Most, but not all, Roman Catholics stood with the colonies, and volunteers served in signing the Constitution and the Declaration of Independence. Membership in the young republic at the close of the war stood between 19,000 and 24,000. The first bishop was appointed for the American church in 1789 with Baltimore selected as the first American see.

The Baptists Baptists were foremost in the struggle for freedom of worship and the separation of Church and State, and were strong in their support of the war. They were responsible for the abolishment of religious inequalities, but had been so absorbed in the battle over separation of Church and State that they suffered spiritual decline.

12

Many stumbled and fell and simply lost interest in spiritual things.

The Methodists During the early years of the struggle, the Methodists were still associated with the Anglican Church. In the central and northern colonies they were suspected of being in sympathy with the English. Consequently, for years the Methodists watched their membership slide downward, and John Wesley contributed to this loss.

Suspicion and hard feelings were created when Wesley issued his "Calm Address to the American Colonies" urging obedience to the King of England. When the Revolution started, he encouraged Methodist preachers in the colonies to remain neutral. Soon his English-born preachers sailed home, with the exception of Francis Asbury, who was convinced that the thirteen colonies would obtain their freedom. In contrast, the native-born Methodist preachers were sympathetic with the struggle though most chose not to be combatants as a matter of principle. "Methodists recovered rapidly at the close of the war and were one of the first religious groups to form a national organization" (Qualben 1942:448).

The Quakers, Mennonites and Moravians The Quakers, Mennonites and Moravians were misunderstood because they were conscientious objectors by belief and principle. They suffered greatly as a result.

These were the churches in existence through the Revolutionary War. All suffered devastating losses and were ill equipped to face the challenge of leading the new nation following the conflict.

Turmoil, Revolution and Unbelief

It was still doubtful in the year of 1800 whether Christianity would succeed in becoming a universal world religion

(Stephen Neill 1966:243). The closing years of the eighteenth century have been called "the darkest period spiritually and morally in the history of American Christianity" (Murch 1962:19). "The period under consideration was one of the lowest eras spiritually in the history of America" (Dowling 1964:9). "Again it looked as though Christianity were a waning influence, about to be ushered out of the affairs of men" (Latourette 1971: vol. 3, 454). "At that time Voltaire was predicting that Christianity would be forgotten in thirty years, and Tom Paine was gleefully repeating the assurance to English speaking folks on both sides of the Atlantic" (Orr 1975:6). Welshimer speaks of "the dark pall of infidelity that had settled over the nation" (1935:31). "There probably never was a time, before or after, when there was so large a percentage of religious indifference and of positive hostility to organized religion in America as during the last two decades of the eighteenth century" (Garrison and DeGroot 1948:70). "The beginning of the nineteenth century was a period of blatant unbelief" (Davis 1915:19).

Reasons for the Decline

There was a crumbling of dependable government, an erratic economic system and sense of apathy and religious skepticism. The entire population had been involved in the Revolutionary War and were either for or against independence. The moral breakdown, always accompanying war, militated against any concern for the Christian message (Latourette 1964:1006).

Influences Out of Europe In Europe rationalistic thought was predominant in intellectual circles, and it entertained a disdainful aversion to Christianity. It was the consequence of humanism and it was antagonistic to the Christian faith. Thus rationalistic philosophy advocated that it is through the initiative and intellect of man that truth is to be found, while the advocates of Christianity asserted that the redemption of man from ignorance and sin was the work of God through God's revealed Word, and not the work of man (Latourette 1971: Vol. 3,445). A sense of self-confidence in the inherent goodness and unlimited abilities of man and the conviction that without supernatural help he could attain to perfection if only the bonds of ignorance and the imposition of preachers and priests and rulers were removed, was widespread. It was not uncommon for the advocates of "rationalistic humanism" to attack and heap vindictive upon the adherents of Christianity and the churches of the day. The faith and zeal of ministers and priests as well as the membership of churches was contaminated by this humanistic philosophy, and spiritual enthusiasm cooled to freezing point in too many cases.

Circumstances in the American Republic The people of the young republic had suffered through years of war. French Roman Catholic Missions were placed on the defensive when Canada and portions of the Mississippi Valley were claimed by Britain following the Seven Years War, 1756-1763. In the following years the thirteen colonies were freed from British control by the Revolutionary War. The quarter century of the war and years following were a time of spiritual disturbance. Worship, Bible reading and religious life all but disappeared.

Many renounced Christianity as superstition and lie thrust upon the masses by religious swindlers. Revelation was rejected for want of evidence and authority. Moral responsibility was a web that the wise and strong avoided. Assuming the possibility of God, and man as a created being, then he had been made only to be happy. In the eyes of the unbeliever, animal pleasure was the only happiness. Consequently this was the purpose of man's creation (Murch 1962:19).

The Lure of the Frontier Other things contributed to this relapse besides the disturbed condition of the population following years of conflict. Independence for many meant anarchy as expressed in the assertion of self. There was a radical change in social conditions. The appeal of the western frontier across the Alleghenies was a lure, and an unbroken stream moved southwest and west on the national roads and waterways.

In the latter eighteenth and early nineteenth centuries numbers streamed into the Ohio and Mississippi River valleys and into the mountains of Kentucky and Tennessee. This wave of white population to the frontier was from the older states, but also, in part, directly from Europe. Those from the older states, while not members of any church, were largely Protestant and Catholic. There was a rough-hewn character about the men and women of the frontier, and there was an erosion of family solidarity and brotherhood within the churches, the result of migrating to the west.

Some, cut off from the rules and customs accepted by the society out of which they had come, rejected all religious and moral standards. Gambling, drunkenness, immorality, quarrelling, brawling and murder were the result. Tyler agrees (1962:19) that there "is still much justice in the emphasis upon coarseness and violence of frontier life." Williams (1904:31) recounts that when Raccoon John Smith was

16

a boy in Kentucky, "a notorious band of outlaws from North Carolina named the Harpes, had made their appearance the year before in the neighborhood of Stanford, and had marked their path through the valleys of the Cumberland and Green River with pillage and murder." Logan County in southern Kentucky was a refuge for the most base and corrupt criminals (Sweet 1973:225).

Factors in the decline of morality and religion were all of these, but all combined were hardly a match for the influences of aggressive, French infidelity which flooded the new nation. English deism, French naturalism and atheism had a devastating impact on the whole of the Western world, fanning hatred against the Church, her ministries and her institutions. Voltaire (1694-1778) had as his motto: "Crush the infamous thing," that is, the Church. Rousseau (d.1778) "maintained that the right to govern came not from God but from the people" (Qualben 1942:449).

Alliance with France The alliance between France and the thirteen states released a flood of infidelity that none could control. Through it came the French revolutionaries with their spirit of atheism. They were warmly received. Skeptics and political extremists were hospitably entertained and infidels claimed the place formerly held by moderate evangelicals in the spiritual arena of the young nation. The fashionable attitude towards religion and morals was one of infidelity, particularly with students and the educated. In 1782 it is said there were two students professing Christianity at Princeton, one at Boudoin, and five at Yale College in 1783. Skepticism raged at William and Mary. Infidel clubs prospered (1942:449). Unconcern for things religious and moral described the poor and middle classes, but among them atheistic pamphlets and books were in ample supply.

17

Aftermath of the Revolution It is reported that 300,000 of the 5,000,000 population were drunkards. Fifteen thousand were buried or "were eaten by dogs or hogs" each year. Religion and morals were never at such a low level.

The Revolution brought political freedom and independence for the thirteen states, but the land was ravaged and the people impoverished. Every denomination underwent severe trials. Houses of worship were burned or otherwise destroyed. Preachers and priests were driven from their homes and parishes. Some were killed and many beaten, imprisoned or otherwise persecuted. Congregations were rent, never to come together again. Priests of the Anglican Church and preachers of the Methodist societies, loyal to the King, returned to England. Groups such as the Mennonites, Moravians, and the Quakers, who refused military service, endured persecution from both the English and the colonial armies.

Apathy in the Churches Some felt that the Church was too far gone to be revived. Bishop Samuel Provoost of New York felt the situation so helpless that he quit functioning (Orr 1975b:10). Chief Justice Marshall and Bishop Madison of Virginia were of the same conviction that "the church was too far gone to be revived."

Nor was this apathy only an Eastern phenomenon. Towns in Kentucky were named after infidels. Logan County, Kentucky, was so populated with criminals that they controlled the county (Murch 1962:20).

By 1800 communities from twenty to fifty thousand people were found west of the Alleghenies. There was neither a church or a minister among them, but they were amply supplied with atheistic literature. While the churches

18

of the east were wallowing in apathy, the atheists of France collected a sum of three million francs to underwrite the cost of infidel literature for the people of America.

Sober-minded Leaders Become Alarmed In 1796 a close friend of George Washington wrote expressing apprehension for the future of the country with greater uneasiness than he had felt during the war, and Washington concurred (Strickland 1934:40). Washington was one of that diminishing minority who continued to cling to the ancient moral and spiritual order of things.

Patrick Henry wrote a reply to Thomas Paine's *Age of Reason*. The work was not published. Paine wrote a tract and sent it to Benjamin Franklin to be printed. Franklin, sometimes called an enemy of religion, refused to publish it, advising Paine to "burn this piece before it is seen by any other person" (1934:31).

The Positive Side of the Picture

However, on the positive side, several factors were potential advantages to the propagation of religion. The land was young and there was a feeling that one could start anew. This instilled a responsiveness to the gospel and created a soil for planting the growing churches in fields yet to be cleared and plowed in preparation for the harvest.

Furthermore, Christianity was not unknown. Pioneers from the older states, whether they were at one time church members or not, were acquainted with basic Protestant concepts. Whatever may have been written earlier, it says much for the vitality of Christianity that it followed the populations westward and that numbers were won to a

19

rapidly spreading Christian faith, adaptable to the conditions of the frontier.

There are cases where congregations were organized before beginning their westward march, and they took their church with them. Often the settlers' new home became a house of worship with little outside help from anyone, a common practice among the Baptists.

The Presbyterians were well situated to propagate Presbyterian doctrines, many of their adherents being Scotch-Irish stock.

The Methodists were uniquely equipped. By the beginning of the nineteenth century, the Methodist Episcopal Church had already formed a structured organization enabling it to reach every settlement, however remote.

The frontier fields were ripe unto harvest, and the laborers were soon to come.

A Moving of the Spirit of God

This devastating religious and moral depression adversely affecting every part of the new nation had gone too far and grown too large for solution by mere human efforts. The churches, singly or combined were not equal to the crisis. They were overwhelmed with a sense of malaise and despair that made impossible any renewal from within. The spiritual prognosis offered no hope, but disillusionment was turned to anticipation and victory. How did it happen? One recourse was open. A small group of men began to pray. Prayer was the only weapon available to them, and they turned to God.

This circumstance has not been overlooked by those who have taken note of the late eighteenth, early nineteenth century revivals. Orr has noted (1965:21) that "when the

tide turned it did so imperceptibly at first in scarcely noticeable gatherings of just a handful of students for prayer."
Qualben has written (1942:470), "in the period from 1789
to 1830 American churches experienced a general religious
awakening which brought fresh life and checked the current infidelity." Walker observed (1947:578) that "a mighty
reawakening of religious interest began" and the last ten
years of the eighteenth century "saw a marvelous transformation initiated." Sweet (1973:226-231) speaks of "infidelity effectively checked" in the east and of "revival in
the west attended by such excitement and such strange
manifestations as were never before seen in America." Orr
recounts the circumstances leading to spiritual awakening
through the prayers of a few students at Hampden Sydney
College in Virginia in 1787 (1971:25), and in six chapters
of *The Eager Feet* examines the Evangelical Awakenings
from 1790 to 1830, all these in America (1975). Latourette
has said, "but revival came. In no other land in the nineteenth century did the churches have so large a numerical
increase" (1971:Vol. 4,177). "The revivals . . . broke out
afresh with augmented fervor and swept various parts of
the country" (Latourette 1964:1036).

The Focus of This Study

Out of this crucible of infidelity and unbelief followed
by revival, every denomination was severely tested and,
through the revivals, strengthened. New religious bodies
were established. One of them, called the Reformation
by its immediate founders, and more familiarly called the
Restoration Movement, had its beginnings through the
Awakenings.

21

Chapter Two

NEW CHRISTIAN MOVEMENTS
IN THE NEW REPUBLIC

Antecedents of These New Movements

Less than two-fifths of America's population lived in the Southern States in 1790 (Orr 1975a:65). The Methodists, Anglicans, Baptists and Presbyterians claimed the greatest strength in the territory of Mississippi, Georgia, South Carolina, North Carolina, and Virginia. Other denominations had a sprinkling of members.

The Presbyterians were strong in the south and west (Garrison and DeGroot 1948:72). They could be found on every trail that pointed west, and the Presbyterian church followed the Irish-Americans southward across Virginia and into the Carolinas.

There were three streams of Baptists, the Particular Baptists, believing that Christ died only for the elect, the Arminians, who insisted that Christ died for all, and the Separate. All were evangelistic. The Baptists grew rapidly in the south, even before the war, and particularly in Virginia, North Carolina, and Kentucky. "In 1785 a revival began in Virginia which added thousands to the Baptist churches and many to other denominations" (Latourette 1964:1036-1037).

Shortly after 1766, Methodist societies were formed in Maryland. In the 1770's aided by one of Wesley's missionaries, a revival broke out in Virginia under the preaching of the evangelical Anglican priest, Devereux Jarratt. Jarratt was converted by the preaching of Presbyterians. He was evangelical to the core. In 1763 he was appointed rector of the parish of Bath in Dinwiddie County, Virginia, and was sympathetic with the lay preachers of the Methodist church, working in association with them. His church was soon filled as a result of his preaching as he labored to evangelize the Establishment (Sweet 1973:152).

Reasons for the Beginnings of These Movements

After the new country gained its political freedom, there was a new sense of individual independence and religious liberty. A large segment of the population was outside the membership of existing churches. Systems of "free thought" had been introduced from France particularly, but from England as well. Refugee religious groups gained in popularity, the idea having come from Germany. Small independent fellowships from England in the eighteenth century encouraged the concept. Numbers of people had lost confidence in credal statements and bold orthodoxy and were revolting in opposition to them. There was a loss of confidence in members of the clergy and an ignoring of their teaching. The ordinary man was gaining confidence in his competence to make his own decisions, to do his own thinking, and if his attention was drawn to the Bible, to interpret it for himself. For numbers moving to the frontiers, these motivations had ample field for their implementation.

All of America was a frontier when the thirteen states, after the war, became a nation. Consequently, eastern seaboard city dwellers, as well as the frontiersmen to the west, loved simplicity, and with their suspicion of tradition, systems of authority, devious procedures and self-acclaimed experts, welcomed anyone who could offer a new system. This was particularly true in the field of religion.

23

New movements anchored their thrust in a rediscovery of the New Testament, in the reaffirmation of the Protestant freedom to interpret it individually, and in the determination to get away from the enslavement of the "traditional creeds and ecclesiastical authorities" (Garrison and DeGroot 1948:80).

In the year of 1800, pietists of the German Reformed Movement came together and the United Brethren in Christ was the result. The Warwickites in 1801 came out of the Reformed Dissenting Presbyterians. Jacob Albright, a Lutheran, led in the formation of the Evangelical Church in 1803. The Cumberland Presbyterian Church, with a desire for a simple and free style of religion, defected because of theological and administrative differences, and became a recognized body in 1810.

In the southeastern states, revivals of the last decade of the eighteenth century following the First Great Awakening, were encouraged by "New Light" Presbyterians, who in like manner emphasized "the simple and common elements of the gospel" (1948:81).

Though rigid forms of life as related to the life of a Christian and a polity that leaned toward authoritarianism soon developed among the Methodists, in the beginnings of the young nation, their appeal was towards those who longed for simplicity in faith and worship. They encouraged a heart religion anchored in the Word of God, without theological complications and allowing room for the believer's own personal experience. Among the Free Will Baptists, there was a comparable inclination, and many discarded their "denominational terminology."

An emphasis upon free will as opposed to election, predestination, and limited atonement was common among these budding movements, but it was more than a theological affirmation with them. When they spoke of freedom of the will, they were expressing their conviction that a person had the freedom to accept the gospel for himself; to read and interpret the Word for himself.

Background of the James O'Kelly Movement

Two thirds of the Methodist membership by 1777 were to be found in six circuits in Virginia and one in North Carolina. All had to depend upon Jarratt for the sacraments (Latourette 1964:1038). As a consequence, the Methodist societies were drastically handicapped.

Immediate measures had to be taken because of lack of Anglican clergymen to administer communion. There was an opportunity in this new land, and the societies were growing. John Wesley moved to solve the problem.

John Wesley and Francis Asbury — 1790

Wesley, priest of the Church of England, never intended that Methodism would be more than a spiritual awakening within the Church of England, and there it remained until after the War.

Methodists in America first came as members of the Anglican Church and on their own as settlers, not as clergymen or missionaries. A captain in the British army, who had been appointed to preach by Wesley, built the first Methodist Church in New York in 1768, and in the years following made many converts in the eastern cities of Philadelphia, Baltimore and various parts of Maryland.

Other preachers also shared in the growth of the movement. Aware of the need for ministers, Wesley, between 1769 and 1771, sent three men, including Francis Asbury, to America. Asbury was to become a central figure in the development of American Methodism. These three men, however, were laymen as were other preachers who soon volunteered for service.

Ten preachers reported 1,160 members in New York, Pennsylvania, New Jersey, Maryland and Virginia in 1773 when the first conference was held in Philadelphia. The conference was called by Francis Asbury.

> The following rules were agreed to by all the preachers present: 1) Every preacher who acts in connection with Mr. Wesley and the brethren who labor in America is strictly to avoid administering the ordinances of baptism and the Lord's Supper. 2) All the people among whom we labor to be earnestly exhorted to attend the church, and receive the ordinances there; (Anglican Church) but in a particular manner to press the people in Maryland and Virginia to the observance of this minute, etc. (Townsend, Workman and Eayrs 1909:Vol. 2:73).

Seventeen hundred and seventy-three members were added in 1776. In spite of the war, there was an increase of more than 2,000 in membership in 1777; but because of the desolation of the war in 1778, there was a loss of 873 members. By 1778 the Methodist had grown to 15,000 members (1909: Vol. 2,76).

However, "their societies still did not consider themselves churches; they could not have the sacraments because they had no ordained ministers, and even Asbury himself was still a lay preacher" (Garrison and DeGroot 1948:83).

This situation was far from bright in the southern states. The complaint of those of Anglican affiliation was that multitudes had never heard the name of Christ but through oaths and curses. Thousands had never seen a Bible or heard a chapter read, and tens of thousands had never heard a sermon preached or been baptized (Orr 1975a:65). All were denied the privilege of partaking of the Lord's Supper.

There was a growing demand that the right of administering the Lord's Supper be granted to their preachers. It had been months, in some instances years, since they had partaken of the loaf and the cup. "The demand was not only urgent, it was logically right; but by the majority of preachers it was not deemed expedient" (Stevens 1878:532). As a consequence, the societies were encouraged to wait until John Wesley, in England, could give his judgment in the matter, and thus they waited for one year. The problem unresolved in 1778, was postponed for another year so that by 1779 a division had developed, those preachers of the south insisting upon the right to administer the communion while those in the north pled for patience.

The consequence of this schism was that the southern Methodists, by the laying on of hands of three of their older and more respected men, ordained themselves. No longer would they be denied the privilege of the Lord's Supper nor would the children and probationary members be denied the rite of baptism.

At their annual conference in 1780, Asbury persuaded the leaders of the southern churches to suspend the administration of the Lord's Supper and baptism until some word should come from Wesley.

At the ninth conference held in 1781, all the preachers except one adhered to the original position and refrained from administering the Lord's Supper and baptism. In 1782, the conference was again divided into two segments, the northern segment in this year choosing Francis Asbury in harmony with "Wesley's original appointment, to act as general assistant to preside over the American conferences and the whole work" (Townsend, Workman and Eayrs 1909:Vol. 2, 77-78).

Asbury's position was settled at the twelfth conference in 1784 by a letter from Wesley to the brethren in America. In this letter written from Bristol and dated 10th September, 1784, Wesley wrote: "I have accordingly appointed Dr. Coke and Francis Asbury to be joint superintendents over all brethren in North America . . ." (1909:Vol. 2, 87-88).

By 1784 the War of Independence was safely concluded.

> Wesley's American preachers had been careful in most cases to remain neutral in the struggle, and some had openly backed the American side. They were therefore welcome in the new America. But none of them were ordained (Davis 1963:128).

Francis Asbury took his office seriously after Wesley released American Methodism from his control, and on November 3, 1784, he was ordained bishop (Stevens 1878:* 534). However, several who were willing to follow Wesley were reluctant to accept Asbury's oversight. James O'Kelly was chief among these dissenters.

James O'Kelly

The first "Christian" movement, in relation to the American Reformation (Restoration Movement) was the James O'Kelly secession in the latter eighteenth century.

O'Kelly was born about 1735 and educated in Ireland, coming to America while a young man, and living for some time in Surry County, Virginia, before moving to

---

* MacClenny adds this significant note: "And it came to pass, about the year 1787 Francis (Asbury) directed the preachers that whenever they wrote to him, to title him Bishop. They did so, and that was the beginning of our spurious Episcopacy" (1950:69).

North Carolina (MacClenny 1950:15). He was married in 1760 and converted about 1774.

Shortly after O'Kelly's conversion, he recounts that preachers sent from God came to his area under the oversight of John Wesley. He writes of Wesley:

> His writings magnified the Bible and gave it preference and honor. He declared he regarded the authority of no writings but the inspired. He urged the sufficiency of the Scripture for faith and practice, saying, 'We will be downright Christians.' This doctrine pleased me and so did the conduct of the Holy preachers. I entered the connection, and soon entered the list among the travelling ministers, where I labored day and night (1950:19-20).

James O'Kelly became a lay preacher on January 2, 1775, and served until the Christmas Conference of 1784 in Baltimore as a member of the Anglican Church. At Baltimore he was ordained as a deacon and elder along with twelve other men. With that act he was no longer a member of the Church of England, and he was no longer a lay preacher in the Methodist societies to which he had been appointed almost a decade earlier. The Methodist Episcopal Church of America had now been organized, and he was an elder of that church. He was a member of "Asbury's Ironsides," shock troops, the cutting edge of Methodism in Maryland, Virginia and North Carolina. He saw the necessity for separating from the Anglican Church and was leader of a movement, before 1784, urging a break with the Anglicans. Wesley and Asbury thwarted the move (Garrison and DeGroot 1948:85).

The "Christian" Movement in Virginia

Townsend, Workman and Eayrs (1909:Vol. 2,102) say that "O'Kelly had been a trouble breeder almost from the time he was ordained." He was leader of a minority group who protested Asbury's assumption of the powers of the episcopacy. Though the bishop appointed him a presiding elder, he continued to lead the discontented who objected to Asbury's autocratic leadership of the church.

The first meeting of O'Kelly and Asbury in 1780 was cordial, but ten years later, Asbury noted that O'Kelly was objecting to the bishop's power and threatening to "use his influence against the bishop if he did not stop for one year."

At the general conference in 1792, O'Kelly put forward the following resolution:

> After the bishop appoints the preachers at the conference to their several circuits, if anyone thinks himself injured by the appointment, he shall have the liberty to appeal to the conference and to state his objections; and if the conference approve his objections, the bishop shall appoint him to another circuit (1909:Vol. 2,103).

The resolution was adroitly broken into two parts. The first, Should the bishop appoint the preacher to his circuit? was accepted with hardly an argument, but the second, Should the preacher, if dissatisfied, have the right to appeal? was not so easy to resolve. For a week the debate continued but when the vote was taken, Mr. O'Kelly's resolution lost.

> O'Kelly thereupon withdrew with such others as he could persuade; and although a committee was named to treat with him, their overtures were in vain, and O'Kelly set out for Virginia where he wrought such havoc as he could; but his influence gradually waned, and the schism practically came to nought. Several of his preachers seceded, and in less than ten years they became so divided and subdivided that it is hard to find two of one opinion (1909:Vol. 2,103).

The Republican Methodist Church
That Soon Became the Christian Church

In 1793 O'Kelly and those with him organized the Republican Methodist Church. Eight months later, in August of 1794, a conference was held in Surry County, Virginia to resolve the problem of forming "a plan of government." A committee was appointed. It met and struggled "earnestly with tears," but no resolution came.

O'Kelly, in his *Apology* (MacClenny 1950:115) wrote as follows:

> At length it was proposed that we should lay aside every manuscript and take the Word of God as recorded in the Scriptures. And it was right; because the primitive church had no government besides the Scriptures, as written by the apostles.

Relating to the same problem, Freese observed,

> The first question that naturally arose was, by what name shall we be known hereafter. At first they took the name 'Republican Methodists,' highly significant of their republican principles and form of government; but at a subsequent conference, remembering that 'the disciples were called Christians first,' and wishing to carry out, not only the principles, but even the name of the early followers of Christ, they resolved 'to be known as Christians only' (not Christ-ians, as their enemies have seen fit to style them,) to acknowledge no head over the Church but Christ, and no creed or discipline but the Bible! (Freese 1852:22-23).

It is reported that one Rice Haggard stood before the conference with a New Testament in his hands and said,

> Brethren, this is a sufficient rule of faith and practice, and by it we are told that the disciples were called Christians, and

31

I move that henceforth and forever the followers of Christ be known as Christians simply (MacClenny 1950:116).

The O'Kelly secession did not dissipate as quickly nor with so little impact as Townsend, Workman and Eayrs indicate above. Though many preachers who stood with his earlier protests yielded to the majority will of the conference, in 1793 there were as many as 1,000 members with approximately thirty ministers.

A statement by the Methodist historian, Buckley, gives some idea of the impact of the O'Kelly movement on the Methodist Episcopal Church.

The secession of O'Kelly reached its height in 1795, and, combined with other impediments caused (for the Methodists) a decrease of 4,673 members among the whites (and . . . 1,644 among the colored) (Buckley 1903:346).

It is true that the majority gained by the Christians during the first year or two came at the expense of the Methodists, but it is doubtful that the O'Kelly movement "reached its peak" in 1795 because this year corresponded with the year of the Methodists' greater losses. It is more dubious that the statement is accurate, that "in less than ten years they became so divided and sub-divided that it is hard to find two of the same opinion" (Townsend, Workman and Eayrs 1909:103).

The breakaway did not impair the Methodist movement, for within half a century it was the largest religious body in the United States, due to the indefatigable labor and vision of Bishop Francis Asbury.

The "Christians" did not "divide and sub-divide and soon disappear." By the time the Kentucky movement got under way during the first decade of the nineteenth century, the O'Kelly movement in Virginia had 20,000 members "in the southern and western states" (Garrison and DeGroot 1948:87), but the future of the movement was limited. O'Kelly was a champion of infant baptism and sprinkling. A number of his preachers became convinced that immersion was biblical baptism, and a division came. The immersionists organized the Virginia Christian Conference, which in 1811 united with the New England Christians. This union collapsed over the slavery question in 1854 at which time it reunited with the O'Kelly group. In 1890 the New England and southern Christians came together once again.

Recounting this significant secession is important. There are areas where this movement touched the pending Barton Warren Stone movement. Examination of this break from Methodism reveals that within it there was no dissent from doctrine or departure from Methodist methods in gospel presentation. The one cause for dissension was the system of government. Following the break, the theology, teaching and preaching continued as before.

> But the new church's declaration of independence was not only a repudiation of Asbury. It was a rejection of the whole system of one-man control. With that went rejection of any type of ecclesiastical control, whether by bishop or by conference, over the individual's doctrinal position (1948:86).

The "Christian" Movement of New England

In the first year of the nineteenth century, a "Christian" movement, having no connection with other movements in the south or on the frontier, began in New England. It originated among the Baptists. This movement was the consequence of the independent rejection by two young

Baptist pastors of Calvinistic doctrines prevalent among Baptist, Congregational and Presbyterian churches of that time.

These men rejected the Calvinistic Theology of

. . . original sin, the immutable decrees of God by which some men are predestined to be saved and others to be damned, the limitation of Christ's atonement to the elect, and the inability of man to do anything for his own salvation (Garrison and DeGroot 1948:88).

Elias Smith, born in 1769 at Lynne, Connecticut, and Abner Jones, born at Royalton, Massachusetts, in 1772, grew up in the backwoods of Vermont, and under similar conditions of frontier hardship with its lack of schools.

Smith became member of a Baptist church and began to preach at the age of twenty-one. Though he was self-taught, having no theological training, he was ordained two years later. For ten years he preached. As he did so he continued independently to study the Scriptures. The result was that he became dissatisfied with Calvinism, believing that not only this system, but all standardized systems of doctrine, or creeds, as tests of fellowship, were wrong and should be discarded. He advocated the restoration of the faith and practice of the church revealed in the New Testament.

Abner Jones also became a member of a Baptist church and, with a few weeks' study to qualify him as a medical practitioner, through the Thompsonian system of medicine, began preaching among Baptist churches as he had opportunity. He too sought to find an escape from Calvinism. In his early twenties, he heard Elias Smith preach. It was the motivation he needed to break with the Calvinistic Baptists.

Jones organized an independent church of twenty-five members in Lydon, Vermont, in September, 1801. He called it a Christian church, refusing to give it a denominational name. Jones was motivated not only by his own thinking but by Smith's influence as well. This church is recognized as the first Christian church in New England. Two years later he "gathered another church in Bradford, Vermont" and in March of 1803 another at Piermont, New Hampshire (Freese 1852:27).

The New England movement grew rapidly. By 1827, through the efforts of both Smith and Jones, and others, it was reported there were

nearly one hundred companies of free brethren that meet together to worship God in the name of Christ without the addition of any other name (Garrison and Degroot 1948:90).

Freese reveals that from the established congregations a number of young preachers of ability, through their traveling and zeal were soon preaching throughout the New England states, New York, Pennsylvania, Ohio, and subsequently in New Jersey, Michigan, New Brunswick, Canada, and elsewhere. The result was the organization of churches and the building of meeting houses (Freese 1852:27-28).

Those churches with reasonable consistency clung to the Baptist practice of believer's baptism by immersion though they had little understanding of its meaning.

According to Barrett, in New England, baptism was by immersion, and in the south both sprinkling and immersion were practiced (Barrett 1908:47).

Freese took exception. He observed that it was an unusual circumstance in the rise of the three branches of the Christian

35

Church (by which he has reference to the Christian Connection of New England, the O'Kelly movement of the south and the Stone movement of the west) that all three

> altogether entirely unknown to each other, adopted the same views with regard to the mode and efficacy of baptism . . . it seems, almost, that as an overriding Providence had directed their minds in the way of truth and thus, from the study of the Bible, they were lead to adopt these sentiments, the truthfulness of which will stand while the world stands (Freese 1852:66).

The New England Christian Churches had several likenesses to the Unitarians, and numbers of their members affirmed as much, insisting, however, that they chose not to be called Unitarians but simply Christians (Garrison and DeGroot 1948:91).

Similarity in views with the Unitarians led the New England Christians in 1844 to share with them in the establishing of the Meadville, Pennsylvania, theological school (Murch 1962:33). This cooperative effort in ministerial training did not last long, however.

Universalism did plague the Christian Churches of the east. According to Freese, the denomination acted at once to eliminate the threat, though it had affected one of the original leaders of the movement.

> In 1817, Elder E. Smith came out a Universalist. This gave a shock to the whole, and the question was asked at once, What shall be done to check these evils . . . At the conference at Portsmouth, (N.H.) many subjects of deep interest were presented; and as Universalism was believed to lead to licentiousness, it was agreed that they could not hold in fellowship any man that preached that doctrine. Elder E. Smith

36

was therefore declared to be no longer in fellowship (Freese 1852:176;177).

By 1827 these churches were known throughout the United States. They were said to have a membership of thousands with several hundred ministers known by the name of Christian only.

The "Christian" Movement in Kentucky

Barton Warren Stone

James DeForest Murch (1962:19,22-23,30,32-33) attributes the Stone Movement to a "tremendous moving of the Spirit of God that appeared in America as the eighteenth century drew to a close," as does William Garrett West (1955:xv) and Charles Crossfield Ware (1932:ix).

The most important of the "Christian" movements in relationship to the Restoration Movement was the one of which Barton Warren Stone was the influence. This development came from a Presbyterian background, and its beginnings, as did the O'Kelly movement, go back to the "New Light" stirrings of Virginia and the states of the south and the east.

Barton Warren Stone was born at Port Tobacco, Maryland, on December 24, 1772 (Rogers 1847:1). He was a fifth generation American and a lineal descendent of William Stone, the first Protestant governor of Maryland (1648-1653), his great, great, great grandfather. His father died shortly before the beginning of the Revolutionary War and the estate was left to his family. Disposing of her property, his mother moved with her children to Pittsylvania County, Virginia.

Stone Attends David Caldwell's Academy Young Barton used his inheritance to finance his education at David Caldwell's academy at Greensboro, North Carolina. Caldwell's school was known and respected throughout North Carolina and Virginia. This Carolina log cabin college was called "Academy, a College and a Theological School" (West 1954:3). It was said of Caldwell that he was "one of the greatest natural teachers that America has ever produced" (Konkle 1922:12f). He was a graduate of the College of New Jersey and was a New Light Presbyterian (Hall 1954:17). His academy radiated a "warmly religious atmosphere and was hospitable to the revivalism of the Methodists, Baptists and New Light Presbyterians" (Garrison and DeGroot 1948:93).

The Influence of James McGready Many evangelists came to Caldwell during the three years that Stone was there. The spiritual atmosphere of the school attracted them. James McGready, a strict Calvinist, was most popular. Shortly before Stone arrived at Caldwell, McGready preached at Greensboro and most of the students had been converted. The consequent atmosphere was disturbing to young Mr. Stone. He was attracted and repelled at the same time.

Stone soon heard McGready himself and was impressed with the evangelistic power of the man, so much so that he thought seriously of becoming a Christian. However, Calvinism of the day had so walled in salvation that it took the penitent a long time to obtain the assurance he sought for. Captive of the prevailing beliefs of the time, Stone knew no better, and for a year he wrestled with the problem. Again he heard McGready as "he thundered divine anathemas" at the unsaved. The result was deep depression at his lost condition about which there seemed to be no remedy.

> While McGready had radically advanced from Calvinism in some evangelical aspects of his message, still, in personal conference with the terrified Barton, he reiterated the impending horrors of the Calvinist's hell. And Barton testified, He left me without one encouraging word (Ware 1932:28).

The Preaching of William Hodge In the spring of 1791 Stone attended a meeting at the Alamance New Light Presbyterian Church, and, for the first time, heard the appeal of preaching focused on the love of God. The revival spirit of George Whitefield had influenced the Alamance church (1932:28). It was the kind of preaching that won Barton Warren Stone's heart and soul.

William Hodge was also trained by David Caldwell. Hodge "was the exact reverse of McGready . . . His great excellency appears to have been his skill, under God, to heal the broken hearted and bind up their wounds" (Smith 1930:668).

Hodge and McGready were leaders in both Kentucky and Tennessee, and McGready was especially influential in Logan County, Kentucky. "This evangelism centering at Caldwell's school, was of far-reaching importance in view of its development of leaders for America's 'Second Awakening' which came beyond the Alleghenies" (Ware 1932:29).

Young Hodge's preaching on the occasion of Barton W. Stone's conversion centered on the text, "God is love," and Stone spoke of Hodge's animation and tears "as he spoke of the love of God for sinners and of what that love had done" (Rogers 1847:10). The young penitent's heart was warmed for the person of Jesus whom Hodge described, and hope and joy came to his heart and mind. Following the service he retired to the forest with his Bible in hand, and with the text of the sermon, "God is love," still ringing in his ears, he gave himself to the Lord.

Stone's Conversion As he himself tells the story:

> I yielded and sunk at his feet a willing subject . . . I now saw that a poor sinner was as much authorized to believe in Jesus first, as at last . . . that now was the accepted time, the day of salvation (Rogers 1847:11).

"His was not an orthodox conversion according to the preaching of his time, but it was real. From this commitment he never departed" (Murch 1962:84).

Stone Decides that He Wants to Preach Barton Warren Stone's first intention was to study law, but after his conversion he decided to preach, if he could be in the same mold as William Hodge (Garrison and DeGroot 1948:94). However he had no miraculous call from God, and this troubled him. His teacher, David Caldwell, assured him that his longing to preach was enough and assigned him a text to be developed with its theme "The Trinity." This sermon was to be delivered before the Orange Presbytery in order that Stone might be granted a license as a preacher. The subject was difficult and one that Stone wrestled with all his life. Through his own studies he was acquainted with the Bible, but until this time his mind had been "undisturbed by polemic and obscure divinity" (Ware 1932:30). After considerable study, Stone found a book by Isaac Watts that provided the help he needed, and the discourse was prepared and presented to the presbytery. Henry Patillo, who accepted the views of Isaac Watts, presided at the meeting. Patillo's questions were carefully phrased, and

40

Stone passed the examination. His license was granted at the next meeting of the presbytery, which met every six months.

While waiting, Mr. Stone visited his brother in Georgia, becoming ill enroute and requiring months to recover (1932:34). His stay was prolonged at a school called Succoth Academy at Washington, Georgia. He served as professor of languages for one year from January, 1795.

His Association with Hope Hull Succoth Academy was founded by Hope Hull, who "before and during the conference of 1792, supported James O'Kelly's campaign against Bishop Francis Asbury's autocracy" (Garrison and DeGroot 1948:95).

Hull and Stone soon became good friends. At the invitation of Mr. Hull, young Mr. Stone travelled with him to Charleston, South Carolina, to attend a Methodist district conference. The association with Hope Hull is of significance in its influence upon Barton Warren Stone, particularly as one notes the time sequence of events in this period of his life. The O'Kelly secession had occured three years prior to this time. The Republican Methodist Church had been established but two years, and the Christian Church, one year before Stone's association with Hull in 1795 (MacClenny 1950:116).

Three years had passed since Hull shared in O'Kelly's protest, and though he remained in the Methodist Church while O'Kelly and other insurgents withdrew, he was aware of what was taking place and why. These events were often a topic of conversation with Stone and Hull.

John Springer, a Fellow New Light Presbyterian Another influence at the time was John Springer, a New Light Presbyterian preacher. A few miles separated his parish from the academy where Stone taught. Springer was an ardent evangelist and a man of broad sympathies and tolerance. He paid little attention to sectarian lines, having fraternal relations with his Methodist and Baptist neighbors alike. He was one of Stone's dearest friends and trusted counselors. His "influence on Barton Warren Stone was decisive" (Ware 1932:42).

The spiritual climate in which Stone lived during this year was to have a tremendous influence upon his future ministry. Distinctions between denominations were of no significance. Carefully defined expressions of divisive theologies were neither remembered nor discussed. Attention was given to the unifying truths of the gospel.

Stone returned to North Carolina and to the Hawfields church in Alamance County where the Orange Presbytery was holding its spring meeting. Indication of the forces influencing Mr. Stone was the fact that the Hawfields church was within ten or fifteen miles of where he had been converted through the preaching of William Hodge. Within the same radius was the first Christian Church of the O'Kelly movement, and the church in which Stone was licensed to preach.

The Unconventional Henry Patillo His license was granted by the unconventional Henry Patillo on April 6, 1796. Patillo was an unusual Presbyterian. He believed that all Christians, including ministers, should be allowed to hold differing doctrinal views without permitting their differences to bring division among them. He denounced division and affirmed that it was the name "Christian" which was first given to the disciples at Antioch and by divine authority, and it was "that name which is the great glory of disciples to wear . . . that new name promised to the New

Testament Church, which the mouth of the Lord should name" (1932:42).

Concerning orthodoxy in matters of doctrine, he said,

Men will think differently in the affairs of common life, politics, philosophy, and religion: Let them differ in a friendly manner. The sheep of Christ must not forget their nature and worry each other. The wolves of earth and the lions of hell will do that for them (1932:52).

His views on church polity were equally unconventional.

I have often thought that the popular congregational government of the independents joined to the Presbyterian judicatures, as a final resort, would form the most perfect model of church government that the state of things on earth will admit of (1932:53).

That Patillo was ahead of his day is beyond doubt, but his background helps to explain this. He had been trained by the outstanding minister, Samuel Davies, of Virginia, who led in "The Great Awakening" in that state. This it was that ushered in the revival of personal religion, emphasizing the new birth and the importance of emotional manifestations, so appealing to all.

Other Significant Influences in the Life of Stone Garrison and DeGroot list a number of the important influences that shaped the life of Barton Warren Stone.

They give first place to the Great Awakening beginning about 1740 through the preaching of George Whitefield and William Tennant's Log College trained preachers. This brought about a revival that "echoed for more than half a century in the middle and southern seaboard colonies" (Garrison and DeGroot 1948:96). They emphasize the place of the Methodist Church which began as an Anglican revival but became a separate church with the revival continuing unabated. Its emphasis upon a heart-centered faith made great impact upon Barton Warren Stone.

The "Christian" Church in North Carolina and Virginia influenced him as he was seeking answers to the problems confronting him. It came into existence through the secession of James O'Kelly from the Methodists during the developing period of his ministry.

There were also the influences of men like David Caldwell, James McGready, William Hodge, Hope Hull, John Springer and Henry Patillo, Presbyterians and Methodists alike who were preachers of revival and a part of that spiritual climate when denominational and sectarian differences were of little consequence.

Stone Moves to the Western Frontier Having received his license to preach, Stone and another licentiate, Robert Foster, were sent to eastern North Carolina on a missionary tour. They enjoyed so little success that Foster decided his call had been a mistake. Stone, made of sterner stuff, and certain of his calling, decided to move to the western frontier. He joined the cavalcade on the wilderness road. By horseback he travelled through Knoxville, encountering nonviolent Indians before reaching the village of Nashville. There he met the New Light Presbyterian, Princeton-trained preacher, Thomas Craighead, brother of Rachel Craighead Caldwell, wife of David Caldwell of Caldwell's Academy at Greensboro, North Carolina (Ware 1932:61).

Craighead was known because of his freedom of thought and his attitude of independence towards presbyteries and creeds. When Stone was later branded a heretic, Craighead was accused of corrupting him. When Craighead was brought to trial in 1815 and interrogated about the nature of his faith, he answered, " 'It is of the testimony of God" —

44

which sounds like Reformer's (Restoration) doctrine, except that he went on to say that the Word of God alone does not produce it without additional aid from the Spirit" (Garrison and DeGroot 1948:97).

His Appointment and His Ordination. In October of 1796, six months after he had been granted his license, Barton Warren Stone was appointed as supply minister of two central Kentucky churches, one at Cane Ridge and the other at Concord, northeast of Paris, Kentucky. He was not yet twenty-four years of age.

During the following year, he was called to the settled pastorate of the two churches he had supplied, and it was required that he be ordained. This made necessary his affirmation of the Westminster Confession.

Up to this time, he had avoided the difficult doctrines of the confession by ignoring them as mysteries, preaching the gospel and avoiding the problems of the creed. Now he had to stand before the interrogation of the presbytery and reveal his personal views, which he had, so far, withheld.

He saw the confession as a unified system. If one block were removed, it would crumble. So perplexed he was by the dilemma that he resolved to postpone the service, and he expressed his apprehensions on October 4th, the day of the ordination, to James Blythe and Robert Marshall, two of the examining preachers. They could not resolve his unbelief, nor would they delay the ordination. However, a possible solution was suggested.

The place of the ordination was Cane Ridge, and when, before the eleven men of the Transylvania Presbytery, Robert Marshall solemnly asked Stone, "Do you receive and adopt the confession of faith, as containing the system of doctrine taught in the Bible?" Stone answered, "I do, as far as I see it consistent with the Word of God" (Rogers 1847:29-30) (Richardson 1868:Vol.2,190).

Theological Problems that Plagued Mr. Stone. Barton Warren Stone was ordained, October 4, 1798, though the answer was not recorded in the minutes with the consequence that difficulties did later arise. His ordination did not remove the dilemma plaguing his mind and heart. Many years later he wrote,

> I at that time believed and taught that mankind was so totally depraved that they could do nothing acceptable to God, till his Spirit, by some physical, almighty and mysterious power had quickened, enlightened, and regenerated the heart, and thus prepared the sinner to believe in Jesus for salvation (Rogers 1847:30).

Stone began to comprehend that if the Lord did not save all men, it must be that he deemed to save some and not others, and this was dependent on his own sovereign will. He then was able to understand that this doctrine was inseparably bound with unconditional election and reprobation as enunciated in the Westminster Confession of faith. Stone saw that they were practically one and the same thing, and said this was the reason why he admitted the decrees of election and reprobation, having admitted the doctrine of total depravity (1847:30-31).

He recalled that protestations flooded his mind against the system. He was preaching on the doctrine of total depravity, man's inability to believe, and the necessity for God to act to produce faith, and then he was urging the helpless to repent and believe. His enthusiasm would be chilled by the contradiction (Rogers 1847:31).

He made the Bible his source of knowledge and he sought for truth, determined to obtain it, if need be at the cost of everything else. "From this state of perplexity," he says, "I was relieved by the precious Word of God" (1847: 32-33).

From meditating upon the Scriptures, Stone became convinced that God did love the whole world, and the reason God did not save all men was because of their unbelief. They believed not because they had neglected to accept God's testimony given in His Word concerning His Son. Stone said, "I saw that the requirement to believe in the Son of God was reasonable; because the testimony given was sufficient to produce faith in the sinner; and the invitations and encouragement of the gospel was sufficient, if believed, to lead him to the Savior . . ." (1847:33).

The Presbyterians, Baptists, and Methodists were present on the frontier. However, the power of religion over the majority of the population was nil. Deism and atheism had captured the minds of the people. In 1800, population statistics for Kentucky revealed only 10,000 church members out of 221,000 residents. This constituted the fertile soil out of which the impending awakening would come.

Chapter Three

BARTON WARREN STONE AND HIS PLACE IN THE NEW REFORMATION

James McGready and Logan County, Antecedent to Cane Ridge

James DeForest Murch (1962:85) called James McGready the "John the Baptist" of the Great Awakening of the west. He and Barton Warren Stone arrived in Kentucky in 1796. McGready had been licensed to preach in 1788. The following year he was influenced by the revival at Hampden-Sydney College in Virginia, on his way back to North Carolina, with the result that he became an evangelist. The Hampden-Sydney College revival started when a few students, not one a professing Christian, tried to hold a prayer meeting. Rowdies attempted to stop it with the result that the president opened his study to the intercessors for prayer. In a short time, a movement started with the majority of students converted and local churches moved as well (Orr 1975a:66).

Mr. McGready began his evangelistic preaching at Caldwell Academy. Barton Stone, William Hodge, William McGee and others in the Kentucky revival were influenced by his preaching. He moved to Logan County, Kentucky, in 1796 and began serving the Gasper River, Red River and Muddy River churches near Russellville. Few areas in America of 1800 could compare with Logan County. It was a raw and lawless frontier filled with thieves and murderers.

In 1797 McGready made a covenant with God to set aside every third Saturday of the month for one year for prayer and fasting for conversion of the lost in Logan

County and the world, and to devote one half hour each Saturday evening and a like period every Sabbath morning beseeching God to revive his work. There was an "awakening of many at Gasper River Church in May. Similar results occurred in 1798, 1799, and 1800. So great was the awakening that all which had gone before was as an introduction and like a few drops before a mighty rain" (Ware 1932:79).

Barton Warren Stone and Cane Ridge

Stone returned to Virginia and North Carolina in late 1800. On his way back to Kentucky, he met leaders of the Shiloh church in Tennessee and received his first knowledge of the Logan County revival.

In the states south and east of the mountains, continuous evangelistic appeals were conducted by the New Light Presbyterians, Methodists and Baptists, and more recently by the Christians (O'Kelly secession); but among older religious communities revivalism had been of little consequence. The first Methodist revival in Virginia was in 1772.

In Concord and Cane Ridge, Stone noted the lack of spiritual concern growing each year. He resolved to go to Logan County to participate in the revival, and hopefully, would bring it back to Bourbon County. He went in early spring of 1801.

Numbers of people encamped at the edge of the prairie, fifteen miles northwest of Russellville, all to hear revival preaching. Stone observed carefully, going from person to person among those struck down, questioning them about their experiences. He was convinced it was the work of God.

Stone now had the dynamic for a message that, until then, was new to him. Back at Cane Ridge he preached on the Great Commission according to Mark, emphasizing that the gospel was universal, that faith was the stated condition and thus urged sinners to believe and be redeemed.

Cane Ridge and Concord were a repetition of Logan County. Christian workers had been alarmed by the wickedness of the people of Kentucky. Now, those participating in the revivals were overjoyed. Many had prayed for a spiritual awakening, but when it came, it was beyond their expectations. Denominational lines melted away. Stone shared in preaching day and night alongside Methodist, Baptist, Presbyterian and independent preachers. Multitudes came from great distances, clogging the roads as they travelled on foot, horseback, and by wagons and carriages (Stone in Rogers 1847:37).

In his biographical sketch years after the Cane Ridge revival, Mr. Stone wrote, "This memorable meeting came on Thursday or Friday before the third Lord's Day in August, 1801" (1847:37). The Cane Ridge meeting possibly lasted six days. Though the date is uncertain, it likely took place from the seventh to the twelfth of August, 1801 (Ware 1932:105-107).

Not until all food supplies were exhausted did the meeting end. It was "probably the greatest demonstration of revival power ever seen in America" (Murch 1962:39).*

---

* Church historians outside the Restoration Movement have also taken note of the Cane Ridge Revival. William Warren Sweet observed (1973:228-229), "Perhaps the greatest of all the single phases of the western revival was what has come to be known as the Cane Ridge Meeting." Orr touches upon the revival, (1965:25) and then looks at it in detail (1975a:60-63). Latourette speaks of it (1964:1041, and 1970: Vol. IV,193), and there are others who, together with those of the Restoration Movement, give Cane Ridge not only a permanent place in the beginnings of the Restoration Movement, but in the larger development of American Christianity.

The Accompanying Revival Excesses

It was Stone's conviction through his life, though he did come to question some aspects of revival (see appendices) that the phenomenon of Logan County and Cane Ridge was the work of God. He affirms that much which he saw was, in his opinion, fanaticism, but he insists that this should not condemn the work. He points out that Satan has always attempted to mimic the work of God to bring it into question. But, he says,

> That cannot be Satan's work, which brings men to humble confession and forsaking of sin, to solemn prayer . . . fervent praise and thanksgiving, and to sincere and affectionate exhortation to sinners to repent and go to Jesus the Savior (Rogers 1847:34-35).

A part of the description of what Mr. Stone observed is recorded here.

> . . . At a meeting, two gay young ladies, sisters, were standing together attending to the exercises and preaching at the same time. Instantly they both fell, with a shriek of distress, and lay for more than an hour, apparently in a lifeless state . . . After awhile, the gloom on the face of one was succeeded by a heavenly smile, and she cried out, 'precious Jesus,' and rose up and spoke of the love of God . . . the preciousness of Jesus, and the glory of the gospel to the surrounding crowd, in language almost superhuman, and pathetically exhorted all to repentance . . .
>
> The jerks cannot be so easily described . . . When the whole system was affected, I have seen a person stand in one place and jerk backward and forward in quick succession, their head nearly touching the floor behind and before. All classes . . . were thus affected. They could not account for it; but

some have told me that they were among the happiest seasons of their lives.

The dancing exercise . . . The subject, after jerking awhile,
began to dance, and the jerks would cease . . . While thus
exercised, I have heard their solemn praises and prayers
ascending to God.

The barking exercise (as opposers contemptuously called it)
was nothing but the jerks. A person affected with the jerks,
especially in his head, would often make a grunt or a bark,
if you please, from the suddenness of the jerk.

The singing exercise . . . The subject in a very happy state
of mind would sing most melodiously not from the mouth
or nose, but entirely in the breast, the sounds issuing thence.
Such music silenced everything, and attracted the attention
of all (1847:39-42).

No effort is made to explain these phenomena, nor is
there need to explain them. Historians unanimously acknowledge that they did take place, and they must not be ignored.

They have been an embarrassment to many in the Restoration Movement, and for this reason Barton Warren Stone
has been denied what should have been a more prominent
place in the movement.

Benjamin Lyon Smith's judgment (1930:311) is correct
when he writes, "Alexander Campbell, had he been in this
country, would have had no part in this fantastic hysteria,"
but Alexander was a lad of twelve years and eleven months,
living in Northern Ireland in August of 1801. The circumstances at Cane Ridge have to be viewed in the context
of eighteenth century frontier and not in the context of
the 1830's and eastern Ohio. It is historically dishonest to
compare Cane Ridge, 1801, with the Mahoning Valley
of 1828.

Barton Warren Stone's Views on
Revival Exercises in Relation to Conversion

Stone's views must be seen today in light of his own judgment of Calvinism and the process by which one became a Christian (Rogers 1847:35).

> Stone encouraged the pattern of conversion which broke the Calvinistic scheme developed by Presbyterians in Kentucky, a scheme which asserted that man must wait until God was ready to strike with the sword of the Spirit. Stone cried out that God had already struck the hour of salvation and continued to strike. The revival was his proof (West 1955: 41).

Stone believed that the Calvinistic emphasis on man's helplessness created a sense of hopelessness, and so he focused on what he saw to be man's part in salvation as well as upon what God had done (1955:92).

It seemed useless, hopeless and wicked to invite his hearers to turn from their wicked ways, and to believe in the Lord if God had already predestined those to be saved and those to be lost and if those still in sin were helpless in moving away from their deserved doom (Latourette 1971:Vol. IV, 197).

Stone approved of revivals but the New Light theology which advocated sudden invasions of the Holy Spirit he was inclined to repudiate. In his approach to conversion he tended to believe there was a gradual fanning of the divine spark in man into a full flame. His theology looked for a gradual but accelerating new life rather than a sudden upheaval (West 1955:211). He believed his was a prophetic ministry and that he was called of God, for he had seen numerous examples of God's grace. "His commitment was complete, and like the Apostle Paul, neither height nor depth nor things present nor things to come could separate him from his fellowship with Christ in the salvation of precious souls" (Murch 1962:91).

Mr. Stone carefully described the doctrine preached, that

> God so loved the world . . . the whole world, and sent his Son to save them, on condition that they believed in him . . . that the gospel was the means of salvation . . . but that this means would never be effectual to this end, until believed and obeyed by us . . . We urged upon the sinner to believe now, and receive salvation (Rogers 1847:44-45).

Stone's legacy to the Restoration Movement is not only in the revivals surrounding Cane Ridge, though they were important, but also in his concern for lost men everywhere. This was Mr. Stone's plea:

> Let all Christians, therefore, unite in prayer, that God would send forth laborers into his harvest; that the Word of the Lord may have free course and be glorified; that his Spirit may be poured out upon his ministers and people; that through them he may reprove the world of sin, of righteousness, and of judgment (1847:220-221).

The Revival Acknowledged by Other Restoration Movement Historians

Restoration Movement historians have observed the Awakenings and have seen the relationship between those Awakenings and the beginnings of the Reformation, though, almost without exception, they have minimized that relationship.

John Williams relates that

In 1799, McGready lifted his warning voice in the hills of Tennessee, and thousands flocked to the forests to hear him . . . The excitement continued to spread like a conflagration through the land. In 1800 it broke out in Kentucky . . . (Williams 1904:34).

Barton Warren Stone describes the Logan County and Cane Ridge revivals.

There on the edge of a prairie in Logan County, Kentucky, the multitudes came together . . . The scene to me was new, and passing strange (Rogers 1847:32-38).

Richardson notes that from Logan County, Mr. Stone returned to Cane Ridge, and there

similar effects occurred under his own labors, and a protracted meeting being appointed in August, the interest felt throughout the community brought together a multitude estimated at more than twenty thousand (Richardson 1868: Vol. II,192-193).

Archibald McLean (1909:37) noted that Barton Warren Stone "was one of the principal speakers at the great Cane Ridge revival."

W. T. Moore (1909:235-242), focuses on Mr. Stone's account of the revival scenes and concludes they are not of God.

Benjamin Lyon Smith (1930:310) referred to "this period in American religious history when emotionalism was at its highest peak."

P. H. Welshimer (1935:78) viewed the frontier revivals with favor.

55

There were a great many strange things happening that baffle description, and although not in accord with all that was done, he (Stone) believed it was a good work . . . the Cane Ridge revival has become notable in history. Three thousand were converted.

William Garrett West spoke of the influence of James McGready and Henry Patillo on Stone (1955:5).

Enos Dowling devoted several paragraphs to Cane Ridge. A unique aspect of the revival was that doctrinal standards that had so long divided the denominations were forgotten and Methodists, Baptists, and Presbyterians labored together.

The revivalists themselves laid aside their denominational differences to lift a united voice in proclaiming the love and mercy of God for the penitent sinner (Dowling 1964:27-29).

M. M. Davis commented that it resembled another Pentecost.

Like fire in stubble, the influence of the meeting swept abroad until a wide scope of country was involved. Doubtless there was fanaticism here, but it was not all fanaticism, or good and permanent results would not have followed as they did (Davis 1915:111).

Garrison and DeGroot add that Stone

rejoiced in the conversion of sinners and the rousing of slumbering saints. He must have rejoiced also that, in the heat of the revival, all sects seemed to be fused into one body and that body — Christian (Garrison and DeGroot 1948:101-102).

J. D. Murch begins his book *Christians Only* with the statement, "As the eighteenth century drew to a close in

America, signs of a tremendous moving of the Spirit of God appeared . . ." (1962:19).

Robert Richardson placed his evaluation on the revivals by saying,

> It cannot be denied that great good resulted from the intense religious excitement which thus prevailed in various portions of Kentucky and Tennessee, nor were its effects by any means transient" (Richardson 1868:Vol. II,193).

Revival Influences That Positively Affected the Forthcoming New Reformation

James DeForest Murch (1962:86 judged the Cane Ridge revival to hold a place of significance in the Reformation.

> It had its proper setting in the great western revival without which it is altogether likely the Restoration Movement in America might not have come into being at this time.

Significant persons and events, both before and following Cane Ridge, bear out Mr. Murch's conclusion.

Springfield Presbytery

Antecedents of the Springfield Presbytery. Richard McNemar, Presbyterian minister who had been one of the participants at the Cane Ridge meeting and who, when the occasion permitted, cooperated with Methodists in evangelistic endeavors, had charges laid against him by the Washington, Kentucky, Presbytery three months after Cane Ridge. Prosecution of the charges was postponed on several occasions because there were more revivalists at Presbytery meetings, taking his side, than there were accusers.

The matter hung unresolved until September, 1803, when the Synod of Kentucky pressed the charges.

Stone recounts (Rogers 1847:44) that five men of the Presbyterian affiliation held to doctrines different from that taught by the Confession of Faith. Those men were McNemar, John Thompson, John Dunlavy, Robert Marshall, and Barton Warren Stone. Stone also names David Purviance, who was then a candidate for the ministry in the Presbyterian Church.

Prior to the trial, John Thompson was also charged, and so Thompson and McNemar stood accused of Arminianism (Freese 1852:34).

Before the synod had time to voice its judgment, all five men appeared with a document protesting the pending action and affirming their right to "appeal from the creed to the Bible" on any doctrinal issue, and formally renouncing jurisdiction of the Synod of Kentucky (Rogers 1847:47), (Garrison and DeGroot 1948:103).

This protest contained three assertions: first, the five men insisted that McNemar was misrepresented with regard to his beliefs. Secondly, they claimed the privilege of interpreting the Word of God by itself. They believed "that the supreme judge by whom all controversies of religion" were "to be determined . . ." could "be no other but the Holy Spirit speaking in the Scriptures." Thirdly, while they asserted no wish to take themselves from communion with the Presbyterians, they said, "We declare ourselves no longer members of your Rev'nd Body, or under your jurisdiction, or that of your Presbyteries," and "we bid you adieu until through the providence of God it seems good to your Rev'nd Body to adopt a more liberal plan respecting human creeds and confessions" (1948:104). The document was dated, Lexington, Kentucky, September 10, 1803, and was signed by the five men, Marshall, Dunlavy, McNemar, Stone and Thompson. Emissaries were commissioned at the next General Assembly to meet with the dissidents, but the gulf was too great to span.

The dissenters were suspended on September 13, 1803, on the grounds that they 1) had separated themselves from the jurisdiction of the synod; 2) had seceded from the Confession of Faith; 3) had refused to return to the doctrines and standards of the church; and 4) had constituted themselves into a separate presbytery (Murch 1962:87).

From the date the declaration of independence was signed, the chasm was too broad, for it was an affirmation that Presbyterian preachers had the right to interpretation of Scripture without approval of the church and thus were not forced to cling to the Presbyterian confession of faith. This was a fundamental question. The changes suggested were radical.

Barton Warren Stone, at his ordination five years previously, indicated this same tendency. He accepted the Westminster Confession only "as far as he could see it consistent with the Word of God" (Rogers 1847:30). In any case, Stone and his companions saw that the action of the Synod with regard to Stone,

> However just their decision might be with respect to the other four . . . was improper with regard to him, seeing he had not received that book at his ordination, nor ever before, more than any other book, i.e., as far as he saw it agreeable to the Word of God (1847:48).

There is no word of this exception in the account of Stone's ordination in the minutes of the Presbytery. They say only that he answered·affirmatively the "Questions appointed to be put to candidates previous to their ordination" (Sweet 1936:181). In his biography he declares that in reply to their query, he answered aloud, "so that the whole congregation might hear" (Rogers 1847:30).

Whether Stone was the first to make this exception, he was not the last. A similar statement was being made by many within two years of the withdrawal of Stone and his friends, and the Cumberland defection, to become the Cumberland Presbyterian Church, was the result (Garrison and DeGroot 1948:105). Something very different, however, was to happen to Stone and his cohorts.

Presbyterians had been known to dissassociate themselves from existing presbyteries in the past. Often this had happened in Scotland. However, the breach created by McNemar, Thompson, Dunlavy, Marshall and Stone carried deeper implications. It was an attack on Calvinistic theology. It rejected the principle that the church could enforce doctrinal uniformity by requiring adherence to a creed. When they denied the right of the church to determine doctrines contained in Scripture and to summarize its conclusions in a creed to be enforced upon its membership and when they insisted on the right of interpretation regardless of the creed, this was a drastic move fraught with danger to the Presbyterian Church.

The Short Life of the Springfield Presbytery. The Springfield Presbytery was informally structured. It was a loosely organized group of independent ministers whose object was to rectify and reform.

After they had separated from the Synod, the five brethren communicated with the churches under their oversight to tell their side of the story. In January, 1804, they published a booklet entitled *An Abstract of an Apology for Renouncing the Jurisdiction of the Synod of Kentucky, Being a Compendious View of the Gospel and a Few Remarks on the Confession of Faith* (1847:49).* The apology was divided into three equal parts. Robert Marshall detailed the circumstances to the time of the breach; Stone enumerated and amplified the points at which the Presbyterian Confession misinterpreted Scriptural teaching; and Thompson formulated his arguments to affirm that all creeds and confessions, when used as standards, are of potentially great harm.

The apology was widely read and exerted favorable influence. It said nothing about restoration, but there were affirmations that were close to the doctrinal stance taken by Thomas Campbell five or six years hence.

These five men stood on solid ground in asserting that they were not the only Presbyterians viewing the doctrine of atonement differently from the Confession. Leaders like David Caldwell, Henry Patillo and James McGready held a broad interpretation of the Confession, but that could be tolerated. It was a different matter for a group to organize itself to launch an attack against the whole system for which the Presbyterian Church stood and to reject the authority of the Synod.

The Last Will and Testament of the Springfield Presbytery. Less than one year after the secession and five months following the *Apology*, the Springfield Presbytery met at Cane Ridge to vote itself out of existence. The act had particular significance.

---

* The complete text of this one hundred page booklet can be found in the biography of Barton Warren Stone (Rogers 1847:147-247).

The instrument has been recognized as one of the charter documents of the Restoration Movement.

The Last Will and Testament

The Presbytery of Springfield, sitting at Cane Ridge, in the county of Bourbon, being, through a gracious Providence, in more than ordinary bodily health, growing in strength and size daily; and in perfect soundness and composure of mind; but knowing that it is appointed for all delegated bodies to die; and considering that the life of every such body is very uncertain, do make, and ordain this our last will and testament in manner and form following, viz.:

Imprimis. We will, that this body die, be dissolved, and sink into union with the Body of Christ at large: for there is but one body, and one Spirit, even as we are called in one hope of our calling.

Item. We will, that our name of distinction, with its Rever'd title, be forgotten, that there be but one Lord over God's heritage, and his name one.

Item. We will, that our power of making laws for the government of the Church, and executing them by delegated authority, forever cease; that the people may have free course to the Bible, and adopt the law of the Spirit of life in Christ Jesus.

Item. We will, that candidates for the gospel ministry henceforth study the Holy Scriptures with fervent prayer, and obtain license from God to preach the simple gospel, with the Holy Ghost sent down from heaven, without any mixture of philosophy, vain deceit, traditions of men, or the rudiments of the world. And let none henceforth take this honor to himself, but he that is called of God, as was Aaron.

Item. We will, that the church of Christ, resume her native right of internal government — try her candidates for the ministry, as to their soundness in the faith, acquaintance with experimental religion, gravity and aptness to teach; and admit no other proof of their authority but Christ speaking in them. We will that the church of Christ look up to the Lord of the harvest to send forth laborers into his harvest; and that she resume her primitive right of trying those who say they are apostles, and are not.

Item. We will, that each particular church, as a body, actuated by the same spirit, choose her own preacher, and support him by a free will offering, without a written call or subscription — admit members — remove offences; and never henceforth delegate her right of government to any man or set of men whatever.

Item. We will that the people henceforth take the Bible as the only sure guide to heaven; and as many as are offended with other books, which stand in competition with it, may cast them into the fire if they choose; for it is better to enter into life having one book, than having many to be cast into hell.

Item. We will, that preachers and people, cultivate a spirit of mutual forbearance; pray more and dispute less; and while they behold the signs of the times, look up, and confidently expect that redemption draweth nigh.

Item. We will, that our weak brethren, who may have been wishing to make the Presbytery of Springfield their king, and wot not what is now become of it, betake themselves to the Rock of Ages, and follow Jesus for the future.

Item. We will, that the Synod of Kentucky examine every member, who may be suspected of having departed from the Confession of Faith, and suspend every such suspected heretic immediately; in order that the oppressed may go free, and taste the sweets of gospel liberty.

Item. We will that Ja__ _____, the author of two letters lately published in Lexington, be encouraged in his zeal to destroy partyism. We will, moreover, that our past conduct be examined into by all who may have correct information; but let foreigners beware of speaking evil of things which they know not.

Item. Finally we will, that all our sister bodies read their Bibles carefully, that they may see their fate there determined, and prepare for death before it is too late.

Springfield Presbytery,
June 28th, 1804

L.S.

Robert Marshall
John Dunlavy
Richard McNemar
B. W, Stone   Witnesses
John Thompson
David Purviance

The Christian Churches of New England were aware of the Stone Movement of Kentucky and Tennessee. Freese credits Stone, McNemar, Thompson, Dunlavy and Marshall, through the blessing of God, for bringing about a mighty revival, and he was aware of their withdrawal from the Presbytery and the formation of the Springfield Presbytery.

> For awhile, after their withdrawal, they continued the Presbyterian form of church government, and formed themselves into an independent organization, which they called the 'Springfield Presbytery,' but they believed this smacked too much of sectarian control and so dissolved the organization in 1804 'to allow each church to be entirely independent — each member thereof to teach and believe those principles which, from a careful and candid examination of the Scriptures, they conceived to be true — and last but not least, to be known as "Christians" only' (Freese 1852:35-36).

In the study of the impact of revival upon the men who shared in the founding of the Reformation or the Restoration Movement, conspicuous features stand out. There was an emphasis upon the responsibility of every Christian to appeal to the Scriptures. There was a demand, noted in the developing theology of the Restoration Movement and similar movements, for the independence of each local church, free from any body of wider scope having delegated authority. "Union with the Body of Christ at large," expressed in the first item of the Will was a longing voiced by other leaders such as John Glas, Robert Sandeman, the Haldane brothers, Elias Smith, Abner Jones and James O'Kelly as well as the Campbells. Emphasis to restore the doctrines of the apostolic church is absent from the document, and yet deductions can be made from the desire expressed by the signers to imitate those doctrines and practices . . . "no title Reverend,* no contracts or stated salaries for ministers, no requirement of secular education or the approval of any agency except the local church as a condition of ordination or license to preach" (Garrison and DeGroot 1948:111).

Party Names and Creeds Cast Away, the Young Movement Adopts for Itself the Name, Christian. Barton Warren Stone wrote in his autobiography,

> Under the name of Springfield Presbytery we went forward preaching and constituting churches; but we had not worn our name more than a year before we saw it savored of a party spirit. With the man-made creeds we threw it overboard, and took the name Christian — a name given to the disciples by divine appointment at Antioch (Rogers 1847:50).

---

* In *The Last Will* the word 'Reverend' was intended to apply to The Springfield Presbytery. Garrison and DeGroot are wrong in suggesting that the authors were objecting to it as a title applying to an individual.

This new association became a fellowship of churches as well as ministers. Most of the congregations served by Stone and his associates followed them in rejecting allegiance to the Presbyterians. With the exception of two, it is said that in southwestern Ohio, all the Presbyterian Churches became Christian (Garrison and DeGroot 1948: 112). New Churches were established. The leaders were already known as revival men, and it is not surprising that they exercised their fervor in this exciting new development. Presbyterian preachers of the New Light type and Christian preachers from the east, besides Rice Haggard, soon affiliated with the movement so that by the end of 1804 eight Christian Churches could be found in north central Kentucky and seven in southwestern Ohio (McNemar 1808:69).*

The Question of Baptism. With those men influenced by revival many came to hold carefully defined views regarding baptism. John Glas defended the pedobaptists position (Glas 1782:Vol. V,421-424). James Haldane wrote a treatise of 115 pages justifying his changed views of believer's baptism by immersion (Haldane 1809). Elias Smith and Abner Jones were strong advocates of believer's baptism while James O'Kelly clung to pedobaptist practice (MacClenny 1950:157-159). The Campbells, father and son, yet to be observed, advocated baptism by immersion and for the remission of sins, as did Walter Scott.

After decreeing the demise of the Springfield Presbytery, baptism became a subject for discussion among the churches.

---

* Two of the best known and significant teachings of The Restoration Movement are its emphasis on the importance of Bible names and its plea for Christian unity. Both can be traced back to the Stone Movement in 1804 and beyond. Because of the relationship between the use of the name "Christian" and men recognized a part of the Awakenings, going back to the Great Awakening, Chapter Four is devoted to "The Sacred Import of the Christian Name."

Robert Marshall became so persuaded of the correctness of the Baptist position that he wrote the same to Mr. Stone. Fearing that Marshall would be lost to the Baptists, Stone penned an urgent reply striving to prove that he was wrong. Marshall's answer presented "believer's immersion" as opposed to pedobaptism. Stone's mind was brought to question infant baptism, and he resolved to practice it no more.

Baptism soon became a subject for discussion and action. Some, like Barton Warren Stone

> began to conclude that it was ordained for the remission of sins, and ought to be administered in the name of Jesus to all believing penitents. I remember once about this time, we had a great meeting at Concord. Mourners were invited every day to collect before the stand in order for prayers (this being the custom of the times). The brethren were praying for the same people, and none seemed to be comforted. I was considering in my mind, what could be the cause. The words of Peter, at Pentecost, rolled through my mind. "Repent and be baptized for the remission of sins, and you shall receive the gift of the Holy Spirit." I thought, were Peter here, he would thus address these mourners. I quickly arose, and addressed them in the same language, and urged them to comply. Into the spirit of the doctrine I was never fully led, until it was revived by Brother Alexander Campbell some years after (Rogers 1847:61).

Stone recounts that congregations and ministers multiplied, and then, he adds, "We became puffed up with our prosperity" (1847:61).

The Shaker Schism

Their pride was soon brought low in an extraordinary way through three missionaries from the mother church of the Shakers of New York City. The shakers were a communistic sect beginning in mid-eighteenth century England. Shakerism was imported to America in 1774 by Ann Lee or "Mother Ann" and a number of adherents (Andrews 1963:18). Soon, modest communities came into existence. Marriage, to the Shakers, was the basis of all evil (1963:20), (Sweet 1973:234-235). Theirs was the true church possessing all the apostolic attributes. Their name was given because of their worship, unique in its dancing and hand clapping by which they manifested their joy in the Lord.

The three missionaries, Benjamin Seth Youngs, Isaachar Bates and John Meachem, were sent from the New York church upon its hearing of the Kentucky revival. Richard McNemar and John Dunlavy of the Christian preachers forsook the movement, renounced their marriage relationships and joined the Shakers (Rogers 1847:61-62), (Andrews 1963:72-77), (McNemar 1808:79-94).

The beliefs of the Shakers were an admixture of asceticism, spiritualism, paternalism and communism. Marriage and the perpetuation of mankind were forbidden (Andrews 1963:8-9,12,20,22-23,81,97,178,230-231). Their worship centered in dancing, a holy exercise (1963:140-141). Through their "United Society of Believers in Christ's Second Appearing" under the oversight of elders and eldresses, they invited all the people of God to unite with them. They required a pledge of union which began,

> We do by these presence covenant and agree to renounce and disannul every bond, tie and relationship of the flesh, and to hold ourselves free and separate from all that pertains to the corrupt generation of fallen man.

Seven principles incorporated the essence of their faith and practice: innocence, purity, love, peace, justice, holiness, goodness and truth.

By 1805 the Shakers reported great progress in winning the Christians to Shakerism (McNemar 1808:92-94).* During this crisis Mr. Stone exerted himself more than at any other time, laboring day and night to "save his people from this vortex or ruin." He comments,

> Our broken ranks were once more rallied under the stand-ard of heaven, and were soon led on once more to victory. In answer to constant prayer, the Lord visited us and com-forted us after this severe trial. The cause again revived, and former scenes were renewed (Rogers 1847:63).

Cane Ridge became "the center of an anti-Shaker move-ment" (McNemar 1808:101-102), (Andrews 1968:73, 80).

Shakerism did not flourish long. In the years of its pop-ularity it built a number of villages that, in a few years began to shrivel and die. Stone sadly relates that John Dunlavy, who for a time was useful and popular with the Shakers, "died in Indiana raving in desperation for his folly in forsaking the truth." McNemar was, before his death, rejected by the Shakers, poverty stricken Rogers (1847:63).

The greatest disappointment for Barton Warren Stone was the return of Robert Marshall and John Thompson to the Presbyterians (1847:65-67). Marshall had persuaded Stone on the Baptist position on baptism (1847:60). Now he had returned to the pedobaptist Presbyterian Church. Only David Purviance stood with Stone (Murch 1962:91).

And yet Stone refused to give up and quit. His call came from God, and he had experienced His amazing blessings. He was committed to preach the gospel, and he was at his best as an evangelist.

---

* It is interesting that John Dunlavy, in his *Manifesto*, reminded Barton Warren Stone that when Shakerism was first introduced, he too, apparently approved, but for some reason turned away (Dunlavy 1847:458).

Growth of the Christian Churches

William Warren Sweet (1973:234-235) records that the "Christian Church" grew rapidly throughout the state of Kentucky and spread across the Ohio River to the state of Ohio. Stone travelled widely, preaching the gospel and establishing churches. Embracing immersion as Scriptural baptism opened the doors of Baptist Churches which, in numerous cases, came into the Christian Church (Rogers 1847:71).

Stone details a journey into Ohio to Meigs County where the separate Baptists, after requesting him to preach

> agreed to cast away their formularies and creeds, and take the Bible alone for their rule of faith and practice — to throw away their name Baptist, and take the name Christian — and to bury their association, and to become one with us in the great work of Christian union . . . After this the work gloriously progressed, and multitudes were added to the Lord (1847:72).

In 1811 in Preble County in the village of Eaton almost the whole town was converted (1847:73). Matthew Gardner in Adams County became a giant in evangelism after Stone converted him. Numerous churches were planted. For twenty years Stone visited them annually without a break. In Meigs County, Ohio, almost every Baptist Church in the county affiliated with the Christian Churches (1847: 71-72). Scores of new churches were established in southern Indiana following revival there in which hundreds were converted (Murch 1962:91).

Stone's greatest evangelistic outreach continued in Kentucky. Audiences attended wherever he went, and he preached. Many were saved. Numerous churches were planted.

In 1826 Mr. Stone started publishing *The Christian Messenger*. It came off the presses monthly, with few exceptions, for the balance of his life and for some time following his death. It radiated a plea for unity and centered on evangelism, and the churches were blessed by its message.

To arrive at accurate statistics concerning the Christian Church is perhaps impossible, but Garrison and DeGroot (1948:115-116) give the following communicant membership by states for the year of 1827: Kentucky, 3,350; Tennessee, 1,800; Alabama, 600; Ohio, 4,390; Indiana, 1,200; Illinois, 600; Missouri, 1,000; for a grand total of 12,940. This report is likely quite accurate.

Murch (1962:94) estimated that by 1830 the Christian Churches had a membership of 15,000. West of the Appalations people were on the move. Families from the east would settle in Kentucky for a year or more, and while there, affiliate with the Christian Churches, only to take their new faith with them as they moved on. In this way, numerous churches were organized in Tennessee and Alabama to the south, in Indiana, Ohio and Illinois in the north, and in Iowa and Missouri in the west, and the Stoneites became increasingly well known throughout the new west.

This growth through revival and evangelism would soon make an impact upon a similar movement in western Pennsylvania, northern Virginia and eastern Ohio.

Chapter Four

THE SACRED IMPORT OF THE CHRISTIAN NAME

The first of the two "main" streams of the Reformation of the early nineteenth century took for itself the name "Christian" at Cane Ridge, Kentucky, under the direction of Barton Warren Stone; the date was June 28, 1804 (Rogers 1847:53). Before this time, the followers of Stone were a part of the Presbyterian Church.

Circumstances surrounding their disassociation with the Presbyterians are well known. The *Last Will and Testament* through which they willed that the Springfield Presbytery should die was the break. "We will that our name of distinction, with its Rever'd title, be forgotten, that there be but one Lord over God's heritage and his name one" (1847:51), made the break final.

As a result of this move, they were cut off from other groups, and they stood alone. Now it was necessary to think of a new name and they were ready. Rice Haggard, a brother recently arrived from Virginia, was with them. Haggard suggested the name "Christian" from Luke's record in Acts 11:26, "the disciples were called Christians first in Antioch." His proposal was unanimously accepted.

As a consequence, they adopted a New Testament name, and this three years before Thomas Campbell and five years before Alexander Campbell arrived in America. It would be twenty years before Stone and Alexander Campbell were to meet face to face and twenty-six years before the Campbells had cause to consider a new name.

From June 28, 1804, their houses of worship were called "The Christian Church," and the proclaimers affixed to their signatures "E. C. C.," meaning "elders, Christian Church." "Or it might be Church of Christ, for those brethren were

72

Greek scholars, enough to be above the hyperliteralism of discriminating between the adjective and the genitive idioms. For nearly a century those two names were used interchangeably without question" (Hall, The *Christian Evangelist*, 1954:271).

The Importance of Rice Haggard

Rice Haggard can best be described as a man with an idea. He had not studied systematic theology and was not a theologian; nor was he an historian.

On page one of his *Address on the Import of the Christian Name* (1804), to be examined later, he had written, "the name Christian is now nearly eighteen hundred years old and almost lost in party names and distinctions . . ." In the previous eighteen centuries every name that came into usage did so, not to designate the church as one and united but to define a party, usually carrying the distinction of the founder, or a doctrine that was unique to that party. There were groups that did not take to sectarian names, but their opponents would give them party distinctions. Rice Haggard refused to be bound by sectarian names. He looked at the Church as one united Church. To him, the only Scriptural name was "Christian." The Reformers of the early nineteenth century were in agreement with Haggard.

Three separate groups, already described, took the name Christian. The first sprang from the Methodists.

Rice Haggard was present at that meeting. The Republican Methodist Church in Surray County, Virginia, in August of 1794 under the leadership of James O'Kelly, adopted its new name, "Christian Church," at Haggard's suggestion.

The second movement, under the leadership of Elias Smith and Abner Jones, beginning in 1801, was located in

New England, and came out of the Baptists. Haggard's influence was apparent once again.

Elias Smith's attraction to the name "Christian" was demonstrated in 1809 in the reprinting of *An Address . . . on the Sacred Import of the Christian Name*, written, we now know, by Rice Haggard.

The Stone group in Kentucky, beginning in 1804, came out of the Presbyterians, and Rice Haggard was there.

The above makes it obvious that "the three main divisions of the Christian Church had some acquaintance and a sense of being part of one enterprise" (Garrison 1946:59). W. E. Garrison in 1931 wrote, "Thus Haggard became a connecting link between these two 'Christian' organizations, one originating among the Methodists and the other among the Presbyterians." Information available today, which Garrison did not have in 1931, reveals that Rice Haggard was an influence between three movements; not two.

Rice Haggard was born in 1769 in Norfolk, Virginia, eighty years after his grandfather, the progenitor of the American Haggards, arrived from England. It was a period of conflict, and Haggard was influenced by the turbulence of the times. He observed the political struggle and the birth of the new nation. He also lived in a climate of religious revolution with its corresponding emphasis upon reformation of the Church.

The family of an uncle of Rice Haggard was Baptist. His own family was Methodist, possibly due to the preaching of Francis Asbury, for Asbury preached in Norfolk during that period. Rice Haggard joined the Methodist Church in 1787 in his eighteenth year, and soon became a Methodist preacher. He was ordained in 1791 by Bishop Francis Asbury (Barrett 1908:269). He was a preacher with great ability, a good man and an able leader, but about 1803 or 1804, when he became convinced that the doctrine was not in full accordance with Bible teachings, he returned to Virginia and received his release from the Methodist Church. According to the journals of Bishop Francis Asbury for November 25, 1792, Rice Haggard, on that Sunday, had sent to Asbury his resignation.

From the time James O'Kelly, in 1793, seceded from the Methodist Church and the domination of Bishop Asbury, Rice Haggard stood with him. The two men travelled together, continuing to preach. They and their followers assumed the name of Republican Methodists. One year later, on August 4, 1794, at Old Lebanon, Surray County, Virginia, Haggard stood before the Conference with his New Testament in hand and suggested the name "Christian" and the Scriptures as sufficient rule of faith and practice (MacClenny 1910:116).

David Haggard, brother of Rice, also remained a preacher in the James O'Kelly movement, after 1794 known simply as the Christian Church. In 1798 David moved across the Alleghenies into Cumberland County, Kentucky. In a few years, Rice followed him. The first account of a "Christian" Church in Kentucky was recorded in the court records of Cumberland County for the year of 1800 (Wells 1947:61), the result of labors of David Haggard and a part of the O'Kelly movement.

Rice Haggard settled near Burksville before moving to Kettle Creek, Kentucky, where he made his home in 1803 or 1804. Possibly he met Barton Warren Stone as early as the Cane Ridge revival in 1801. He obviously knew Stone and the other men of the Springfield Presbytery. It is likely he was at the meeting of the Presbytery in June of 1804 where, as Barton Warren Stone recalled years later in his autobiography, Haggard proposed the adoption of the name "Christian."

At this time the pamphlet, *An Address to the Different Religious Societies, On the Sacred Import of the Christian Name* was written. It was printed in Lexington, Kentucky, in 1804 by Joseph Charless. Less than five years later, it was reprinted in the *Herald of Gospel Liberty* published by Elias Smith. Many believed that Rice Haggard was its author, yet there was no proof.

Between 1806 and 1808, Haggard married the widow, Nancy Grimes Wiles. Four children were born into their family.

Haggard published a Christian hymn book in 1818.* One year later, on a preaching and business tour in Champaign County, Ohio, he took ill and died at the age of fifty years.

An Address to the Different Religious Societies on the Sacred Import of the Christian Name

It is true that a number of scholars suspected Haggard was the author of *An Address . . . on the Sacred Import of the Christian Name,* but it had not been proven. Known was his association with O'Kelly and the Republican Methodist Church and his suggestion concerning the name Christian, resulting in the Republican Methodist Church taking the name, Christian Church. Ten years later, he was present at the meeting of the Springfield Presbytery when it willed itself out of existence, and he proposed again the adoption of the name Christian, by which the churches of the Stone

---

* A Selection of Christian Hymns, by Rice Haggard, John Norvell, Printer, Lexington, 1818.

movement were called. Known also has been the information (Rogers 1847:50) that Rice Haggard had written a pamphlet on the name Christian. There was also a tract on the Christian name, but its author, whoever he was, had left his name off the document.

The Question of Authorship

At the beginning of the tract, its author had written,

Some may, perhaps, be anxious to know who the author of the following pages is, his name, and to what denomination he belongs. Let it suffice to say, that he considers himself connected with no party, nor wishes to be known by the name of any — he feels himself united to that one body of which Christ is head, and all his people fellow members (1804:12).

Nothing more regarding the authorship of *An Address to the Different Religious Societies on the Sacred Import of the Christian Name* came to light for many years.

Confirmation of Authorship Determined

In 1953 John Neth, a research student from Butler University, discovered the following paragraph on page 198 of Davidson's *History of the Presbyterian Church in the State of Kentucky*, published in 1847. This was forty-three years after the *Last Will and Testament of the Springfield Presbytery* had been written and executed.

Filled with the pleasing dream of an approaching universal kingdom, which was to embrace the whole earth, they proposed to establish a grand communion, which should agree to unite upon the simplest fundamental principles according to a plan drawn up by Rice Haggard, such as worshiping one God, acknowledging Jesus Christ as the Savior, taking the Bible for the sole confession of faith, and organizing on the New Testament model. To this union of all the disciples of Christ, they gave the name of "The Christian Church," and it recognized no sectarian appellation. Their views were communicated to the world in the promised *Observations on Church Government* and *An Address to the Different Religious Societies on the Sacred Import of the Christian Name.*

That Haggard was the author can be further confirmed from evidence found in the address itself. There a plan was suggested for reuniting the divided church. The proposal is summarized in nine points, the first four of which the historian, Davidson, has referred to above. In abbreviated form they are 1) We are to worship one God; 2) Acknowledge one Savior, Jesus Christ; 3) Have one confession of faith, and let that be the Bible; 4) Let us have one form of discipline and government and let this be the New Testament. This fourth point at least suggests the likelihood that Haggard's plan preceded *The Last Will and Testament of the Springfield Presbytery*, and was the basis for item one.

> We will, that our power of making laws for the government of the Church, and executing them by delegated authority, forever cease; that the people may have free course to the Bible, and adopt the law of the Spirit of life in Christ Jesus (Rogers 1847:51-52).

Through associating Barton Warren Stone's statement (1847:50), the place (Lexington, Kentucky), date of publication (1804), confirmation of the evidence from Robert Davidson's History, and internal evidences of the work itself, the work attributed to Elder Rice Haggard had at last been found.

The above find was significant, and did not go unnoticed by leaders within The Restoration Movement. Examples of reaction of Restoration scholars are Colby D. Hall's piece in *the Christian Evangelist* (1954:271) and his pamphlet on Rice Haggard, published in 1957; and Dr. C. C. Ware's article in *The Harbinger and Discipliana* (1954: Vol. XIV,No.11).

Other Significant Proofs of Authorship
The previously discussed evidences of the authorship of *An Address . . . on the Sacred Import of the Christian Name*, are not the only proofs available. The author of this volume in researching the Cane Ridge Revival and events following, found the following paragraph.

> And as the groundwork of this vast kingdom, which must include the whole earth, they proposed to seize upon the sacred name "Christian," exclusive of all other names; and so draw into union and one grand communion, all who wished to be called by that worthy name. The plan of this great kingdom was drawn up by Rice Haggard, and published in the year of 1804: which proposed, as the leading foundation principles, simply to worship one God — acknowledge one Savior, Jesus Christ — have one confession of faith, and let that be the Bible — one form of discipline and government, and this to be the New Testament — the members of one church, etc. (see *Address to the Different Religious Societies on the Sacred Import of the Christian Name*, p. 21), (McNemar 1808:97).

The Place of Richard McNemar. Richard McNemar was one of the co-signers of the *Last Will and Testament* at Cane Ridge on June 28, 1804, and thus was intimately acquainted with Rice Haggard, who was also present on that occasion. McNemar wrote his *The Kentucky Revival* in 1808, only four years after Haggard's pamphlet was printed. Robert Davidson's history was not published until 1847, forty-three years after the demise of the Springfield Presbytery.

It is significant that Davidson, in 1847, summarizes the nine points of Haggard's plan for Christian unity to four emphases. McNemar, who knew Haggard personally, did the same thing, thirty-nine years earlier, suggesting that Davidson gathered his information from McNemar's book.

Richard McNemar has already been mentioned in regard to *The Last Will and Testament of the Springfield Presbytery* and with reference to the Shaker schism. A co-signer of *The Last Will and Testament* he, with John Dunlavy, soon forsook Barton Warren Stone and affiliated with the Shakers, creating havoc with the young Christian Church (Rogers 1847:62).

Perhaps this explains why McNemar's work has been little noticed. By the year of 1900, the Shaker movement had run its course (see Andrews 1968:224). What literature it had produced was forgotten, and few were aware that Richard McNemar had written a book that throws light on the Cane Ridge revival and its antecedents. Whatever the reason, no Restoration Movement historian has taken note of the McNemar statement.

The Implications of Haggard's Authorship

The confirmation of authorship has far reaching implications. Haggard's relationship with the James O'Kelly movement and his link with Elias Smith and the Christian movement of New England (both adopted the name "Christian Church," as did the Stone movement and ultimately the New Reformation itself) make Rice Haggard a firm link between the eighteenth, early nineteenth century Awakenings and the Restoration Movement. This can be established in determining where Haggard got his great idea. It seems certain that his thinking was influenced by a number of circumstances and outstanding religious leaders.

Influences of Religious Leaders of the Time
James McGready. It is reasonable to surmise that Haggard was acquainted with James McGready, and the Logan County, Kentucky revival. McGready's expectations of heaven and his anticipation of the union of all believers was enunciated in his sermon, *The Christian's Journey to the Heavenly Canaan.* In that sermon, McGready said:

> But in the heavenly country all disputes and suspicions are banished; the names of Presbyterian, Episcopalian, Methodist, and Baptist shall be known no more. Luther, Calvin and Zwinglius shall agree. Toplady and Wesley shall quarrel no more; but shall adore the matchless grace and the splendid glories of Jehovah; and love divine emanating from God, will unite all together, and continually draw them nearer and nearer to Christ, their living head (James Smith 1835:Vol. 1,332).

Henry Patillo. It is likely that Rice Haggard knew of Henry Patillo and perhaps was acquainted with him. Both were residents of North Carolina and Virginia. Both had labored in the same area. Both were personally acquainted, at some time in their lives, with the same men. In 1788 Patillo, then of Greenville, North Carolina, published a sermon entitled, *On Division Among Christians.* It is probable that Haggard read that sermon. In it Patillo said,

> His (Paul) holy soul takes the alarm, left by these names and distinctions, that name should be lost at Corinth, which

81

was first given to the disciples by divine appointment at Antioch; that name, which it is the great glory of disciples to wear, the name Christian; that new name, promised to the New Testament Church, which the mouth of the Lord shall name.

Patillo entertained the same views as Samuel Davies. This is understandable for Patillo was a student of Davies, and they shared a warm friendship when Patillo was a young man.

John Wesley. Rice Haggard's first thoughts regarding the name Christian were revealed while he was in association with James O'Kelly and the Republican Methodist Church. He could have known of the thinking of John Wesley concerning party names and the name Christian.

It is related that once John Wesley, in the visions of the night, found himself, as he thought, at the gates of hell. He knocked and asked who were within. 'Are there any Roman Catholics here?' he asked. 'Yes,' was the answer, 'a great many.' 'Any Church of England men?' 'Yes, a great many.' 'Any independents?' 'Yes, a great many.' 'Any Presbyterians?' 'Yes, a great many.' 'Any Baptists?' 'Yes, a great many.' 'Any Wesleyans?' 'Yes, a great many.' Disappointed and dismayed, especially at the last reply, he turned his steps upward and found himself at the gates of paradise, and here he repeated the same questions. 'Any Wesleyans here?' 'No.' 'Any Presbyterians?' 'No.' 'Any Church of England men?' 'No.' 'Any Roman Catholics?' 'No.' 'Whom have you here, then?' he asked in astonishment. 'We know nothing here,' was the reply, 'of any of those names you have mentioned. The only name of which we know anything here is Christian. We are all Christians here, and of these we have a great multitude, which no man can number, of all nations, kindreds and peoples, and tongues' (Barrett, 1908:20 f.n.).

82

The Certain Influence of Samuel Davies

Perhaps Haggard had access to Benjamin Grosvenor's *An Essay on the Christian Name: Its Origin, Impact, Obligation, and Preference to All Party Denominations,* published in London in 1728. There were a few copies in America in the 1780's and 1790's. Samuel Davies was well acquainted with Grosvenor and his essay, from which he borrowed "several amiable sentiments" (Davies 1828:Vol. I,210 f.n.), and Davies influenced Haggard. An examination of Davies' sermon, *The Sacred Import of the Christian Name,* and Haggard's *An Address to the Different Religious Societies on the Sacred Import of the Christian Name* provides proof.

Shortly after it was proven that Rice Haggard was the author of *An Address. . .,* Charles Ware pointed out the "idiological and philosophical parallelism" between Haggard's essay and Davies' sermon (Harbinger and Discipliana XIV:157).

The Log College Movement

Samuel Davies was a product of the Great Awakening following the preaching of Jonathan Edwards and George Whitefield.

The greatest single influence on Rice Haggard and his associates was that of the New Light Presbyterians. The Christians in Kentucky were given the same designation, but this influence had greater results than that. The New Lights were the evangelistic wing of the Presbyterian Church. In 1726 at Neshaminy, Pennsylvania, William Tennent, graduate of the University of Edinburgh, began a revival in cooperation with the Dutch Reformed Dominie Thodorus Frelinghuysen. The community and people of neighboring

83

areas were moved by the spirit of this revival which predated the Massachusetts revival of 1734 under the preaching of Jonathan Edwards (Hall 1957:17).

The stirring result of the revival made the dearth of fervent, spirit-filled preachers so apparent that William Tennent and other ministers were no longer content with sending their best young men to the universities of England or Europe or Yale or Andover. His four sons and fifteen other young preachers, Tennent educated in his own home. To accomplish this work, he constructed on his own property a log house which came to be known, often in derision, the "Log College."

George Whitefield. Shortly after George Whitefield's first arrival in America in 1739, he visited Neshaminy, Pennsylvania, the home of William Tennent and the location of the Log College. Whitefield writes of that occasion:

It is surprising how such bodies of people, so scattered abroad, can be gathered at so short a warning . . . I believe there were nearly a thousand horses. The people, however, did not set upon them to hear the sermon, as in England, but tied them to the hedges; and thereby much disorder was prevented.

We had sweet communion with each other and spent the evening in concerting measures for promoting our Lord's kingdom. It happens very providentially that Mr. Tennent and his brethren are appointed to be a presbytery by the Synod, so that they intend breeding up gracious youths, and sending them out into the Lord's vineyard. The place wherein the young men study now is in contempt, called the college. It is a log house, about twenty feet long and nearly as many broad . . . From this despised place, seven or eight worthy ministers of Jesus have lately been sent forth; . . . Carnal ministers oppose them strongly; and because people, when awakened by Mr. Tennent of his brethren, see through them and therefore leave their ministry, the poor gentlemen are loaded with contempt, and looked upon as persons who turn the world upside down (Whitefield's Journals: 354-355; Dallimore 1971:437-438).

Other log colleges soon came into existence. Disapproval from the older synod, the consequence of its opposition to the zeal of the evangelists, led the younger preachers, Gilbert, William Jr., John and Charles Tennent, sons of William, and Samuel Blair to establish the New Brunswick Presbytery, through which they sent preachers in sympathy with their revival-motivated position.

At Fagg's Manor in Chester County, Pennsylvania, Samuel Blair founded a log college after the pattern of William Tennent's school. Its first graduate was Samuel Davies. Similar colleges were established at Nottingham, at Pequea, in Lancaster County, and in the Redstone country of western Pennsylvania.

McAllister and Tucker, first historians of the Disciples of Christ to see connections between the Awakenings of the eighteenth and nineteenth centuries and the formation of the Christian Churches, note that the most prominent figures in the revival were New Light Presbyterians such as William Tennent, "one of the secondary leaders of the Great Awakening," Samuel Blair who was trained by Tennent, and Samuel Davies, "a tower of strength for the revival movement" (McAllister and Tucker 1975:56-57).

Virginia was Anglican-dominated from its beginnings. It was the oldest by thirteen years, of the thirteen colonies and was most loyal to England and the established Church, and Anglicanism was firmly entrenched. As a state church its regulations were enforced by laws of the House of Burgesses of the colony.

The first dissenting denomination to gain entry into Anglican-dominated Virginia was the Presbyterians. Two factors contributed to their influence, one, through a group of Scotch-Irish, settled beyond the mountains to the west, and the other the result of the skillful leadership of Samuel Davies. Davies was sent to Hanover County in 1748 by the New Light Presbyterians, New Brunswick Presbytery, in Pennsylvania.

Samuel Davies was an outstanding man and remarkable minister. He was successful, with his culture, temperament and diplomacy, in securing recognition for the Presbyterians. He exercised care in working with colonial officers,, never commencing a new enterprise until he had secured permission to do so.

The College of New Jersey

In 1746, the year that William Tennent died, and his log college was closed, the New York Synod obtained a charter for the College of New Jersey in Elizabethtown. Jonathan Dickinson, a graduate of Yale, had joined the evangelical wing and became a part of the revival in 1740. The academy opened in 1747 in Dickenson's home, and Dickenson died in the fall. Aaron Burr was called as president of the new school, and it was moved to Newark. In 1755, the college was relocated, this time permanently, at Princeton, and became Princeton University. Burr died in 1757 and his father-in-law, Jonathan Edwards, assumed the presidency (Sweet 1973:140-145). Edwards died at Princeton on March 11, 1758 (Edwards [first printed 1834] 1976:Vol. I,clxxviii).

Samuel Davies, President of the College in 1759. Samuel Davies was called to be president of the College of New

Jersey in 1759. His life was short (1724-1761). He died at the age of thirty-seven and was president of the College for only two years, but his ministry and labors made an impact upon the forthcoming Restoration Movement.

Davies' Sermon, *The Sacred Import of the Christian Name.*

Davies impinged upon the movement through his influence on Rice Haggard. His sermons, published in three volumes, are entitled *Sermons on Important Subjects.* *

Davies' spirit was expanded through David Caldwell and Henry Patillo who had such influence on Barton Warren Stone. Through Rice Haggard, the impact of Davies upon the Restoration Movement left its permanent mark (McAllister and Tucker 1975:80-81).

Its Influence on Rice Haggard. In Volume One is found sermon XII on *The Sacred Import of the Christian Name.*

Davies' sermon and Haggard's tract have significant similarities. Their parallelism is worth noting, and it establishes the influences on Rice Haggard leading him to emphasize the importance of the Christian name.

It also provides a link between the forthcoming Restoration Movement and Davies, a true child of the First Great Awakening, as well as the revival influences of Jonathan Edwards, John Wesley, George Whitefield and others.

---

*A fourth edition, a copy of which is in the Carolina Discipliana Library, was published in London in 1792. The three volumes are also in the library of Austin Theological Seminary in Austin, Texas, and they were published in New York by Dayton and Saxton in 1841. The author of this study has examined copies found in the library of Lexington Theological Seminary, Lexington, Kentucky, published in New York by Collins and Hammay, Collins Company, in 1882.

*Examples of Parallelism Between
Haggard's Tract and Davies' Sermon*

The Use of the Name, Christian

Haggard	*Davies*
An address to the Different Religious Societies on the Sacred Import of the Christian Name.	The Sacred Import of the Christian Name.
Acts xi:26	Acts xi:26
The disciples were called Christians first at Antioch.	The disciples were called Christians first at Antioch.
Hence, they were called Christians, and the original . . . strongly intimates that they were called by divine appointment. For it generally signifies an oracular nomination, or declaration from the mouth of the Lord . . . See Matt. 2:22, notwithstanding being warned of God.	The original word which is here rendered called, seems to . . . intimate that they were called Christians by divine appointment, for it generally signifies an oracular nomination or declaration from God. Matt. 2:22 (footnote) being warned of God.
Luke 2:26, And it was revealed unto him by the Holy Ghost.	Luke ii:26, it was revealed unto him by the Holy Ghost.
Acts 10:22	Acts x:22
Cornelius the centurian . . . was warned from God.	was warned from God.
Heb. 8:5, as Moses was admonished of God.	Heb. viii:5, Moses was admonished of God.
Chapter 11:7, By faith, Noah, being warned of God.	Heb. xi:7, Noah being warned of God.

Heb. 12:25. For if they escaped not, who refused him that spake on earth . . .

In this view . . . Isa. 62:2

Thou shalt be called by a new name, which the mouth of the Lord shall name.

And call his servants by another name . . . Isa. 56:5.

Though the name Christian is now nearly eighteen hundred years old and almost lost in party names and distinctions

yet it may be worth while to further its original import . . . to recover not only the name but also the thing.

This name should stand as a distinction.

A patronymick name

A badge of revelation to Christ, as his servant, his bride, etc., and as intimating their unction by the Holy Ghost.

for as Christ was anointed

Heb. xii:25, If they escaped not, who refused him that spake on earth . . .

And in this view . . . Isa. lxii:2.

Thou shall be called by a new name, which the mouth of the Lord shall name.

The Lord shall call his servant by another name . . . Isa. lxv: 15.

Such is the Christian name; a name about seventeen hundred years old . . . almost lost in party distinctions

it may be worth our while to consider the original import . . . to recover both name and thing.

Now we may consider this name in various views, particularly as a name of distinction.

A patronymic name

As a badge of our relation to Christ as his servants, his children, his bride; as intimating our unction by the Holy Spirit.

as Christ was anointed

89

It is a catholic name intended to bury all party denominations.

The name Jew is odious to the Gentiles, and the name Gentile to the Jews.

But the name Christian swallows up all other names in one common and agreeable appelation. He who broke down the middle wall of partition has taken away partition names and united all his followers in his own name as one common denomination. And it is but a due honor to the Lord Jesus Christ, the founder of Christianity, that they who profess his religion, should wear his name.

Those, therefore, who take their denomination from his subordinate ministers, pay an extravagant, and almost an idolatrous compliment to them.

The Roman Catholics, having corrupted and lost the thing, acted consistently in laying aside the name. In these days it is not enough but we must be something more . . . rigid

As a catholic name, intended to bury all party denominations.

The name Gentile was odious to the Jews, and the name Jew was odious to the Gentiles.

The name Christian swallows up both in one common and agreeable appelation. He that hath taken down the partition wall has taken away partition names, and united all his followers in his own name, a one common denomination. It is but due honor to Jesus Christ, the founder of Christianity, that all who profess his religion should wear his name.

And they pay an extravagant and even idolatrous compliment to his subordinate officers and ministers, when they take their denomination from them.

The popish church . . . having corrupted the thing, they act very consistently to lay aside the name.

To be a Christian is not enough now-a-days, but a man must

bigots to some party, and the whimsies entertained by that party.

also be something more, and better; that is, he must be a strenuous bigot to this or that particular church.

I believe some things, which great and good men have believed and taught, but I believe them not on their authority, but on the sole authority of Jesus Christ.

I may indeed believe the same things that Luther and Calvin believed, but I do not believe on the authority of Luther and Calvin but on the sole authority of Jesus Christ.

The requisites to constitute a Christian.

What is it to be a Christian?

A Christian, in a good degree, imitates the character of Jesus Christ.

To be a Christian indeed, to be a Christian is to be like Christ.

Who was holy, harmless, undefiled, and separated from sinners (Haggard, 1804).

He was "holy, harmless, undefiled, and separated from sinners" (Davies 1828:Vol. I, 209-220).

Rice Haggard's Influence on the Stone Movement

There is no doubt that Haggard had before him Samuel Davies' sermon on *The Sacred Import of the Christian Name* when he wrote *An Address to the Different Religious Societies on the Sacred Import of the Christian Name.* Nor is there any doubt as to the influence Haggard exerted in the beginning of the young Reformation, later to be called the Restoration Movement, with its churches called Christian Churches and its adherents content to be called Christians only. Its plea for Christian unity was on the basis of Scripture, using the Christian name as the rallying point.

The name Christian and the name Christian Church come down to the present day from the Barton Warren Stone movement. This was not a product of the Alexander Campbell stream at all. Campbell advocated the name, disciple, for the followers of Christ and the name, Disciples of Christ for the Church.

Barton Warren Stone got the idea from Rice Haggard.

We . . . took the name Christian — the name given by the disciples by divine appointment first at Antioch. We published a pamphlet on this name written by Elder Rice Haggard . . . (Rogers 1847:50).

Questions That Arise over the Parallelism. A sufficient number of statements have been harmonized to demonstrate the irrefutable literary equation of Haggard and Davies.

Why hadn't someone following Haggard's pamphlet noted this equation? Haggard's piece came out in 1804, forty-three years after the death of Davies. At least four editions of Davies' sermons had been published between 1770 and 1804. Rice Haggard was a native of Virginia where Samuel Davies had enjoyed tremendous success as a Presbyterian preacher and scholar. Likely, Davies had first preached these sermons in Virginia. It seems safe to assume that Haggard had access to them because of their availability, which could have inspired him to suggest the adoption of the name Christian at Lebanon Church, Virginia in 1794 as well as at Cane Ridge one decade later.

What was the reason Haggard kept the authorship of his article anonymous? Perhaps he was afraid of being criticized for not revealing the source of his material. Perhaps he so identified with Davies' thinking that he made it his own.

How was it that this parallelism escaped the attention

of Presbyterian scholars in Virginia and Kentucky after 1804? Sufficient time had passed between 1804 and 1847 when Robert Davidson wrote his *History of the Presbyterian Church in the State of Kentucky*, where he mentions (page 198) the pamphlet *On the Sacred Import of the Christian Name*, and its author, Rice Haggard, for him to have known of this parallelism. Perhaps Davidson's knowledge of Haggard and his pamphlet came through Richard McNemar's book, *The Kentucky Revival*, published in 1808, and he never saw the Haggard piece at all.

It has been suggested by Charles Ware (*The Harbinger and Discipliana*, Vol. XIV,157) that because "the most forward of them despised in their hearts this creed of Haggard as associated with the 'Christians,'" that they simply ignored it. Or if they did examine it carefully, they would allow no reference to Samuel Davies sharing in an apparent agreement at a critical point with Barton Warren Stone. "Far be it from them to recognize this fugitive canard as being a clever corollary to a renowned sermon by one of their Christian brilliants." Ware did not know in 1954 that Richard McNemar in his *The Kentucky Revival*, published in 1808, had also revealed the authorship of the pamphlet *On the Sacred Import of the Christian Name*, some thirty-nine years before Davidson's history was published. He was unaware that Davidson had summarized in 1847 the same four emphases of Haggard's piece that McNemar had noted in 1808.

It seems possible that Davidson depended upon McNemar and he likely never saw the Haggard pamphlet at all. This should not be surprising, for the men responsible for publishing the Haggard piece were poor men. Possibly not many copies were printed. While it was a document of great import, it was not widely read because of limited circulation. Furthermore, Haggard was unknown, and not a scholar, while Samuel Davies was a college-educated divine, who by the time his sermons were published in 1770, had served as president of the College of New Jersey which had become Princeton College, later to become Princeton University. Richard McNemar, of course, knew about the Haggard tract because he was one of the signers of *The Last Will and Testament*, and Rice Haggard was present on that June 28th, 1804, day.

Haggard's suggestion (Rogers 1847:50) was little noticed in those early years of the nineteenth century. It was not until the tiny Reformation had exploded into a movement of national consequence that the Christian name, as taken by adherents of the Restoration Movement, was taken note of by other religious bodies. It can be traced to Rice Haggard, a product of the Second Great Awakening, and, to Samuel Davies, a true son of the First Great Awakening.

Other Noteworthy Men Stress the Importance of the Christian Name

George Whitefield

At the Presbyterian Church in Elizabethtown, New Jersey, in April of 1740, George Whitefield preached, and in his journal (page 414) referred to that occasion. He said

> I care not for any sect or party of men. As I love all who love the Lord Jesus, of what communion soever, so I reprove all, . . . who take His Word into their mouths, but never felt Him dwelling in their hearts (Dallimore 1971, 549).

Whitefield was one of the most catholic-spirited ministers of his time, and could cooperate with Quakers, Baptists, Lutherans, Moravians, Presbyterians, Congregationalists, Dutch Reformed, and all others so long as they, like himself, advocated vital religion, and preached conversion (Sweet 1973:141). On one occasion, preaching from the balcony of the courthouse in Philadelphia, Whitefield cried out,

> Father Abraham, who have you in heaven? 'Any Episcopalians?' 'No!' 'Any Presbyterians?' 'No!' 'Have you any Independents or Seceders?' 'No!' 'Have you any Methodists?' 'No, No, No!!' 'Whom have you there?' 'We don't know those names here. All who are here are Christian — believers in Christ — men who have overcome by the blood of the Lamb and the word of his testimony.' 'Oh, is this the case? Then God help us, God help us all to forget party names, and to become Christians in deed and in truth.'

John Wesley '

Wesley, as has been noted, said essentially the same as Whitefield (Barrett 1908). Both Whitefield's and Wesley's sentiments found amplification in the pamphlet of Rice Haggard.

The Influence of Benjamin Grosvenor
on Samuel Davies

Samuel Davies' sermon, *The Sacred Import of the Christian Name*, contains a footnote, referring the reader to "Dr. Grosvenor's excellent essay on the Christian name" (1882:Vol. I,210). Benjamin Grosvenor had published this essay in London in 1728.

Parallelism Between Grosvenor, Davies and Haggard

The title of Benjamin Grosvenor's pamphlet was *An Essay on the Christian Name: Its Origen, Import, Obligation, and Preference to All Party Denominations*. The text for the essay was, as with Davies and Haggard, Acts 11:26. One finds in Grosvenor's work a parallelism with Davies' sermon published later, and there is evidence that Davies had Grosvenor's essay before him when he wrote his sermon *The Sacred Import of the Christian Name.*

Grosvenor wrote (page 3), "The love of the world has, in a great measure, eat out the thing; (by which he meant Christianity, p. 9) and party-denominations have almost devoured the name; what shall we do to recover both name and thing?" Davies, writing some thirty years later, ". . . It may be worth our while to consider the original import of that sacred name, as a proper expedient to recover both name and thing" (1828:Vol. I,209). Haggard, following Davies, wrote, "It may be worth while to consider further its original import, as a happy means to recover not only the name but also the thing" (1804:13).

Again, Grosvenor wrote in his essay, (p. 23), "It is a name of distinction from all the rest of the world, whether Jews or Gentiles that were unbelievers." Borrowing from Grosvenor, Davies said, "Now we may consider this name in various views; particularly as a name of distinction from the rest of the world" (p. 210). Haggard, after Davies, wrote, "This name should stand as a distinction between the followers of Christ and the world" (p. 14).

According to Grosvenor (p. 24), "the name Christian is a badge of relation to Christ . . ." Davies followed by saying, ". . . as a badge of our relation to Christ as his servants . . ." (p. 210), and Haggard, after Davies has it, ". . . a badge of relation to Christ, as his servants" (p. 14).

"It seems designed to bury all denominations," penned Grosvenor (p. 28). "Let us consider the Christian name as a catholic name, intended to bury all party denominations," wrote Davies in his sermon (p. 210). Haggard, borrowing from Davies phrased it, "It is a catholic name intended to bury all party denominations" (p. 14).

Davies (p. 210-211), quotes Grosvenor word for word (p. 28), "the name Gentile was odious to the Jews, and the name Jew was odious to the Genitles." The only difference between Haggard and his predecessors was that he worded the sentence, "The name Jew was odious to the Gentiles, and the name Gentile, to the Jews" (p. 14).

Again Grosvenor writes (p. 30), "I could wish that the insolence of lifting Christians under men's names, were only to be found among papists. They are very just, in quitting the name Christian, for Dominican, Franciscan, etc. who have so corrupted or destroyed the thing." In a similar vein Davies puts it (p. 211), "Not to take notice of Jesuits, Jansenites, Dominicans, Franciscans, and other denominations and order in the papish church, where, having corrupted the thing, they act very consistently to lay aside the name . . ." Haggard similary said (p. 14), "The Roman Catholics, having corrupted and lost the thing, acted consistently enough in laying aside the name."

There are other parallelisms as well, but the above offers ample evidence of the similarity in thought regarding the name Christian, between Grosvenor in the early eighteenth century, Davies in the mid-eighteenth century, and Haggard, late eighteenth and early nineteenth century. The years between Grosvenor's work, 1728, and Haggard's pamphlet, seventy-six years start near the First Great Awakening, and reach into the Second Great Awakening with all three men the product of those Awakenings.

The Leaven of Revival at Work

The influence of Grosvenor on Davies, Davies on Haggard, Haggard on Barton Warren Stone and Stone on the budding Reformation, soon to become The Restoration Movement, is undeniable, and the Restoration Movement can trace its use of the name Christian back to these men.

The idea of the import of the name Christian did not begin with Grosvenor more than with Davies or Haggard or Stone. Grosvenor made reference to an earlier paper written by a Dr. Fuller of London entitled, *Best Name on Earth* (p. 17). He quotes from Tertullian, pleading for the Christian name (p. 27), from Luther who protested against any man calling himself by Luther's name, and from Calvin who insisted that "the Apostle does so assert the mastership in the Church to Christ alone, upon which we should all depend, that among us there should be but one only Lord and Master named, and no man's name opposed to it" (p. 51).

Benjamin Grosvenor quotes a Mr. Baxter in answer to those who queried what party he was of:

I'll tell you, I am a Christian, a mere Christian, of no other religion, and the Church that I am of, is the Christian Church; and has been visible, whenever the Christian religion and Church has been visible. But must you know what sect or party I am of? I am against all sects and dividing parties . . . I am sorry that you are not content with mere Christianity, and to be a member of the catholic Church, and hold the communion of saints, but that you must needs also be of a sect, and have some other name (2nd Pref. to his Church history, p. 53).

This was the nature of the leaven at work, the kind of idea considered by godly men for hundreds of years but which swelled into a ferment of major proportions through the fervor generated by the Great Awakenings.

Chapter Five

THE CAMPBELL MOVEMENT BEGINS — 1807

Thomas Campbell Arrives in Western Pennsylvania

Thomas Campbell, from Northern Ireland, but of Scottish lineage and education, had been a Presbyterian preacher in County Antrim where he was introduced to the writings of James Alexander Haldane.

At the advice of his doctor, in 1807, Campbell came to America in search of his health. He landed in Philadelphia on May 13, 1807, to find the Anti-Burgher Synod meeting in the city (Smith 1930:47). Warmly welcomed by the session, he was appointed to Washington, Pennsylvania, as a home missionary on the western frontier. It would be his responsibility to bring scattered members of the Anti-Burgher Presbyterians into the Anti-Burgher fold, to organize them into congregations, and to pastor them until permament preachers could be appointed.

The appointment pleased Thomas Campbell, and he accepted it as a manifestation of God's grace. On the 27th of May, two weeks after his assignment, he wrote to his family:

> Be sure you make it your chief study to do all to please and nothing to offend that great God who has raised such friends and conferred such friendships upon your father, both at home and abroad, and especially when he became a stranger in a strange land. But what do I say? A minister or a member of Christ's Church is a citizen of the world, as far as the Church extends (Richardson 1886:Vol. I,86).

Immediately upon his arrival in western Pennsylvania he found a number of his neighbors from Ireland, and his ministry promised early success.

99

Sectarian Division on the Western Frontier

Thomas Campbell was an Old Light, Anti-Burgher Seceder Presbyterian, a graduate of the University of Glasgow and of the theological school of the Anti-Burgher Seceder Presbyterian Church (McAllister 1954:24-30). Though he belonged to the Seceder sect, he revealed a firm independence and a balanced spirit of catholicity.

William Warren Sweet (1973:235-236) speaks of problems encountered by Mr. Campbell soon after his arrival in the west. In Ireland he had been distressed by the division within the Presbyterian Church and hoped he might get away from these sectarian practices. However, the associate synod of the Anti-Burgher Synod in the United States was more rigid than was the original body in Scotland. "Occasional Communion" with other groups of Presbyterians had been prohibited by an act of Synod in 1796. This decree Thomas Campbell refused to obey. Presbyterian families were scattered throughout this frontier, but they were of different persuasions. None had partaken of the Lord's Supper for years, and Campbell, friendly to independents and members of other denominations, found that his ministry was sought after by many. At Cannamaugh on the Allegheny River near Pittsburgh, he was invited by a number of Anti-Burghers to administer the Lord's Table. Other segments of the regular Presbyterian Church, as well as the Seceder branch, were present to receive the emblems (Smith 1930:48).

Population in this part of Pennsylvania was scattered. It was rare when the services of a minister were available to the several denominations represented.

Most were Presbyterians and Thomas Campbell, concerned with the spiritual destitution of some, belonging to

100

other branches of the Church that had not enjoyed the Lord's Supper for years, expressed his conviction that all who desired to do so, who were prepared, should partake, regardless of the divisions keeping them apart, and this Mr. Campbell encouraged.

Seceder Presbyterian Minister John Anderson refused to cooperate with Mr. Campbell in dispensing the Lord's Supper at Buffaloe and, at the regular session of the Presbytery which met in October, 1807, gave as his reason, Campbell's deviation from the orthodox stance of the associate synod of the Anti-Burghers in America. A Mr. Wilson confirmed that he had heard Thomas Campbell's vocalized exceptions to the orthodox position of the Anti-Burghers, and the circumstance was exaggerated to become an ecclesiastical disgrace of consequence (Hanna 1935:32-34) (Minutes of the Chartiers Presbytery, 122-124).*

The accusations, discussion, and decisions made by the presbytery and synod portray Thomas Campbell, not as a sentimentalist sympathetic with the scattered flock, but as a man with a meticulously thought out theology that incorporated carefully formulated beliefs which took exception to major doctrines of his denomination.

Five men, four of them preachers, were appointed by the Chartiers presbytery to examine the charges, and if the evidence appeared sufficient, to bring libel suit against Mr. Campbell. Thomas Campbell protested verbally and by letter, but the presbytery refused to consider his dissent, and he was restricted from preaching in November and December while the committee functioned.

---

* A comparison of Hanna 1935:37, who relies on the minutes of the Chartiers Presbytery, with Richardson Vol. I, p. 224 makes interesting reading.

Mr. Campbell Charged with False Teaching

At the January, 1808, session of the Chartiers presbytery, the appointed committee leveled a libel action at Mr. Campbell. He was charged

> with false teaching concerning the nature of saving faith; rejecting creeds as lawful terms of fellowship; urging ruling elders (laymen) to pray and exhort in public meetings when no minister was present; that it was permissible for the Seceders to hear ministers of other communions when there were no services in their own churches; repudiating the substitutionary concept of the atonement; that it is possible for one to live a sinless life; and preaching in congregations assigned to other ministers (Dowling 1964:37).

Mr. Campbell heard each charge and a copy of the libel was presented to him. When the presbytery next met, he was found guilty of virtually every count and was suspended in mid-February, 1808. After the session had concluded and many had returned home, three members still present voted to make Thomas Campbell's suspension a permanent one. In March he asked for a review of his case, and his request was denied.

Mr. Campbell Appeals to the Associate Synod of North America

Mr. Campbell directed his appeal to the highest court, the Associate Synod of North America, which met on May 19-21 and 23-27, 1808. He pled

> I only beg leave, for my own part, to walk upon such sure and peaceable ground that I may have nothing to do with human controversy about the right or wrong side of any

opinion whatsoever, by simply acquiescing in what is written, as quite sufficient for every purpose of faith and duty; and thereby to influence as many as possible to depart from human controversy, to betake themselves to the Scriptures, and in so doing, to the study and practice of faith, holiness and love . . . Say, brethren, what is my offence, that I should be thrust out from the heritage of the Lord, or from serving him in that good work to which he has been graciously pleased to call me? For what error or immorality ought I to be rejected, except it be that I refuse to acknowledge as obligatory upon myself, or to impose upon others, anything as of divine obligation for which I cannot produce a "Thus saith the Lord?" (Richardson 1868:Vol. I,227).

Upon review, the synod revoked the suspension of the Chartiers presbytery and declared their actions with regard to Mr. Campbell improper (1886:Vol. I,229).

It was decided that there were such informalities in the proceedings of the presbytery to afford sufficient reason to the synod to set aside their judgment and decision, and to release the protestor from the censure inflicted by the presbytery; which they accordingly did.

The synod then launched its own inquiry. The judgment of the committee appointed by the synod to investigate the case concluded:

Upon the whole, the committee are of the opinion that Mr. Campbell's answers to the first two articles of the charge, especially, are evasive, unsatisfactory and highly equivocal upon great and important articles of revealed religion as to give ground to conclude that he has expressed sentiments very different upon these articles from the sentiments held and professed by this church; and are sufficient ground to infer censure (1868:Vol. I,229).

The motion was made and seconded that Mr. Campbell be "rebuked and admonished." An effort was made to reduce the censure, to "admonish" only, but it failed. Mr. Campbell then requested that the judgment be postponed one day, and the request was granted. For many within the Seceders he entertained an abiding love, and it was with reluctance that he viewed this separation with men he cherished as brothers. In a protest filed against the synod, he expressed his reluctance to bow to censure on the charges that his replies were "evasive, unsatisfactory and highly equivocal" (Dowling 1964:38).

Before Mr. Campbell's case was taken up the following day, he forwarded a letter to the synod charging it with partiality and injustice and "informing the synod that he declined their authority" (Garrison and DeGroot 1954: 138). Called before the synod, he retracted the letter and admitted he acted in haste. Judgment was reconsidered in the morning hours. "Evasive" was stricken from the record, but the decision remained "rebuke and admonish." Mr. Campbell agreed to submit, a prayer was offered, and by the moderator he was rebuked and admonished. Later in the same session, Mr. Campbell, as recorded in the minute book, was appointed to Philadelphia for June and July and then back to the Chartiers presbytery for further appointments until the next meeting of the synod.

Mr. Campbell Withdraws From the Presbytery and Synod
There was much ill feeling among the presbytery of Chartiers. It had suffered rebuke from the synod, Mr.

Campbell's suspension had been lifted, and this was a constant vexation. He returned to Washington and the Chartiers presbytery for his continuing appointment to find that none had been made and no intention of making any. He was under the presbytery but it would not use him. When he sought definition of his relationship, he was informed that he was only a member by order of the synod, with the veiled suggestion that he was not welcome nor wanted (Rowe 1894:132).

The minutes of the presbytery for September 13, 1808, say that Thomas Campbell

> in his own name and in the name of all who adhered to him, declined the authority of the presbytery for reasons formerly given, the authority of the Associate Synod of North America and all courts subordinate thereto, and all future communion with them (Garrison and DeGroot 1954:139).

One is justified in asking if the providence of God may be seen in all this (Moore 1909:102). What if he had chosen, for the sake of peace, to remain with the Seceders? Thomas Campbell could never have led the Seceder Presbyterians from their sectarianism. The movement, the principles which he enunciated, would never have started except as he was forced out of the Presbyterian Church.

"The fire burned in his heart and there came to him a vision, of the Holy Spirit . . . a concept of the union of all God's people upon the Bible alone" (Smith 1930:49).

Mr. Campbell delivered to the presbytery the same letter he sent to the synod and immediately withdrew, in July. The decision was now irrevocable. The Presbytery acted to suspend him, and the separation was complete. The synod was informed and his name was taken from its roll.

105

The date was May 23, 1809, two years and ten days from the date he arrived in America. The highest censure of the Chartiers presbytery was recorded on April 18, 1810. It expresses the disposition of that body regarding the troublesome Mr. Campbell.

> Accordingly the presbytery did and hereby do depose Mr. Campbell from the office of the holy ministry, and from sealing ordinances for the reasons above mentioned. Agreed to send an extract of this disposition of Mr. Campbell to the synod and to intimate it to the congregations under our inspection (Dowling 1964:49).

Before the above minute was recorded, Thomas Campbell had been reunited with his wife and family, and with his first son, Alexander.

Thomas Campbell's separation from the Seceders created no hindrance to his work of the ministry (Richardson 1868: Vol. I,230). Already he was known and respected through the reputation and warm influence he had earned in western Pennsylvania, Wherever he went, he attracted crowds who felt the appeal of his plea for Christian union on the basis of Scripture. Almost a year he preached wherever the opportunity afforded, but he made no effort to organize a church or to attract preachers or laymen away from the Presbyterian denomination.

After a time, Thomas Campbell observed that many of his Irish neighbors, still holding membership in Seceder Presbyterian Churches, who were regular in inviting him to preach in their homes, were in attendance at every service and obviously in sympathy with the principles advocated. Mr. Campbell suggested to the leaders that a meeting should be called to consider the contemporary situation and to plan the movement they all had been sharing, though there was no formal structure. He longed for the fulfillment of his aspirations to mold a union of believers upon the Scriptures alone (Moore 1909:104).

His suggestion was accepted, and a time agreed upon for the objects in view. Abraham Altars offered his home. He was not a member of any church, but he was a sympathetic friend. The meeting was one of major consequence (Richardson 1868:Vol. I,231).

The Christian Association of Washington

Until this moment, the friends of Thomas Campbell gathered with him to worship and hear him preach, and his sermons related to the situation in which they found themselves. Though the all-sufficiency of the Word as a rule of faith and practice was advocated, there was no common agreement as to principles or action. No withdrawal from denominational factions had been suggested, and no pledge of unity had been asked for among those attending. Only the example and personality of Mr. Campbell and the ill-defined longing for Christian brotherhood bound them one to another (Moore 1908:104).

There was no desire by any affiliated with the fellowship of starting a new religious party. The object of the scheme, by all means, was to do away with partyism and to persuade the factions to seek for unity upon the basis of Scripture and to put behind them their quarrels over differences of opinion.

Thomas Campbell in 1809 had no objections to their systematized doctrines. There was little in the Westminster Confession that he objected to. His problem with the Confession was that "it gave to the clergy a position and an authority which he thought unauthorized, and which, as he had found by experience could be readily abused" (Richardson 1868:Vol. I,232). The Protestant prescriptions were agreed that the Bible was the only rule of faith and practice. Mr. Campbell knew this and believed it his right to encourage all religious factions to adopt the principle. The demands of the day were that it should be embraced by all as the one foundation for Christian unity. He was encouraged that when isolated from his own denomination, there gathered around him well-informed people who were unhappy with contemporary partyism, and in their concern over the intolerance and sectarianism intermeshed into them, were, as never before, inclined to embrace the Word of God as the only compass in things spiritual.

There was agreement by those dubious of the outcome of the proposal and by those sympathetic to it when Mr. Campbell suggested a meeting to formulate a declaration of the concepts he proposed.

The exact date of a meeting at the Abraham Altar's farm is uncertain, though it was sometime in the early summer of 1809 that a group came together to make plans for a future organization. All present felt the occasion was of importance. At that meeting Mr. Campbell proposed a rejection of every item of religion that could not be justified by the sanction of Scripture, and he plead with concern for a return to the teaching of the Word of God. At last he pronounced with emphasis, the underlying faculty upon which he believed they were acting, and that was that "Where the Scriptures speak we speak; and where the Scriptures are silent, we are silent " (Richardson 1868:Vol. I, 236. McAllister 1954:98).

It was from the moment when these significant words were uttered and accepted that the more intelligent ever afterwards dated the formal and actual commencement of the Reformation which was subsequently carried on with so much success, and which has already produced such important changes in the religious society over a large portion of the world (Richardson 1868:Vol. I,237).

A Key Principle Easily Embraced in Theory. In fact, it proved more difficult to apply. Immediately after it was approved, a Mr. Andrew Munro stood to declare, "Mr. Campbell, if we adopt this as a basis, then there is an end to infant baptism" (1868:Vol. I,238). Differences arose, and a number ceased attending the meetings, fearful of the principle they had adopted, lest it lead them into theological seas beyond the depth of their understanding (Moore 1909:105-106).

As committed as Mr. Campbell was to Christian unity and believing that in the divided condition of the religious community perhaps some concessions were needed, he was of the opinion that infant baptism, as with other questions, should remain a matter of private judgment and for the sake of harmony kept in the area of non-essentials. However, regarding specific questions, the brethren saw themselves joined together for the purpose of advocating union in the Christian world.

A second meeting was convened on August 17, 1809 at the headwaters of the Buffaloe. The group of about twenty-one persons, representative of the community regardless of denominational affiliation, named themselves "The Christian Association of Washington" after the county of their residence. Their first need was to publish a declaration of the purposes and objectives of their new organization. Thomas Campbell was to write it. The famous

Declaration and Address was the result (McAllister 1954: 100-101).

The Declaration and Address

These twenty-one persons were commissioned to compare views, with help from Mr. Campbell, to formulate an acceptable way of putting into motion the objects of the organization (Rowe 1894:139).

The members built a log meeting house near Mount Pleasant, to be used also for a needed school in the area. Nearby was the home of a friend, and Mr. Campbell lived in an upstairs room and met regularly with his followers. In the quiet of his apartment he filled his hours with study and writing, and from his pen came *A Declaration and Address*. On September 7, 1809, and before members of the association, the document was carefully read. It had their unanimous approval, and arrangements were made for its publication (Richardson 1868:Vol. I,241).

It was "a statement of principles and program for the Christian Association of Washington." The paper consisted of four parts: the declaration stating the purposes for which the association was formed; the address containing thirteen proposals focusing on arguments for the unity of all believers and giving attention to methods by which it could be accomplished; the appendix giving response to criticisms made or anticipated and amplifying particular emphases in the address; and a postcript added after three months offering proposals for the implementation of the plan (Garrison and DeGroot 1954:145).

Specific principles in the declaration are fundamental. They reveal the basis for Mr. Campbell's rationale and suggest his conclusions regarding matters of belief (Murch 1962:43). These principles emphasized 1) the authority of

110

the Scriptures; 2) the Christian's responsibility before God and the right of private judgment; 3) the evil of sectarianism, and 4) the way to peace and unity in the body of Christ is through conformity to the teachings of Holy Scriptures.

Nine propositions were put forward, designed to provide the association with a constitution and plans for the proclamation of the gospel and the extension of New Testament Christianity.

The salutation and address exudes the love Mr. Campbell entertained for all Christians. Towards all who loved the Christ as Savior and Lord, he held no ill feelings. The declaration would go first to friends among the Presbyterians who had shoddily dealt with him, and then to denominations of several persuasions. He appealed to them all by writing,

> It is the great design and native tendancy of our holy religion, to reconcile and unite man to God, and to each other, in truth and love to the glory of God, and their present and eternal good . . . insofar then as this holy unity and unanimity in faith and love is attained; just in the same degree is the glory of God, and the happiness of man promoted and secured" (1962:43-44).

Mr. Campbell revealed by contrast the heart-rending consequences of this perpetual contention in and among neighboring congregations, often in the same denomination, while numbers of people over vast areas neither heard preaching nor shared in worship, and all of this in a land where democracy guaranteed freedom of religion and worship. Mr. Campbell wrote,

> Dearly beloved brethren, why should we deem it a thing incredible that the Church of Christ, in this highly favored

country, should resume that original unity, peace and purity, which belongs to its constitution, and constitutes its glory? Or is there anything that can be justly deemed necessary for this desirable purpose, but to conform to the model, and adopt the practice of the primitive church, expressly exhibited in the New Testament?" (Richardson 1868:Vol. I, 253-254).

Mr. Campbell shared the dream he entertained of a united Church, its unity determined by the Bible only, with all churches agreeing essentially on matters of doctrine. He said,

It is, to us, a pleasing consideration that all churches of Christ, which mutually acknowledge each other as such, are not only agreed in the great doctrines of faith and holiness; but are also materially agreed, as to the positive ordinances of Gospel institution; so that our differences, at most, are about the things in which the kingdom of God does not consist, that is about matters of private opinion, or human invention. What a pity that the kingdom of God should be divided about such things! (1868:Vol. I,254).

Thomas Campbell had no intention of establishing another denomination. He regarded his friends in the religious groups in the community as brethren in Christ. His concern was that his brethren who were so separated, might be united, and he believed that among many there was this same hunger for unity that so held his prayerful concern.

You are all, dear brethren, equally included as the object of our love and esteem. With you all we desire to unite in the bonds of an entire Christian unity, Christ alone being the head, the center; his word the rule . . . (1868:Vol. I,255).

112

Mr. Campbell, hesitatingly, put forward thirteen propositions to be weighed in the light of Scripture.

He had cause for second thoughts concerning the principles he was suggesting. He realized that application of his proposals would make it necessary to renounce practices long cherished. Others saw their implications, and a number who too lightly accepted the proposals, turned back when they realized the price to be paid (Moore 1909:108).

Each proposal focused on the restoration of the Church revealed in the New Testament, the purpose being that all born again believers "might stand with evidence upon the same ground on which the Church stood in the beginning."

Few propositions, outside Scripture, have been as important as these. This statement is accepted as "one of the greatest contributions that American Christianity has made. It has been called the religious Declaration of Independence . . . declaring the Church free from bondage to human creeds, human names, and human lordship" (Smith 1930: 52).

Its Thirteen Propostions

1. That the Church of Christ is essentially, intentionally and constitutionally one.

2. That although this unity presupposes and permits the existence of separate congregations or societies, there should be perfect harmony and unity of spirit among all of them.

3. That the Bible is the only rule of faith and practice for Christians.

4. That the New Testament alone contains the authoritative constitution of the Church of Christ.*

---

* Comparison of proposition four as J. D. Murch gives it, with Richardson, indicates that Murch was in error.

113

5. That no human authority has power to amend or change the original constitution and laws of the Church.

6. That inferences and deductions from the Scriptures, however valuable, can not be made binding upon the consciences of Christians.

7. That differences of opinion with regard to such inferences shall not be made tests of fellowship or communion.

8. Faith in Jesus Christ as the Son of God is a sufficient profession to entitle a man or woman to become a member of the Church of Christ.

9. That all who have made such a profession, and who manifest their sincerity by their conduct, should love each other as brethren and as members of the same body and joint-heirs of the same inheritance.

10. That division among Christians is anti-Christian, anti-scriptural, unnatural and to be abhorred.

11. That neglect of the revealed will of God and the introduction of human innovations are and have been the cause of all the corruptions and divisions that have ever taken place in the Church of God.

12. That all that is necessary to secure the highest state of purity and perfection in the Church is to restore the original ordinances and constitution as exhibited in the New Testament.

13. That any additions to the New Testament program which circumstances may seem to require, shall be regarded as human expedients and shall not be given a place of higher authority in the Church than is permitted by the fallible character of their origin (Richardson 1868: Vol. I,258-262; Murch 1962:47).

114

Thomas Campbell concluded the address with the conviction that all who loved the Lord would be as anxious for the unity of the Church as he.

Ye desire union in Christ, with all them that love him; so do we. Ye lament and bewail our sad divisions; so do we. Ye reject the doctrines and commandments of men that ye may keep the law of Christ; so do we. Ye believe the alone sufficiency of his word; so do we. Ye believe that the word itself ought to be our rule and not any human explication of it; so do we. Ye believe that no man has a right to judge, to exclude, or reject, his professing Christian brother; except in so far as he stands condemned, or rejected, by the express letter of the law: so do we. Ye believe that the great fundamental law of unity and love ought not to be violated to make way for exalting human opinions to an equality with express revelation, by making them articles of faith and terms of communion: so do we (Murch 1962:48).

An appendix followed. It had one objective, to clarify in detail the emphases found in the Address. Mr. Campbell was apprehensive lest the purpose of the Christian Association of Washington be misinterpreted. The appendix was an effort to give answers to objections raised regarding the associaton.

As to creeds and confessions, although we may appear to our brethren to oppose them, yet this is to be understood only in so far as they oppose the unity of the Church, by containing sentiments not expressly revealed in the word of God; or, by the way of using them, become the instruments of a human or implicit faith, or oppress the weak of God's heritage (Richardson 1868:Vol. I,264; Moore 1909: 118-119).

115

The postscript was written after December 14, 1809, following the meeting of the twenty-one. Proposals were made for the implementation of the program. The first suggested the formulation of a catechism "Upon the entire subject of Christianity." The second proposed a monthly magazine to be called *The Christian Monitor* (Garrison and DeGroot 1954:152).

Nothing came of either suggetion. By the time the Declaration and Address was ready for publication, Alexander Campbell, with the rest of Thomas Campbell's family, arrived, and his father asked him to proofread the original copies of the manuscript. Both proposals were eliminated (Moore 1909:127).

There Were Other Pleas for Unity as Well

The life of Thomas Campbell has been documented by several Restoration Movement historians. His *Declaration and Address* is one of the great documents of the movement. A fact too long overlooked is that there were pleas for the unity of believers and the restoration of the Church revealed in Scripture before either Thomas or Alexander Campbell began propagating their concepts to people of Pennsylvania, Virginia, and Ohio in the early nineteenth century.

The Christian Baptist, edited by Alexander Campbell, contains portions of a sermon preached by James Madison before the convention of the Protestant Episcopal Church in Virginia on May 26, 1786 (*The Christian Baptist* 1829: 578).

Bishop James Madison

James Madison was born near Staunton, Virginia, on August 27, 1749. He was the son of John Madison and a

116

cousin of James Madison, fourth President of the United States. He graduated with honors from William and Mary College in Williamsburg, Virginia, in 1771. He studied law under George Wythe, signer of the *Declaration of Independence*, who was the first professor of law in America and Chancellor of Virginia. Though admitted to the bar, he did not practice law.

James Madison became professor of natural history and mathematics at William and Mary in 1773, and two years later went to England for advanced studies and for ordination to the ministry of the Church of England. Back in Williamsburg, now a full professor, he was, in 1777, chosen president of the college, an office held until his death in 1812.

Madison supported the Revolutionary cause. In 1777 he was commissioned captain of a company of college students, and he saw active service at times during the war.

Because Madison was one of the best scientific men of his day, he was drawn to Thomas Jefferson, and the two carried on considerable correspondence on scientific subjects. While Jefferson was Governor of Virginia, Madison, with the governor, brought a number of organizational reforms at William and Mary.

Near the close of the war, Madison's position as president of the college became difficult. Classes were dismissed. The campus was in the hands of the British and later in control of the French and Americans. Following the war, the college was plagued with lack of income and students, but under his presidency, was brought back to strength and prosperity.

After the war, Madison took part in the reorganization of the Episcopal Church and in the formation of the diocese of Virginia, serving as president of the first convention in 1785. He was elected Bishop in 1790 and was consecrated at Canterbury by the Archbishop of Canterbury in Lambeth Chapel. Madison was third of three bishops, White and Provoost the other two, by means of whom the Church of England espiscopate was brought to the United States.

Madison's responsibility as Bishop of Virginia was superhuman. The Episcopal Church, before the war, was never allowed to have its own bishop or to determine its own affairs. Until the Revolution, it had been supported by government of the colony which created new parishes as it created new counties. Following the war, the church, with neither training nor experience in corporate government, was hardly more than a conglomerate of disestablished parishes. It was confronted with antagonism from parts of the population who attempted to possess its glebe lands and other properties.

The Episcopal Church in Virginia, from 1785 to the time of Madison's death, was unable to solve its post-war problems, and it weakened, almost to the point of death. Through this, James Madison's convention addresses were outstanding, reflecting deep devotion, conviction and love for the church.

Madison's Sermon Noted by the Editor of The Christian Baptist

Alexander Campbell, on September 7, 1829, in introducing James Madison's sermon says,

> The following expose of many sentiments for which I have been called a heretic, coming from a man who was, in his days, and died in the Office of Bishop in the whole

THE CAMPBELL MOVEMENT BEGINS

state of Virginia, will to the minds of many, afford much more evidence of truth than if I had said them . . . I have not met in any one extract so many of the sentiments advanced in this work: nor have I seen so exceptional an exposition of my "peculiar views" from any pen; nor did I know, till yesterday, that any man in the United States had spoken so much good sense on these subjects, in the year of 1786, as appears in the following extract *(Christian Baptist* 1829:578).

The Sermon of James Madison

The text of Madison's sermon was John 4:24: "God is Spirit: and they that worship him must worship him in spirit and in truth."

The purpose of the sermon was to stress the importance of Christian unity and the destructive nature of creeds in creating and perpetuating divisions among Christians.

God grant that she (The United States) may never prove herself unworthy of being an instrument in the consumation of a plan, so capable of restoring the human race to its true and original dignity. God grant that those political institutions which she has adopted, institutions, which have ever exhibited human nature in its greatest perfection, may not only be preserved in that purity in which they originated, but may still receive those improvements which experience and wisdom may suggest, and render America that land of happiness, where men shall be no longer considered superiors and inferiors, but as equals and as brethren; where at length the doctrine of Christ, uncorrupted by views of state or the ignorance of fallible and presumptuous men, shall flourish in its primitive excellence, when the principles of a morality so sublime, so pure, so godlike, shall conduct men to that sum of greatest felicity which they were doubtless designed to establish upon earth.

119

. . . This is the principal consequence, I wish to draw from what has been as yet delivered. May the minds of all here, be conscientiously impressed with the particular duty of applying the opportunity which is now offered, in such a manner, as to institute a Christian Church upon principles, truly consentaneous to that spirit of charity and benevolence which dictated Christianity itself; a Church whose liberal, rational enlarged views, unrestrained by the schemes of political ambition, and uncorrupted by the doctrines of fallible men, may prove the superior excellence, nay, the divine origin of our holy religion; by ultimately accomplishing that arduous task of uniting all the individuals of the human species in the most powerful and sacred of all ties, in that brotherly love, that universal charity which is the bond of all perfection, and which the gospel would inspire, nay kindle with a divine ardour in the souls of men. Here then let us rear on the foundation of the gospel alone, the temple of universal charity.

. . . Would to God, those dissentions, which too much abound amongst Christians, could at this moment be banished from amongst us! Would to God, instead of those that often arise from subjects with which obedience to the doctrine of Christ is by no means connected, that union and church fellowship could everywhere be established. This union is often recommended by St. Paul as "the bond of peace and of all perfection," and is enjoined as a duty of strict obligation on all Christians; there being, as he saith, but "one Lord, one faith, one baptism, one God, and Father of all, who is above all, and through all, and in you all." Could the followers of Christ once be persuaded of the importance of this duty; could they, imitating the noble example of meekness and humility which has been set before them, range themselves under the banners of love, abandon as trifles, unsubstantial as vanity, when compared with the

sublime, but simple morality of the gospel, those idle controversies, those dotings about questions and strifes of
words, those perverse disputings, which have too long
occupied the minds of Christians, and which serve only to
execute envy, strife, railings, evil surmisings, shameful to
the professors of religion, whose basis is universal charity;
could men be persuaded to embrace the substance of so
pure a religion, the wholesome words of our Lord Jesus
Christ, and not dispute about the shadow; could they be
persuaded as Christians who acknowledge the same God,
the same Jesus; as Christians who look forward to the same
celestial commonwealth, at this moment to unite in one
church; could they, at this moment, be incorporated as
brethren in one happy and glorious society, assemble themselves under the same divine standard, and with conspiring
voice, send forth their united prayers, like incense to the
Throne of Grace, might we not then, my brethren, anticipate the blessings of heaven itself; might we not, in pious
confidence, at length raise our eyes to that signal, which
should aloft display peace, happiness and victory to the
Christian world.

. . . To promote this great event is the bounden duty of
every church. It is our duty, and a golden opportunity
invites to the performance of it.

Permit me then, to make some observations upon the means
most likely to forward such an event . . . Fortunately for
Christians, those means are altogether of the negative kind,
They depend upon the rejection, not the adoption of any of
those human systems of belief, or rules of faith, which
have often usurped the place of Christianity itself. They
only require Christians to revert to the gospel, and to abandon every other directory of conscience. I will then venture
earnestly to recommend to Christians to reject every system,

as the fallible production of human contrivance which shall dictate articles of faith, and adopt the gospel alone as their guide.

. . . I will take the liberty to advance a general proposition, the evidence of which I persuade myself, may be established by the most incontestible proofs. The proposition is indeed simple and plain; it is, "that those Christian societies will ever be found to have formed their union upon principles the wisest and best, which impose the fewest restraints upon the minds of their members, making the scriptures alone, and not human articles or confessions of belief, the sole rule of faith and conduct."

It is much to be lamented that the venerable reformers, when they burst the cords of popish tyranny, ever departed from the simplicity of this scripture plan, and that instead of adhering to it, they thought theological systems the only means of preserving uniformity of opinion, or of evincing the purity of their faith. The experience of more than two centuries hath proved, how far they are capable of producing either effect. On the other hand, the consequences which such institutions have been productive of, have been more or less severely felt in every part of the Protestant world, from the diet of Augsburg, to the present time. They have, in former as well as in latter ages, caused a religion, designed to unite all men as brethren in the sacred bonds of charity and benevolence, too often to disseminate amongst them jealousies, animosities, and rancorous hatred. They have nursed the demon of intolerance; nay, aided by the civil power, they have led martyrs to the stake, and have offered up as holy sacrifices to the God of mercy, Christians, who had the guilt to prefer, what they esteemed the doctrines of Christ, to the commandments of men.

. . . It is a maxim, self-evident, to everyone, and which was held sacred by the fathers of Protestanism, "that the scriptures contain all things necessary to salvation, and are the sole ground of faith of a Christian." This maxim, the basis of the Reformation, and which is acceded to by all Protestants, is alone sufficient, independent of what experience hath taught, to induce every Protestant church, to reject all systems of belief, unless conceived in the terms of Scripture, not only as unwarrantable, and in the highest degree oppressive to the rights of private judgment, but as presumptuous, and as calling an unworthy reflection on the Scriptures themselves.

. . . Did not our Savior constantly enjoin his followers to search the scriptures themselves? Do we not find, that the Bereans were commended for their conduct in not receiving even the doctrine of the inspired apostles until they had first searched the scriptures to see whether these things were so or not? . . . Doth he [Paul] not everywhere recommend to Christians the duty of examining the ground of their faith "to prove all things, and to hold fast that which is good?" . . . No, my brethren, we may be assured that Christ and His apostles did not esteem any other summary necessary, than the gospel itself; and that whatever is essential either as to faith or practice is there expressed with that clearness which a revelation from heaven required. We are directed there to search, and to judge for ourselves; for religion, to be profitable to the individual and acceptable to God, must be the result of free enquiry and the determination of reason. This right of free inquiry, and of judging for ourselves, is a right natural and unalienable.

. . . The very attempt, in matters dark and disputable, to prevent diversity of opinion, is vain and fruitless . . . to attempt there to prevent diversity of opinions upon such subjects, is to oppose the very laws of nature, and consequently vain and fruitless . . . those things alone should be held as

123

essentials, which our Lord and Master, hath fully and clearly expressed, and which therefore cannot require the supposed improvements and additions of men. So long as men agree in these essentials, or fundamental articles of our religion, in those great and important truths and duties, which are so clearly expressed that every sincere inquirer must readily apprehend them, where is the necessity, or the reasonableness of attempting to compel men to be of one mind, as to other matters of infinitely inferior moment, and which we may suppose, were designedly less clearly expressed. That Christian unity, so strongly recommended to us, as the bond of perfection, does not consist in uniformity of opinion upon abstruse, metaphysical subjects, but upon the great fundamentals of our religion, and in that unanimity of affections, love, peace and charity, which is enjoined the brethren in Christ Jesus, who all walk by the same rule, and acknowledge one and the same Lord.

. . . I conceive, moreover, that no Christian Church hath a right to impose upon its members, human systems of belief, as necessary terms of communion. For what, I beseech you, do we understand by a Christian Church? According to the most general acceptation, "every Christian Church is a voluntary society of men agreeing to profess the faith of Christ and stipulating to live according to the rules of the gospel." From this definition we find the destructive terms of union, or the fundamental law of such a society, is to embrace the scriptures alone, as the rule of worship, faith and conduct.

. . . What then, it may be asked, shall not a church prescribe to itself, terms of communion, shall it not have its particular confessions or articles of belief, provided they be agreeable to the Word of God? How many Protestant churches have been built on this foundation of sand, unable to resist the winds and tempests which beat against them!

The condition is inadmissible. For who shall determine with certainty, that those terms are agreeable to the Word of God? How is it possible that all the members of the Church should be sufficiently assured of this important point? Or is private judgment to be entirely annihilated; if so, to what end, did the benign author of our being grant reason to men? Is the conscientious Christian to forget, that it is his duty to search the scriptures themselves, or are those human expositions to usurp the place of the Word of God? What then is the consequence? The difference between them is surely a proof, that infallibility is not the attribute of all of them. Truth, like the Eternal, is one. In which church then shall we find it? I will presume to say in none of them. He who would search for the truth must search for it in the Scripture alone.

. . . I will endeavor briefly to place in one point of view, some of the many objections which may be made against the introduction of human articles of belief in the Christian Church.

1st. Then, they are to be avoided, because the Scriptures, being the sole ground of faith, afford the only test by which purity of doctrine is to be ascertained.

2nd. Because, the attempt to establish them, is an assumption of power, which can of right, belong to no Christian Church.

3rd. Because they impose shackles upon the human mind which not only effectively impede the progress of Christian knowledge, but destroy the essential rights to private judgement.

4th. Because, they tend, instead of producing harmony and unity of opinion amongst Christians, to excite dissentions and animosities.

5th. Because, they corrupt the pure fountain of Christianity and impregnate the living waters of truth with the impure conceits of men.

6th. Because, they are nowhere enjoined in scripture, as essential to the Christian Church.

7th. Lastly, because, the great and important doctrines of revealed religion, being delivered with sufficient perspicuity, an attempt to express them in a mode, different from that in which they are delivered, supposes an imperfection in the scriptures, which should be avoided.

. . . Those Christian societies will ever be found to have formed their union upon principles the wisest and the best, which impose the fewest restraints upon the minds of their members, making the scriptures alone, and not human articles or confessions of belief, the sole rule of faith and conduct.

Let us then abandon all those systems, which to say the least can only involve us in error. Our venerable forefathers erred, or why a reformation? Their descendents will err. Nor shall the resurrection of true Christianity be seen amongst men, until it shall appear in the white garment of the gospel alone.

. . . These worthies would not in vain have exhausted the thunder of their eloquence, could they have occupied the ground on which I now stand. They would have exulted with joy that the opportunity was at length arrived of restoring Christianity to its primitive purity. They would have told us, that now was the time to break down all those vain barriers, which have so long opposed the union of Christians; now was the time to establish the worship of Spirit and of truth, and to evince the superior excellence of our holy religion. But why suppose we what the best or the wisest of men would have said or done? Imagine to yourselves the love of God, in all the lustre of His own meekness and humility, again descending to visit the Christian world. Behold in His hands and His side those wounds which he endured for your salvation, and hearken once more to the salvation of peace. What think ye, my brethren, will now be the first sacred lesson which shall flow from the lips of your once crucified Savior? But, already I perceive, you anticipate Him. Already you hear His divine voice calling men to return to the gospel, and to receive it as the only rule of faith and conduct; already you hear Him, with tears of compassion, lamenting those dissentions, which prevail amongst His followers; and with eyes lifted up to heaven, exclaim, 'O righteous Father, I pray for them which believe on me, that they all may be one; as thou Father, art in me, and I in thee, that they may be one in us; that the world may believe that Thou has sent me. I have given them thy word, sanctify them through thy truth. Thy word is truth.'

James Madison's Sermon and Thomas Campbell's Declaration and Address

In comparison of Madison's sermon and Campbell's *Declaration*, the examples of parallelism are not so evident as between Rice Haggard and Samuel Davies and Samuel Davies and Benjamin Grosvenor. No effort is made to imply that Thomas Campbell had Madison's sermon before him as he wrote his *Declaration and Address*, though chronologically that would have been possible with Madison's sermon preached and published in 1786 in Virginia and Campbell's *Declaration and Address* written and published in western Pennsylvania in 1809, twenty-three years later.

Remarks of the editor of *The Christian Baptist* (1829:578) state that Madison's sermon had not come to his attention until early September of 1829. Therefore, it seems unlikely that Thomas Campbell became aware of the sermon until the same time. However, there is such a close comparison between Madison and Thomas Campbell as to demand the quoting of the high points of Madison's sermon and earlier in this chapter, of Campbell's *Declaration and Address*. A detailed comparison of the emphases of the two men is also needed.

Both Madison's and Campbell's pleas for unity were anchored in affirmations that demonstrate just how much they were thinking alike. Relying on Campbell's statement as the point of comparison does not minimize the importance of Madison's assertions made twenty-three years earlier. Far from that, Madison's sermon demands a place of first importance in the formative years of the American Republic and the American Church. However, the *Declaration and Address*, written by Thomas Campbell in 1809, is the document known and associated with the beginnings of the Reformation, later known as the Restoration Movement. For that reason, Madison is compared with Campbell, for adherents of the Restoration Movement know Thomas Campbell and his work.

Thomas Campbell wrote in 1809	James Madison wrote in 1786
Where the Scriptures speak, we speak; where they are silent, we are silent.	Those Christian societies will ever be found to have formed their union upon principles the wisest and best, which impose the fewest restraints upon the minds of their members, making the scriptures alone and not

human articles or confessions of belief, the sole rule of faith and conduct.

It is a maxim, self evident to everyone, and which was held sacred by the fathers of Protestantism, 'that the scriptures contain all things necessary to salvation, and are the sole ground of faith of a Christian.'

'Thus saith the Lord,' either in express terms or by approved precedent, for every article of faith and item of religious practice.

We may be assured that Christ and his apostles did not esteem any other summary necessary, than the gospel itself; and that whatever is essential either as to faith or practice is there expressed with that clearness which a revelation from heaven required.

Those things alone should be held as essentials, which our Lord and master, hath fully and clearly expressed, and which therefore cannot require the supposed improvements and additions of men.

They [human articles of belief] are to be avoided because the scriptures, being the sole ground of faith afford the only test by which purity of doctrine is to be ascertained.

Nothing ought to be received into the faith or worship of the church or to be made a term of communion among Christians, that is not as old as the New Testament.

I will then venture earnestly to recommend to Christians to reject every system, as the fallible production of human contrivance, which shall dictate articles of faith, and adopt the gospel alone as their guide. He who would search for the truth must search for it in the Scriptures alone.

No Christian Church hath a right to impose upon its members, human systems of belief, as necessary terms of communion.

The destructive terms of union, or the fundamental law of such a society [the Christian Church], is to embrace the scriptures alone, as the rule of worship, faith and conduct.

An agreement in the expressly revealed will of God is the adequate and firm foundation of Christian unity.

Those Christian societies will ever be found to have formed their union upon principles the wisest and the best, which impose the fewest restraints upon the minds of their members, making the Scriptures alone, and not human articles or confessions of belief, the sole rule of faith and conduct.

An assumed authority for making the approbation of human

They have [theological] systems in former as well as in latter

130

opinions and human inventions a term of communion, by introducing them into the constitution, faith, or worship of the Church, is and has been the immediately obvious, and universally acknowledged cause of all corruptions and divisions that have ever taken place in the Church of God.

ages, caused a religion, designed to unite all men as brothers in the sacred bonds of charity and benevolence, too often to disseminate amongst them jealousies, animosities, and rancorous hatred.

The attempt to establish them [human articles of belief] is an assumption of power which can of right, belong to no Christian Church.

They [human articles of belief] impose a shackle upon the human mind which not only effectively impede the progress of Christian knowledge but destroy the essential right of private judgment.

[Human articles of belief] tend, instead of producing harmony and unity of opinion amongst Christians, to excite dissentions and animosities.

The restoration of pure, primitive, apostolic Christianity, in letter and spirit, in principle and in practice, as the only cure for sectarianism.

Would to God, those dissentions, which too much abound amongst Christians, could at this moment be banished from amongst us.

[Human articles of belief] corrupt the pure fountain of Christianity and impregnate the living waters of truth with the impure concerts of men.

They [our venerable forefathers] would have told us that now was the time to break down all those vain barriers, which have so long opposed the union of Christians. Now was the time to establish the worship of spirit and truth, and to evince the superior excellence of our holy religion.

Absolute and entire rejection of human authority in matters of religion.	[Human articles of belief] are nowhere enjoined in Scripture, as essential to the Christian Church.

The Quiet Imprint of Awakenings

There is no intimation that Campbell borrowed from Madison, and yet, examination of the above confirms that the two men were thinking alike. They did not express themselves in the same way, but they were close to saying the same thing.

The question of how and why these two men, so far apart secularly and religiously could be so close theologically, is a logical one.

Thomas Campbell was a product of the second Great Awakening (Orr 1965:55; 175:140; Latourette 1974:Vol. IV, 198; MacAllister 1954:60-64). James Madison of William and Mary College in Williamsburg, Virginia, a generation earlier than Thomas Campbell, was a product of the first Great Awakening. Madison, born in 1749, a son of Church of England parents in the colony of Virginia, grew to manhood immediately following the year of George Whitefield's American preaching.

Whitefield had visited Williamsburg, Virginia, ten years prior to James Madison's birth, and he recounts that he visited a Reverend Mr. Blair who was primarily instrumental in building a beautiful college (William and Mary) in Williamsburg where "the gentlemen of Virginia send their children . . . . The present masters came from Oxford" and were Whitefield's contemporaries at Oxford (Whitefield's Journals 359, Dallimore 1971:442).

However, during the lifetime of James Madison, there was little within the Protestant Episcopal Church to inspire him. From 1777 until his death in 1812 Madison was President of William and Mary, and in 1790 he was elected Bishop of the Episcopal Church of Virginia. So desperate were the fortunes of the church during this period that James Madison, in agreement with Chief Justice Marshall, also a devout churchman, believed that the Episcopal Church was beyond being revived (Sweet 1973:224). But the Episcopal Church did not die, and in Virginia the fact that it lived is due, to a great degree, to the work of President and Bishop James Madison.

Madison's sermon must be seen in the context in which he lived, just as Thomas Campbell's *Declaration and Address* has to be seen in the context in which Campbell lived. Their theologies of the Church, so much alike, affirm that both men were products of the Awakenings.

Madison's 1786 sermon confirms, however, that following the war in the atmosphere created by the founding of the new nation and the uniting of the thirteen colonies, there was a similar leaven, or ferment present in the minds of godly, thinking men, focusing on the unity of Christians on the basis of Scripture.

133

Thomas Campbell's *Declaration and Address* is better known than Madison's sermon because of the successful beginnings of the Christian Church which has succeeded, at least in a limited way, in enunciating Campbell's great principles. Madison's sermon, on the other hand, was little heeded by his own church, and therefore, has been forgotten, but his clear expression of Biblical truths is no less important because of it.

Not only were Thomas Campbell and James Madison the products of the Great Awakenings, but the concepts they so clearly proclaimed found expression because of the Awakenings.

Chapter Six

JOHN GLAS AND THE RESTORATION MOVEMENT

Alexander Campbell Was Acquainted with John Glas

Early in 1826, in an article in *The Christian Baptist*, Alexander Campbell wrote,

> While I am pretty well acquainted with all this controversy, since John Glas was excommunicated by the high church of Scotland, for preaching that Christ's kingdom is not of this world, which is now more than a century ago, and while acknowledging myself a debtor to Glas, Sandeman, Harvey, Cudworth, Fuller and McLean; as much as to Luther, Calvin, and John Wesley, I candidly and unequivocally avow, that I do not believe that any one of them had clear and consistent views of the Christian religion as a whole (*The Christian Baptist* 1826:229).

Was Campbell a Glasite, Sandemanian or Haldanean?

The question as to what extent John Glas influenced the founders of the Restoration Movement and particularly Mr. Campbell, has long been debated. Some of his own critics branded him with Sandemanianism, charging that he borrowed from John Glas, the Scotch Baptists and the Haldanes.

In 1825 his Baptist critic, R. B. Semple, accused him of being "substantially a Sandemanian or Haldanian" (1826: 229). Sixty years later, Dr. W. H. Whitsitt made a similar charge, asserting that the Disciples of Christ, commonly called Campbellites . . . are an offshoot of the Sandemanian sect of Scotland (1891:51, 3rd ed.:Longan 1889:13).

Alexander Campbell denied he was a follower of Glas, Sandeman, McLean or Haldanes or that the Restoration Movement was to any degree in the debt of those men.

"While I thus acknowledge myself a debtor to those persons, I must say, that the debt, in most instances, is a very small one. I am indebted, upon the whole, as much to their errors as to their virtues . . ." (*The Christian Baptist* 1826:299).

In 1827 Mr. Campbell denied the relationship once again.

> To call me a Sandemanian, a Haldanean, a Glasite, an Arian or a Unitarian, and to tell the world that the Sandemanians, Haldaneans, etc., etc., have done so and so, and have been refuted by such and such a person, is too cheap a method of maintaining human traditions, and too weak to oppose reason and revelation. You might as well nickname me a Sabellian, an Anthropomorphist, a Gnostic, a Nicolaitan, or an Anabaptist, as to palm upon me any of the above systems. I do most unequivocally and sincerely renounce each and every one of these systems (1827:399).

Mr. Campbell was acquainted with John Glas' book, *King of Martyrs*, before he began his own work of reformation. He attributes that book, rejected by the Synod of Angus and Mearns in 1728, "as the foundation of the Edinburgh reform school" (*The Millennial Harbinger* 1835:305).

William Jones of London wrote to Campbell in March, 1835, "The Scotch Baptist Churches, out of which yours in America took their origin, as I think you will not deny . . . arose during that period" (1835:300).

The pronouncement that Campbell's movement was an offshoot of the Sandemanian sect or that he was a disciple of Glas, Sandeman or the Haldanes, was to go too far. G. W. Longan rightly affirms that the Reformation of Campbell, Scott and Stone was never associated with the Sandemanian movement or any part of it (Longan 1889:26).

Mr. Campbell did not deny that, to some degree, he was a debtor to earlier advocates of a return to the teaching of the apostles and the order of the church revealed in the Scriptures. He affirms his debt to Archibald McLean who "had drawn largely and liberally from the writings of John Glas" and others. "I may, therefore, indirectly be indebted to Archibald McLean . . . much more than I am aware" (*The Millennial Harbinger* 1835:304). It is his conclusion, after acknowledging his "debts to the great and wise and good men who have gone before us," that in the Restoration Movement "there will be found views of the Christian Institution wholly new as far as the works of all the schools to which I have attended are concerned" (1835:306).

The Life and Ministry of John Glas

His Early Life

John Glas was born on September 21, 1695, at Auchtermuchty in the county, Fife, in Scotland. He was the fifth son in an unbroken clerical succession. His early education was obtained at Kinclaven in Perthshire. He attended the school at Auchtermuchty, and from there studied at the grammar school at Perth, where he continued until he went to the University of St. Andrews and earned his A.M. He completed his studies at the University of Edinburgh (*Memoirs of John Glas* (1813:ii). In 1719 he was ordained minister of Tealing in the Presbytery of Dundee. He was married in 1721 and had fifteen children, all of whom preceded him in death.

The Controversy Over the Covenants

His thinking at the time of his ordination is evident from his own words. He says,

Though I was educated for the ministry, and could never apply myself to any other employment, yet I could never allow myself to think that I was fit for that work; and therefore, I was so far from making any motion toward my entering upon it, that it was a surprise for me, when I was pressed by a presbytery to enter upon trials, in order to preach; and because I thought I had gone but a very short way in the study of divinity, and the time prescribed by the assembly was not yet elapsed, and my ineptness in all respects was evident to me, I was therefore truly averse from it; but being prevailed upon to undergo the usual trials, I was brought through them, and came the length of subscribing the Formula, which I had not till then considered. I had looked a little into the Episcopal controversy, and was fully satisfied that in the Word of God there was no foundation for prelacy, and that the Presbyterians had the better of them by the Scriptures. I had not then considered the controversy between the Presbyterians and them of the congregational way, but took up the common report against the congregational business, that it is near confusion. And further, I thought I saw a subordination of church courts in the fifteenth chapter of Acts, without considering whether it was this national subordination, or something else; or whether it was a stated subordination, or occasional only; of whether there was any discipline in the case or not . . . . Thus I thought myself a sound Presbyterian, and accordingly declared myself so, by subscribing to the Formula. And when I entered upon the work of the ministry, and was settled in a parish as a public teacher, I again declared myself a Presbyterian, and subscribed to the Formula (1816:iii-iv).

Glas was determined to make the Scriptures his only rule of conduct and so began his ministry. He did not forsee that holding to such a rule would bring him into opposition with the precepts of his own denomination. His mind was possessed "by the doctrine of the glorious gospel of the grace of God," and this he preached in the church and homes of his people. He was soon aware that his ministry little affected his hearers. Doubts assailed him, that he was not fitted for the ministry, and this compelled him to prayer and study. His preaching improved, and he not only held forth the teachings of Scripture, but he also tried to acquaint his people with the articles of the national church with the object of demonstrating how these articles in the Westminster Confession agreed with the Word of God. These lectures began in the first year of his ministry. He proceeded from the beginning of the shorter catechism to that question, "How does Christ execute the office of a king?" At this point he discovered he could not harmonize the biblical answer to that question with the doctrine then popular which advocated the still binding obligation of the national covenants — "that these kingdoms were by that covenant married to the Lord — that the judgment of God was impending because of that Covenant having been violated and disregarded" (1816:vi).

It is essential to observe, that the nature of the controversy might be understood, that the national covenant had been instituted to establish Scotland after the pattern of the church of Israel. The first confession of faith of the King of Scotland was ratified in July of 1560, and this became the basis for the second. This second was referred to as the King's Confession, having been subscribed by James the First in January of 1580 and imposed on all his subjects in the following year. In 1638 this confession or covenant was renewed, its adherents declaring by oath to maintain religion as it was when the confession was made and to oppose all changes brought in since that time. As a result of the court party, and the continuing strength of the pope and prelacy, stronger action was essential for the defense of the reformed religion in both Scotland and England.

The Solemn League was approved in a meeting consisting of "commissioners from the Parliament and assembly of the Divines of England, and commissioners of the Convention of Estate and the General Assembly in Scotland" (1816:vii). The Solemn League moved further than the national Covenant. It bonded Scotland and England together, with Ireland also included. Many subscribed to it, rejecting all popery, and they agreed to proceed in unison for their common defense and for the elimination of all heresy.

According to John Glas,

> Thus is pleased the holy and wise God to order things so, that this was the first thing I had to contend with, as a considerable bar lying in the way of edification of such as professed religion in the place. It is true, some that were of more discretion stood with me in this matter, and showed me much kindness; but I was grieviously persecuted with the tongues of those I have been describing when I began to set myself against their way: and if it had not pleased the sovereign Lord to stand by me, and go forth with me in preaching, so as to bring some to a professed subjection to the Gospel of Christ, I had undoubtedly sunk under the opposition I met from that sect (*A Narrative of the Rise and Progress of the Controversy About the National Covenants* 1828:4).

"I resolved," he said, "if possible, to be at the bottom of this controversy, and that it should be determined to me by the word of the Lord Jesus, and by that only" (1828:3).

As a result of his study, John Glas was led to those conclusions later enunciated in his significant theological study, *The Testimony of the King of Martyrs.* There his argument was "that the Kingdom of Christ is essentially spiritual, and as such is completely independent of state sanctions and control, as well as the support of the secular arm" (Hornsby 1936:10). "Then," said Glas, "I had done with national covenanting, under the New Testament, according to all views that they who are truly zealous for our national covenants have had of that convenanting" (*Narrative* 1828:4).

All the while there was an expansion of Glas' own thinking regarding the constitution of the church. From his conviction concerning the spirituality of the Church, he moved to the view that such a church was made up of believers who were possessers of an experience of God's saving grace and who, in obedience to Christ, had separated from the world. Unaware of it, he arrived at approximately the same position as the English Congregationalists, who advocated "gathered Churches" as distinct from parochial congregations.

The doctrines Glas would now preach were new in Scotland, and they were opposed by those anxious to defend the national covenants. Every occasion was used to condemn the new doctrines and their author, but he clung to his stand. Brethren urged him to keep his position to himself for the sake of his wife and his family. He labored with considerable anxiety, believing that he was alone. However, when his wife and members of his parish informed him that they understood and embraced his teaching, he determined to gather those with him into a little society or separate congregation. At Tealing in July of 1725, this

141

fellowship was established with membership under one hundred, a few from other parishes. They agreed to unite in the Christian profession, "to follow Jesus Christ the Lord, as the righteousness of his people, and walk together in brotherly love, and in the duties of it, in subjection to Mr. Glas as their overseer in the Lord." They

> agreed to observe the ordinance of the Lord's Supper once every month . . . on the 12th of August following, several were added; and the Lord's law for removing offences, Matthew 18, being laid before them, they professed subjection to it. On the 9th of December, it was agreed, that at all public meetings there should be a collection for the poor and for professors of Christ's name in other places as were in straits; and at a subsequent meeting, they enjoined' brethren nearest each other to form societies, and to have a meeting once a week for prayer and exhortation (*Memoirs* 1816:x-xi).

Mr. Glas felt that he was not inconsistent with his role as minister of the national church. However, many disagreed with him. The creation of his fellowship, in their judgment, meant establishing an independent church in his parish, while he continued in the contradictory dual role as minister of a parochial charge. The result was that after soul searching and study, he acknowledged his sympathies were more with the Independents than with the Presbyterians.

The Progress of the Controversy

All this created much excitement. Those with zeal for the covenant resolved that war should be declared against Glas' doctrines and divisiveness. The battle was joined in August of 1726 with John Willison, champion of the Covenants. Both Glas and Willison were to preach on

August 6, a fast day. Crowds came from all parts of the country. The text of John Glas' sermon was John 6:69, and the message contained Glas' confession of faith which he stated in three ways:

> I confess my adherence to the good confession of the King of Martyrs before Pontius Pilate concerning his kingdom, John 18:36-37; and I reckon his blood, where with that his dying testimony was sealed, of more worth than the blood of all the martyrs that ever was shed upon the earth. He testified plainly that his kingdom, which he used to design the kingdom of heaven, is not a worldly kingdom, and that it is not set up advanced or defended, as the king-doms of this world, either, 1st by human policy, for it is by the truth; or 2ndly, by human eloquence, and the words of man's wisdom, for it is by bearing witness to the truth; or thirdly, by worldly force or power, for his subjects are all of those, and those only, who are of this truth. And he says, "If my kingdom were of this world, my servants would fight, but now is my kingdom not from thence . . ." Next, I confess my adherence unto the testimony of the apostles of Christ after his ascension, which they gave to the spirit-uality and heavenliness of the kingdom of Christ, in oppo-sition to Jews and Judaizing teachers, who set up for a temporal kingdom to the Messiah, and minded earthly things. Lastly, I confess my adherence to our fathers and martyrs in their testimony to the kingdom of Christ, in opposition to any earthly head of the church not appointed by the Lord Christ; and thus I acknowledge them to be the martyrs of Jesus: but as far as they contend for any such national covenants, as whereby Christ's kingdom should be of this world (his church and world mingled together, and his people who are of the truth, and hear his voice, divided from one another) and such as he hath

143

not appointed under the New Testament, but set aside, so far they were not enlightened (1816:xiii-xiv; *Narrative* 1828:9).

In his response, Mr. John Willison used Luke 13:34 as his text:

> O Jerusalem, Jerusalem! which killeth the prophets, and stonest them which are sent unto thee, how often would I have gathered thy children together, as a hen doth gather her brood under her wings, and you would not.

Entering upon his theme he affirmed his advocacy of the national covenant, to propagate it "as the glory of our land, and our forefathers entering into it, as the fruit of the down-pouring of the Spirit upon our Kings, nobles, barons, and the whole nation" (*Memoirs* 1816:xiv). Mr. Willison affirmed that the effusion of the Holy Spirit accompanied the covenant, to the converting of multitudes. He magnified the national covenant as a confession of faith, deploring the divisiveness and schism the result of opposition to the covenants (*Narrative* 1828:35-36).

Progression to Glas' Deposition

The controversy was too public and important in its consequences to any longer be ignored. The Presbytery, meeting at Dundee on the 7th of September, 1726, felt they must take note of the problem. Glas and Willison were asked to defend their differing opinions. Willison portrayed Glas as rejecting "the doctrine and authority of the church and martyrs, and mentioned an act of Assembly enjoining the deposition of them who spoke against the covenants." Glas responded by saying,

> If the national covenant was the doctrine of the church and of the martyrs, so was the solemn league; and that if Mr.

144

Willison affirmed not the lawfulness and obligation of the solemn league, he himself had not the doctrine of the Church and the testimony of the martyrs, for which he seemed so much concerned (*Memoirs* 1816:xvi).

The matter was unresolved after considerable argument and was postponed until the next presbytery meeting. At this gathering, following bitter debate, it was determined that Mr. Glas should be prohibited from speaking further on the subject of dispute. Mr. Glas refused to adhere, "because he was convinced that what he had preached was a glorious truth of the New Testament, the testimony of our Lord; — a truth of great importance, and in his view, no way so inconsistent with the present establishment as the covenants were" (*Narrative* 1828:75-76).

The matter was next brought before the synod at Aberbrothick in April of 1727. It was proposed to bring in a decree enforcing obligation to the covenants which was agreed upon. An act was drafted which many felt too general and too smooth, with the consequence that the matter was tabled until the next synod where it "should be enacted in a full meeting of that synod" (*Memoirs* 1816: xviii).

A proposal was placed before the synod of Angus and Mearns, meeting at Montrose on October 17, 1727, appointing the Presbytery of Dundee . . . to make inquiry concerning the deportment of Mr. Glas with respect to the reports brought against him" (1816:xx). After the synod had investigated the matter, they were to bring it before the Assembly for its direction, to be reported to the next synod. In the meantime the synod was to prohibit its members from discussing the controversy, publicly or in private.

The synod next met at Brechin on April 16, 1728. Mr. Glas was called to answer questions which dealt with such issues

> as the power of the civil magistrate within the sphere of religion, the use of the secular arm in defense of the church, the nature of the church, the sanction for national covenanting, the place and authority of the local congregation, the membership of the church, the qualifications for admission to communion and the religious education of children (Hornsby 1936:34).

Mr. Glas argued that the magistrate has no authority in the church. The kingdom of the Lord was not of this world; the kingdom could not be promoted by the civil power or defended by the military arm or civil sanctions; the Word of God in no way approved the national covenant, and only the Holy Spirit brought true reformation. The New Testament in no way warranted a National Church; churches in the New Testament were congregational churches; only those whose Christian character was consistent with the gospel of Christ were true members of the visible church; only the consent of the local congregation could allow one to be admitted to the Lord's Table; the inclusion of visible unbelievers into the fellowship damages the fellowship; and a church of Christ with its eldership is, in its practice and discipline, subject to no jurisdiction under heaven.

Twenty-six questions were put to Mr. Glas. The last was, "Do you think yourself obliged, in conscience, to teach and publish these, your opinions, differing from the received doctrine of this church, unto the people, or not?" In his reply Glas asserted,

> I think myself obliged in conscience to declare every truth of Christ, and keep nothing back, but to speak all the words

of this life, and to teach his people to observe all things whatsoever he commands, so far as I can understand; and that notwithstanding of others their differing from me, and my being exposed to hazard in the declaring of them (*Memoirs* 1816:xxvii).

Because of the nature of his replies the synod passed sentence upon him, suspending him from any exercise of his ministry. Believing he had been grievously wronged, Mr. Glas appealed to the General Assembly which met in Edinburgh on May 2, 1728. His appeal, accompanied by a further appeal from his congregation at Tealing, was considered by the assembly on May 11. The assembly, after considering his appeal and the petition from the Tealing church authorized their commission to act upon its corporate judgment, "and the commission thought fit to continue the suspension, but at the same time, appointed a committee to confer with Mr. Glas and to endeavor to give him light as to those points wherein he was said to have erred . . ." (1816:xxix-xxx).

The Concluding Stages of the Process

At the meeting of the commission in August, 1728, they reported,

> . . . that they have been informed by a letter from him [Mr. Glas] . . . that notwithstanding of the commission's sentence, he was in the exercise of his ministry, and resolved, through grace . . . to continue in it; but that he was still willing to receive light from the committee.

As a consequence, the committee resolved,

> . . . that he should be appointed by letter that the committee's opinion was, that as the affair now stood . . . if he inclined to confer with them, they could not decline to do so (1816:xxx-xxxi).

The matter was brought before the presbytery of Dundee, in September, after proceedings "in different judicatories." There a libel, including further accusations, was brought against Mr. Glas. Following his response and after he had been removed from the presbytery, the question put forward, "Sustain the said libel relevant, notwithstanding of these answers, or not?" When the votes were in, it carried, "sustain."

Again the matter was put forward to the next synod which met on October 15. After considerable preliminary work, and the Court authorized to proceed with further censure, the proposition to be voted upon was revealed: "Depose the said Mr. John Glas from the ministry, or not?" Though there were dissenting votes, the proposal was carried affirmatively. "The synod did accordingly depose him from the office of the ministry, prohibiting and discharging him to exercise the same, or any part thereof, in all time coming, under pain of the highest censures of the church" (1816:xxxiv). When Glas heard the sentence, he responded that he

> was satisfied in his conscience that the synod of Angus and Mearns had no warrant from the Lord Jesus Christ for this sentence. He wished that it may be well known, that he intended not the contempt of any authority, but desired to regard the authority of the Lord Jesus Christ, who had ordered him to fulfill his ministry; that he was resolved, through his grace, at all hazards, to fulfill the same.

Finally, he indicated his intention to appeal to the next General Assembly.

The proceedings were brought before the Assembly in May, 1729, but it was not until March 12, 1730, that the final sentence was given.

148

Glas's Later Ministry

The sentence stirred up antagonism against Mr. Glas. He was branded a heretic who had renounced his pastoral agreement and split the church. He was blamed by his friends for being so candid in his discussion of the issues. It gave his enemies ground for further attack.

The adherents of Mr. Glas at Tealing, some years before, met with him, agreeing to walk together in love, and to observe the breaking of bread once a month. They soon learned they had as little authority for this practice as did the church of Scotland for theirs, because "the disciples came together on the first day of the week for breaking of bread" (Acts 2:42; Acts 20:7). They agreed that with this practice, as with others, they must follow the pattern of the apostolic churches, being taught and led by the Scriptures only.

Some practices were embraced without question. Others, which did not have approval of human authority, created much controversy. Some were not ministering as the Lord had prospered them and were judged according to the Lord's teaching regarding covetousness.

This determination to adhere only to the word worked like a fan in the hand of the Master Thresher who will thoroughly purge his floor, separating the chaff from the corn. Many who left became his bitter enemies, but never was he deterred from exercising the teachings of Christ upon such people.

Until this time, Mr. Glas presided over the congregation, with the help of designated lay-elders. Through their investigation of Scripture, they learned that in the primitive churches there was a plurality of elders. Consequently, in July of 1728, a Mr. Archibald and Mr. Glas were appointed to the office of elder together. The concept grew, but as further congregations were considered, the question of how they were to supply qualified elders defied answer.

With this problem, they were forced to consider the character of elders as defined by the Apostle Paul in letters to Titus and Timothy. They found no requirement for a university degree or familiarity with Greek and Hebrew. They were equipped to see several of their number blessed with characters described by the Apostle. In a meeting for fasting and prayer, they appointed two, godly men, one to serve with Mr. Glas at Dundee and one to serve with Mr. Archibald at Guthrie.

Opposition created by the action is impossible to describe two and one half centuries after the circumstances — that humble men, weavers, spinners and farmers should claim to understand the Bible and stand before the public and preach, was the height of presumptuousness, and little less than blasphemy itself. The clergy generated public agitation, describing things initiated by Mr. Glas in the worst way. The consequence was reaction against the clergy, the louder their clamor, the more curiosity was created, and many went to hear for themselves. Numbers were amazed to discover how they could apply the word and reveal the doctrines of the Lord Jesus, with its affect upon penitent believers.

In spite of the above, prejudice against the uneducated preachers was general, and wherever churches were built, Glas and his associates found opposition. They were sometimes in danger for their lives. In Perth, in 1733, when the church was built, the clergy attempted, through local magistrates, to expel them from the community. While the preachers were in the church, an attempt was made to burn it. A friend thwarted the attempt.

The Glas schism was followed by a secession, designed to attract multitudes of people, led by six or eight popular ministers of the established Church. The threat to the establishment was great. Instead of denying authority in Scripture for the national covenants, as Glas had done, they affirmed its obligation upon all people of Scotland. They asserted there was a relaxation of discipline in the Established Church. They complained against the laws of patronage and agreed that the people ought to be permitted to choose their own ministers. Though accused of being schismatics, they denied the charge, claiming their rigid loyalty to Presbyterian principles. They lamented the necessity forced upon them of seeking help from the church courts of the establishment as being repugnant to the constitution of the Scotish National Church. The General Assembly of 1733 and 1734 deposed these ministers on account of such principles (1816:xlviii).

The matter was not settled, and many pro-establishment became alarmed because of the number of followers of the deposed leaders.

Following the removal of Mr. Glas, there were those who believed his case served as precedent for deposing the leaders of the secession. It was apparent that the number of Mr. Glas' adherents would never pose a threat to the National Church. The principles he taught would always be rejected in any state church. The Established Church had little to fear from him. Modification of the censure imposed upon him while unlikely to bring harm to the establishment, perhaps could help friends of the deposed leaders of the secession in seeking modification or repeal of the deposition against them. In May of 1739, nine years following his deposition, and without any petition from Mr. Glas or his brethren, the General Assembly

> did take off the sentence of deposition passed by the Commission, 12th March 1730, against Mr. John Glas, then minister at Tealing, for independent principles; and did restore him to the character and exercise of a minister of the gospel of Christ; but declaring, notwithstanding, that he is not to be esteemed a minister of the established church of Scotland, or capable to be called or settled therein, until he shall renounce the principles embraced and avowed by him, that are inconsistent with the constitution of this church (1816:xlix-1).

In spite of antagonism and opposition experienced by Mr. Glas in the beginning, churches were established and buildings erected in various towns in Scotland and following, in England and America. These congregations in Scotland have been called Glasites, but in England and the New World, Sandemanian, after Mr. Robert Sandeman.

Possible Influences from George Whitefield

A further note, has to do with the relationship of the secession referred to above and the ministry of George Whitefield. Both John Glas and Robert Sandeman were aware of the evangelical awakening, with its ingathering of thousands.

Throughout 1742, events transpired which generated considerable interest in the religious world. These events also created much party spirit in Scotland. In the contention to which the above developments gave rise, the secession was largely responsible, though the part played by the leaders was by no means a credit to them. George Whitefield's ministry during the year of 1740 had created much excitement in parts of the country. Many had been greatly influenced by his preaching and appeals to conscience. In villages and large towns alike, he gained an unprecedented popularity with the consequence that revivals of religion became the subject of much conversation.

One of the followers of Whitefield was William Mc-Culloch, minister of Cambuslang. McCulloch was a pious man, and with the intention of exciting spiritual concern among his parishioners, he distributed printed reports of revivals having taken place under the preaching of George Whitefield. For almost a year, Whitefield had preached to them "on the nature and necessity of regeneration" (Mc-Kerrow 1854:161). He was laboring to further their spiritual welfare. An extraordinary concern was soon expressed by them.

Ninety families, desiring more than Sabbath day ministrations, petitioned him to initiate a weekly lecture among them as well, and he gladly complied. Little happened in the first two meetings, but during his message on Thursday, February 18, the congregation was affected in an unusual way. Some fainted. Others were overcome with convulsions. Still others clapped their hands and beat their breasts, crying that they heard the screams of the condemned as hell opened before them (1854:163; *The Works of Jonathan Edwards*, 1976:Vol. 1,lxxii).

Such circumstances drew the interest of ministers from distant areas, and multitudes made their way to Cambuslang from near and far to participate in these spiritual activities. Mr. Whitefield visited Scotland a second time in June. Immediately he was invited to Cambuslang, and his first day, preached three times.

During his subsequent visits to Cambuslang great numbers from many areas came to observe but went home "convinced and converted unto God." Near the minister's home there was a brae or hill suited for accommodating a large congregation, and Whitefield preached to thousands who, regardless of the weather, sat unwearied until two in the morning to hear his sermons and who "were melted down under the word and power of God." During August, at the dispensation of the Lord's Supper, an estimated thirty thousand people were in attendance with more than three thousand partaking of the Supper.

These developments were looked upon in a critical way by the Seceders. The work at Cambuslang and Mr. Whitefield, who had motivated it, were soundly condemned. Whitefield was stigmatized in the most opprobrious terms. He was called deceiver and destroyer of the souls of men; one of the false Christs prophesied in Scripture; Satan transformed into an angel of light; "and the religious revival which he had been instrumental in producing, was described as the present awful work upon the bodies and spirits of men," a "black affair," as "a gangrene that had overspread the land." Numerous pamphlets flooded the countryside condemning the whole affair, and the pulpits echoed noisy and often repeated warnings against the ministry of the dangerous Mr. Whitefield (McKerrow 1854:166).

The situation was looked upon in such a somber light by the Associate Presbytery that at a conference held on July 15 at Dunfermline, a day of humiliation and fasting was set for August 4, when all the congregations under their oversight would gather because of the "works of delusion" in progress (1854:167).

Actions of the Presbytery regarding these events did not escape considerable criticism. In his narrative recounting the matter, Mr. Robe described the list of reasons published by the Presbytery as "full of swelling words, altogether void of the spirit of the meek and lowly Jesus, and the most heaven-daring paper that hath been published by any set of men in Britain these hundred years past" (1854:168). The conduct of the Presbytery was condemned in a pamphlet entitled, "A Friendly Caution to Seceders." Their actions were charged with standing in direct opposition to a great work which had all the evidences of the blessing of the Holy Spirit.

McKerrow's own evaluation is worthy of note.

> In taking a review of the whole of the proceedings, after the lapse of nearly a century, when it may be supposed that party feelings have in a great measure subsided, we are enabled to form a more calm and dispassionate judgment of events, than they did who lived in the heyday of contention; and were I, taking such a review, to attempt a vindication of the harsh and unwarrantable language which the Presbytery employed with regard to Mr. Whitefield, and with regard to the work that took place at Cambuslang and Kilsyth and in other parts of the country, I would act in opposition to the decided convictions of my own mind (1854:168).

The above account throws light on the spiritual ferment evident through the labors of George Whitefield and John Wesley during the latter years of John Glas and the youthful years of Robert Sandeman. It seems apparent that neither Glas nor Sandeman were personally involved in the evangelical awakening of Whitefield. However, the people whose lives Glas and Sandeman touched with their teaching were aware of the revival, and it is a safe assumption that the movement of Glas and Sandeman was affected by the Whitefield awakening of the 1740's.

In 1749 John Glas' wife died of consumption. Until then, under the adverse circumstances, because of his large family, he continued to serve the churches in Scotland, which service ended only when his life ended in November of 1773.

A Note About Robert Sandeman

Robert Sandeman had been given by his parents to the ministry of the Church of Scotland and was student at the University of Edinburgh while the persecution of Mr. Glas was progressing with much publicity. Mr. Sandeman was a strong advocate of the doctrine of the covenants, and therefore he examined Mr. Glas' teaching very carefully as well as the action of the established church against him, and the grounds on which that action stood. He came to see that his favorite doctrines could not be defended. Consequently, after completing his studies, he rejected the Church of Scotland ministry and moved to London to operate a loom, and though ridiculed, associated himself with Glas and his few associates. Advocating the same doctrines as Mr. Glas and his friends, Robert Sandeman became a noteworthy champion.

Sandeman married a daughter of Mr. Glas, by whom he had no children. In the church at Perth and later in the church in Edinburgh, he served as an elder. He became popular as an author, expressing those doctrines found in the writings of Mr. Glas. In 1760, he moved to London at the invitation of friends. A church was planted there, and sister congregations sprang up in other cities of England. Later an invitation was extended to Mr. Sandeman to visit America. He went to Boston in 1764, where he remained, preaching the gospel and exhorting obedience to the faith. Fruits came from his labors so that new churches were planted in different areas of North America. Sandeman and his followers suffered because of the opposition, prevalent at the time, to the British government, and this persecution continued until his death in 1770.

The Influence of the Glasites on Alexander Campbell

As one reads Mr. Campbell's correspondence with William Jones of London, he is impressed with Campbell's effort to minimize his own debt and to substantiate his own originality.

> . . . the cause that we plead is at least something in advance of even the Scotch, or English, or American Baptists . . . We only claim some new discoveries and these are only so far new to us, as we have combined and arranged certain ideas derived from the Book, possessed by myriads before we were born . . .(*The Millennial Harbinger* 1835:307).

It would seem probable that Alexander Campbell was more in the debt of those who had gone before him than he supposed. It is doubtful that he would have left the doctrines of the Seceder Presbyterians except for his contacts and association with the Independents of Ireland and Scotland. In Ireland, his contacts, with the encouragement of his father, with his neighbors and their friends, made him aware of a religious perspective other than Presbyterian. The year in Glasgow, his thinking was influenced by Greville Ewing, James and Robert Haldane and others. He admits that he had studied and was conversant with the history and doctrines taught by the Glasite movement, before he commenced his labors as an advocate of return to primitive teaching and order (1835:305). No effort is made to suggest that Alexander Campbell was an imitator of John Glas, Robert Sandeman, or Robert and James Alexander Haldane. However, the movements put forward

157

by these men helped Campbell to shape his own thinking and to establish the character of the American reformation. If Robert Sandeman or Archibald McLean had any claim as the "real leader to whom our divine movement owes its origin," it is due only to "priority of discovery" (Longan 1889:32). The question to be asked is this: Would Alexander Campbell, apart from this "priority of discovery" of men like Glas, Sandeman, the Haldanes and McLean, have arrived at precisely the same position regarding the truths he enunciated all his life? Perhaps, but it cannot be denied that it was due to the rediscoveries of men before his day, that his interest was first drawn to those truths.

Mr. Campbell comments on this.

> Most unhesitatingly can I say, that all my previous reading and study of theology greatly disqualified me from understanding the Book, although I had no doubt derived an immense revenue of ideas, critical and theological, from the labors of all the reformers. But not one of them ever gave a hint, and from the best of my recollections, there is not to be found in all these reformers a hint upon the true and rational reading of the Book of God. I think I hazard the assertion, and certainly from all my prefaces to the historical and epistolary books of the New Testament, and my hints to readers on the proper method of persuing the oracles, are not to be met with in all the writings of the school of 1728, or of the Edinburgh school of 1768, nor in the Wesleyan school of from 1721 to 1775 (*The Millennial Harbinger* 1835:305).

That Alexander Campbell was a person of independent judgment, not willing to embrace any teaching until he was persuaded it was scriptural can hardly be questioned. When he discovered such instruction grounded in Scripture, he was eager to join others as a defender of the truth. There were precepts and practices of John Glas, Robert Sandeman, Archibald McLean and Robert and James Haldane with which he took exception, but with their main principles, he was in agreement.

More significant than any other likeness is their understanding of saving faith. Mr. Campbell defines saving faith as embracing the testimony of Scripture that Jesus is both Lord and Christ.

> For faith is only the belief of testimony, or confidence in testimony as true. To believe without testimony is just as impossible as to see without light. The measure, quality, and power of faith are always found in the testimony believed. Where testimony begins, faith begins; and where testimony ends, faith ends (Campbell 1866:113).

Campbell was in agreement with the position taken by Glas, Sandeman, the Haldanes and others. "Regarding the nature of faith, as then debated, he agreed with Sandeman, McLean and Fuller, as they confessedly, agreed with each other" (Longan 1889:67). On further query as to whether regeneration came before or after faith, Mr. Campbell agreed with Sandeman and McLean, that faith preceded regeneration. In Longan's judgment, Alexander Campbell's understanding of the priority of faith "was the most fundamental conception of what may be called his theology. It determined his view of divine influence and conversion and sanctification, as he defined those terms, beyond any shadow of doubt" (1889:73). Campbell asserted: "The question whether regeneration — meaning thereby change of heart — is before faith, or through faith, is the chief theological issue we make with the denominations of our time. Other questions are subordinant to this, or are involved in this" (1889:76). The above well reveals Mr. Campbell's understanding of the beginnings of the life of faith. The dangerous but accepted mistake

> . . . that the nature or power and saving efficacy of faith is not in the truth believed, but in the nature of our faith, or in the manner of believing the truth . . . as if there could be any faith without history, written or spoken. Whoever believed in Christ without hearing the history of him? "How shall they believe in him of whom they have not heard?" Faith never can be more than the receiving of testimony as true, or the belief of testimony; and if that testimony be written, it is called history, though it is as much history when flowing from the tongue as when flowing from the pen (Campbell 1866:114).

To believe a fact is to accept it as true. There is no other way. If the fact is not accepted, it is not believed.

In the debate ignited by Sandeman's *Letters on Theron and Aspasio*, Alexander Campbell believed Sandeman conducted himself as a giant among dwarfs. "He was like Samson with gates and posts of Gaza on his shoulders," and yet Campbell did not approve of Sandeman's definition of faith as a bare belief of the testimony of Gospel (*The Christian Baptist* 1825:228). To Mr. Campbell this appeared a frigid and purely intellectual perspective.

> I disclaim Sandemanianism as much as I do any system in Christendom; but I agree with Sandeman in making faith no more than the belief of truth . . . but I differ from Sandeman in making this belief the effect of physical influence 1829:615).

Mr. Campbell approached closely the position of the Haldanes which added to the acceptance of the testimony the

idea of faith and trust in Jesus Christ as Lord. The principles of faith he looked upon, not as doctrinal or theoretical,
but rather as personal and experimental. He asserted that no
man can be saved by the belief of any theory, true or false;
no man will be damned for the disbelief of any theory. Religion may be defined as a relationship established through
belief in Christ and obedience to His will: it is a personal
relationship between the man of faith and his Master.

> Faith in Christ is the effect of belief. Belief is the cause; and
> faith in Christ, the effect. 'The faith' sometimes means the
> truth to be believed. Sometimes it means "the belief of the
> truth; . . . accepting what Christ says about himself results
> in trust or confidence in him, and as the Christian religion
> is a personal thing, both as respects subject and object, that
> faith in Christ which is essential to salvation is not the be-
> lief of any doctrine, testimony or truth, abstractly, but
> belief in Christ; trust and confidence in him as a person,
> not a thing (Campbell 1866:52-53).

In *The Christian Baptist* he writes, I would not give a grain
of wheat for any faith that does not purify the heart, work
by love and overcome the world" (1829:615).

Like the followers of John Glas and the Scotch Baptists,
the followers of Campbell, Scott and Stone desired the
restoration of New Testament Christianity. Mr. Campbell's
mind was filled with great issues. He was concerned with
the spirituality of the fellowship, the unity of believers
and the proclamation of the Gospel. The foundation of the
fellowship of believers was not so much in creed and order
as common faith and allegiance to Jesus Christ. Cooperation should have at its base, "In essentials, unity, in non-
essentials, liberty, in all things charity."

Mr. Campbell observed that customs of a locality and temporary expediency not binding on the church for all time, were the cause for early church practices. Consequently, in such as abstaining from eating blood, the kiss of charity, the keeping of love feasts, and other insignificant matters, the disciples of Mr. Campbell have not followed the Glasites. In a number of details, as their conviction that the church is a society of believers ordained by God, the independence and autonomy of the local church, their keeping of the Lord's Supper each first day of the week, a plurality of elders in each congregation and the practice of mutual exhortation, they have followed the Glasites. In several factors, they disagreed with Mr. Glas. They advocated the baptism of believers only, for "the remission of sins"; they emphasized the duty of evangelism, and they believed and preached the importance of Christian unity.

Chapter Seven

THE HALDANE BROTHERS AND THE RESTORATION MOVEMENT

Impact of Haldanes on Alexander Campbell Noted by His Biographer and by Mr. Campbell Himself

Robert Richardson discusses

> the eminent men concerned in the reformatory movement then progressing in Scotland — a movement from which Mr. Campbell received his first impulse as a religious reformer, and which may be justly regarded, indeed, as the first phase of that religious reformation which he subsequently carried out so successfully to its ultimate issues (Richardson 1868:Vol. I,149).

Richardson's attention is directed to the Haldane brothers, Robert and James Alexander.

In 1843 Alexander Campbell published an article in two parts, furnished by a friend in New York, entitled "Memoirs of Robert Haldane" (*The Millennial Harbinger* 1843:173-177; 201-204). The piece concluded,

> But it is interesting to contemplate and trace the first streaks of light — the first dawning of the day which has brightened since then, and shall continue to increase till the full orb of light and glory shall shine in meridian splendor, and diffuse fullness of light and of blessing on this still imperfectly illuminated and churchless world.

Thus Mr. Campbell acknowledged the influence of Robert Haldane in helping him shape his understanding of the Scriptures and the church, early in his life and ministry.

Early Life of Robert and James Haldane

Robert Haldane was born on February 28, 1764, in London. James Alexander Haldane, his younger brother, was born at Dundee on July 14, 1768 (Haldane 1852:1). The elder Haldane entered the Royal Navy in 1779 when he was seventeen years old (*Edinburgh Advertiser*, December 20, 1842). James Alexander went to sea five years later at approximately the same age (Haldane 1852:28).

Robert served with distinction in the navy from 1780 until peace was attained in 1783. The purpose of his life did not manifest itself for another twelve years when James Alexander also quit the sea with a sense of the shortness of life and the magnitude of eternity (1852:39). In 1786, Robert, with his wife, settled at Airthrey, the family estate. It was here that his religious interests were revived by daily examining the Scriptures. Robert Haldane attributed his surrender to Jesus Christ to a conversation he had with a stone mason while walking through the forests of Airthrey, "in which he began to discern more clearly that in the matter of justification, faith must cast away all reliance on the shifting sands of frames or feelings, and fasten only upon the Rock of Ages" (1852:96). He committed his life and estate to the furtherance of the gospel (Richardson 1868: Vol. I,151).

Robert Haldane's views had been centered in politics until about 1794. Like many at that time, he was enthralled with the prospects "of a new order of things at a time when politics ran high" (*Edinburgh Advertizer*, December 20, 1842). Of himself he wrote,

> Before the French Revolution . . . I contented myself with the general profession which is common and so worthless, and that form of godliness which completely denies its power . . . Sometime after this, when I trust I had been led to choose that good part which cannot be taken from

> anyone, and to adopt the views of religion I at present hold,
> I first heard of the Baptist Missionary Society, and their
> mission in Bengal. It immediately struck me that I was
> spending my time in the country to little profit, while,
> from the command of property, which through the good-
> ness of God, I possessed, I might be somewhere extensively
> useful (Robert Haldane 1800:13-14).

In the following months Robert Haldane and his wife determined to go to India as missionaries. The East India Company refused them leave to go (*Edinburgh Advertizer*,
December 20, 1842).

James Alexander Haldane, the younger brother, was not
motivated to Christian service until, at the General Assembly of the Church of Scotland in 1796, he heard the
discussion and vote to reject the resolution, "that it is the
duty of Christians to carry the gospel to the heathen world"
(Haldane 1852:133).

In the summer of 1796 the Church of England divine,
Charles Simeon, toured the highlands of Scotland. James
Haldane was his riding companion (1852:138-144; Moule
1956:120). The friendship of Haldane with Simeon proved
a blessing to James Haldane. Because of it, "it is not difficult to conclude, that James Haldane's progress in the
Divine life had been both rapid and decisive" (Haldane
1852:145).

Both Robert and James Haldane, through their study
of the Scriptures and through continuing growth were
led, at about the same time, to devote themselves to religious matters. They were attached to each other and of a
similar mind in the changes taking place in their lives and
in their projected undertakings in the future.

Their Ministry Begins

James Haldane's first sermon was preached at Gilmerton, Scotland, in May, 1797. Present was Dr. Charles Stuart of Dunearn, who was impressed with Haldane's sermon and who became his admirer and friend. Stuart had considerable influence on James Haldane.

Charles Stuart had gone from Divinity Hall in Edinburgh and was associated with a Dissenting Academy in London, where he expressed disapproval to the union of church and state. He believed he could no longer baptize children of unbelievers or admit to the Lord's Table those inconsistent in the profession of faith (1852:151).

Numerous Preaching Tours

James Haldane, in a series of tours, preached in "almost every town or populous village of Scotland, and to tens of thousands of people" during the following nine years (*Edinburgh Advertizer*, December 20, 1842).

> Upon the tour north in 1797, there was poured out a blessing which can never be mistaken, and whatever may be said of the regularity of their commission, it will be safer to adopt the sentiments so beautifully expressed in one of Mr. Simeon's letters to Mr. James Haldane, which will be hereafter given at large: "I think immortal souls of such value, that I should rejoice if all the Lord's people were prophets. If mercy and sacrifice stand in opposition to each other, we may choose mercy; and if David and his men be perishing with hunger, they may eat the forbidden bread" (Haldane 1852:153).

Following his return from his first tour, James Haldane's life as a preacher was determined. No longer did he consider the life as a country gentleman. He embraced new responsibilities and excited the attention of all of Scotland. The godless clergy was shaken, multitudes across the highlands were aroused, and while the Gospel was embraced by many, a larger number were seeking the answer to, "What must I do to be saved?" (1852:191).

On the 26th of July, 1798, James Haldane met the English preacher, Roland Hill, for the first time. Hill would bless James and Robert Haldane with his winsome influence. Both traveled with Roland Hill through August.

A short time before Hill's visit to Scotland, Robert Haldane assumed responsibility for bringing thirty or thirty-five African children to Britain where they would be educated and sent back to Africa as missionaries. Twenty African boys and four girls arrived at Portsmouth in June of 1799. Robert Haldane promised to underwrite the scheme—from six to seven thousand pounds—with the understanding that he would be in charge of educating the children. After their arrival in England he learned that because of his religious views, in contrast to the Established Church, he would be opposed in his plan to equip them as missionaries to go back to their own people. Denied the right to school them, he refused to finance the project altogether. Other monies were found and the children were educated, with more attention to their secular than to their religious training, and returned to Sierra Leone. Some good was accomplished in the experiment (1852:249-253). "The whole affair, however, serves to place in a strong light the Christian enterprise and munificent liberality of Robert Haldane" (Richardson 1868:Vol. I,165; *Edinburgh Advertizer,* December 20, 1842).

In 1787 Robert Haldane rented the Circus building in Edinburgh for religious purposes, but he found it difficult to secure good ministers to preach. He determined to establish a school for educating pious young men for the ministry, "who might be selected, as in primitive times, from the various occupations of life, on account of their piety and promising talents to receive instruction" (Haldane 1800:82-84: Haldane 1852:233; *Edinburgh Advertizer*, December 20, 1842). In selecting these men, natural ability was one requisite, but the indispensable consideration must be evidence of a "state of grace." In October, 1798, Robert Haldane wrote to his friend, Mr. John Campbell,

> I intend to give one year's education to ten or twelve persons, of any age that may be fit for it, under Mr. Bogue, with a view to the ministry. Will you and my brother be looking out for suitable persons to be ready by the time I return? (1852:233).

At this same time, while traveling with Roland Hill, Robert Haldane determined to provide tabernacles for preaching in the chief towns of Scotland (Robert Haldane 1800:81-82). With his brother consenting to preach in the circus in Edinburgh, Robert travelled to Glasgow where he purchased a large building and converted it into a tabernacle for a congregation over which Mr. Greville Ewing would preside. In Dundee, similar arrangements were made. Back in Edinburgh he arranged for the construction of a "spacious place of worship," called the tabernacle where James Haldane would preach, which would accommodate four thousand people. The building opened in 1801, and the congregation which had occupied the circus for three years, took possession of it. The work grew so that a second tabernacle was soon erected in the Old Town of Edinburgh, near the college (1852:302-303).

The seminary for training young men was not to be the responsibility of Robert Haldane's friend, Dr. Bogue. Instead Mr. Greville Ewing was employed by Mr. Haldane to head the school, which opened in Edinburgh, but shortly moved to Glasgow. It began with twenty-four students, all Presbyterians. The choice of Mr. Ewing "was unfortunate, both for Mr. Haldane and Mr. Ewing, who were not at all calculated for such mutual cooperation" (1852:247). Mr. Haldane assumed full responsibility for maintaining the students. A second class of forty and third of twenty-two followed, entirely under Mr. Haldane's support. In 1802 the Glasgow Seminary closed under Mr. Ewing and another was opened in Edinburgh on a larger scale, under the control of the Haldane brothers.

The first class under Mr. Ewing began in January 1799. Through "December of 1808, when the Seminary was grown up" almost three hundred ministers were trained and sent out (1852:329-330). For almost ten years, this program was conducted entirely at Mr. Haldane's expense.

James A Haldane, in 1797, shared in the cost of publishing and distributing twenty thousand tracts. From this time Robert Haldane provided an unlimited supply of tracts to all who would make use of them (1852:273; Robert Haldane 1800:64-67). In the same year Mr. John Campbell founded the first tract society in Edinburgh. He was responsible for starting a Sabbath-school society and was successful in opening a number of evening Sabbath schools. In cooperation with James A. Haldane, it was not long "till there was not a single town in Scotland which was not provided with those most useful seminaries" (Richardson 1868:Vol. I,159).

The Impact of the Preaching Tours

The ministry of the Haldanes affected Scotland, England and Northern Ireland. Noteworthy were their preaching tours that excited attention of tens of thousands of listeners. In 1797 James Haldane, in the company of Mr. Rate "visited almost every place in the north of Scotland and the Orkney

Islands, distributing tracts, preaching in the open air to great multitudes" (Haldane 1852:157-190). A second tour in the west and south of Scotland was made by James Haldane and John Aikman in 1798. "People came to hear in crowds." The same year Roland Hill and Robert Haldane traveled through Perth, Kinross, and Glasgow. In Kinross Mr. Hill preached "to a large congregation" and in Glasgow to "five thousands at least." In Edinburgh, Mr. Hill, with Robert Haldane, preached to fifteen thousand on the Calton Hill. In September, 1798, Roland Hill, accompanied by James Haldane, toured England, travelling through Dunbar, Berwick, Alnwick, Newcastle, Durham, Leeds, Rotherhand, Sheffield, Derby, Coventry, Warwick, Painswick to Wotton-under-Edge in Gloucestershire (1852:220-224). A fourth tour by James Haldane, accompanied by John Campbell, in 1800, took them from Edinburgh to Peebles, Biggar, Douglas and Ayr as they preached in every place. At Ayr they preached to "congregations in the open air, amounting to three thousand and even five thousand souls," who heard the word with much attention (1852:280-281). In 1801 James Haldane travelled to Dumfries where he preached in the city and in neighboring towns and villages. Concluding his labors, he travelled across to Ireland in company with George Hamilton of Armagh. At Portadown he preached to large audiences. Time was spent in Belfast. Again and again he preached to crowded congregations (1852:305-306). During his tour James Haldane preached at Rich Hill. Thomas Campbell was resident there (Richardson 1868:Vol. I,60). During the summer of 1802, Mr. Haldane "devoted himself to long and laborous itinerancies, for the purpose of preaching the gospel." In Derbyshire his proclamation resulted "in a season of revival and awakening . . . Everywhere his preaching was acceptable, and often it was manifest that the word was with power" (Haldane 1852:314-315). He focused attention in 1803 on those parts of Scotland where Gailic was spoken. The consequent revival "was as plainly the work of God." In 1804 James Haldane travelled into England and over to Dublin.

Throughout this period, not only the Haldanes but many noteworthy persons, while not in full agreement, were laboring together to propagate the gospel. Their fellowship and cooperation, in person and by correspondence, contributed to their knowledge of the Scriptures which they all regarded as the only truth in matters of religion (Richardson 1868:Vol. I,172). It is unlikely that any were as biblical, in all of these labors, as were Robert and James Alexander Haldane. Their efforts were successful as a consequence of their scriptural emphasis. Without the generosity of Robert Haldane, the doctrines he and his brother labored to advance would have taken a longer time. Before Alexander Campbell's fortuitous studies in Glasgow in 1808-1809, Robert Haldane had already given sixty thousand pounds for the spread of the gospel at home. Other ministries were initiated which, when joined with the effective labors of his younger brother James, "produced a most powerful impression, which was felt throughout almost all the whole Protestant world" (1868:Vol. I,173).

Robert Haldane's Ministry in Europe

One of the significant contributions of Robert Haldane came as the result of his labors in Geneva, Switzerland, in 1816. His intention was to labor in Paris, but finding no opening there, he proceeded to Geneva where he found a number of young men desiring to study the Scriptures. Mr. Haldane met with the group three times a week, teaching from the Epistle of Romans, devoting himself to the task through the winter and to the close of the session the following summer. In his class he had most of the theological students, along with others, including residents in the city.

The consequence was opposition from the clergy and professors in the faculty who taught that the Lord was the first of all created beings, that the gospel was useful but not indispensable to salvation, and other philosophies, Arian, Socinian and Arminian (Haldane 1852:422). Mr. Haldane gave answer to all their falsehoods, proving to the students their inconsistency with scripture. Subsequent contentions were therefore the cause for excitement and considerable persecutions of the clergy. Many students came to comprehend the nature of salvation and were strengthened to bear the suffering from the clergy. It was "largely to these labors of Robert Haldane at Geneva that the continent of Europe was blessed with that religious awakening by which . . . a mighty barrier has been erected against that flood of Rationalism which threatened to obliterate all the teachings of the Lutheran Reformation" (Richardson 1868:Vol. I,173-174).

Greville Ewing

Alexander Campbell was resident in Glasgow in late 1808 and early 1809, when differences between Robert Haldane and Greville Ewing were creating much excitement. The problem had come because of differences over the amount Ewing expected Haldane to give to the Glasgow Tabernacle (Haldane 1852:363-364). Mr. Campbell was convinced that Ewing was wrong (Richardson 1868:Vol. I,175).

Ewing was unhappy that Robert Haldane had removed the Glasgow Seminary from his oversight because of differences entertained by Mr. Ewing, and had relocated it in Edinburgh. So far as Mr. Haldane was concerned, these divergencies had to do with church order and the ordinances (Haldane 1852:363).

The Impact Upon Alexander Campbell

Alexander Campbell was impressed with the information he obtained from Greville Ewing concerning the reformation then in progress in Scotland. Factors characteristic of the movement were in harmony with his own convictions. He noted the devotion of the reformers to the Bible and the Haldane brothers' independency of spirit, which motivated them to proclaim the gospel to every hamlet, town and city through a scheme of lay preaching and itineration: this in spite of continuing opposition from the clergy. Mr. Campbell admired the generosity of Robert Haldane and the labors of the younger brother. He could see no way of imitating the former, but he could follow the pattern of the latter and preach the gospel without remuneration. This he did all through his life, asking nothing for his labors and even providing his own travel expenses (Richardson 1868:Vol. I,176-178).

It would be a mistake to imply that the Haldane brothers advocated the above practice for all. James Haldane, refering to Gal. 6:6, "Let him that is taught the word, communicate unto him that teacheth, in all good things," commented,

> Here the duty of supporting those who teach in the churches of Christ is inculcated. The laborer is worthy of his hire, and the Lord applies this proverb to those whom he sent out to preach. The situation of the elders of a church is somewhat different, but although they are not to be actuated by

the love of money, they are entitled to support. "Let the elders who rule well be counted worthy of double honor, especially they who labor in the word and doctrine. For the scripture saith, Thou shalt not muzzle the ox that treadeth out the corn. And the laborer is worthy of his reward" (James Haldane 1848:238-239).

In significant doctrinal areas, Mr. Campbell was in substantial agreement with the Haldane brothers. They held that faith rested upon evidence provided by the Holy Spirit in Holy Scripture, embracing the understanding but also the heart. This view Mr. Campbell adopted, and he advocated it throughout his lifetime.

The Haldanes had no intention of separating from the Church of Scotland. They longed to motivate all who professed faith in Christ to greater spiritual vigor. Theirs were simple views of the gospel, and they desired to give proper emphasis to "the divinity, dignity and the glory of Christ, and the all sufficiency of the works of salvation which he accomplished; and to enforce the great principle of justification by faith (Richardson 1868:Vol. I,178).

It was Greville Ewing more than any other who effected the transition from the Church of Scotland structure to an independent or congregational form of church government. In this he was influenced more by John Glas and Robert Sandeman than by the Haldanes. "As a whole, the Glasite, or Sandemanean system was abhorrent to their principles and feelings" (Haldane 1852:381). Keeping the Lord's Supper every Lord's Day was introduced by Mr. Ewing in Glasgow. The practice was embraced by the church in Edinburgh and soon by other new churches.

At this time William Ballantyne published his *Treatise on the Elder's Office*. The piece created widespread division in the new churches, but his views were adopted by the Haldanes. Ballantyne advocated a plurality of elders in each church. To add to the dissatisfaction, in the spring of 1808, James Haldane informed his Edinburgh congregation that he could no longer baptize infants. In the month of April he was immersed. Immediately the church in Edinburgh divided, some returning to the Established Church, some going to College Street, and a number determined to become a separate church. Two hundred continued on with James Haldane. In a few months Robert Haldane was also immersed, as were Mr. Innes and Dr. Carson.

These divisions, deprecated by both of the Haldanes, had occurred the year before Alexander Campbell's attendance at the University of Glasgow. The problems surrounding the controversy were frequent items for discussion with Mr. Ewing.

In their labors for advancing the cause of religion at home, Robert and James Haldane "proceeded hand in hand." "Between both there was a remarkable harmony of design, and oneness of spirit, and never, during their long and honorable course of mutual cooperation was there one jarring feeling to damp their zeal for the common object which they steadily pursued" (*Edinburgh Advertizer,* December 20, 1842).

It was the judgment of Robert Richardson that the Haldane movement was the first phase of the American Reformation or Restoration Movement. If this is so, then the work of the Haldanes affirms the historical truth "that restoration is a continuing mark of the divine order" (Murch 1962:18). Work had progressed far when Robert and James Alexander Haldane came on the scene. It has come far since their day. The task, yet incomplete, will remain so until the Lord's return, shared by devout men across the world.

175

Doctrinal Emphases of the Haldanes

It is necessary to note material written by the brothers Haldane. Both were prolific writers, discussing a number of issues deeply relevant to The Restoration Movement.

They were responsible for introducing significant doctrinal changes. One was their emphasis upon "the authenticity and inspiration of the Holy Scriptures." They took the Bible and the Bible alone as their rule of faith and practice (Murch 1962:17). In Volume One of his *The Evidence and Authority of Divine Revelation*, Robert Haldane said:

> The canon and inspiration of Holy Scriptures are subjects of the highest importance to every Christian. The divine books contain the only information with respect to the salvation of sinners; and the duties, privileges, and hope of the heirs of heaven. All that can be known of the mind of God, and the future state of man, must be learned from them. The theories of men with respect to the things of God, and all reasoning respecting revealed subjects, grounded on any other foundation but the divine declarations, are not only fallacious as far as concerns their immediate objects, but prevent an accurate acquaintance with the ways of God, by opening innumerable devious paths, which deceitfully promise to lead to heavenly knowledge.

> The Bible not only contains things that are divinely accredited as true, but it contains all the truth on divine subjects that is accessible to man. Hence, everything that respects the particular books comparing the canon, and the inspiration of these books, is of the liveliest interest to the Christian. Whatever tends to invalidate the authority of any particular book of the canon, or adds other books to the number, ought to be met with the most decided opposition, as threatened to rob us of the most precious revealed truth,

or to impose on us the traditions of man as commandments of God. To reject a book whose authenticity rests on the authority of the canon, is not only to give up the portion of every other book standing on the same authority. If one book of the canon is given up, how shall any other be retained on the authority of that canon? (Robert Haldane 1839:Vol. I,9-10).

Mr. Haldane wrote (1827:34),

The Scriptures of the Old and New Testament are not only authentic, but also inspired writings. The claim of inspiration which they advance, is a claim of infallibility and of perfection. It is also a claim of absolute authority, which demands unlimited submission.

In the same book he wrote, "Christians ought to beware of giving up the smallest degree the inspiration of the Bible. That precious deposit is now delivered to their keeping . . ." (1827:74).

One of "the radical decisions made by the Haldanes was the rejection of extra congregational church" (Murch 1962: 17). In the early years of the Edinburgh Tabernacle there was no presbytery or plurality of elders "according to the views entertained of apostolic times, in every church."

In an 1809 pamphlet, James Haldane, speaking of the beginnings of the Edinburgh Tabernacle in those days, took it for granted that the apostles, with reference to church order, left matters to our discretion. He believed there were outlines which they had drawn, but what they were and their implications he neither knew nor cared. Gradually he began to take note of the order defined for the churches in the Scriptures. Becaused the Edinburgh

Church had no standard of organization, they made their appeal to the Word of God (J.A. Haldane 1809:3).

The Haldanes were finally left with no other recourse, because of the resistance of the Established Church clergy, than to form separate congregations. In so doing they were led to introduce another chapter in church reform, and from the teaching of Scripture. Following the Scriptures, which they referred to as the only authority, they adopted an independent or congregational form of church government with a plurality of elders. From then onward, "it was adopted as a principle that ecclesiastical usages should be conformed to the practice of the apostolic churches" (Richardson 1868:Vol. I,179).

In 1822, James A. Haldane, in a letter to his son who was moving to London, expressed himself on church government.

> The liberality which chiefly prevails, I think, in England is most unscriptural. It is an idea that Scripture has laid down no rules for church order, and that we are to do what appears to us most calculated for usefulness. If I adopted this sentiment, I should myself be much disposed to join the Established Church, for in many respects, the field of usefulness there is greatest. But I see plainly that the order of a Church is not unimportant, and that, although at present there are many defects in all parties, we ought to love all who love the Lord Jesus Christ, and that our love to them ought to abound in proportion as we see the great features of the kingdom of God . . . (Haldane 1852:379).

Already noted, in the spring prior to Alexander Campbell's brief sojourn in Glasgow, James Haldane made public his decision to no longer baptize children, and in April he had been baptized by immersion. Later his brother Robert followed his example with others to do the same. From

178

that time both brothers became advocates of baptism by immersion of believers only.

In a letter to the Reverend Dr. John Brown, James Haldane expressed his and his brother's position regarding baptism.

> There is no ordinance respecting which we have fuller instruction than that of baptism.
>
> 1st. The law of baptism is clear and explicit; he that believeth and is baptized shall be saved. Here we are clearly taught that only believers are to be baptized, and are also guarded against considering it a matter of little importance; a mere ritual observance, as some ignorantly or presumptuously speak. Baptism is the only ordinance, the observance of which the Lord has connected salvation.*

In his rather detailed study of baptism, J. A. Haldane said,

> Baptism is described as referring to the remission of sins, Acts 2:38; 22:16. This idea is also intimately connected with our having fellowship with Christ in his death, by whom we have received the atonement, Romans 5:11. Hence we are said to be saved by baptism, I Peter 3:21, because it represents the way in which we are justified by having fellowship with Christ in his death. "He that is dead is freed [or justified] from sin," Romans 6:7. Thus we are reminded, that "God is just, and the justifier of him that believeth in Jesus." Romans 3:26.

Further, in writing to Mr. Brown, James Haldane said,

---

*The Haldane brothers did not see as Walter Scott, Alexander Campbell and Barton Warren Stone believed they saw, the relationship between baptism and the remission of sins, nor did they teach it as did the founders of the early 19th century Reformation, but nonetheless, they were more than vaguely aware of the connection.

Two things are necessary, confession with the mouth, and believing in the heart, Romans 10:9; now baptism is the appointed mode of confession.

2ndly. We have more instances of baptism than of the observance of any other ordinance, and they are all in perfect accordance with the Lord's commandment. Who were baptized? Those that gladly received his word, Acts 2:41 — those who believed — both men and women, 8:12 — those who had received the Holy Ghost, 10:47; the Corinthians believed and were baptized, 18:8. When one asked to be baptized, the reply is, "If thou believest with all thine heart, thou mayest" 8:37.

3rdly. That believers only should be baptized, appears by what is denoted by the ordinance. Its meaning is fully explained in the Scriptures. It is being baptized into Christ's death; being buried with him by baptism into death and rising to walk with him in newness of life, Romans 6:3-4; it is putting on Christ, Galatians 3:27; it is the profession of our faith, Hebrews 10:22-23; and you substitute for this ordinance, the sprinkling of water on an unconscious infant! He is the very root of the National Churches. Infants are made Christians, and members both of the Established and Secession Churches, by what is termed baptism. Let there not then be any strife between these bodies, for they are brethren. So long as you continue to defend infant baptism, so long you condemn yourself in opposing National Churches.

You may allege that households were baptized; but households do not necessarily include infants; and, supposing there were infants in all the households mentioned in the New Testament as having been baptized, they were excluded from baptism by the law of the institution, and by what is represented in the ordinance. Whether there were infants in the household of Stephanus, I know not; but of one thing I am sure, — the infants did not addict themselves to the

180

ministry of the saints, I Corinthians 16:15. I am equally sure that infants were not baptized, because believers are exclusively the subjects of the ordinance. The baptism of households would never have been alleged as a warrant for infant baptism, had not Jewish children been circumcised; but those who rely on this argument, do not "distinguish things that differ." An Israelite was by birth a member of the Jewish Church, as the child of one who makes a profession of the true religion is of the Secession Church; but those only are members of Christ's Church, who are born of God and he has commanded that none should be received into fellowship, but those upon whom this great change appears to have taken place. The antitype of a Jewish child is a believer; and as the Jewish child was by circumcision recognized as being within the bond of the covenant, so does the believer put on Christ, and is recognized as a child of the new covenant by baptism. Hence it is written, "For as many of you as have been baptized into Christ have put on Christ. There is neither Jew nor Greek, there is neither bond nor free, there is neither male nor female: for ye are all one in Christ Jesus. And if ye be Christ's then are ye Abraham's seed, and heirs according to the promise" Galatians 3:27-29 (Letter from James A. Haldane to John Brown, n.d.).

In his commentary on Romans, first published in 1835-1839, and referring to chapter six and verse three, Robert Haldane observes,

The rite of baptism exhibits Christians as dying, as buried and as risen with Christ . . . . By faith believers are made one with Christ: they become members of his body. This oneness is represented emblematically by baptism. In baptism, they are represented as dying in Christ . . . they have died with him who bore their sins (Haldane 1960:244).

181

The Haldanes, Leaders of the Awakening in Scotland, Touch Alexander Campbell

The knowledge which he gained while with Greville Ewing in 1808 and 1809 impressed the young man, Alexander Campbell. Of importance was the expansion of his knowledge of the reformatory movement. The time spent in Glasgow became the link between Alexander Campbell and the movements of the Haldane brothers, John Glas and Robert Sandeman.

There were several causes for Mr. Campbell's dissatisfaction with the Seceder Presbyterian Church, but chief among them was the movement initiated by Robert and James A. Haldane, and the personal influence of Greville Ewing (W. E. Garrison 1931:80, 84).

Dr. J. Edwin Orr refers to the Haldanes as "outstanding leaders of the Awakening in Scotland about the end of the eighteenth and the beginning of the nineteenth centuries . . ." (Orr 1975:33).

Chapter Eight

ALEXANDER CAMPBELL: LEADER OF THE
MOVEMENT — 1809

His Arrival in America

On September 29, 1809, two years, four months, two weeks, and two days after Thomas Campbell arrived in America, his wife and family, in the care of the oldest son, Alexander, sailed into New York Harbor. It had taken eight weeks and one day to make the crossing on a leaky vessel amidst storms so ominous that all aboard despaired of survival. Alexander renewed his commitment to his Lord, dedicating his life to preaching the Gospel (Richardson 1868:Vol. I, 198; Sweet 1952:223).

Six days were spent in New York City, affording Alexander the opportunity on Sunday, October 1, of hearing Dr. John M. Mason, preacher of the Anti-Burgher Secession Presbyterian Church. His views on more frequent participation of the Lord's Supper and other subjects were in agreement with the Campbells, father and son (Richardson 1868:Vol. I,205 f.n.). Two days by stagecoach brought the family to Philadelphia, and on Monday, October 9, by wagon, they began the 350 miles across the mountains to Washington in western Pennsylvania.

Reunion with His Father

Ten days' west of Philadelphia the family, with the teamsters with whom they were traveling, stopped for the night at an inn. That same evening, fifteen miles west, at another hotel on the same east-west road, a young man, arriving on horseback, and traveling eastward, stopped to spend the night. Shortly, two other gentlemen, traveling the same direction, on horseback but leading two horses with side-saddles, made their appearance. During the evening, Mr. Thomas Campbell, one of the two traveling together, let it be known that he was a minister traveling eastward to meet his family, recently arrived from Glasgow. This the single young man noted without divulging that he, too, was a minister. Early the following morning he resumed his journey towards Philadelphia. Ten miles along the way he met the wagon carrying the Campbell family, taking note of the young man Alexander. Bowing to them, he continued on his way little knowing that in another eighteen years he would be associated, as one of the forces in the movement, with the Campbells, father and son, in introducing what Walter Scott was to call the Ancient Gospel into the Western Reserve. That young man was Adamson Bentley, who by God's providence was granted a silent acquaintance with the two men who were so significantly to alter his outlook and witness (1868:Vol. I, 214-217).

Shortly after Mr. Bentley left the hotel, Mr. Campbell and his companion, Mr. McElroy, continued their eastward journey. In a short time, they came in view of the wagon traveling towards them. With joy and surprise, the family recognized Thomas Campbell and a tender reunion, after more than two years' separation, occurred.

Getting Acquainted Again

The family was still three days from their destination. As they travelled, the father and son were comparing notes and recounting their similar spiritual journeys from the time of their separation.

Tradition has it that Thomas Campbell had a proof sheet of his *Declaration and Address* with him when he met his family. This seems unlikely for Alexander has written, "The first proof sheet that I ever read was a form of my father's *'Declaration and Address'* in press at Washington, Pennsylvania, on my arrival there in October, 1809" (Moore 1909:126). In any case, it is certain that the statement was discussed as they traveled towards their new home. The younger man was pleased with the concepts enunciated by the *Declaration and Address*. "While Thomas Campbell had outlined the principles of restoration, his son was to propagate and defend them" (Dowling 1964:50).

Referring to his arrival Alexander wrote, "I commenced my career in this country under the conviction that nothing that was not as old as the New Testament should be made an article of faith, a rule of practice, or a term of communion amongst Christians" (Moore 1909:126). Neither was aware that the other had recently resolved a spiritual crisis in his relationship with the Seceder Presbyterian Church. The father soon rehearsed his disappointment in America, surrounding the charges he was forced to meet before the presbytery and synod, how he had rejected and withdrawn from both and of his labors from that time as an independent. Alexander then revealed his spiritual journey and his conclusions, the result of his Glasgow decision. To their surprise and relief, the two men discovered they were unified in their convictions. Alexander was a young man committed to the ministry but a member of no church. Now he had a cause (Garrison and DeGroot 1948:144).

Alexander Soon Involved in the Infant Movement

Once settled in his Pennsylvania home, there was little about the movement of Thomas Campbell to give encouragement, and yet Alexander was filled with enthusiasm, giving himself in preparation that he might serve within it. An hour for Greek, another for Latin, half an hour for Hebrew, two hours for Scripture memorization and study, and time each day for church history was his self-appointed routine (Richardson 1868:Vol. I,278-279).

Effort to Establish Fellowship with the Redstone Presbytery

Thomas Campbell still clung to the hope of remaining in the fellowship of his Presbyterian brethren. He saw no reconciliation with the Seceders, but the Synod of Pittsburgh was not the Seceder Synod and was associated with the main Presbyterian body which had been in southwestern Pennsylvania since 1781. Members and ministers had approached Mr. Campbell suggesting he bring the Christian Association into union with the Presbyterian Church and gave reason to believe that the Presbytery would receive him and the Association on the principles they enunciated. Alexander doubted the wisdom of his father's efforts.

The Synod of Pittsburgh convened at Washington, on October 2, 1810, and rejected Mr. Campbell's request "to be taken into Christian and ministerial communion," and the following reasons were given:

> for expressing his belief that there are some opinions taught in our Confession of Faith which are not founded in the Bible, and avoiding to designate them; for declaring that the administration of baptism to infants is not authorized by Scriptural precept or example and is a matter of indifference, yet administering that ordinance; for encouraging and continancing his son to preach the gospel without any regular authority; for opposing creeds and confessions as

injurious to the interests of religion (Richardson 1868:Vol.
I,325-338; Garrison and DeGroot 1948:154-155; Rowe 1895:
156-157).

The Brush Run Church

Alexander Campbell was not a member of any church
and was neither licensed or ordained as a preacher. His
first sermon, preached on July 15, 1810, in a home, brought
criticism from the Presbyterians. There is little doubt that
his sermon was an expression of rebellion against the closed
shop of the clergy and the presbytery.

As the antagonism of the religious bodies did not slacken,
it became apparent to Thomas Campbell that the Christian
Association should claim the attributes of a free and independent church (Richardson 1868:Vol. I,365). The brethren
should enjoy the blessings and claim the right to respond
to those ministries that were the possession of the church.
It was not easy to widen further the breach between himself
and his brethren, but the move had to be made.

Alexander Becomes Leader of the New Movement

Alexander Campbell had by now been associated with
his father for one year and had preached many times since
his first sermon in the previous July. He was twenty-two
years of age, and for the first time entered the ground of
conflict. On November 1, 1810, he publicly examined the
proceedings of the Synod, approved the action his father
had taken, and assumed a stance more advanced than the
position of the older man. Before the Christian Association
he enunciated the proposals of the suggested reformation
and gave answer to the criticisms of the Synod (1868:Vol. I

335-346; Rowe, 1895:159-160). "The vigor of his championship did much toward winning recognition of him as the most competent and energetic advocate of the movement of which he was soon to become the acknowledged leader" (Garrison and DeGroot 1948:155).

Brush Run Church Organized

The Christian Association established itself as a Church at the following semi-annual meeting on May 4, 1811, at the meeting house near Mt. Pleasant (Richardson 1868: Vol. I,367). Thomas Campbell felt that as a condition for entering this new relationship, each member should be required to satisfactorily answer the question, "What is the meritorious cause of a sinner's acceptance with God?" (1868:Vol. I,366-367). Two members failed to satisfy and their entry was delayed. Alexander was unhappy with his father's question. He doubted its wisdom and authority though he deferred to the will of the older man. The query was never raised again (Smith 1930:97-98).

Four deacons were chosen: John Dawson, George Sharp, William Gilcrist, and James Foster; Thomas Campbell was appointed an elder, and Alexander was licensed to preach. A portion of the 118th Psalm was sung "in the old metrical version, which, as Seceders, they had been in the habit of using" (Richardson 1868:Vol. I,367).

With the condemnation and rejection of the ecclesiastical community around them, they longed for, in their new relationship, a conclusion to the unhappy circumstances of the past. In spite of those experiences, they were confident of the presence of the Holy Spirit and his direction in their exertions to further Christian unity.

The following day was the Lord's Day, and the Lord's Table was spread, to be commemorated each week. This was the pattern established by the Apostles. Alexander preached on John 6:48 and 58 (1868:Vol. I,368-369). Thus a church had been established. It was brought into being, as were similar churches in widely separated parts of the young Republic, to restore the church after the pattern revealed in the New Testament, determined to be instructed in all things by Scripture alone (Murch 1962:51).

Within weeks a new church had been constructed. It was located two miles south and east of the village of West Middletown, Pennsylvania, on a stream called Brush Run, which gave the church its name. Alexander preached the first sermon in the building on the 19th of June.

The Problem of Baptism

Shortly after Alexander Campbell's June 19th sermon in the newly constructed Brush Run meeting house, the problem of baptism arose. No longer would the question be resolved by Protestant tradition, if the principle enunciated by the *Declaration and Address* was followed. To the Word of God would they go. Three members declined to partake of the Lord's Supper and when asked to explain, replied that they could not partake as they had never been baptized (Richardson 1868:Vol. I,371-372; Garrison and DeGroot 1948:159-160). For the first time, the mode or action of baptism became an issue.

Thomas Campbell held doubts about baptizing those whom he considered already members of the Church. The present difficulty did not trouble him, for the three had so far not been baptized by any mode and when they requested to be immersed, Thomas Campbell agreed to perform the ordinance. On July 4, 1811, in Buffalo Creek, the baptism took place. The pool was shoulder-deep. Standing on a root that extended over the stream, Thomas Campbell dipped the head of each candidate until he was buried in water, pronouncing at the moment of each act the baptismal formula.

Some did not approve the way the baptisms were done. Some doubted that Mr. Campbell, who was not immersed himself, should presume to immerse others. Nonetheless, Thomas Campbell was first to introduce immersion, soon recognized as a "distinguishing feature in the progress of the Reformation" (Richardson 1868:Vol. I,373).

Baptism now grew to an issue of increasing importance. Alexander married on the 12th of March, 1811, and March 13, 1812, his first child was born. Immediately he was faced with the matter of baptizing his own baby, with the urging of his Presbyterian parents-in-law and his wife (1868:Vol. I,391).

Alexander had been inclined to look upon baptism as a matter of little consequence, willing to let the matter go undecided in his own mind. On three occasions in the past three years, he had preached on baptism using Mark 16:15-16 as his text. Each time he had "distinctly stated . . . 'as I am sure it is unscriptural to make this a term of communion, I let it slip. I wish to think and let think on these matters' " (1868:Vol. I,392). With the birth of his child, and with the fear expressed by his wife that the infant, if it were to die would be condemned to hell, the question could no longer be postponed.

Alexander turned to the Scriptures and investigated from the Greek the words transliterated baptism and baptize. It soon became his conviction that translated, these words meant immersion and immerse, and with further study he concluded that believers were the proper subjects of baptism.

If this were true, then his having been subjected to sprinkling as a baby was not baptism and he was not baptized al all. It was a matter of major consideration that he, an unbaptized person, could not consistently preach baptism to others.

The younger Campbell was not alone in this study about baptism. The membership of the Brush Run Church was probably about thirty members, but among them there was a growing opinion that baptism was a factor of greater significance than they had so far accepted. A command so important in the Lord's commission to his disciples that he would link it directly with salvation in the understandable affirmation, "He that believeth and is baptized shall be saved," could not be viewed as an insignificant opinion which might be postponed indefinitely.

Richardson says,

> Admitting that infant baptism was without warrant, the question began to assume quite a different aspect, and was no longer, "May we safely reject infant baptism as human invention?" but, "May we omit believer's baptism, which all admit to be divinely commanded?" If the baptism of infants be without warrant, it is invalid, and they who receive it are, in point of fact, still unbaptized. When they come to know this in after years, will God accept the credulity of the parent for the faith on the part of the person baptized, but will God sanction the omission of baptism on the part of the believer, on the ground that in his infancy he had been subject of a ceremony which had not been enjoined? On the other hand, if the practice of infant baptism can be justified by inferential reasoning or any sufficient evidence, why should it not be adopted or continued by common consent, without further discussion? (1868:Vol. I 393-394).

Alexander Campbell came to the decision that he must be immersed. He must obey that which he understood, through the teachings of the Word of God to be a command of the Lord. So he informed his father. Arrangements were made for a Baptist preacher to do the baptizing. On June 12, 1812 in Buffalo Creek, "Thomas and Alexander Campbell and their wives, Alexander's sister, and a Mr. and Mrs. James Hansen were immersed on the simple confession of their faith into Christ " (1868:Vol. I, 397-398; Garrison and DeGroot 1948:160).

The creekside service was seven hours long. The majority of the Brush Run Church were there, as well as a crowd of onlookers, for the service had been publicized. Joseph Bryant, before the baptisms took place, had to leave to "attend a muster" of men volunteering for the war with Great Britain which was to be declared by Congress on June 18. After making his appearance at muster, he returned to the baptismal pool in time to hear an hour of preaching and to watch the baptism service.

Of the small membership of Brush Run, ten were now immersed. At the following assembly thirteen others asked to be immersed. Several more were to make the request later. The few who chose not to follow the practice dropped out.

The Reformers Join the Baptists

The Baptists became very cordial to the small community because the reformers adopted immersion. Barriers between themselves and other churches rose higher.

Never had there been any intention of establishing another denomination. Relationships between Baptist Churches of the Redstone Association of Pennsylvania and the Brush Run Church were cordial, and Alexander Campbell was happier with the Baptists than any other group. Many were urging the Reformers to unite with the Redstone Association. In the fall of 1813, Alexander put the matter before the Brush Run Church. The decision was made to apply for membership in the Association. A careful statement defining Brush Run's opposition to man-made creeds as restraints for communion and affirming the desire to fellowship in union with the Baptists with the condition that they might be permitted to preach as taught from the Word, was put forward and approved by considerable majority (Richardson 1868:Vol. I,436-441; *The Millennial Harbinger* 1848:344). Minutes of the *Redstone Baptist Association* for September 2, 1815 read, "A letter was received, making a similar request (for union with the Redstone Association), from a church at Brush Run, which was also granted."

The Founding of the Wellsburg Church

In 1815 Alexander Campbell proposed the building of a Church in the village of Charleston, Virginia (now Wellsburg, West Virginia). Between December 12, 1815, and the early months of 1816 he traveled as far as Philadelphia, Trenton, New York and Washington City, and when he returned he had approximately one thousand dollars, a considerable amount for the times. With this money and gifts from folk in Charleston, a site was secured and a comfortable church house was constructed (Richardson 1868:Vol. I,468-469).

This was a Baptist Church. Money solicited for its construction came from Baptists in the East. An Elder Pritchard, minister of the Baptist Church at Cross Creek, three miles north and also a member of the Redstone Association, took exception to the action of Mr. Campbell. The Wellsburg Church was an intrusion into his parish, and he was gravely offended (Garrison and DeGroot 1948:164-165).

193

The Sermon on the Law

The regular meeting of the Redstone Baptist Association convened at the Cross Creek Church on August 30, 1816. There was anxiety on the part of many people and preachers present that Alexander Campbell should be one of the preachers at the Sunday services. There was considerable opposition led by Elder Pritchard because of the above. After much discussion agreement was achieved that the younger Campbell might have the second sermon of the day.

His text, taken from Romans 8:3 read, "For what the law could not do, in that it was weak through the flesh, God sending his own son in the likeness of sinful flesh, and for sin, condemned sin in the flesh." This was Alexander Campbell's famous "Sermon on the Law."

Recounting the circumstances, Mr. Campbell later wrote of the occurrence.

> At the impulse of the occasion, I was induced to draw a clear line between the Law and the Gospel, the Old Dispensation and the New, Moses and Christ. This was my theme. No sooner had I gotten on my way than Elder Pritchard came up into the tent and called out two or three of the preachers to see a lady suddenly taken sick, and thus created much confusion amidst the audience. I could not understand it. Finally, they got composed, and I proceeded. The congregation became much engaged; we all seemed to forget the things around us and went into the merits of the subject. The result was, during the interval, (as I learned long afterwards) the over-jealous elder called a council of the preachers and proposed to them to have me forthwith condemned before the people by a formal declaration from the stand — repudiating my discourse as "not Baptist doctrine." . . . Thus originated my Sermon on the Law (*The Millennial Harbinger* 1848:345-349).

194

This was a carefully structured discourse. Following the meeting, Mr. Campbell recorded it in detail and printed it in pamphlet form. Years later he had it published *in extenso* (1846:493ff.). James DeForest Murch called it "a sort of declaration of independence for the whole Christian Church" (Murch 1962:62).

Alexander Campbell introduced his theme by showing that the law implied the total dispensation of Moses, and he continued by arguing that although there were unchangeable concepts upon which the law was grounded, the law did not initiate them. It incorporated implications of these concepts, but was a unique institution created for particular purposes for a particular age.

These fundamentals were underscored by Jesus Christ. As Campbell said in his sermon:

> There are two principles, commandments or laws that are never included in our observations concerning the law of Moses, nor are they ever, in Holy Writ, called the law of Moses: These are, "Thou shalt love the Lord thy God with all thy heart, soul, mind and strength; and thy neighbor as thyself." These our Great Prophet teaches us are the bases of the law of Moses and of the prophets. Indeed the Sinai law and all Jewish laws are but modifications of them. These are of universal and immutable obligation (*The Millennial Harbinger* 1846:493ff.).

Alexander Campbell affirmed that the nature of God and man makes imperative that these principles be incorporated into any covenant between God and man. That they have persisted under the new covenant is in no way a validification of any portion of the old (1846:496-501; Garrison and DeGroot 1948:165).

195

Under the second point of his sermon, he emphasized the things the law could not do. Righteousness and eternal life are perpetually joined. If the first is missing, there can be no enjoyment of the latter. Mr. Campbell asserted that the law of Moses could not give righteousness and life. "For if there had been a law given which could have given life, verily righteousness should have been by the law," Galatians 3:21. "If righteousness came by the law, then Christ is dead in vain" (1846:Vol. I,513). Nor could the law portray the cancerous and debilitating nature of sin. Deeds such as theft, adultery and murder it declared sinful, offending God and injurious to man, deserving death; how far-reaching and massive their destructiveness, the law could not demonstrate. It could not cope with the sin problem underlying all the actions of man. The law was an unsatisfactory rule of life for man in his corrupted state. Its precepts were designed only for the Jews and were inadequate for the needs of all men (1846:513-520).

These weaknesses God corrected when he sent his only begotten Son in the likeness of sinful flesh to make reconciliation for iniquity so that "all the spiritual seed of Abraham might find righteousness and eternal life, not by legal works or observances, but through the abundance of grace and the gift of righteousness which is by him."

Thus it was that Christ is the end of the law for everyone who believes. He is not, by this fact, the minister of sin, for this righteousness of the law is fulfilled in us who walk not after the flesh but after the Spirit. Do we thus make void the law or destroy the righteousness of it by faith? God forbid: we establish the law.

Mr. Campbell next amplified aspects of the Lord's life including his atonement, and stressed the destructiveness of sin, with its consequences in contrast to the eternal mercy, love and grace of our God. The weakness of the law in its failure as a rule of life was corrected through Jesus Christ and his perfect teachings and life. Mr. Campbell continued, that Moses, the lawgiver, and Elijah, who restored the law, were present with the Lord and Peter, James and John on the Mount of Transfiguration and heard the pronouncement of the Heavenly Father, "This is my beloved Son, in whom I am well pleased. Hear ye him." The Lord was thus appointed in the place of the law of Moses through a new dispensation of truth and grace. Mr. Campbell then infers several conclusions, for example, the necessary distinction between the law and the gospel, and Christians lived no longer under law but under grace (Richardson 1868:Vol. I, 476).

Another conclusion was that it was unnecessary to proclaim the law as a means of preparing men and women to accept the Gospel. "This conclusion," said Mr. Campbell, "corresponds perfectly with the commission of our Lord to the apostles, and with their practices under the commission" (1868:Vol. I,477). The apostles were appointed ministers by the Lord and not by Moses, and they served under the new covenant and not the old. Christ and not the law was to be the beginning and ending of their preaching.

The young preacher then focused on what he believed were seven weaknesses of Protestantism of his day, weaknesses the result of formulating creeds and doctrines on arguments taken from the Old Testament. The baptism of babies, the keeping of fasts and days in preparation for the Lord's Supper, consecration of the seventh day, establishing religion by ordinance; all these he condemned. Practices not authorized or permitted by the teachings of Christ were not to be continued (1868:Vol. I, 478).

In the conclusion of his sermon, Mr. Campbell said:

We are taught from all that has been said, to venerate in the highest degree the Lord Jesus Christ. To receive him as the great prophet, of whom Moses in the law, and all the prophets did write: to receive him as "The Lord of Righteousness, and to pay the most punctilious regard to all his precepts and ordinances. If we continue in his word, then are we his disciples indeed, and we shall know the truth, and the truth shall make us free: and if the Lord shall make us free, we shall be free indeed" (*The Millennial Harbinger* 1846: 520).

If this sermon were preached today before many Baptist Associations or other denominations, it would create little protest. The majority of Christians accept the distinctions between the institutions and statutes found in the Old Testament and the Christian Church with its ordinances, found in the New Testament, with symbolism those ordinances could not have had before Christ. It is accepted today that the New Testament is the norm by which the Old Testament is interpreted.

Alexander Campbell himself observed, thirty years after the sermon was preached,

I may further say at present, that I do not think there is a Baptist Association on the continent that would now treat me as did the Redstone Association of that day, which is some evidence to my mind that the Baptists are not so stationary as a few of them would have the world to believe (1846:493-494).

The Baptist ministers of the Redstone Association were so displeased with the discourse and with Alexander Campbell that attempts were made at the next meeting held at

Peter's Creek in 1817 to bring the sermon to trial and condemnation. The effort was dismissed but not without
charges of heresy and heterodoxy (Richardson 1868:Vol.
I,479).

At the meeting at Cross Creek where the sermon was
delivered, twenty-seven of the Association's thirty-three
churches were represented. "After that he itinerated less
and confined his labors to three or four little communities
constituted on the Bible, one in Ohio, one in Virginia, and
two in Pennsylvania" (Garrison and DeGroot 1948:167).
Mr. Campbell said of the "Sermon on the Law,"

> This unfortunate sermon afterwards involved me in a seven
> year's war with some members of the said Association, and
> became a matter of much debate (*The Millennial Harbinger*
> 1846:493).

However, he looked upon his presence at Cross Creek in
1816 and his preaching the controversial sermon as providential work of God.

The discourse was of significance to the development of
the tiny Reformation. Of its importance Campbell wrote,
"It is, therefore, highly probable to my mind, that but for
the persecution begun on the alleged heresy of this sermon,
whether the present reformation had even been advocated
by me" (1846:493).

Mr. Campbell's Letter to the Redstone Baptist Association

Mr. Campbell's circular letter published in the minutes,
was written for the churches in connection with the meeting
of the Redstone Baptist Association at the Peter's Creek
Church in Washington County, Pennsylvania, September 2,
1817. The letter, accepted without amendment, set forth the

doctrines of election and reprobation and the divine purposes of God as Alexander Campbell advocated those
doctrines, one year after his famous *Sermon on the Law.*

In this letter, Mr. Campbell wrote with reference to the
apparent contradiction between God's sovereignty and
man's free will,

Another mistake of the objector is manifest in the objection,
viz.: that God cannot make a creature who shall always act
freely, and yet all his actions be known and determined of
God. That this is within the compass of the Divine power,
the Scriptures fully evince. That God is not the author of
sin; that he cannot be tempted of evil, neither tempteth he
any man, is most obvious; and that man acts freely, and yet
of necessity, is equally plain — not however in metaphysical
proposition in the Scriptures, but in certain and incontest-
able facts. For instance, no man ever acted more freely than
Judas Iscariot in betraying Christ for thirty pieces of silver,
and yet no action was ever more certainly determined than
that very action. For Christ was delivered by the deter-
minate counsel and foreknowledge of God. A thousand
actions recorded in Scripture, indeed all prophecy contained
in them, demonstrate that men act freely in all that they do,
and all their actions are fixed as certain as that Christ shall
come again, or that time shall end.*

Though Alexander Campbell had obviously moved from
influences of his youth and young manhood, he was still
wrestling as the circular letter of 1817 indicates.

The Debate with John Walker on the Mode and Subject of Baptism

Charges of heresy were regularly brought against Mr.
Campbell by the oppostion in the Redstone Association

---

* Minutes, Redstone Baptist Association, 1817:15. Copy in Lincoln Christian
College library, Lincoln, Illinois.

following his *Sermon on the Law*, but each year they failed. Whatever differences the Baptists had with him over other matters of doctrine, they believed him to be sound with regard to baptism.

Mr. Campbell was widely recognized as a powerful speaker, and with the confidence Baptists had in his views on baptism, they urged him to meet Seceder Presbyterian minister, John Walker, of Mount Pleasant, Ohio, to debate the subject. His reluctance to become involved in religious argument, partly in deference to his father's feelings, led him to refuse, but the Baptist brethren persisted until he agreed to meet Mr. Walker (Moore 1909:165; Richardson 1868:Vol. II,14).

Archbishop Purcell, who afterwards debated with Mr. Campbell, refers to Campbell the debator. He says:

> Mr. Campbell was regarded as a kind of religious Goliath, and was met at every crossroad and tollgate by well intentioned half informed preachers of the different denominations and challenged to produce his credentials, to enter into a discussion in defense of his original and peculiar views. Our hero was nothing loth to do so. Such opportunities were precisely what he desired. A vast audience would gather together to hear what to them was vastly more attractive than a great battle to the death between two celebrated gladiators.

> These debates were brief and decisive. Campbell floored his opponents in a few moments. Their arguments fell to pieces as if they had no more strength than a potter's vessel. So quickly was all this accomplished that they could hardly realize their discomfiture. The people saw all of this and it made Campbell thousands of proselytes; and their children and their children's children have to this day stuck to his

church like grim death, and they will stick for generations to come (*The Christian* 1926:423-424).

Hayden, (1875:18) a contemporary of Alexander Campbell, began his *History of the Disciples in the Western Reserve* with the Campbell-Walker debate held at Mount Pleasant in June of 1820. The public dispute, recorded and published, was the most significant event of the period.

Mr. Walker, who had the first speech used but few minutes of his time. He commenced as follows:

> My friends — I don't intend to speak long at one time, perhaps not more than five or ten minutes, and will therefore come to the point at once: I maintain that baptism came in the room of circumcision — that the covenant on which the Jewish Church was built, and to which circumcision is the seal, is the same with the Covenant on which the Christian Church is built, and to which baptism is the seal — that the Jews and the Christians are the same body politic, under the same lawgiver and husband; hence the Jews were called the congregation of the Lord — and the bridegroom of the Church says, "My love, my undefiled is one" — consequently the infants of believers have a right to baptism (Campbell 1822:9).

Having so spoken, stating the premise upon which he would maintain his argument throughout the debate, he sat down.

Early in his reply, Mr. Campbell suggested that the paedobaptists did not put baptism in the room of circumcision. They did not confine it to males only and extend it to servants and children. They did not do it on the eighth day. He then underscored several differences between baptism and circumcision which made the substitution of the one for the other an impossibility.

He stressed that circumcision only demanded fleshly descent from Abraham and its blessings were temporal. Baptism required faith in Jesus Christ as a precondition, and its promised blessings were spiritual. "Baptism," Mr. Campbell said, "is connected with the remission of sins, and the gift of the Holy Spirit—circumcision had the promise of Canaan's land, and a numerous family, as its peculiar blessings" (1822:13).

These were the emphases for the first day. Richardson in his evaluation of Walker said that he "used considerable repetition and often recurred to his argument from the covenants without considering the refutation given by Mr. Campbell . . ." (Richardson 1868:Vol. II,21).

The second day Mr. Walker referred to the four examples of household baptism revealed in the New Testament as proof for infant baptism (Campbell 1822:65). In response, Mr. Campbell gave evidence that there were no infants in those households.

All the house of Cornelius feared God and received the Holy Spirit. The household of Lydia were comforted as brethren. The word of the Lord was spoken to all in the jailor's house, and they all rejoiced, believing in God as well as himself. All the house of Crispus believed on the Lord, and the house of Stephanus are said to have addicted themselves to the ministry of the saints (Richardson 1868: Vol. II,22; Campbell 1822:70-72).

Because Mr. Walker continued his agruments from the covenants, Mr. Campbell formulated questions for Mr. Walker so that Mr. Campbell might have affirmation regarding the ground on which his Presbyterian opponent stood. They were:

Proposition 1st — "That the covenant of circumcision is the same with the New Covenant or Covenant of Grace" — Does Mr. Walker admit and maintain this proposition? Mr. Walker answers, "Yes."

Proposition 2nd — "That the Old and New Testament Church are the same, with only some accidental or circumstantial differences" — Does Mr. Walker admit and maintain this proposition? Mr. Walker answers, "Yes" (1822:67).

Campbell responded that the covenanters of Europe maintained that all the blessings enjoyed by mankind were enjoyed through the righteousness of Christ, but that the Seceders of Scotland opposed this, maintaining that it was derogatory to the redemption of Christ to suppose that he died "to purchase food and raiment for mankind, which the Almighty has given to the brutes that perish" (1822:76). The Seceders argued that it was a dangerous error to think that corrupt, unrepentant mankind had shared in any portion of the redemptive purchase of Christ (Richardson 1868:Vol. II,23).

Thus does Mr. Campbell point out that Mr. Walker, a Seceder Presbyterian, had abandoned his own church. To Mr. Campbell this was an insignificant matter compared to the fact that Mr. Walker also opposed both Moses and Paul. The claim of advantage under the bond of circumcision was nothing more than fleshly descent from Abraham. The affirmation of the Jews was, "We have Abraham to our father." On grounds far different, the new covenant located the source of its blessings, "If ye be Christ's, then are ye Abraham's seed and heirs, according to the promise" (Campbell 1822:76-77). To the natural descendants of Abraham in the covenant of circumcision, regarding temporal blessings promised, the assurance was, "If you be Abraham's seed through Sarah, then you are heirs according to the promise." Of the eternal blessings assured the spiritual seed of Abraham, Gen. 12:3, "And in thee shall all families of the earth be blessed," this covenant between God and Abraham was made twenty-five years (see Gen. 12:4 and Gen. 17:1) prior to the covenant of circumcision (Gen. 17:10). It made clear reference to Paul's promise (Gal. 3:29) "And if ye be Christ's, then are ye Abraham's seed, and heirs according to the promise," and Mr. Campbell affirmed, "This distinction is abundantly evident, and should forever terminate the controversy betwixt the Baptists and Paedobaptists, on the subject of baptism" (1822:77).

It was Mr. Campbell's object, in placing such stress upon the successive dispensations, not only to cast doubt upon the analogy of baptism to circumcision but particularly to release Christianity from Judaistic precedents. What he said in this debate had great influence on men who were part of the Restoration Movement in its beginnings (Garrison and DeGroot 1948:170).

Mr. Walker, having moved from his arguments on the covenants, turned next to the ancients to prove that infant baptism was practiced in the early church.

Mr. Campbell did not deny that both baptism and sprinkling of babies were of ancient date, but he insisted that antiquity did not prove them right, as other things as well were introduced at the same time, admitted to be corruptions.

He affirmed, however, that infant baptism was not taught or practiced for many years after the apostolic age, there being no record extant that mentions it for at least one hundred and fifty years after the Christian era, the testimony

205

of the primitive fathers bring up to this time, exclusively in favor of believer's baptism (Richardson 1868:Vol. II, 25).

Campbell discussed in detail the views of the church fathers in response to Mr. Walker. He referred to Tertullian

> And I will frankly own he mentions infant baptism. Whether boys or babies, is however, controverted; but with this dispute I shall not intermeddle — Tertullian flourished from the year 194 until 216; he is ranked among the writers of the third century. From the quotation read out of Mr. J. P. Campbell [authority quoted by Mr. Walker to prove the early antiquity of infant baptism], it is obvious he was no friend of infant baptism, though he has the honor of first mentioning it in history, sacred or ecclesiastical — he appears like one opposing an innovation of recent date, not an established custom (Campbell 1822:106).

So the debate continued until two p.m. on Tuesday, the second day. After a half hour's recess, Mr. Campbell was informed that Walker requested the disputants speak once each on the action or mode of baptism and that the debate be concluded. The request came as a surprise. Walker and his moderator had, that very morning, "proposed adjourning from day to day until everything should be fully discussed" (1822:121). Though amazed by the decision, Campbell consented, provided each should speak twice.

Mr. Walker's final arguments were designed to authenticate that "pouring and sprinkling are Scriptural modes of baptism," contending that 'in water' could be read as accurately 'with water.' He alleged that βαπτιζω need not of necessity be translated 'dip' for it often implied 'washing,' as adaptable to sprinkling and pouring as to the verb, 'to dip.'

Mr. Campbell responded by quoting Dr. George Campbell, Pedobaptist, Presbyterian professor of Greek at the College of Aberdeen, Scotland, who affirmed that βαπτιζω ought to be translated to dip, to plunge, to immerse and that in conjunction with it the Greek preposition, εν, should always be rendered "in" and never "with" (1822:123-132).

Alexander Campbell urged,

> If you desire to know about baptism, don't look for information concerning the subject by investigating some supposed correspondence to an earlier command with other beginnings, forms, purposes and subjects, but investigate those scriptural passages that speak precisely about baptism itself.

The debate came to a rather early ending. It was the consensus of the Baptists, though they were displeased with the arguments Mr. Campbell used to support immersion, that he had won the contest, and his reputation was enhanced throughout the territory (Garrison and DeGroot 1948:170).

The debate was providential. For one thing, it provided the opportunity for him to amplify the themes of his Sermon on the Law preached four years previously at the Cross Creek Church. His elaboration of the differences between the Jewish Covenant and the Christian were penetrating the minds of thinking people, many of whom would soon find their way into the Reformation. His reputation as a scholarly preacher spread far and wide, and the arguments revealed in print only extended it more rapidly.

Chapter Nine

THE IMPACT OF
ALEXANDER CAMPBELL'S LEADERSHIP

Consequences of the
Campbell-Walker Debate

The factor that precipitated the Campbell-Walker debate was the number of Pedobaptists immersed following Baptist evangelistic services held at Mount Pleasant in the fall of 1819 (Richardson 1868:Vol. II,14-15). At the conclusion of the dispute, many more asked to be immersed.

The debate was immediately published (1,000 first edition) and republished (3,000 second edition). Invitations now came to Mr. Campbell from Baptist Churches of eastern Ohio. Many were fearful of his teaching. Some called it heresy. Others expressed apprehension at what was believed an explosive innovation as he taught about the several dispensations. However, the majority joyously heard him, traveling many miles when they knew he was to preach.

Adamson Bentley of Warren, Ohio, who had silently met the Campbell family as they were traveling across the mountains of Pennsylvania to their new home, eleven years earlier, was one of those extremely favorable to Alexander Campbell's doctrinal position. Bentley was a preacher of great ability. He loved the Scriptures, and he loved God's people. He had a major influence among the Baptists of the Western Reserve of Northeastern Ohio.

The Beginning of the Mahoning Baptist Association

The Western Reserve was heavily populated for the times, and Baptist Churches had already been planted. Adamson Bentley persuaded the ministers of these congregations to

208

come together each year to examine their own progress, to aid one another in their preaching and to study the Scriptures. It was also the consensus of the preachers that they ought to create a formal fellowship. On August 30, 1820, the Mahoning Baptist Association was organized, a bit more than two months following the Campbell-Walker debate.

Early the following year Adamson Bentley acquired a copy of the debate, and he was impressed with what he read. Bentley was aware of efforts being made in the Redstone Association of Pennsylvania to censure Mr. Campbell, because of his strange doctrines enunciated in his *Sermon on the Law*. In Bentley's judgement, no other man in the West had done more for the Baptists than Alexander Campbell, and it was his intention to visit and become acquainted with Mr. Campbell (1868:Vol. II,44).

This meeting came in the summer of 1821 when Adamson Bentley and his brother-in-law, Sydney Rigdon, visited Campbell at his own home. Their discussions began following tea in the evening and continued through the night. Campbell recounted the meeting.

> Beginning with the baptism that John preached, we went back to Adam and forward to the final judgement. The dispensations — Adamic, Abrahamic, Jewish, and Christian — passed and repassed before us. Mount Sinai and Arabia, Mount Zion, Mount Tabor, the Red Sea and Jordan, the Passovers and the Pentecosts, the law and the Gospel, but especially the ancient order of things and the modern, occasionally engaged our attention (*The Millennial Harbinger* 1848:523).

Campbell spoke of Sydney Rigdon as the great orator of the *Mahoning Baptist Association*, but in the judgment of members of the churches Rigdon was always second to Adamson Bentley.

Campbell's meeting and friendship with Rigdon and Bentley opened the way for invitations to speak throughout the Western Reserve with opportunities to preach to the "uncommitted community" and to the Baptist Churches. Campbell reported that within a year they had persuaded the entire association to hear him with the result that from that time he attended association meetings.

The study of Scripture, a regular part of these gatherings, resulted in greater understanding of Bible truth, and the evidences of Reformation began to appear within the association. It would be incorrect to credit this movement to one influence. There were other dynamics at work such as the admixture of people from other states with the predominant New England population with its comparisons, differences of opinion and the desire to investigate to find the source of truth. But one of the obvious influences in this desire for the restoration of "the divinely established order of the gospel" was the pen and labors of Alexander Campbell (Hayden 1875:21).

There was an accelerating interest in the ministerial meetings due largely to Mr. Campbell's presence. He helped to resolve many problems through his comprehension of the Word of God. He defined the differences between matters of faith and matters of opinion, pointing out that suppositions of men concerning areas where the Scriptures are silent must never be made tests of fellowship or allowed to cause division and strife. He taught them that by studying the Scripture in its own context, it became its own best interpreter.

From time to time, Mr. Campbell was able to return to Pittsburgh. On these occasions as a member of the Redstone Association, in spite of opposition within it, he preached at the Baptist Church which had grown to one hundred or more members, many of whom were sympathetic to the concepts of reformation. Sydney Rigdon, from Warren, Ohio, became a pastor of the church in 1822, due to Mr. Campbell's influence. Because of Rigdon's interest in the Reformation, Mr. Campbell hoped to introduce him to Walter Scott, who was serving the small New Testament Church in Pittsburgh over which the late Mr. Forrester had presided. Mr. Campbell for the first time met Mr. Scott but a few months previously and was impressed with him, and he hoped that the Baptist Church and the congregation led by Walter Scott might unite. For a considerable time, because of distrust on both sides, the union did not take place.

Decisions that Affected Alexander Campbell's Ministry

By early 1823, Alexander Campbell was prepared to make decisions that would change his pattern of life. He had witnessed the impact of the Campbell-Walker debate. It was being read far and near and provided the avenue for enunciating his views of the Reformation of the Church. He and his father had suffered disappointment at their lack of success to reform the divided denominations upon the concept defined by the *Declaration and Address.* They had lost hope of ever witnessing any transformation of divided Christendom. Though Alexander continued to give himself to the object that he advocated, it was without hope of doing more than perhaps establishing one church advocating his principles.

In the last article written for *The Christian Baptist* one decade later, Campbell wrote,

> An unsuccessful effort by my father to reform the presbytery and synod to which he belonged, made me despair of reformation. I gave it up as a hopeless effort: but did not give up speaking in public assemblies upon the great articles of Christian faith and practice. In the hope, the humble hope, of erecting a single congregation with which I could enjoy the social institutions, I labored. I had not the remotest idea of being able to do more than this (*The Christian Baptist* 1829:661).

Alexander Campbell considered devoting his time to farming, and teaching gratuitously those who came within his sphere of influence, when he was persuaded to enter the debate with Mr. Walker.

Having observed the impact of the debate and the published account, Mr. Campbell reexamined his position. There was still hope that in a more expansive way the population might be awakened. "Guided providentially step by step, he had been brought to an eminence from which he could survey the wide field in which he was destined to labor, and he began at once to nerve himself for the undertaking" (Richardson 1868:Vol. II,49).

There was little about his debate with Walker to make it stand out, and yet, through the providence of God, it was the most important for Mr. Campbell and the religious world. It displayed his ability in public dispute on spiritual matters. It convinced him of the excellency of this method to reveal what he thought to be truth and error. Opportunities for preaching multiplied. The debate with Walker led to his further discussion with W. L. MacCalla. This enhanced his reputation among the Baptists even more, providing entry into numerous Baptist Churches of Kentucky.

212

Mr. Campbell's principles of reformation soon blanketed much of the state. Through his journeys into the state, he met and became acquainted with Barton Warren Stone, and the publication of his debate with MacCalla spread far and wide his teaching on baptism (Dowling 1964:59).

The Christian Baptist

In the summer of 1823 Alexander Campbell distributed through the mails the prospectus of a magazine he was planning to publish. Already he had discussed with his father, Walter Scott and others the proposed design and purpose of the journal, and they enthusiastically gave the project their approval. Mr. Campbell doubted the wisdom of attaching the word "Baptist" to the name, because he felt it had a denominational connotation. He preferred the name "Christian," but Walter Scott persuaded him to name the journal *The Christian Baptist*. Mr. Campbell was still a member of the Baptist Church and Scott felt he ought to avoid, as far as possible, exciting religious prejudice.

Mr. Campbell explained the proposed purpose of the publication.

The Christian Baptist shall espouse the cause of no religious sect, excepting that ancient sect "called Christians first at Antioch." Its sole object shall be the eviction of truth and the exposing of error in doctrine and practice. The editor, acknowledging no standard of religious faith or works other than the Old and New Testament, and the latter as the only standard of the religion of Jesus Christ, will, intentionally at least, oppose nothing which it contains and recommend nothing which it does not enjoin (Richardson 1868:Vol. II,50).

The first edition of *The Christian Baptist* came from the press in August, 1823. The publication continued through July, beginning January, 1830. It was superseded by *The Millennial Harbinger*. The influence of the magazine was tremendous. Mr. Campbell flooded its pages with principles he had discovered through his study of the Scriptures since his boyhood. Many truths he propounded from the first. Other things, advocated early in his career, he rejected as he came to a greater knowledge of the truth. The impact of his pen was earth shaking. Until he began writing, his followers were few, but now his fame spread, and numbers saw his position and accepted it.

Among those minds prepared by sectarian divisiveness, *The Christian Baptist* was like a beacon in the storm. In following years the journal was to maintain its popularity through several republished editions as it was read and reread from generation to generation (Smith 1930:136).

Many opposed Mr. Campbell. Predominant were the clergy. To them *The Christian Baptist* was the enemy of churches, and they did all they could to persuade their people not to read it, with minimal success.

With sarcasm, Campbell described the denominational institutions as they "manufactured" clergy. He denounced the acquiring and increasing of salaries, the securing of offices and titles. He was caustic in his criticism of councils, synods, assemblies, associations and conferences, and he documented his reasons for opposing missionary giving with high overhead and minimal funds for reaching the heathen. Expensive church buildings, musical instruments, stalls and boxes and tithes and offerings all felt the prick of his pointed pen (Richardson 1868:Vol. II,54-55). A paid clergy was a memento of popery. Paid preachers were stall fed preachers. It must be remembered that the antagonism and bitterness was not one-sided. If there was intolerance on his part, it had too often been incited by the bigotry manifested by the denominational churches against him. In fairness to Mr. Campbell, it must also be remembered that what he was attacking was a wicked spirit which had been appealed to in toleration and godly love. It had revealed itself impervious of any other treatment than the fiery blasts Campbell was so well fitted to ignite (Smith 1930:151).

Before Alexander Campbell entered western Pennsylvania, his father, with gentleness, intreated the synods to exercise compassion towards those of their own denomination, and the clergy treated his appeals with disdain. They refused to relinquish the offices they had attained and the bounty they longed to acquire. Mr. Campbell concluded that he had no other recourse than to employ something more rigid and striking that he might demand their attention.

> It is to be particularly noticed that he did not include among the clergy whom he denounced the ministers of the Baptist and other independent churches. These, being appointed by the churches, and acting as elders and preachers of the gospel in subordination to just, scriptural authority, he constantly recognized as a lawful ministry in the church, for the accomplishment of the purposes for which it was established on earth (Richardson 1868:Vol. II,61).

Attached to the above reference to the clergy, Mr. Campbell added,

> In our remarks upon the Christian clergy we never include the elders and deacons of a Christian assembly, or those in

the New Testament called the overseers and servants of the Christian Church. These we consider as very different characters, and shall distinguish them in some future number (*The Christian Baptist* 1829:8).

The Redstone Association Attempts Excommunication of Mr. Campbell

With all the resistance applied by an antagonistic system, Alexander Campbell's principles of reformation were embraced by many people over a wide area, and changes were to be seen. Their acceptance only strengthened opposition from the clergy. This was true with Mr. Campbell's antagonists in the Redstone Association, and because of his activities elsewhere, his enemies, during his absence, did all they could to strengthen the opposition from the clergy. His now famous *Sermon on the Law*, provided his adversaries with cause, from their perspective, for charges of heresy with the object of throwing Mr. Campbell and his adherents out of the Association.

Knowledge of what his enemies were planning was gained by Mr. Campbell in August of 1823. He became aware of an effort to bring messengers from the churches, unfriendly to him, to the next Association meeting, with the intention of removing him from the organization.

The meeting of the Association was but a month away and time was short. Mr. Campbell, in adherence to Baptist practice, but in a fashion his adversaries could hardly anticipate, resolved to thwart their efforts.

Elder Adamson Bentley of Warren, Ohio, had been urging Campbell to withdraw from *The Redstone Association* and to affiliate with the *Mahoning* of northern Ohio. Mr. Campbell had in 1816 aided in establishing a Baptist

216

Church in Wellsburg, Virginia, one of the reasons for the antagonism of the Redstone Association. He requested the Brush Run Church, where he still had his membership, to grant him and thirty members of the congregation (brethren who now lived in or nearby Wellsburg) letters of dismissal in order that they might constitute a church in Wellsburg. The letters were granted in respect of Mr. Campbell's request.

In contrast to what usually would have been the case, Alexander Campbell attended the meeting of the Redstone Baptist Association in September of 1823, not as a messenger of the Brush Run Church but as a spectator. Great was the amazement when, in the regular order of business, the letter from Brush Run was read, and Alexander Campbell was not listed as a messenger. A motion was made inviting him to a seat and a lengthly debate resulted taking considerable time. Mr. Campbell listened in silence until requested to explain why, as in the past, he was no longer a representative of Brush Run.

He then stood to voice concern that the association should devote so much time to a trivial problem. He then stated the cause for not having been chosen a messenger from the Brush Run Congregation. No longer was he a member of that church, and the congregation with which he was now affiliated was not a part of the Redstone Association.

His opponents were crestfallen. Their plans to make an example of Mr. Campbell through disfellowshiping him had crumbled. He had escaped excommunication and blocked any effort to limit his activities. He was free to promulgate those concepts of reformation which would give new life to the people of the Christian community, if embraced by them (Richardson 1868:Vol. II,68-70).

The Campbell-MacCalla Debate

At the conclusion of the Campbell-Walker debate Mr. Campbell publicly announced,

> I have now accepted the invitation or challenge of the Seceders, and having fully satisfied their most eager desires for an interview of this kind, I conceive it is my time to give an invitation or challenge to any Pedobaptist minister; and to return the compliment with the utmost ceremoniousness, I this day publish to all present, that I feel disposed to meet any Pedobaptist minister of any denomination, of good standing in his party, and I engage to prove in a debate with him, either viva voce, or with the pen, that infant sprinkling is a human tradition and injurious to the well being of society, religious and political (Campbell 1822:141).

This was the one occasion when Alexander Campbell published such a challenge (Garrison and DeGroot 1948: 191). A former attorney, known for his ability in debate, the Reverend W. L. MacCalla of Augusta, Kentucky, responded. Conditions necessary were agreed upon only after bitter correspondence, and the debate took place in October, 1823, in the village of Washington, Kentucky.

Because the Ohio River was too low for the navigation of steamboats, Mr. Campbell had to travel three hundred miles through Ohio and into Kentucky by horseback. On many occasions he would later visit the state, but this was his first time. Sydney Rigdon from Pittsburgh traveled with him, wishing to hear the argument himself. The discussion began on the fifteenth.

Mr. Campbell opened the debate.

> As my opponent contends for infant sprinkling, he must think that some benefit is communicated in it. Now as we

know of none, it not only becomes him for the sake of consistency to point out numerically, in the first place, in the second, third, and fourth, etc. the advantages resulting from the practice, but it will also add to our zeal, and engage our attention, in discussing the subject. Let us see what is at stake, and then we shall enter into debate with spirit and energy (MacCalla-Campbell 1842:38).

In Mr. MacCalla's response he stated,

That faith is not essential to baptism, and that immersion is not essential to baptism. That the infant of a believer is a proper subject, and that sprinkling or pouring is valid baptism. In the establishment of the first proposition or first branch of this subject, I will observe the following method:

In the first place I will produce a divine command for infant baptism; a command of God authorizing infants to be baptized — the infants of believers.

In the second place I will produce probable evidence of apostolic practice of infant baptism.

In the third and last place under this head, I will produce positive evidence of apostolic practice of infant baptism (1842:42).

Mr. MacCalla, speaking to numbers of Pedobaptists, referred to Mr. Campbell and the Baptists in general as "our adversary," "our accuser" in what Campbell and others believed an attempt to unite the audience against Mr. Campbell. The situation the first day became so obvious that Bishop Vardeman, one of the moderators, observed,

. . . that he thought it very illiberal to represent the Baptists as accusers and adversaries of the Pedobaptists, and to call his opponent, Mr. Campbell, an adversary and an accuser. Mr. MacCalla must know that these are names given in

219

Scripture of Satan, who is called "the adversary" and "the accuser of the brethren." He thought that Mr. MacCalla should treat his opponent as a gentleman and as a Christian, although he differed from him on the questions under discussion (1842:51).

Because of this manner of Mr. MacCalla, Mr. Campbell, in an effort to narrow the chasm between himself and his Pedobaptist friends, proceeded in his response from the foundation laid down by the Westminster Confession of Faith. He purposed to take the Confession which Presbyterian minister MacCalla had sworn to teach, and according to his faith had affirmed to be the system of truth taught in the Bible, and from it to choose precepts relevant to the debate. Mr. Campbell then quoted from the Westminster Confession and from section seven of chapter one.

All things in Scripture are not alike in themselves, nor alike clear unto all; yet those things which are necessary to be known, believed and observed for salvation, are so clearly propounded and opened in some place of Scripture or other, that not only the learned but the unlearned, in a due use of the ordinary means may attain unto a sufficient understanding of them (1842:46).

Campbell then called his audience to keep in mind, that according to the confession MacCalla adhered to, he accepted his hearers to be capable judges of biblical testimony by exercise of ordinary study. Furthermore, his confession affirmed, according to Campbell, that without a religious teacher, though his audience be uneducated, they could learn all required things "to be known, believed and observed for salvation; because all those things are so clearly propounded and opened in some place of Scripture or other" (1842:46).

Mr. Campbell continued,

In the same confession, and in the same chapter, section nine, you will find the following most excellent sentiment: "the infallible rule of interpretation of scripture is the scripture itself; and, therefore, when there is a question about the true and full sense of any scripture which is not manifold, but one, it may be searched and known by other places that speak more clearly" (1842:46).

This statement, said Mr. Campbell, contained the most excellent rule of interpretation he had ever observed. To this principle he would appeal in differences over the understanding of Scriptures arising during the debate. He then quoted the first clause of the first verse of the twenty-eighth chapter of the Westminster Confession, referring to it as his text: "Baptism is a sacrament of the New Testament, ordained by Jesus Christ" (1842:47).

In the application of this text, Mr. Campbell promised two things: he would draw from the New and not the Old Testament to determine the nature of the ordinance of baptism, and for the institution of baptism he would heed the words of Christ for, as Campbell underscored, the Confession of Faith declared that baptism was a command of Christ (1842:47).

Through the course of the contest, it was fought on this ground with the judgment that the contest was won here (Murch 1962:77).

Mr. MacCalla proceeded to keep his promise to show there was a divine command for infant baptism, first by observing "that there is a difference in divine commands; some of them express, and others not express," and then by adding, "When we propose to produce a divine command

221

for infant baptism, you are not, my friends, to expect that we shall produce, in so many words, a command for parents to have their children baptized" (MacCalla-Campbell 1842: 53). He stated that by five propositions, which he enunciated, which would clearly "infer a divine command for infant baptism."

The five propositions were as follows:

1. Abraham and his seed were divinely constituted a true visible church of God.
2. The Christian Church is a branch of the Abrahamic Church, or in other words, the Jewish society before Christ, and the Christian society after Christ, are one and the same church in different dispensations.
3. Jewish circumcision before Christ, and Christian baptism after Christ, are one and the same seal, though in different forms.
4. The administration of this seal to infants was once enjoined by divine authority.
5. The administration of this seal to infants was never prohibited by divine authority (1842:53-54).

Mr. Campbell responded that Mr. MacCalla had rejected his Westminster confession, stating that his text was taken from the Confession on the assumption that Mr. MacCalla both believed and accepted it as his authority. Campbell suggested that possibly Mr. MacCalla had renounced the confession.

Has he not solemnly vowed his belief of it as the system of doctrine taught in the Bible? Has he not promised, solemnly promised to teach the doctrines which it contains? Does it not say that baptism is an ordinance of the New Testament? Why then does he go to the Old Testament to find it? Does

222

it not say that baptism was ordained by Jesus Christ? Why then does he go to Abraham and to Moses to authorize it? Does he not, in his first proposition, make it an ordinance of Moses, or of the Jewish Church? Does he not originate it in the law of circumcision? Why then pledge himself to teach that "baptism is an ordinance of the New Testament ordained by Jesus Christ?" or does the phrase New Testament mean both the Old and the New? And does the name, Jesus Christ, mean both Moses and the Messiah? (1842:58).

Mr. Campbell allowed MacCalla no respite at this point, and "MacCalla could not extricate himself from the web of his own Westminster Confession in which Campbell had enmeshed him" (Murch 1962:77).

MacCalla had antagonized the Baptists for some time before the debate by attacking their practices. Feeling that Mr. Campbell had vanquished him gave the Baptists much pleasure and elevated Mr. Campbell in their sentiments (Richardson 1868:Vol. II,87), so that they pled with him to tarry in Kentucky to preach in their largest churches. His debates contributed to his stature as a scholar, (Davis 1930:87) and opened the doors to the Baptist Churches in Kentucky where his concepts of reformation spread like a prairie fire.

Here he met and became acquainted with Barton Warren Stone and Elder "Raccoon" John Smith. He had been impressed with the Kentucky reformers for years. In time, a large segment of the Stone movement with Mr. Stone's encouragement would unite with the Campbell reformation to constitute a purely indigenous movement on American soil.

The editions of the Campbell-Walker Debate were quickly sold and avidly read, and the Campbell-MacCalla Debate

223

was also widely circulated, particularly in Kentucky and Ohio, but further afield as well. Alexander Campbell's popularity grew tremendously, primarily among the Baptists.

By the conclusion of the debate with MacCalla, the design of the Reformation to become the Restoration Movement, was beginning to reveal itself in the following ways:

1. There was no desire or plan to create another denomination. Rather, they would encourage a reformation within churches already in existence.
2. Essentially, it would be a restoration of existing churches, in an effort to bring them closer to "the ancient order."
3. By purposeful determination it would be a unity movement.
4. Unity and fellowship grounded upon God's Word, separate from all human creedalism would be their plea.
5. Their rigid stand against creeds was anchored to their opposition to human opinions.
6. Three "ordinances," baptism, the Lord's Supper and the Lord's Day, found emphasis in their call for reformation.
7. Necessary for the restoration of the Church, they would, more and more, advocate Christian piety and the development of Christian virtues, particularly an in depth knowledge of God's Word (Garrett, 1981:195-197).

In Kentucky, following the debate with MacCalla, Mr. Campbell became acquainted with Barton Warren Stone and Elder "Racoon" John Smith. He had been impressed with the Kentucky reformers for years.

Chapter Ten

WALTER SCOTT, A GREAT LIEUTENANT

His Preparatory Years

"It is often said that without the ministry of Walter Scott, the work of the Campbells might soon have been forgotten" (Murch 1962:97).

Walter Scott was born into a Scotch Presbyterian home in Moffat, Dumfrieshire, Scotland, on the last day of October, 1796 (Hayden 1875:61).

Walter was one of five sons and five daughters. His father was a music teacher and his parents were Presbyterians. In that church the children received careful tutoring. His mother was a spiritual woman with a sensitive nature.

A university education was often limited to the rich, yet his parents out of their means arranged for him to attend the University of Edinburgh where he prepared for the ministry in the Presbyterian Church.

In the years of his young manhood, he lost his parents. His father died suddenly at Annan, Scotland. Word got back to his mother, and she fell dead from shock. Both parents were buried in the same grave (Baxter 1874:30; Hayden 1875:61).

Shortly after he completed his education, an unexpected turn of events occurred that affected his life. A brother of his mother, living in New York City, arranged for Scott to come to the United States, something far removed from his plan of life. He sailed from Greenock on the ship Glenthorn and arrived in New York July 7, 1818.

For a time he taught on Long Island, but hearing tales out of the west, beyond the Alleghenies, he and a companion walked from New York City to Pittsburgh, arriving there on May 7, 1819 (1875:62).

He soon found employment as an assistant to a fellow Scotsman, Mr. George Forrester, principal of an academy (Richardson 1868:Vol. I, 503; Hayden 1875:62).

The Influence of George Forrester

Alexander Campbell noted that

Sometime in 1814 or 1815, I have not a very certain recollection of the precise date, a certain Mr. Jones, from England, and a Mister George Forrester, from Scotland, appeared in Pittsburgh — the former an English Baptist; the latter, rather a Haldanean than a Scotch Baptist. They were both much in advance of the regular Baptists of Redstone Association, and I had hoped for assistance from them. But neither of them could found a community in Pittsburgh. Elder Jones migrated westwardly, and Mr. Forrester went into secular business. Neither of them, however, had progressed beyond the limits of James Haldane or Andrew Fuller (*The Millennial Harbinger* 1848:349).

Robert Richardson observed that about 1815 a Haldanean preacher arrived in Pittsburgh from Scotland, opening an academy in Pittsburgh and preaching occasionally. Forrester was restricted in his views. He did not hold that "enlarged conception of the Gospel plan of salvation" attained by Mr. Campbell.

It was thus, however, that several phases of the Haldanean movement were at this time, on a small scale, represented in Pittsburgh, but though they aided in some respects in preparing the ground, none of them were capable of rendering any great assistance to Mr. Campbell (Richardson 1868: Vol. I,486-487).

About 1815 there were two or three small congregations of Christians in various places in Pittsburgh. Each cast off human creeds and had taken the Bible alone for their rule of faith and practice. Each in the beginning was independent of the others, but as time passed, they united as individual believers creating the larger congregation known as the Christian Church in Pittsburgh. Apparently, George Forrester brought together the first of these groups. He was both teacher and preacher having already opened an academy in the city. A number of stalwarts, members of the tiny church in New York City, had come to Pittsburgh. They began at once meeting around the Lord's Table. Forrester opened his home and school to them. He was a follower of Robert Haldane (*The Christian Standard,* October 16, 1909:4).

None of the historians reveal the exact time when the small congregation which met with him was organized. It probably took place shortly after his arrival in Pittsburgh in the fall of 1814. Walter Scott verifies that Forrester was the minister of the church.

> I myself had been baptized on the Apostolic Confession in 1819, eight years anterior, by a man of stern integrity, but of very imperfect views of the true Gospel, and who, without the least reference to baptism for remission and the Holy Spirit, received me into the fellowship in the Church (*The Evangelist,* December 1838:227).

Without doubt, Scott was referring to Forrester.

Goodnight and Stevenson reveal further spiritual activities of Forrester.

> When Thomas Campbell left Pittsburgh in the summer of 1817, Robert (Richardson)* was enrolled in a private academy conducted by George Forrester, who was also a lay minister of a tiny independent congregation of Haldanean

---

*This is the same Robert Richardson who wrote in the *Memoirs of Alexander Campbell.*

Christians, who met in the courthouse. At thirteen years of age he was still a pupil in that same school. . . . (Goodnight and Stevenson 1949:50).

By the spring of 1820, Forrester found that his church was demanding too much of his time. Observing that Walter Scott was an able teacher, he determined to leave the academy in the care of Scott so that he could give his time to the ministry (Stevenson 1946:26). This relationship was to be a short one. George Forrester was drowned in the Allegheny River on July 7th, 1820.

In 1840, D.S. Burnet referred to George Forrester as "a Scotch Haldanean, familiar with the labors of McLane (sic), he early contended for the proximate principles of the reformation and upon their fuller development, became very active in their advocacy" (*Christian Age and Protestant Unionist* 1840:123).

Thomas Campbell became acquainted with George Forrester, elder of a Haldanean Scotch Baptist Church in Pittsburgh in 1816. Campbell was attracted to the objectives of Mr. Forrester. He was repelled by his legalism. The acquaintance grew into warm friendship. Through Forrester, Mr. Campbell was introduced to Walter Scott (Walker 1935:27).

With certainty Alexander Campbell knew George Forrester, and well enough to have confidence in his abilities to serve as examiner for examinations given to students at the Buffalo Seminary. Forrester's name is included in the list of prominent literary gentlemen invited by Mr. Campbell to be present for those exams (*The Pittsburgh Mercury.* January 7, 1820:2).

Alexander Campbell and George Forrester had much in common. Forrester was a Haldanean. Mr. Campbell, for one year, studied at the feet of Greville Ewing: "Among those connected with the Haldanes, Mr. Ewing himself stood deservedly high" (Richardson 1868:Vol. I,148-149).

George Forrester was acquainted with a Christian Church, after the Haldane persuasion, in New York City. This is confirmed by references to a certain tract concerning baptism. As already seen, Walter Scott was baptized by George Forrester. After Forrester's drowning, a tract on baptism written by Henry Errett of the New York Church, came into the possession of Mr. Scott and Mr. Campbell. Scott says,

> The pamphlet [Errett's on Baptism] containing the above piece was put into my hands in the spring of 1821. It only remains to be shown that Brother Campbell received it in the same year. The person who gave it to me was Mrs. Forrester, of the church in Pittsburgh . . . and he who gave it to Brother Alexander Campbell was Brother John Tate, Sen., now of Rising Sun, Indiana, who also received it from Sister Forrester (*The Evangelist*, Dec. 1828:286).

Walter Scott, in 1835, implies that George Forrester played an important part in the development of the Pittsburg Church, "ordered on the ancient model." He recounts that when he and Mr. Campbell came forward to "plead for the Ancient ecclesiastical or Church order," that they stood to plead "an order to which our churches had already returned" (April 1835:81), which suggests that the congregation planted by George Forrester was, from near its beginning, patterned after the model of the ancient order.

The above affirms that George Forrester served as another bridge between the Scotch movement of the Haldanes and The American Restoration Movement.

George Forrester more than touched the lives of the Campbells, father and son, and he certainly greatly influenced Walter Scott.

Walter Scott, Student of the Scriptures

Though Mr. George Forrester was a truly spiritual man, his religious views were different from what Scott thought to be true.

Mr. Forrester's peculiarity consisted in making the Bible his only authority and guide in matters of religion, while his young friend had been brought up to regard the Presbyterian standards as the true and authoritative exposition and summary of Bible truth (Baxter 1874:37).

Careful study soon convinced Mr. Scott that standards determined by men were, like their formulators, faulty, and he was impressed with the conclusion that the only safe guide was the revelation of God. Following their teaching responsibilities, he and Forrester would search the Scriptures with a hunger to know God's will and a determination to follow wherever it should lead.

By now, the Bible had a meaning it never had before. Now it meant what it said. It was no longer a collection of texts from which to draw, but it was God's Word, God's will, a message to be believed and obeyed to be a Christian.

Change of Views Regarding Baptism

He was not long in making the discovery that infant baptism was without the vestige of a divine warrant; that wherever baptism was enjoined, it was a personal, and not a relative duty; that it was a matter that no more admitted of a proxy than faith, repentance, or any other act of obedience; and as he had rendered no service, obeyed no command, when he had been made the subject of that ordinance as taught

230

and practiced by the Presbyterians, he had not obeyed the command "be baptized" 1874:38; Hayden 1875:62-63).

But how was he to obey the command? He exercised his knowledge of Greek, examining the New Testament, and he discovered that sprinkling and pouring were substitutions which satisfied neither going down into or coming up out of the water described with the ordinance in Scripture. Mr. Scott also noted that the modes referred to failed to agree with Scripture where baptism was called a burial. Consequently, in harmony with his convictions, he was immersed by his employer and then united with the congregation brought together by the labors of Mr. Forrester. He was a valuable addition to the tiny fellowship.

Begins Preaching

Awareness of what the Gospel had done for him filled him with an urge to bring others to the truth he had discovered. A great part of his time was devoted to instructing all who would heed. Often his efforts were crowned with success (1875:63).

The small fellowship of believers were growing in the faith under his and Forrester's teaching. He found among them a nearness to the purity of the New Testament church which he had never believed possible on earth.

A change in Mr. Forrester's plans made it necessary for him to step out of this position in the school, and Mr. Scott was given his place (Stevenson 1946:26). Scott's relationship with Mr. Forrester continued. With him he would walk to worship and then sit at his feet as he expounded God's Word, but a heartbreaking end came to their association. George Forrester was drowned in the Allegheny River. Scott lost a beloved friend. The congregation lost its faithful pastor.

New responsibilities were now thrust upon Walter Scott. He would care for the widow and her children, and he would, the best he knew how, minister to the saddened church.

At this time the tract mentioned above in connection with George Forrester, came to the hands of Mr. Scott, published by a small church in New York City. The pamphlet did much to determine the course he would pursue in the future (*The Evangelist*, Dec. 1838:286). The New York congregation was made up primarily of Scotch Baptists who followed the views of Robert and James Haldane.

The pamphlet was published in 1820 and its purpose was to express the beliefs the church adhered to. It was Scott's decision to visit the church responsible for the document. He brought his school to a close and set out for the east, convinced that his studies there would add to his Christian knowledge and further his desire to proclaim the truths he had discovered.

The New York visit was a disappointment. He was led to expect, from the tract, that the church was far advanced from that which he found, and after three months he thought of return to Pittsburgh.

Mr. Scott's absence from Pittsburgh was painfully felt. A Mr. Richardson, father of Robert Richardson, one of Scott's best loved students, forwarded a proposal for the young teacher to come back to Pittsburgh. The invitation met with approval, and he returned, walking a second time from New York, but this time by way of Baltimore and Washington City. Back in Pittsburgh he made his home with the Richardson family (Richardson 1868: Vol I, 504-506).

His Development as a Teacher

His return to Pittsburgh gave cause for rejoicing not only to the school but also to the tiny congregation. Each member of the church was a student of the Word. So anxious were they to obey every admonition that when they read, "Salute one another with an holy kiss," they made it a matter of practice with the result that their community became known as "the kissing Baptists" (1868:Vol. II,129).

After Mr. Scott's return from New York City in 1821, his thoughts were possessed by what became the great passion of his life;

> namely, that the great central idea of Christian religion is the Messiahship; that Jesus is the Christ, the son of the living God; a proposition around which, in his esteem, all other truths revolve as the planets around the sun (Baxter 1874:60).

In his biblical studies he obtained encouragement from books he found in the library of Mr. Forrester. Among them were the works of the Haldane brothers, with those of John Glas and Robert Sandeman. His delight, however, was in the Word, a portion of which he memorized every day (Richardson 1868:Vol. I,507).

His reputation as a teacher spread throughout Pittsburgh and with that, pressure that he should enlarge the school. The decision made, the number of his pupils grew from fifteen to one hundred and forty. Only one difference arose between him and the parents of his pupils. He insisted that the New Testament be read each day; they, predominantly Presbyterian, insisted rather that the Westminster Catechism be taught. This Mr. Scott refused to do, stating

> . . . that he was thoroughly convinced that in regard to Christianity it was his duty to teach it, not as found in

233

creeds and party standards, but just as it was written (Baxter, 1874:63).

Agreement not possible, a compromise was made. The catechisms were laid aside and a chapter of Scripture was read each week. Mr. Scott determined to make the most of this. He resolved that each lesson should be taken from one of the four gospels and that Christ should be the theme of each study. He wanted the great truth that "Jesus is the Christ" to be kept before his students.

Scott Meets Alexander Campbell

Walter Scott met Alexander Campbell in Pittsburgh in the winter of 1821-1822 (Hayden 1875:63). Scott was twenty-five. Campbell was thirty-three (Murch 1962:99). Robert Richardson, as closely associated and fully acquainted with both men as any other person, said of Scott and Campbell

> They conceived for each other, therefore, at once, the warmest personal esteem — an esteem which was based perhaps less on those points in their respective characters in which they agreed than upon those in which they differed. For although their mutual reverence for Divine things, their earnest desire for religious reformation, their zeal and their piety, their devotion, their Christian faith and love, certainly united them strongly to each other, these were qualities possessed also by others, and constituting with them all in common the bond of fellowship and union. But the different hues in the characters of these two eminent men were such as to be, so to speak, complimentary to each other, and to form, by their harmonious blending, a completeness and brilliance which rendered their society peculiarly delightful to each other (Richardson 1868:Vol. I,510).

Walter Scott was married in 1823. He was twenty-six years of age. In that same year Alexander Campbell began his first publication which through its history became justifiably famous. *The Christian Baptist's* (Hayden 1875: 63-64) first issue came off the presses in August, 1823 (Richardson 1868:Vol. II,49-50).

Campbell was convinced when he met Walter Scott that Scott was a most unusual man. At Campbell's invitation, one of the articles in the first issue of *The Christian Baptist* was prepared by Scott (*The Christian Baptist* 1823:11).

This new publication gained a large reading audience and created a climate of discussion not often surpassed. Scott continued his writing, and coupled with the powerful articles from Alexander Campbell and his father, succeeded in establishing a fruitful atmosphere for searching the Scriptures.

The Christian Baptist was circulated in communities of western Pennsylvania, Virginia, and eastern Ohio. Wherever read, there was a reexamination of foundations for faith and practice, and the consequences for many who had viewed religion as something incomprehensible, was that, as set forth in the Word of God, it was harmoniously beautiful.

Moves to Steubenville, Ohio

In 1826 Scott with his family moved to Steubenville, Ohio, where he opened an academy (Richardson 1868:Vol. II,128: Hayden 1875:55). In Steubenville, he found three congregations, each adhering to beliefs similar to his own. One was of the Haldane persuasion and was known as the Church of Christ. The second, following the leadership of Barton Warren Stone, was associated with similar churches in Kentucky. It called itself the Christian Church. The third, related to the Mahoning Baptist Association of northeastern Ohio (the Western Reserve) was organized in 1820 and was affiliated with the Campbell movement. To restore original Christianity was the objective of all three congregations (Murch 1962:100).

In 1832 Mr. Scott described the situation as it was in 1827.

> There are three parties struggling to restore original Christianity: the first of them calling themselves "the Churches of Christ"; the second calling themselves "Christians"; and the third lying at that time chiefly in the bosom of the regular Baptist Churches and originating with the writings and labors of Brother A. Campbell. To the first of these parties up to 1826, belonged your humble servant, W. S. (*The Evangelist*, April 1832:94).

The group to which Walter Scott belonged consisted of churches motivated to restore New Testament Christianity as enunciated by Robert and James Alexander Haldane, John Glas and Robert Sandeman. These independent churches were found both in Britain and America. The "Christian" Church as Scott had seen it in Ohio and heard of it in Kentucky and elsewhere was the Barton Warren Stone movement (See Hayden 1875:57), and the third, lying nervously "in the bosom of the regular Baptist Churches" was the Campbell movement (Garrison and DeGroot 1948:185).

Called to be Evangelist of the Mahoning Baptist Association

The Mahoning Baptist Association annual meeting for 1826 was attended by Walter Scott. He was asked to participate as a "teaching brother" and preached the morning sermon on the eleventh chapter of Matthew, leaving a profound impression on all present. Alexander Campbell was impressed by the eloquence of his presentation and the quality of his address (Murch 1962:100).

The association for 1827 was to meet at New Lisbon, Ohio, on the 23rd of August. Alexander Campbell, on his way, passed through Steubenville and after some urging, persuaded Walter Scott to attend with him. As was the practice in the association, Mr. Scott, though not a member, was invited to take a seat in the association and share as a participant (Richardson 1868:Vol. II,173).

The first item of business on the morning of August 24 was the consideration of a request put forward by the church at Braceville, Ohio.

> We wish that the Association may take into serious consideration the peculiar situation of the churches of this association, and if it would be a possible thing for an evangelical preacher to be employed to travel and to teach among the churches, we think that a blessing would follow (1868: Vol. II,174: Hayden 1875:57).

Walter Scott was only a visiting "teaching brother." He was not a member of the association nor was he affiliated with a church a part of the association. It was with reluctance that he had even attended the 1827 assembly. It is significant that other preachers also present, invited as was Scott to participate, were of the "Christian party," meaning that there were at least three religious parties present, all seeking to restore what Mr. Scott called "The Ancient Gospel."

It was voted,

> . . . that all the teachers of Christianity present be a committee to nominate a person to travel and labor among the

churches, and to suggest a plan for the support of the person so employed (Richardson 1868:Vol. II,174).

Unanimously the committee recommended

. . . that Brother Walter Scott is a suitable person for the task, and that he is willing, provided the association concur in his appointment, to devote his whole energies to the work. 2. That voluntary and liberal contributions be recommended to the churches, to raise funds for his support. 3. That at the discretion of Brother Scott, as far as respects time and place, four quarterly meetings be held in the bound of the association this year for public worship and edification, and that at these meetings such contributions as have been made in the churches in these vicinities to be handed over to Brother Scott, and an account be kept of the same, to be produced at the next association. Also that at any time and at any church where Brother Scott may be laboring, any contributions made to him shall be accounted for in the next association (1868:Vol. II,174-176; Hayden 1875:57-58.

Scott, in 1832, wrote of how he was appointed a preacher or evangelist of the *Mahoning Baptist Association.*

I never made one objection to the nomination, nor to the appointment but saw in it a providence, I believed no mortal then understood but myself. I immediately cut all other connections, abandoned my projected editorship, dissolved my academy; left my church, left my family, dropped the bitterest tear over my infant household that ever escaped from my eyes, and set out under the simple conduct of Jesus Christ, to make an experiment of what is now styled the Ancient Gospel.

I had consulted no mortal on the topic of the Ancient Gospel, the very phrase was unknown, except in a single piece, which was dropped from my own pen about two or three months before. I was prompted to it by no man nor set of men, nor did I get it from men, but from the book of God, and that too by a course of reading, meditation and prayers to God, which he alone knows, and to him alone the practice is due. My essays on the one fact required to be carried out and the matter of them reduced to practice (*The Evangelist*, April 1832:94).

The 1827 meeting was significant, and none present could have foreseen its consequences. The request of the Braceville Church was not anticipated; the course of the conclave in appointing an itinerant evangelist; the unplanned presence of Walter Scott; his consent to give himself to the work; the welcome presence and cooperation of the religious body known as "Christian" who were bringing many converts to the Lord, — all these combined were circumstances that only God could have designed for the fulfillment of a great purpose. Scott saw in it "a providence" that he believed no mortal then understood but himself.

Alexander Campbell was delighted. That one such as Walter Scott, in whom he had such confidence, whom he believed was so eminently qualified to further the reformation, should agree to give himself to the cause, was beyond that which few would have anticipated.

For his part, Scott resolutely overcame his timidity, and disassociating himself from past entanglements, gave himself completely to his new calling. Soon he began to exercise those talents which Alexander Campbell had already observed.

In 1827, the *Mahoning Baptist Association* of eastern Ohio consisted of seventeen churches, one of them, Wellsburg in (West) Virginia. The annual report was depressing. Total baptisms for the year were thirty-four, but thirteen had been excommunicated. The net gain was sixteen. The record for the year earlier was worse with only eighteen baptized (Baxter 1874:89), and this at a time when the population was doubling and redoubling. The churches were not growing. Though the emphasis was upon restoring the Church revealed in the Scriptures, this was not sufficient. Concepts and truths focusing on the Reformation were constantly debated, but there was no growth (Stevenson 1946:53; Garrison and DeGroot 1948:186-187).

The Important Prayer Factor

One factor not to be overlooked has to do with the place of prayer in the events above and those which were to follow.

There were fifteen preachers present at the New Lisbon meeting, twelve of whom served on the committee that chose Walter Scott as evangelist. On the committee were Adamson Bentley, Joab Gaskill, Jacob Osborne, A. Campbell, Abijah Sturdevant, Walter Scott, Samuel Holmes, William West, Sidney Rigdon, J. Merrill, John Secrest, and Joseph Gaston. Besides these men, there were present also Darwin Atwater, Zeb Rudolph and John Jackman, who also were to become prominent teachers of the Gospel.

These brethren were committed in their objectives. An extract from the minutes of the New Lisbon meeting gives much insight: "Met Lord's Day at sunrise, in the Baptist meeting house for prayer and praise and continued till eight o'clock" (Hayden 1875:58).

For more than three hours they directed their petitions to the Mercy Seat while their praises were lifted to God. Great events in the Kingdom often result from great prayer. Developments to follow confirm that this was no exception.

240

From the beginnings of Walter Scott's labors the Reformation gained momentum. Granted a field offering freedom for his religious convictions, where his mind and genius had room for development, Scott thrust himself into the work. He was in the prime of his life, not yet thirty-one years of age. Academically he was well qualified. He was educated at the University of Edinburgh but had added to his literary qualifications by a devotion to his studies through ten years of his teaching career before he was called to be an evangelist. Beyond this he had acquired an accurate knowledge of the Holy Scriptures, combining this with religious experience. His memory was fortified with God's Word, and his faith and love were affectionately attached to the Lord Jesus Christ who was central in his thoughts. He had a fine singing voice, a pleasing manner, and a storehouse of classical and sacred imagery. He was qualified to be an evangelist.

The circumstances into which he entered were filled with promise. The churches of the Mahoning Baptist Association were prepared to receive the teaching from the New Testament.

There had been a growing sense of inquiry with things spiritual, and growing numbers of people were involved in searching the Scriptures. There was an attitude that extended beyond the Baptist Churches into other churches of the area, that made people favorable to religious investigation. Other religious communities also had been laboring to wear down sectarian strength and to put the Word of God, again, in its proper place. One of the more prominent, in a number of ways, was very similar to the Reformation encouraged by Mr. Campbell, and under the support of a number of capable preachers was enjoying

241

significant progress in Ohio. Two of these preachers of the "Christians" attended the recent meeting of the Mahoning Baptist Association and actively participated in the appointment of Walter Scott (Richardson 1868:Vol. II,183).

The Growth of the Churches

From the start of Scott's labors on the Western Reserve, the Reformation gained momentum. It was at New Lisbon in Columbiana County, Ohio, where, earlier he had been chosen as an evangelist. This became the center of his initial presentation of the Gospel first proclaimed in apostolic times (Baxter 1874:103).

His preaching made history. When he arrived at the Baptist chapel in New Lisbon, every seat was filled. Standing room was taken and the doorway was blocked by people eager to hear. His text was "Thou art the Christ, the son of the living God," Peter's good confession found in Matthew 16:16, and Scott was on familiar ground. Years before at Pittsburgh it had been his resolve to proclaim this truth as the creed of the Church. The four Gospels were written to establish this fact; it was this truth to which prophecy had pointed in ages past; this was God's affirmation from heaven following Jesus' baptism in Jordan and the descending of the Spirit upon him, and which was restated again amid the grandeur of the transfiguration (1874:104).

The evangelist showed that the deity of Christ is the truth of the Christian faith and that belief in Jesus Christ was essential to salvation. This belief would bring forth such love in the believer's heart that he would willingly obey all things necessary to the acceptance of Christ as

Redeemer and King. He then revealed that this same Peter was the first to proclaim the conditions of forgiveness and pardon under this new dispensation of mercy and grace.

> It is said that as Scott spoke, he was gripped with the idea that if what he was saying was true, the Spirit-guided answer of Peter to the cry of the people, "What must we do?" was the only answer that any minister of Christ has a right to give to the same question now. With great boldness of spirit, Scott thereupon concluded his discourse with these words, "Repent and be baptized, everyone of you in the name of Jesus Christ, for the remission of sins, and ye shall receive the gift of the Holy Ghost" (1874:105; Murch 1962:101).*

In the city lived William Amend, a God-fearing Presbyterian, who, in his study of the Word of God, had drawn the same conclusions as Mr. Scott. Amend arrived at the service late, as it was being concluded, but when he heard the conditions of pardon in words of Scripture, he made his way forward before the crowded congregation, affirmed his faith in the Lord Christ and declared his intention to obey him in the way of the thousands on Pentecost.

> On the same day, in the beautiful stream at the edge of Lisbon, Amend was buried with his Lord in Christian baptism and rose to walk in newness of life. The city was stirred to its depths. The meeting became the talk of the market place and the point of discussion in every home. Scott used the divine formula with great effectiveness in his evangelistic ministry. He often referred to the date, November 18, 1827, as the time when the ordinance of Christian baptism was

---

*Walter Scott's experience in 1827, in reference to Acts 2:37-38 needs to be compared with Barton Warren Stone's use of the same text as noted in Rogers 1847:61 and in Richardson 1868:Vol. II,197-198.

for the first time in modern history received in perfect accordance with apostolic teaching and practice (Murch 1962:101; Baxter 1874:108).

Scott was perplexed at Amend's simple confession and his desire to be baptized, so much so that as he reflected upon it, he wrote a letter to Mr. Amend requesting that he explain the motives that led him to offer himself. Amend answered in the following fashion.

In order to show these things aright, I must go back a piece. I was at that time a member of that strait sect called Presbyterians, taught many curious things, as elections, foreordination, etc., that belief in these things was necessary; that this faith resulted from some sacred impulse; and worse, that I could not believe; and finally, that I must hope and pray that God would have mercy upon me. In this wilderness I became wearied, turned about and came home to the book of God, took it up as if it had dropped from heaven, and read it for myself for just one year.

This enquiry led me to see that God so loved the world as to give his only begotten Son, that whosoever believed on him might not perish but have eternal life. I then inquired how I must believe. Paul said, "Faith cometh by hearing and hearing by the Word of God." Also that faith was "The substance of things hoped for, the evidence of things not seen." Peter spoke of election, saying, "Save yourselves." Paul said, "I must be dead to sin and be buried and raised with Jesus Christ to newness of life." The Savior said, I "must be born again if I would enter into the kingdom of God."

Now, here it was I discovered myself to stand in the garden of nature and not in the kingdom of heaven, but I learned that of this kingdom Peter received the keys and I was anxious to see what he would do with them. Jesus said, "Proclaim the gospel to all nations; he that believeth and is baptized shall be saved," etc. I then moved a little forward till I found these words, "And they were all pricked to the heart, and said to Peter and to the other apostles, "Men and brethren, what shall we do?" Peter said, "Repent and be baptized every one of you, in the name of Jesus Christ, for the remission of sins," etc. To this Scripture I often resorted; I saw how Peter had opened the kingdom and the door into it, but to my great disappointment I saw no man to introduce me, though I prayed often for it.

Now, my brother, I will answer your questions. I was baptized on the 18th of November, 1827, and will relate to you a circumstance which occurred a few days before that date. I had read the second chapter of Acts, when I expressed myself to my wife as follows: "Oh, this is the gospel; this is the thing we wish — the remission of our sins!" Oh that I could hear the gospel in these same words as Peter preached it! I hope I shall some day hear it, and the first man I meet who will preach the gospel thus, with him will I go. So, my brother, on the day you saw me come into the meeting-house my heart was open to receive the Word of God, and when you cried, "The Scripture shall no longer be a sealed book. God means what he says. Is there any man present who will take God at his word and be baptized for the remission of sins?" — at that moment my feelings were such that I could have cried out, "Glory to God! I have found the man whom I have long sought for." So I entered the kingdom when I readily laid hold of the hope set before me. William Amend (Richardson 1868: Vol.II,213-214; Baxter 1874:112-113).

This practical restoration of that portion of the gospel answering the question, "What must I do to be saved," was not only the result of the prayerful studies of the evangelist. Walter Scott had been prepared providentially, and had been provided with the stamina to proclaim the redemptive word, but that his hearers might accept it was of equal importance, and here "the excellency of the power" must not be credited to any man but to God. In the example of Mr. Amend, the good seed of God's kingdom fell upon fertile soil that only God had prepared.

In *The Christian Messenger* (1828:261) is recorded a letter from Elder J. E. Church, New Lisbon, Ohio, dated July 26, 1828.

> With Elder Walter Scott I fell in company a few days ago, at Fairfield, Ohio. He has made an unusual number of disciples the past year. His method and manner are somewhat novel to me; but in consequence of his extraordinary success in reforming mankind, I feel no disposition at present to pronounce him heretical. He seems to suppose the Apostolic gospel to consist of the five following particulars, viz.: faith, repentance, baptism for the remission of his sins, the gift of the Holy Ghost, and eternal life. Thus you see he baptizes the subject previous to the remission of his sins, or the receiving of the Holy Spirit . . . Brother Scott informed me that in almost every instance, his plan has produced the most salutary effects. He has baptized several hundred of late. I am now with him at his house, in this village, and expect to tarry with him a few days. He was appointed last year by the Mahoning Association of Baptists to travel, and the development of those peculiar principles of his grew out of that appointment. His general principles correspond very nearly with those which are peculiar to the Christians.

From page 262, the editor of *The Christian Messenger* answered Brother Church's letter.

> We have for some time since practiced in this way throughout our country. Many of the most successful Baptists pursue

the same course. I have no doubt that it will become the universal practice, though vehemently opposed.

Years later Mr. Scott wrote of his experience with Mr. Amend giving the circumstance which accompanied "the ordinance of baptism to its primitive place."

The republication of the gospel in the style and terms of the apostles was attended with so extraordinary an excitement as to cause us to forget and sometimes overlook matters and things, which, on common occasions, would have been accounted very singular . . . After vexations not to be mentioned, it was resolved to make a draft upon the audience, that it might be known why the preacher spoke and wherefore they came to hear. Accordingly, bursting away from prejudices and feelings almost as strong as death, and thinking of nothing but the restoration of the Gospel, it was proposed to ascertain immediately who would obey God and who would not. The confusion of all, the preacher not excepted, was indescribable. A person whom I had seen come into the meeting house about fifteen minutes before the end of the discourse came forward. This, as often as I thought about it, had always appeared to me wholly unaccountable, for it was most certain the man could not have been converted to Christianity by anything which he heard during the few minutes he was present. His letter [as recorded above] explains the matter, and will enable you, sir, to judge whether this whole business, as well on the side of the hearer as on the side of the preacher, is not resolvable into the good providence of our heavenly father, to whom be glory through Jesus Christ (Baxter 1874:111-112).

Walter Scott spent several months in evangelizing in the Steubenville area before moving to Canfield. He believed he must be centrally located among the Mahoning Baptists.

Warren, Ohio, was the strongest church. Its minister, close friend of Thomas and Alexander Campbell, was Adamson Bentley. He was suspicious of the kind of evangelism of Scott and closed the doors of his church against him. After a day's consideration, however, he agreed that the evangelist should use the church building. A series of meetings ensued stirring the community with many obedient to the faith (1874:131).

One baptized at Warren was a devout Presbyterian. Clinging to the faith of his fathers before him, he was a man of powerful physique and will. Mr. Tate's wife, having heard Scott's preaching, was determined to confess Christ as her Lord and be baptized. Not only did Tate oppose her decision; he threatened bodily harm to the preacher if he should immerse her. Mr. Scott assured Mr. Tate that if it was his wife's desire to be baptized, he would baptize her, regardless of her husband's threats. Scott then opened the Scriptures and reasoned with Mr. Tate on the subject, and as the evangelist's revealing of the word continued, the agitated man began to understand so that his behavior was transformed, and under deep conviction he asked Mr. Scott to baptize him also. His petition was given, and none were more pleased than Mr. and Mrs. Tate (1874:133-134).

Church after church embraced "the New Testament view" of conversion. The Mahoning River became a second Jordan where hundreds of believers were baptized by Walter Scott (Murch 1962:102).

Though Scott's first visit to Warren was short, the interest ignited continued to grow and to spread. The entire community was shaken. Neighboring towns were exposed to the contagion, and through the winter there continued

248

a growing interest in things spiritual resulting in growth never known in that district before. Many were added at Warren. New converts often had to give defense for the faith recently confessed, and they "fully proved their ability to do so" (Baxter 1874:135).

Rumors reached Alexander Campbell that Scott was advocating a new heresy and Campbell, already apprehensive of Scott's enthusiasm, feared that the evangelist had moved beyond the bounds of propriety. Alexander asked his father to visit the arena of Scott's victories to scrutinize this development personally. Thomas recounted to his son what he saw in the spring of 1828.

> I perceive that theory and practice in religion, as well as in other things, are matters of distinct consideration. It is one thing to know concerning the art of fishing — for instance, the rod, the line, the hook, and the bait, too, and quite another thing to handle them dextrously when thrown into the water, so as to make it take. We have long known the former (the theory), and have spoken and published many things correctly concerning the ancient gospel, its simplicity and perfect adaptation to the present state of mankind, for the benign and gracious purposes of his immediate relief and complete salvation; but I must confess that, in respect to the direct exhibition and application of it for the blessed purpose, I am at present for the first time upon the ground where the thing has appeared to be practically exhibited to the proper purpose. "Compel them to come in," saith the Lord, "that my house may be filled."
>
> Mr. Scott has made a bold push to accomplish this object, by simply and boldly stating the ancient Gospel, and insisting upon it: and then by putting the question generally and particularly to males and females, old and young. Will you come to Christ and be baptized for the remission of your

sins and the gift of the Holy Spirit? Don't you believe this blessed Gospel? Then come away. This elicits a personal conversation, some confess faith in the testimony beg time to think; others consent, give their hands to be baptized as soon as convenient; others debate the matter friendly; some go straight to the water, be it day or night, and upon the whole, none appear offended (Richardson 1868:Vol. II, 219-220; Hayden 1875:148-149).*

From No Growth to Great Growth

Dr. J. Edwin Orr has written,

An Evangelical Awakening is a movement of the Holy Spirit in the Church of Christ bringing about a revival of New Testament Christianity. Such an awakening may, of course, change in a significant way an individual only: or it may affect a larger group of people; or it may move a congregation, or the churches of a city, or a district, or the whole body of believers throughout a country or continent; or indeed the larger body of believers throughout the world.

Again Dr. Orr has said,

The surest evidence of the Divine origin of any such quickening is its presentation of the evangelical message declared in the New Testament and its reenactment of the phenomena evident in the same sacred literature (1970:3).

---

* The author has before him seven histories of The Restoration Movement. All recount in precise detail Alexander Campbell's fears, his father's careful investigation, as he visited New Lisbon, Fairfield, Warren, Braceville, Wingham, Mantua, Mentor and other towns where Scott had been preaching, and the above report written on April 9, 1828. See Davis 1915:95; Dowling 1964:60-61; Garrison and DeGroot 1948:188-189; Stevenson 1946:92-93; Baxter 1874:158-159; Hayden 1875:148-149; Richardson 1868:Vol. II,219-220; Murch 1962:102. There are others.

Never in the history of the Restoration Movement have the definition and divine origin of any evangelical awakening been so exemplified as in the growth of the Churches in northeastern Ohio under the preaching of Walter Scott.

Already noted, the Brush Run Church was organized on June 19, 1811, near West Middleton, Pennsylvania. This was the first church established by Thomas and Alexander Campbell. Its life was short.

As early as April, 1814, the congregation decided it must move because many in the vicinity were too widely scattered to "take membership in the Brush Run Church, which owing to removals, scarcely preserved its original number" (Richardson 1868:Vol. II,69). Several had already located in Wellsburg, Virginia. In latter 1823 Alexander Campbell requested letters of dismissal for himself and his family and others, about thirty in all from the Brush Run Church, that he might organize a congregation in Wellsburg. The petition was granted, and "the second church of the reformation" was at once constituted in the town (1868:Vol. II,69).

Richardson, in assessing the membership of churches in association with the Campbells says that at this time, "those who could be reckoned as actual advocates of the Reformation . . . amounted to not more than one hundred and fifty persons . . . (1868:Vol. II,486) with none capable of assuming leadership but the two Campbells. Until the formation of Wellsburg, Brush Run was the only church founded by the Campbells, father and son (1868:Vol. II,489).

Soon after September 7, 1827, remnants of the Brush Run congregation disbanded because of emigration, its few members "affiliating with the Washington church and new congregation near Buffalo (Bethany), Alexander Campbell's home" (1868:Vol. II,167; Murch 1962:78).

According to Richardson (1868:Vol. II,69), until the time when Walter Scott assumed responsibility as evangelist of the Mahoning Baptist Association in 1827, Thomas and Alexander Campbell had been responsible for planting two churches, the first of which was then disbanded. The Mahoning Baptist Association to which the Campbells belonged, consisted of only seventeen churches, and one of them was Wellsburg. For the combined years of 1826 and 1827 a total of only fifty-two baptisms had been reported with the number of excommunications, dismissals and deaths outnumbering the baptisms.

McAllister says the simple truth is,

> . . . that the movement to restore a church based on the New Testament did not take hold firmly until Walter Scott began preaching on the reserve and Barton W. Stone's Christian movement spread to Ohio. Without the impetus given by those movements, Thomas Campbell's great dream of a Christian Union on a biblical basis would have quickly been passed over on the rapidly growing frontier (McAllister 1954:198-199).

The Significant Revival Factor

The Haldanean movement in Scotland was a direct product of the early nineteenth century Evangelical Awakening in Scotland (Orr 1965:33-36). Through George Forrester, an irrefutable connection between Walter Scott and the Haldane movement was established.

That there were links between the revival through Walter Scott in the Mahoning Valley of Ohio and the Christian

252

movement in Kentucky through Barton Warren Stone is also undeniable. Through the Stone movement, there are relationships with the James O'Kelly, Elias Smith and Abner Jones movement already noted.

Many attributes of revival were to be found in the labors of evangelist Scott: his efforts beginning with concerted prayer, the thought that a long lost fortune beyond estimate was being rediscovered after having been hidden for centuries, that excitement at being able to participate in the birth of this new movement in the history of Christianity. These factors contributed to an awakening of phenomenal significance. Different was this from the frontier revivals of Kentucky and Tennessee of one generation earlier, out of which came the Barton Warren Stone movement or the "Christian Church." In eastern Ohio, there was a careful meeting of reason and authority, of man's capability to understand, and the inspired Scriptures. There were no frenzied exercises here, no uncontrolled emotions.

The reaction of the people was apparent at once, and it was staggering. In a short time the new sound was being echoed by other preachers of the association as well. Hundreds made the confession of faith and were baptized, and new churches came into existence.

The membership of the churches of the Mahoning Baptist Association more than doubled within the year.

Chapter Eleven

A MOVEMENT OF NATIONAL IMPORT

Background of the Campbell-Owen Debate

The following announcement appeared in *The Christian Baptist:*

> It will be remembered that Mr. Robert Owen, of New Harmony, Indiana, did, in the month of January last, challenge the clergy of New Orleans (as he had in effect the teachers of religion everywhere) to debate with him the truth of the Christian religion. In his public discourses, as well as in the words of that challenge, he engages to prove that "All the religions of the world have been founded on the ignorance of mankind; that they have been and are, the real sources of vice, disunion and misery of every description; that they are now the only bar to the formation of a society of virtue, of intelligence, of charity in its most extended sense and of sincerity and kindness among the whole human family; and that they can be no longer maintained except through the ignorance of the mass of the people, and the tyranny of the few over the mass. This challenge I had formally accepted, believing it to be my duty so to do in existing circumstances; and I stand pledged to prove, in a public discussion, that the above positions are every one intenable; that Mr. Owen cannot prove any one of them by any fair or legitimate process of reasoning whatsoever" (1829:469-470).

A flood of infidelity poured into the United States from Europe from the 1780's onward. Men from the Continent and Great Britain, eager to affect a change in human society, invaded America believing its freedom of religion, expression and movement and expanse of fertile lands afforded opportunities for their experimentation. Robert Owen, son-in-law of David Dale, owner of the New Lanark Mills in Scotland, who had done so much for the improvement and uplift of the working classes, had succeeded in directing public opinion to endorse cooperatve societies in several places. Following Owen's philosophy and "social system" principles, a number of communities were soon established. At Kendal, Ohio, New Harmony, Indiana, and other centers also, men were soon engaged in writing, publication and lecture, in promoting the advantages of these new communities. They were accompanied by considerable success.

The advocates and adherents of these societies attempted to eradicate all weight and force of religion. With Robert Owen, this was particularly true and all elements of a spiritual import were to be eliminated. At New Harmony, a community of size was functioning, formed on Owen's concepts of infidelity and communisn (Richardson 1868: Vol. II,233-234).

The United States had no state religion. Consequently, Mr. Owen believed that the states were open for his atheistic experiments. In 1824, he purchased 30,000 acres, incorporating the village of New Harmony, where in a short time several thousand people gathered. It appeared that Owen's social system was destined to match the noblest aspirations of its promoters. Robert Owen repudiated Christianity as "the opiate of the masses" and with skill advocated the principles of atheism.

Alexander Campbell watched these developments, and when he learned that they were bent on the elimination of religion, he responded by means of the written page. Five essays were published under the captions, "Robert Owen and the Social System" (*Christian Baptist* 1829:327-328), and "Deism and the Social System" (1829:343-345; 357-358; 364-366; 373-376).

In late 1827 and early 1828, a Dr. Underhill, proclaiming the philosophy of the New Harmony community, was in Canton, Ohio. In February a friend wrote to Mr. Campbell at Bethany, urging him to meet Underhill in a public debate. Campbell declined because Underhill, in contrast to Owen, was a novice, but he added, if Owen should participate in such a discussion he would be happy to meet him. Mr. Campbell believed the opportunity would come to confront Robert Owen, His intuition was correct.

Three weeks prior to the above, Robert Owen, giving a series of addresses in New Orleans, invited any clergyman who would accept, to debate with him the principles and assumptions of religion.

Alexander Campbell was informed of the challenge and that no one, so far, had responded to it. Immediately, from Bethany, Virginia, on April 25, 1828, he published his willingness to meet Mr. Owen (1829:443-444).

Mr. Owen, a gentleman of very respectable standing as a scholar and capitalist, of much apparent benevolence, travelling with the zeal of an apostle through Europe and America, disseminating the most poisonous sentiments as Christians conceive, finding myriads in waiting to drink, as the thirsty ox swalloweth water, whatever he has to offer against the Bible and the hope of immortality, passes unchecked and almost unheeded by myriads of advocates and teachers of the Christian religion . . .

Impelled by those considerations and others connected with them, we feel it our duty to propose as follows: Mr. Owen says in his challenge before us: "I propose to prove, as I have already attempted to do in my lectures, that all the religions of the world have been founded on the ignorance of mankind; that they are directly opposed to the never-changing laws of our nature; that they have been and are the real source of vice, disunion and misery of every description; that they are now the only bar to the formation of a society of virtue, of intelligence, of charity in its most extensive sense, and of sincerity and kindness among the whole human family, and that they can be no longer maintained except through the ignorance of the mass of the people and tyranny of the few over the mass."

Now, be it known to Mr. Owen, and to all whom it may concern, that I, relying on the Author, the reasonableness and the excellency of the Christian Religion, will engage to meet Mr. Owen any time within one year from this date . . . and will then and there undertake to show that Mr. Owen is utterly incompetent to prove the position he has assumed in a public debate . . . (Richardson 1868:Vol. II, 240-241).

Weeks later Robert Owen visited Mr. Campbell at Bethany. The two men developed a respect for each other, and arrangements were made for the debate to take place in Cincinnati, Ohio, beginning April 13, 1829.

Year of Evangelism in the Mahoning Association

Alexander Campbell's first wife passed away on October 22, 1827. Shortly after Robert Owen's departure from Bethany, Mr. Campbell married again, and he took his wife with him to the annual meeting of the Mahoning Baptist Association held at Warren, Ohio.

This was a meeting of unusual circumstance. Little had anyone anticipated the events that had taken place as a result of the appointment of Walter Scott as evangelist one year previously. Those present looked back with amazement, thanksgiving, and praise. Many believed that the means of presenting the Gospel as proclaimed in the apostolic era had been rediscovered and restored. They were convinced that the power was manifest with almost one thousand added to the church in a small area over the past twelve months. In addition, they had witnessed victories over sectarianism and unity among preachers and laymen of the denominational groups (1868:Vol. II,181-183).

The Campbell-Owen Debate

Interest in the Campbell-Owen debate spread across the nation. People concerned about the subject and knowing the reputation of the two principals, traveled from New York, Pennsylvania, Virginia, Tennessee, and Mississippi and other states to join the crowds. The debate was held in the largest Methodist church in Cincinnati. Accounts of the confrontation were carried in the city newspapers.

Robert Owen was the first speaker. He stated the reason for the debate and gave a review of his experiments on the Continent at which time he claimed to have found "important laws of our human nature" which he believed would abolish . . . "the countless evils which have been engendered by conflicting religions, by various forms of marriages and by unnecessary private property" and make way for ". . . real charity, pure chastity, sincere affections and upright dealing between man and man, producing abundance for all" (Owen-Campbell Debate 1912:2-3).

Mr. Campbell's opening address was the only one prepared prior to the debate. He began by apologizing for even presuming to ". . . bring into public discussion the evidences of Christian religion," fearing that by doing so he might ". . . appear to concede that it is yet an undecided question" which he was not prepared to admit.

Campbell then affirmed that he had consented to the confrontation, ". . . not with any expectation" that Mr. Owen ". . . was to be convinced of the errors of his system."

> But the public, the wavering, doubting, and unsettled public, who are endangered to be carried off, as an apostle says, by the flood which the dragon has poured out of his mouth, are those for whose benefit this discussion has, on my part, been undertaken. They are not beyond the reach of conviction, correction, and reformation (1912:6-7).

Mr. Campbell was ready to demonstrate that there was cause that rational people could request for genuine faith and wholesome acceptance of the Christian Religion. He then reviewed the first exertions of Christianity and its early triumphs and concluded by saying,

> It is not the ordinary affairs of this life, the fleeting and transitory concerns of today and tomorrow; it is not whether we shall live, all freemen, or die all slaves; . . . nay, indeed, all these are but the toys of childhood, the sportive excursions of youthful fancy, contrasted with the question, What is man? Whence came he? Whither does he go? Is he a mortal or immortal being? Is he doomed to spring up like the grass, bloom like a flower, drop his seed into the earth, and die forever? Is there no object or future hope? . . . These are the awful and sublime merits of the question at issue. It is not what shall we eat, nor what we shall drink, unless we shall be proved to be mere animals; but it is, shall we live or die forever? (1912:13).

At the beginning of his next speech, Mr. Owen began reading a two-hundred page manuscript, prepared for the occasion, and to this document he clung through the course of the discussion. From the manuscript he read twelve

259

statements (he called them facts) upon which he constructed his system for society by which he proposed to reform all of humanity (1912:16-17). These were his

> . . . divine moral code — a code abundantly sufficient to produce in practice, all virtue in the individual and in society sufficient to enable man, through a correct knowledge thereof, to "work out his own salvation" from sin or ignorance and misery, and to secure the happiness of his whole race (1912:17-18).

Upon these facts Mr. Owen anchored himself, and no amount of urging from Mr. Campbell or the moderators would move him.

Mr. Owen attempted to establish that religions of every sort were the consequence of man's fear and ignorance. He contended that all religions are in opposition to immutable natural precepts, twelve in number, which Owen himself had formulated. Religions were the fount for vice, conflict and the suffering of man, standing in opposition to the creation of a social order embracing moral excellence, wisdom and goodwill. He contended that only by the control of an unprincipled minority over the masses was religion maintained (*Christian Baptist* 1829:551-554).

Mr. Campbell had to assume the responsibility of defending Christianity and of enunciating the principles of a religious view of the world (Garrison and DeGroot 1948:198).

It was suggested to Mr. Owen by the board that

> all the arguments which he might be about to introduce in support of any one of his positions might have exclusive relevance, and pertinence, and logical conviction with that single position. The Board thought that Mr. Owen

260

was, logicly, bound to exhibit the logical connection and dependence between his proofs and positions (*Owen-Campbell Debate* 1912:28).

To bring Mr. Owen into actual confrontation, Mr. Campbell agreed to the twelve statements "with the exception of the assertion that 'the will has no power over belief,'" and he proceeded to show that these facts alluded only to the animal nature of man, that they were incomplete and provided a dangerous basis for such a system because they ignored man's mutual and moral attributes.

Neither to Campbell's affirmations nor to his refutation of Owen's arguments did Owen pay any attention. Instead, he persisted in reading from his prepared manuscript his explanation of his twelve laws of nature.

Owen's twelve facts could apply to a dumb beast as easily as to a man (1912:46). Any theory was in contradiction to logic and experience, when postulated on a part of man. Campbell contended that all of our conceptualizations were the consequence of stimulation of our senses and our contemplation of those ideas (1912:47). Campbell then asked how a man could conceive any concept, the original pattern or model of which was not revealed in nature. Man believed in a God creating out of nothing, in an incorporeal spirit, in a great first cause, and in life after death. On the basis of Owen's twelve facts, Campbell questions, how could a man acquire these thoughts? Mr. Owen's answer was, "By his imagination."

To Mr. Campbell's arguments, Robert Owen would offer no response except to cling tenaciously to the "gems in his casket."

It soon became evident, indeed, that Mr. Owen could not reason, that he had no just perception of the relation between

261

proposition and proof, and that it was vain to expect from him any logical discussion of the points at issue (Richardson 1868:Vol. II,274).

Owen completed reading his manuscript on Friday, the 17th. Immediately he granted Mr. Campbell the privilege of speaking without interruption until he had completed his argument (Campbell-Owen Debate 1912:278).

Mr. Campbell, having begun his defense of Christianity when Mr. Owen gave way, continued, altogether for twelve hours, revealing his thoughts regarding the purpose, content and defense of Christianity. In this presentation he amazed Mr. Owen and other doubters by distinguishing pure Christianity from the controversial incongruities that had caused so much unbelief in his day and which were the cause of Owen's infidelity. He examined the misleading bases on which systems of unbelief were built and showed that there was no way of building a reformed society on those faulty concepts. Finally, he portrayed the magnitude, the power and the applicability of the Good News everywhere in all possible situations in every culture.

By request, Mr. Campbell preached on Sunday to an overflow audience in the Methodist Church where the debate was held. His twelve hour address was concluded on Monday evening. To this Mr. Owen responded by lauding Mr. Campbell's knowledge, ability, manliness, honesty and fairness, and then filled his time with an obscure harangue against religion, reviewed again the twelve facts upon which his social system would be constructed and described the consequences to follow.

The debate concluded on the evening of April 21 and Mr. Campbell had the closing remarks. He employed an unusual way of determining the reaction of the audience to what it had heard. First, he praised the people in attendance for their conduct throughout the long discussion. He then said:

> Now I must tell you that a problem will arise in the minds of those living five hundred or a thousand miles distance, who may read this discussion, whether it was owing to a perfect apathy or indifference on your part, as to any interest you felt in the Christian religion, that you bore all these insults without seeming to hear them. In fine, the question will be, whether it was owing to the stoical indifferences of fatalism, to the prevalence of infidelity; or to the meekness and forebearance which Christianity teaches, that you bore all these indignities without a single expression of disgust. Now I desire no more than that this good and Christian-like deportment may be credited to the proper account. If it be owing to your concurrence in sentiment with Mr. Owen, let skepticism have the honor of it. But if owing to your belief in Christ, or regard for the Christian religion, let the Christian religion have the honor of it. These things premised, my propositon that all the persons in this assembly who believe in the Christian religion or who feel so much interest in it, as to wish to see it pervade the world, will please to signify it by standing up. (An almost universal rising up.)

Here Mr. Campbell says, You will have the goodness to be seated.

> Now I would further propose, that all persons doubtful of the truth of the Christian religion, or who do not believe it, and who are not friendly to its spread and prevalence over the world, will please signify by rising up. (Three arise.) (1912:503-504).

All parties following the debate felt a debt of gratitude to Mr. Campbell. Several well-known people confessed their faith in Jesus Christ and were baptized. Converted

263

college men travelled by foot and horse and saddle preaching throughout the country, and several churches were planted. Soon published, the debate had tremendous circulation and was read wherever English was spoken (Richardson 1868:Vol. II,283-284).

Baptists and Reformers Separate

That the separation of the Baptists and Reformers (Restorationists) took place precisely in 1830 would be difficult to prove. The separation was a progressive thing that developed over several years. Tensions began between Alexander Campell and the Redstone Association of southwestern Pennsylvania as early as the founding of the Wellsburg, Virginia, Baptist church in 1816 and the Sermon on the Law, preached in August of the same year.

Charges of heresy were brought against Mr. Campbell each year following his Sermon on the Law, by a minority group of the Redstone Association, and for years the charges failed to convict for lack of votes.

In 1823, with thirty members of the Brush Run Church, Mr. Campbell transferred to Wellsburg, Virginia.* He was no longer under the Redstone Baptist Association. In 1824 the Wellsburg Church was received into the membership of the Mahoning Association of Northeastern Ohio (1868: Vol. II,100).

The act of separaton within the Redstone Association, consisting of twenty-three or twenty-four churches, took place in 1827. Thirteen churches were voted out and immediately formed the Washington (Pennsylvania) Association embracing the views of Mr. Campbell (1868:Vol. II,165).**

---

* A new church of the Reformation was promptly organized and joined the Mahoning Association (Garrison and DeGroot, 1948:171).

** There is, however, a discrepancy between Richardson and the minutes of the Redstone Association for 1827.

A minority from the Youngstown, Palmyra, and Salem churches of the Mahoning Association, refusing the teachings of the Restoration Movement, formed an association on Beaver Creek in Pennsylvania. With the assistance of two or three preachers, they began to circulate attacks against the Mahoning Association and Mr. Campbell, accusing them of "disbelieving and denying many of the doctrines of the Holy Scripture" (1868:Vol. II,322-323).

Alexander Campbell wrote to Walter Scott asking about the state of four of the churches, Youngstown, Palmyra, Salem, and Achor. Scott answered Mr. Campbell's queries on April 9, 1830.

> Youngstown Church. — About eight or nine years ago, there was a revival within the bounds of the church; the acting minister was Brother Woodsworth, a regular Baptist. There was a great stir, and many were baptized in the name of our Lord Jesus Christ. Mr. West . . . was elected minister . . . to the resisting and dismissal of Brother Woodsworth, the successful laborer . . . The church declined from that day — conversions stopped, and after the lapse of some years, the meeting was embroiled in family quarrels.
>
> When I called about two years ago, I found the church in a state of entire prostration. For four years they had not eaten the Lord's Supper; all was delinquency . . . For about three weeks I strived to disentangle the sincere hearted, but in vain.
>
> I accordingly looked upon this institution to be entirely lost, and began to preach the ancient gospel . . . All hearts were immediately broken or burnt, and of that sinful people there have been immersed 250 individuals.

At this point it needs to be noted that in his circular letter for the Mahoning Association, in the year of 1829, Mr. Scott wrote,

The Gospel, since last year, has been preached with great success in Palmyra, Deerfield, Randolph, Shaltersville, Nelson, Hiram, etc., by Brothers Finch, Hubbard, Ferguson, Bosworth, Hayden and others. Several new churches have been formed (*Millennial Harbinger* 1830:35).

In Walter Scott's letter to Mr. Campbell, he writes of the church in Palmyra.

I went to Palmyra in company with Brother Hayden . . . Here, too, all was worse than decayed — twas ruin all . . . As at Youngstown, so here also, the church was filled with creeds, swellings, and personal and family quarrels.

We forthwith read the gospel . . . and exhorted to obedience, whereupon many believed and were baptized . . . We afterwards separated the young converts, and informed the old folks, that so many of them as choosed to embrace the new institution, would be admitted with all pleasure, and the church now included about one hundred names.

They break bread every day, having the Scriptures as their sole authority.

Achor Church. This used to be a flourishing church . . . I visited the church about two years ago, but found so much hate from their indecent behavior that I would not preach, and retired from their meeting house.

Salem Church. In no place did I ever experience such deceitful treatment as at Salem . . . The brethren received me with seeming courtesy, and I began to preach . . . Accordingly, I rushed upon the sinful people like an armed man — forty-one were immersed in ten days, and all seemed to rejoice with me in victory; but we had to wait until monthly meeting before we could propose the young converts for admission . . . Those who were secretly or openly opposed . . . had abundance of time . . . to keep out so many . . . as they thought unconverted . . . The meeting came along and none of them were admitted; yet they were many of them their own children, and nearly all of them related . . . At my return to Salem, I was requested to be absent for a little . . . and finally had word sent not to return.

Thus a people who would have cut their own eyes and given them to me, did all of a sudden turn around and separate me from their own relations and townsmen, whom under God, I had been the means of bringing back to the Lord and to righteousness. I never spoke to all the converts again. Signed, Walter Scott (*Christian Baptist* 1829:66-67).

Material of the Beaver Creek Association was widely circulated and republished in Baptist journals. The accusations were recorded in the minutes of the Franklin Association of Kentucky and endorsed by the Appomattox Association in Virginia.

The attacks were set forth in the following terms:
1. They, the Reformers, maintain that there is no promise of salvation without baptism;
2. That baptism should be administered to all who say they believe that Jesus Christ is the Son of God, without examination on any other point;
3. That there is no direct operation of the Holy Spirit on the mind prior to baptism.
4. That baptism procures the remission of sins and the gift of the Holy Spirit.
5. That the Scriptures are the only evidence of interest in Christ;
6. That obedience places it in God's power to elect to salvation;
7. That no creed is necessary for the Church but the Scriptures as they stand; and
8. That all baptized persons have the right to administer the Ordinance of Baptism (Williams 1904:268).

A similar attitude was reflected by the Long Run Association of Bullet County, Kentucky, where the resolution "the Scriptures of the New Testament were the all-sufficient rule of faith and manners," was looked upon with suspicion and finally rejected.

The consequence was to bring things to a head inciting the Baptists in many places to remove the Reformers from their midst (Torbet 1950:291).

By 1830, many within the Reformation were entertaining doubts as to the Scriptural authority of any association as the Redstone, Long Run, Washington or Mahoning. The action of the Redstone and the Beaver Associations in Pennsylvania, in the Long Run and Franklin Associations in Kentucky and the Appomattox Association in Virginia (1950:291) led the Reformers to question the authority for such structures. They observed what they believed were examples of arbitrary power, and they became apprehensive lest these weaknesses be inherent in every such association. There was no authority for them in the Scritpures, and numbers of the disciples viewed them as inconsistent with the principle they advocated. When the Mahoning Association convened at Austintown, Ohio, in 1830, in opposition to the judgment of Mr. Campbell, it resolved that the association, as "an advisory council" or an "ecclesiastical tribunal" should never meet again (Richardson 1868:Vol. II,328). From henceforth, there would continue a yearly meeting for worship, preaching the Gospel and hearing reports from the churches.

The Austintown meeting was occasion for joy, because of growth of the churches. More than thirty were baptized during the association meeting, and approximately one thousand additions had been reported through the previous year (1868:Vol. II,328).

By 1832 or 1833 the separation between the Baptists and the Reformers was complete. The most significant result was that the Reformation which for seventeen years had been a "movement" within the Baptist churches, now became an independent body of Restorationists free to associate with other movements with comparable purposes (Vedder 1897:248-251; Torbet 1950:291-292).

The Millennial Harbinger

Mr. Campbell had concluded, before his debate with Robert Owen, that he would not publish *The Christian Baptist* after July, 1830, and that he would begin a new journal in January, 1830, of larger size and having a different character. The new publication would reveal a more peaceable quality than *The Christian Baptist*. Mr. Campbell was persuaded that the movement he pled for, which advocated a return to the primitive Gospel to restore it in its fullness and perfection, must be the last effort to reach mankind for the final return of the Lord. Thus the name for the new publication, *The Millennial Harbinger*, expressed his conviction that the millennium, eagerly awaited by the Church, would soon come (Richardson 1868:Vol. II,302-303).

Mr. Campbell saw his new magazine as a harbinger of the millennium, and its objectives would be:

(a) To restore the faith, ordinances, organization, and terms of admission of the apostolic church; (b) to do this by resting directly upon the teachings of Scripture; (c) thus to come to what Thomas Campbell had called "simple evangelical Christianity"; and (d) to make this the basis of union (Garrison and DeGroot 1948:206-207).

The Reformers and Christians

An event of significance to both the Reformers under Alexander Campbell and the "Christians" under Barton Warren Stone was the union of the two movements, consumated in Lexington, Kentucky, in 1832(Sweet 1952: 223-224).

Alexander Campbell first traveled to Kentucky in October of 1823 to participate in debate with W. L. MacCalla. The debate, held in Washington and published shortly after, gave Mr. Campbell, with help from *The Christian Baptist*, which also began circulation in 1823, notoriety throughout the state.

In the spring of 1824, Campbell published an article in *The Christian Baptist* on the subject of "Experimental Religion" (*The Christian Baptist* 1824:48-50). Shortly thereafter he visited Kentucky a second time. The above article and other pieces he had written created interest and opposition to his coming (Williams 1904:129). On this tour he met Barton Warren Stone, Elder (Raccoon) John Smith and other preachers, both Christian and Reformer, who were to influence the course of events to come (Richardson 1868:Vol. II,108-112,118).

Mr. Stone writes of the appearances of Mr. Campbell in 1826 where he "caused great excitement on the subject of religion in Kentucky and other states" (Rogers 1847:75). Rumors preceded Campbell wherever he went. Some were persuaded he was a good man. Others said he was a deceiver. Barton Stone heard him often and purposefully became acquainted with him, and he was pleased with what he heard and with the manner in which it was presented.

> I saw no distinctive feature between the doctrine he preached and that which we had preached for many years, except on

270

baptism for remission of sins. Even this I had once received
and taught . . . but had strangely let it go from my mind,
till Brother Campbell received it afresh (1847:75-76).

It was Stone's opinion that Campbell was not specific on
the work of the Holy Spirit. Many of Stone's followers
were persuaded that he denied the influence of the Spirit
altogether and consequently, at the time of union, refused
to join with the Reformers.

Barton Warren Stone started publishing a monthly journal, *The Christian Messenger* in 1826. The union of Christians was the subject for consecutive articles in the first
issues of *The Messenger* and the theme was discussed again
and again.

Several preachers of the "Christian" movement were
present at the Mahoning Baptist Association meeting held
at New Lisbon, Ohio, in August of 1827 when Walter Scott
was chosen evangelist of the Association. These men,
attracted to Scott's way of preaching faith in Jesus Christ,
repentance from sin, and baptism for the remission of sins,
soon adopted Scott's methods (*Evangelist* 1832:94).

Often there were congregations of both Reformers and
"Christians" in the same towns, particularly in Ohio and
Kentucky, but also in Indiana and Tennessee. In Steuben-
ville, Ohio, in 1827, there were three such churches, "The
Church of Christ" of Haldanean influences, the "Christian"
Church of the Barton Warren Stone persuasion, and the
Reformers lying in the bosom of the Baptists, associated
with the Campbells (Richardson 1868:Vol. II,174).

With their views so nearly alike, it is not surprising that
union should be suggested, and it often was. There were
many likenesses, and there were some differences.

The likenesses were significant in their import:

(1) Both held the union of all Christians as one of their definite objectives.
(2) Both held that Christ alone was the object of faith, both rejected creeds as tests of fellowship, and insisted upon liberty of opinion in all matters of doctrine that were not unmistakably revealed.
(3) Rejecting the Calvinistic doctrine of a "limited atonement," they agreed that Christ died for all and that all who would might believe on him and be saved.
(4) With some reservations, they were agreed upon the nature of faith and the ability of sinful man to believe the evidence about Christ without personal assistance from the Holy Spirit (Garrison and DeGroot 1948:208-209).

Point number four caused some difficulty for Stone and the Christian Churches. Many were convinced that Mr. Campbell denied the influences of the Holy Spirit altogether, and for that reason refused to come into union with the Reformers. It is likely that Campbell and Stone never did agree fully upon this question. As Mr. Stone wrote, "in a few things I dissented from him, but was agreed to disagree" (Rogers 1847:76).

(5) The practice of believer's baptism by immersion and the idea of baptism as related to remission of sins were common to both (Garrison and DeGroot 1948:208-209).

But here, too, were rather strong differences of opinion. Mr. Stone made reference to them when in 1843 he wrote his own autobiography, recalling those differences back in 1826 (Rogers 1847:76). Immersion for the "Christians" was not a condition for membership in the church as it was with the Reformers. Though most of them had been immersed,

272

yet they considered it a matter of opinion, and Mr. Stone defended this position as late as 1830, and yet, in that same year he evidenced inconsistency in advocating immersion for the remission of sins and accepting individuals into the membership of the Church without it. "When asked for our divine authority from the New Testament," he wrote, "we have none that can fully satisfy our own minds" (*Christian Messenger*: 1830:200,275).

(6) Opposition to unscriptural and sectarian names for the Church was a pronounced characteristic of both groups (Garrison and DeGroot 1948:208-209).

Here, too, there were differences. Barton Warren Stone preferred the name "Christian" and with good reason. Alexander Campbell, Walter Scott in his earlier relationship with Campbell, and their associates, preferred the name "Disciple." In later years, however, Mr. Scott, with Mr. Stone, advocated the name "Christian" (Baxter 1874:388-390). The difference was not allowed to become a barrier to union.

During the early years, from the *Declaration and Address* in 1809 until 1827 when Walter Scott was chosen evangelist of the Mahoning Association of eastern Ohio, there was little growth and few churches were planted among the Reformers. This underscored the differences between the Christians and Reformers. The proclamation of the Good News among the latter embodied an easily understood message. To fulfill the stipulations upon which the Lord would forgive one's sins and grant the blessings to follow, one must believe on the Lord Jesus Christ, repent of his sins and be baptized. But there was no place for distress and suffering from the uncertainty as to whether one was one of the chosen, the

273

elect, the accepted of God. This, at first, was a matter of amazement and suspicion among the Christians. They were part of a movement that came out of revival. Theirs had been a Methodist type of evangelism and spoke of mourners coming to the mourner's bench, weeping and crying out to God for mercy (Garrison and DeGroot 1948:211).

The Holy Spirit was with Barton Warren Stone and the fast growing Christian movement that came out of revivals of an earlier period via Wesley, Whitefield, Asbury, O'Kelly, Caldwell, McGready, Stone and others. It was a movement blessed of God, for which contemporary churches ought to be thankful. It has much to say to the contemporary church as it seeks the guidance of the Holy Spirit for this day.

The same can be said for the Reformer side of the movement. It, too, developed through the Holy Spirit, though from a different stream of the revival, through Glas, Sandeman, Robert and James Haldane, Thomas and Alexander Campbell and Walter Scott. The movement of the Holy Spirit is plain to be seen, however, a fact about which the contemporary church and its leadership should give more attention.

One other difference existed between the Reformers and the Christians. With the Reformers the Lord's Supper was a weekly occurrence. The Christians observed it less frequently. Not until 1830 did Mr. Stone see that the church should "receive the Lord's Supper every first day of the week."

"Raccoon" John Smith, Extraordinary Preacher

"Next to Campbell and Stone, John Smith did more for primitive Christianity in Kentucky than any other man" (Davis 1915:215). John Smith was a pioneer in the truest sense of the word. He was the Daniel Boone, the Davy Crockett of the Reformation in Kentucky and Tennessee during the first two-thirds of the nineteenth century. What Boone and Crockett did in the social and political arena of those two states, John Smith did in the arena of religion.

He was an unusual person and a unique preacher. How he got his nickname is not known, but it was no more peculiar than the man who wore it.

He was born in a tiny log cabin in eastern Tennessee in 1784. There was little opportunity for education, and what little schooling he obtained came from itinerant school teachers (Williams 1904:15).

At twelve years his family moved across the Cumberlands and into the Stocktons Valley district. Soon after, John began to consider becoming a Christian, but frontier Calvinism was all he knew. The predestinarian views appalled him, but when he was twenty he was baptized into a Baptist Church. Shortly thereafter he was asked to preach, and his fame soon spread.

The catastrophe that transformed John Smith's beliefs occurred in 1814 when two of his children were burned to death, and his wife died of grief. He revolted at the doctrine of infant damnation taught by frontier Calvinism. He believed his children were without sin and condemnation and yet his conscience was ill at ease. He rejected what he felt to be the errors of Calvinisn, but he had found no solution to his dilemma in Scripture.

In 1823 Alexander Campbell began publishing *The Christian Baptist*, and John Smith read each issue critically. Mr. Campbell dealt with the difficulties that had plagued Mr. Smith. When, in 1824, Mr. Campbell visited Kentucky, John Smith spent considerable time with him (Richardson

1868: Vol. II, 108-112). He was led to embrace Campbell's position regarding the ancient gospel.

Mr. Smith believed his Baptist brethren would follow his leading. When the break came between the Reformers and the Baptists, the majority in the churches he served went with him. His zeal knew no bounds. "Converts were numbered by the thousands and new churches by the scores" (Davis 1915:212). He was a great preacher, and a large part of the growing work of the united Reformers and Christians in Kentucky is due to his labor.

The Two Groups Unite

About 1829, John T. Johnson, minister of the Great Crossings Baptist Church near Georgetown, Kentucky, began studying, with the use of his Bible, the teaching called Campbellism. He accepted the doctrine as from the Word of God and began preaching it with zeal. His church would not follow and so resigning, and at the same time giving up a lucrative law practice, in early 1831 he and two others formed a church of the Reformers (Williams 1904:367). His decision brought him into contact with Barton Warren Stone, minister of the Christian Church in Georgetown, and the men were drawn together in an "intimate acquaintance and firm friendship." They discovered that they shared a passion for Christian unity and a desire for fraternity among the members of their respective congregations. The brethren, by mutual agreement, met for worship and found that they stood on the same foundation, were led by the same Holy Spirit and preached the same Gospel.

"Raccoon" John Smith, controversial but powerful preacher of the Reformers in Kentucky, was wholly in accord with this development and saw the tiny group of Reformers at Great Crossing under Johnson and the Christians at Georgetown under the leadership of Stone "as those who seemed to be called, in the providence of God to lead in the work of uniting the two brotherhoods together" (Williams 1904:368).

In November, 1831, John T. Johnson invited John Smith to hold a meeting at Great Crossings. Johnson was a man of stature and a leader in the community. He was injured in the War of 1812 as an officer, had prepared himself to practice law, was a member of the State Legislature and also a member of Congress from Kentucky. In 1832 his brother, Richard, became a United States Senator and under Van Buren, in 1837, became Vice President. All of this had transpired in the life of John T. Johnson before his thoughts turned to spiritual matters (Garrison and DeGroot 1948:213).

Several were added at Great Crossings, increasing the number to about forty. Union was a major subject for discussion, and a conference developed between Stone, Johnson and Smith, along with Stone's dear friend, John Rogers, also with the Christians. Their decision was to reveal plans for union to their congregations to determine if the brethren would approve. Congregational reaction was almost unanimous.

Places and dates for united meetings of Christians and Reformers in each community were publicized by the four men. Christmas fell on the Lord's Day in 1831, and plans were made to honor the birthday of the Lord and to share in a celebration of unity at Georgetown on December 23 through the 26, and to usher in the new year by continuing the celebration in Lexington from December 30 to January 2.

The Christian Church in Lexington was strong and a couple of months before, had dedicated a new house of worship on Hill Street. The Reformers met in a chair factory renovated as a place of assembly. The New Year's meeting of the two congregations took place in the new church and was described as a "multitude of anxious brethren" (Williams 1904:369). John Smith, representing the Reformers, spoke first, followed by Barton Warren Stone speaking for the Christians. Smith emphasized that Christian unity must rest in the one faith anchored on the Word of God. Among other things, he said,

> God has put but one people on the earth. He had given to them but one book and therein exhorts and commands them to be one family. A union such as we plead for — a union of God's people on that one book — must then be practicable (1904:371).

Perhaps apprehending a tendency of Mr. Stone, Mr. Smith expressed opposition to fruitless speculations and non-productive dialogue.

Barton Warren Stone followed John Smith. He addressed the two congregations with irresistible tenderness. He responded to Smith's apprehensions by accepting that brethren could never be united on the basis of speculative theology. His weakness in becoming involved in theological speculation and reflection, he admitted. Said he,

> I perfectly accord with Brother Smith that those speculations should never be taken into the pulpit; but that when compelled to speak of them at all, we should do so in the words of inspiration.
>
> I have not one objection to the ground laid down by him as the true scriptural basis of union among the people of

278

God; and I am willing to give him, now and here, my hand (1904:372).

Mr. Stone then turned, as he was speaking, and offered his hand to John Smith. It was grasped with all the warmth of Smith's heart. Elders and teachers of both congregations surged forward, linking their hands and hearts in happy fellowship. From their lips came a hymn of praise as with joyous affirmation they asserted their union. On January 1, 1832, the Lord's Day, they met about the table, affirming their love for each other as they broke the loaf and shared the cup. Meetings of committees were held and a second fellowship about the Lord's Table took place on the third Sunday of February with plans to consummate the union on the following Lord's Day. However, problems arose. The Christians believed that only an ordained minister could officiate at the table. The elders could not act alone. Union was postponed, but not for long. The Christian brethren came to understand that administering the ordinances was not exclusively the privilege of the minister, and the problem was resolved. The two congregations came together, forming one church, worshiping in the new building on Hill Street, recently constructed by the Christians.

The Contagious Spirit of Union

The spirit of union was contagious. Soon it reached into neighboring churches. The congregations in Paris, Kentucky, also followed, and union was in the air. Soon came union of the Christians and Reformers throughout the state.

279

This was greatly promoted by the efforts of John Smith and John Rogers, who had been appointed at the Lexington meeting to visit all the churches and hold meetings in conjunction with each other, and who were most successful in removing any lingering doubts or prejudices — a result to which Elder Stone's earnest and intelligent advocacy of the movement greatly contributed. Thus, as the latter had foreseen, Christian love resolved, by simple and direct methods, differences and difficulties which would probably have been only augmented by any system of church representation or any formal general convention, and Mr. Campbell rejoiced in an issue which he greatly desired to see accomplished, but which he, for a time, feared was prematurely effected (Richardson 1858:Vol. II,384-387).

Apprehension of Alexander Campbell

Alexander Campbell and Barton Warren Stone shared voluminous correspondence during this period, and the burden of their concern was Christian union. Campbell had heard of Stone's theological vagrancies and the practices of some of the Christians, and he was suspicious. He rejoiced in the prospects of union, but he would oppose it if in any way it implied an overshadowing of "the ancient gospel and the ancient order of things."

Campbell was dumbfounded when the news reached him of the developments at Lexington, Georgetown, Paris and throughout Kentucky. He longed for union but was not prepared for such impetuous consequences.

In the April 2, 1832, *Millennial Harbinger*, Mr. Campbell published a letter dated February 1832, from a Brother H. C. Coon of Lexington. The letter informed readers of the Christmas meeting at Georgetown and the New Year's assembly in Lexington, but it was written before the problem was resolved concerning who could administer the Lord's Supper (*Millennial Harbinger* 1832:191-192).

The following *Harbinger* carried Mr. Campbell's response. His were words of caution and admonishment. He referred to the recent union at Lexington as "an abortion." A part of his problem related to the matter over the Lord's Supper and Mr. Campbell spent time discussing this difficulty. He neither encouraged nor did he oppose it, but he laid emphasis upon the necesssity of leading all committed to union into the revealed truth and practice of Scripture. In the *Harbinger* he wrote,

> To us it appears the only practicable way to accomplish this desirable object, is to propound the ancient gospel and the ancient order of things in the words and sentences found in the apostolic writings: to abandon all traditions and usages not found in the record, and to make no human terms of communion. But on this theme much must yet be said before all the honest will understand it. One thing, however, is already sufficiently plain to all, that a union amongst Christians can be obtained only upon Scriptural grounds, and not upon any sectarian platform in existence (1832:195).

Union Accelerated and Its Results in Evangelism and Church Planting

The union between the Disciples and Christians accelerated. At the time of the developments in Lexington and Georgetown, the Christians and Reformers were uniting in Rush County, Indiana. A letter from Rush County, dated December 24, 1831, written to Mr. Stone said,

> The Reforming Baptists and we are all one here. We hope that the dispute between you and Brother Campbell, about

names and priority, will forever cease, and that you will go on, united, to reform the world (Williams 1904:375).

Several reasons account for the union movement. There was a spirit of unity among the leaders and the churches. There was no ecclesiastical or denominational authority, no confessions or creeds or disciplines demanding adherence, and no church structure to hinder it. There was no debate whether the Christians were joining the Reformers or the Reformers the Christians. The Word of God was embraced as the final authority and a certain standard determination to restore the church revealed in the New Testament in its life and teachings. Man made creeds were renounced and human opinions, being fallible, were discounted.

There were those, however, who refused to participate in the union. The New England movement was opposed to both Stone and Campbell. In the southeast, where among the Christian Churches there still prevailed continuing Republican Methodist doctrine, union was strongly opposed.

Nonetheless, the years following the

. . . historic union of the forces of Campbell and Stone in Lexington were marked by a uniform pattern of evangelism and church planting that exceeded anything that hitherto had been experienced. The travels of the evangelists, the circulation of periodicals, the establishment of colleges, and the mouth to mouth propaganda of converts created a spirit of unity and fellowship in a common cause that was electrifying (Murch 1962:121).

In 1843, Barton Warren Stone, speaking of the contribution he made towards the above said, "This union, irrespective of reproach, I view as the noblest act of my life" (Rogers 1847:79).

Williams writes, "His cooperation with Stone and Johnson in the work of bringing the two parties together, John Smith always regarded as the best act of his life (Williams 1904:374).

A Great New American Religious Movement Under Way

The Holy Spirit of God was in it to direct in the growth of a body of believers that, in another seventy years, would be a million and a quarter strong (Garrison 1909:14 in Disciples of Christ 100th Anniversary).

Chapter Twelve

THE RAPID GROWTH OF THE CHURCHES

Discipling the Lost Not a Major Emphasis of Reformers in the Early Years

Alexander Campbell began publishing *The Christian Baptist* in August of 1823. In its first years, it said little about the planting or growth of churches. Mention of successful evangelistic preaching in the 1827 edition has reference to Elder John Secrest. In the 1826-1827 year, Secrest travelled about three thousand miles, and preached six hundred times. The first half of the year he failed to record the number immersed, but in the last half, he had baptized five hundred thirty persons (*Christian Baptist* 1827:420). John Secrest was a "Christian" preacher of the Stone movement. In the same issue was information about Walter Scott who had begun his work with the Mahoning Association and had reported to the editor that he had started an experiment in preaching the ancient gospel and that the effects were astounding. In ten days, he had baptized thirty persons (1827:420). A note from Columbiana County, Ohio, reported forty immersed in the space of three weeks (1827:434).

A news article in the 1828 edition recounted that from March 22 through June 22, Bishop John Secrest baptized two hundred twenty-two; that on four consecutive Sundays, Bishop Jeremiah Vardeman immersed one hundred eighteen persons in Cincinnati; that in Kentucky, through the preaching of brethren Polson, Anderson, Sterman and others, between three and four hundred had been immersed; that Bishop G. G. Boon, baptized about three hundred fifty; that Bishop William Morton immersed at least three hundred and Bishop Jacob Creath, many besides. In little

284

more than five months, Bishop John Smith had baptized six hundred three persons (1828:478).

From D. S. Burnet of Dayton, Ohio, was a note about growth of the Reformed Churches within the year of 1829. Ten or twelve preachers, partially or altogether Reformed, were with him and all part of a large congregation. Three sermons were preached on Saturday before hundreds of people, and the preachers recounted their progress and reformation (1829:587).

A few other references to evangelists at work may be found in the pages of *The Christian Baptist*, prior to 1829, but they are not many.

First Growth of Reformers in Northeastern Ohio

The growth of the Reformed Baptist Churches of northeastern Ohio, under the evangelistic preaching of Walter Scott in 1827, marks the beginning of substantial growth among those churches so far loosely associated with Thomas and Alexander Campbell.

The Christian Churches under Barton Warren Stone had been in existence for twenty-three years, and wherever the Christian evangelists labored, churches grew.

The Reformers Contrasted with the Christians

Barton Warren Stone began publishing *The Christian Messenger* in November of 1826. Every issue contained exciting news of the growth of the church over the United States. These reports revealed the rapid spread of the gospel.

At Kyle, Ohio, "Above sixty have lately been added to the churches . . ." (*Christian Messenger* 1827:Vol. I,64). From Georgetown, Kentucky, June 25, 1827,

The editor received daily, cheering accounts of the progress and spread of truth from various parts of the United States; especially from the southern and western states. The doctrine of union among Christians prevails and must ultimately triumph in despite of bigotry and intolerance. The light of the sun may be partially obstructed by a few intervening clouds, but those clouds are transient, and the light will break forth in full lustre before long. Let the motto of our lives be holiness to the Lord (1827:192).

In Russell County there is a church . . . that has increased from four to thirty within twelve months (1827:212).

At Florence, Alabama,

Last Saturday and the Lord's Day eight persons were added to the church, and in the few months past, sixteen have professed faith in Christ. Last Sunday evening I baptized six . . . (1827:213).

From Monroe, Tennessee,

With some months past between three hundred and four hundred souls have been added" (1827:213).

In Greencastle, Indiana,

A small Christian Church has formed . . . and from last account it has increased to upwards of two hundred members (1827:213).

In Pennsylvania and Virginia, in a few years, a great number of Christian Churches . . . and large additions (1827:214). At Westchester, Ohio, where John Secrest labored, he had "Baptized fourteen the day before we arrived, and since last winter he has baptized . . . some hundreds" (1827: 275). At Bloomington, Iowa, Delana R. Eckels reported that "between forty and fifty professed faith in the Lord

Jesus Christ" (*The Christian Messenger* 1827:Vol. II,13). In Overton County, Tennessee, "between twenty and thirty believed" (1827:14). "Elder John Secrest . . . told me . . . that since the Mahoning Association last met, he had immersed with his own hands, one hundred and ninety, thus lacking ten of five hundred in about five months" (1828:95). "Elder E. Paraner," of Smithfield, Ohio, "since last May . . . has baptized one hundred thirty" (1828:111). Elder James McVay at Steubenville, Ohio, reports, "About three hundred and fifty . . . the greater part of whom I have baptized" (1828:215). From Isaac N. Walter of Dublin, Ohio, "Reformation is spreading rapidly . . . under the labors of Elder T. L. Campbell. Many are turning to the Lord. . . . Churches have been planted" (1828:281). From David Steward of Tuckersville, Iowa, "Upwards of one hundred of my neighbors have professed faith in the Lord Jesus within two months past" (1828:20). Elder S. Kyle of Miami County, Ohio, reported that "on the head of King's Creek, about sixty souls have, within a few weeks, publicly professed faith in the Lord" (1828:41).

> We have just received accounts that Elder James Challen, the pastor of a Baptist Church in Cincinnati, has renounced the Baptist confession of faith, and with about one hundred of that Church have constituted on the Bible alone, as a distinct Church. A large majority of the Presbyterian Church in Nicholasville, Kentucky, have rejected their preacher, his Calvinistic doctrine and confession, and we understand they are about to build a splendid house of divine worship. Several hundred of the Methodists have withdrawn from the Methodist connexion in Cincinnati (1828:44).

From D. H. Hathaway of Lewis County, Kentucky, "Within ten months I have immersed upwards of one hundred" (1829:Vol. II,118). Matthew Gardner of Brown

County, Ohio reported "Within twelve months I have baptized in this county one hundred fifteen . . . in other places within the same period . . . about seventy more" (1829:162). From Elder William Mavity of Lewis County, Kentucky, "during last winter ninety-five professed faith in Christ and united with the Church" (1829:227).

A letter from Jacob Johnston of Covington County, Alabama, recounted:

> To this work I was ordained by Bishop Asbury. Sometime ago I found fault with human creeds and forms, and for the greater part of my time of late have lived almost alone. I determined to know nothing among the people but Jesus Christ and him crucified. This occasioned serious difficulties between me and sectarians. I have been between two and three years in this state, and have planted three churches in the Christian name; two in this state and one in West Florida. They were received and baptized by immersion on profession of their faith, except three who have been previously baptized by the Calvinistic Baptists. The glorious Emmanuel is riding forth conquering and to conquer, and sectarian parties are crumbling to pieces at a wonderful rate. I have just returned from a preaching tour, on which I have baptized nine. I find many in my travels who profess no religion, yet are fully convinced of the impropriety of human creeds and traditions, and like the Bereans are strongly searching the scriptures for truth (1829:229).

From Elder John W. Roberts of Harrison County, Kentucky,

> On the first Friday of this month I constituted a new church . . . on the North Fork of Licking. . . . On Wednesday following I constituted another church at Russelville, Ohio . . . on the fourth Lord's Day of this month I also constituted a church . . . in Medicine County, Kentucky (1829:259).

From Brother David W. Morris of Park County, Iowa, "in the space of six weeks about two hundred have been added to the Church of Christ . . ." (1829:283). From Henry D. Palmer of Carlisle, Iowa, "I have immersed sixteen in the neighborhood where I live within three weeks past" (1829:Vol. IV,16). From Elder James E. Matthews of Lauderdale, Alabama, "Thirty-one were added to the church" (1829:16). From Elder C. Sine of Back Creek Valley, Virginia, "I have immersed about twenty-three. I have also planted a church near my own residence . . . and another . . . six miles west of Winchester" (1829:17). Elder Barzillia H. Miles of Rutland, Ohio, wrote, "The number of converts amounted to about 100" (1829:18). From Elder John Hooton of Hickman County, Tennessee, "I have received into society, in about two years, three hundred sixty-six members" (1829:18).

A notice from J. G. Ellis to the editor of *The Christian Messenger* for February, 1830, read

> Mr. Stone: I inform you that a number of Christian brethren, some in Indiana, some in Ohio, and some in Kentucky have agreed to hold a conference in August of next, at the Republican meeting house in Campbell County, Kentucky, to be called the Union Conference, and to commence the Friday before the first Lord's Day in August next. You are requested to give notice of the above named conference in the Christian Messenger; and also to request that yourself, Brother Smith, Palmer, Allen and other brethren should attend with us (1830:Vol. IV,72).

From George Alkive of Williamsport, Ohio, "Large additions are made in many of the churches in this part of the country" (1830:119). From James Kinkennon of Tippacanoe County, Iowa, "I have visited several churches called by the Christian name . . . they contained from thirty to fifty members on the average" (1830:141). "In Brother Watson Clark's bounds in Fountain County, Iowa, a great and extensive work is progressing; large additions are daily made to the Churches" (1830:142). From Issac N. Walter of Dublin, Ohio, "I have baptized in twelve months an hundred twenty converts" (1830:191). From Elder Mansel W. Matthews of McMairy County, Tennessee, "Many churches have been planted recently in the western district" (1830:192). From Brother Daniel Long of George's Hill, Maryland, "I have given the right hand of fellowship to about fifty converts, and have baptized thirty-five" (1820: 215). Brother Samuel Rogers from Willmington, Ohio, reported, "Since last May we have baptized nearly two hundred. . . . Some new churches have been formed" (1830: 286).

In February of 1831, T. M. Allen reported "that there were fourteen churches in Fayette and Bourbon Counties, Kentucky, with a total of ten preachers and eight hundred and eighty-nine members" (1831:Vol. V,47-48). "To this list are added twenty-four more churches in seventeen Kentucky counties, making a grand total membership of two thousand seven hundred and ten" (1831:135).

From James B. Taylor concerning revival in North Carolina, "The preaching of Brethren Crudup, Purify, Crocker, Worrell and Bennet . . . is simple, evangelical, and faithful. . . . The number baptized by these brethren since last fall may be safely estimated at not less than four hundred" (1831:188). A letter from John Jones, Jr., from South Fork, Casey County, Kentucky, listed "twenty-three churches in South Kentucky with a total communicant membership of seven hundred forty-two" (1831:191). Minutes from the

Christian Conference north of the Kentucky River listed twenty-nine churches in that part of the state. "Brother Walters also informed us, that he had received into fellowship upwards of five hundred within the last two years, and had also immersed upwards of two hundred and twenty in the same time" (1831:262). A letter from Elder James E. Matthews of Bartons, Alabama, revealed "about sixty churches in Tennessee with probably four thousand members, and in Alabama about twenty churches with about fifteen hundred members" (1831:280).

The first edition of Alexander Campbell's *Millennial Harbinger*, successor to *The Christian Baptist*, was published in 1830. Like its predecessor, in its early years it had little to report concerning the growth of the Reformed Baptist Churches. Few were the references to church growth.

An article on the Mahoning Association reported that through laborers affiliated with the association in 1829, about one thousand were baptized, which was about the annual average for the past three years (*Millennial Harbinger* 1830:415) and from Hopkinsville, Christian County, Kentucky, came a report of a new church at Noah Springs with twenty-eight members, but numbering about ninety at the time of the report (1830:425). Few reports are found in the *Harbinger* during the year of 1830.

The following year was a little better. Reference was made to the church at Nashville, Tennessee, that consisted of two hundred fifty members (1831:121). A report was published regarding the constituting of the new church at Great Crossings, Scott County, Kentucky (1831:179). From the general meeting in New Lisbon, Ohio, it was reported that about five hundred persons were immersed by different laborers during the previous year (down about

five hundred from the year before) (1831:445). From Georgetown, Kentucky, "Brother Johnson has immersed thirteen
persons since last March" (1831:545).

The Evangelical Inquirer, published in Dayton, Ohio,
reported interest stimulated through Christian County,
Ohio, through the ministries of Brethren Rains, Wilson and
Crihfield, resulting in more than fifty persons, through faith,
being baptized within two months (*The Evangelical Inquirer*
1830:47). Reports of the ministry of John Secrest revealed
that he had enjoyed great success in Indiana, Illinois,
and Michigan. In those states, and in Ohio, within three
years he had baptized about three thousand (1830:70-71).

The Union of the Reformers and the Christians

The first announcement of the union of reforming Baptists and the Christians at Georgetown and Lexington,
Kentucky, appeared in the January issue of the *Christian
Messenger* for 1832 along with a rationale for the union
written by Barton Warren Stone (*The Christian Messenger*
1832:6-8). A similar uniting of Reformed Baptist and Christian Churches took place immediately in Indiana, and the
union movement spread like wildfire.

While union was taking place, and afterwards, churches
continued to grow. Latourette recounted that the churches,

> zealously evangelistic, they sought to win the unchurched
> to the Christian faith. With their emphasis upon the union
> of Christians, their ardent preaching adapted to the average
> man, and their democratic form of government, they made
> a strong appeal to the frontier mind. Their message of the
> erasure of ecclesiastical divisions under the simple name
> of Christian or Disciple attracted many from other religious
> bodies (Latourette 1971:Vol. IV,199-200).

Reported Growth by States

Ohio

Northeastern Ohio became the area of greatest growth and strength for the Reformers. Christian Churches were prevalent in the south, but there were Reformer or Disciple Churches as well. The decision was made at Austintown, Ohio, in 1830 that the Mahoning Association should disband at once but there should continue an annual meeting of the brethren for preaching, mutual encouragement and sharing of reports (Richardson 1868:Vol. II,328). These assemblies were attended by two to five thousand people (*The Evangelical Inquirer* 1830:97f.).

Indiana

The first churches of the movement in Indiana came from the Christians and Reformed Baptists, but grew from other sources as well. Greatest growth came not through other churches, but from the world, and by faith and obedience (Moore 1909:340). In 1829 a regular Baptist Church in Clark County affiliated with the Reformers. Other churches joining the movement began at least as early. Scores of independent churches, Dunkards, or German Baptists, and Free Will Baptists joined the growing stream. Many churches were established by the Kentucky Christians. The first union of a Christian Church and a church of the Reformers took place at New Albany, across from Louisville in 1823. Indianapolis entertained the first state convention in 1839. There were one hundred and fifteen churches and seven thousand one hundred and ten members reported at that time (Murch 1962:124-125).

293

Illinois

Illinois was admitted to statehood in 1818. Years earlier, a Christian Church had been established eight miles north of Mt. Carmel. In 1819 this congregation with a number of Reformers was reorganized into the Barney's Prairie Christian Church. In the summer, a second church was planted in the same county. The Christian Church northwest of Vincennes, Indiana, was founded in 1815 and affiliated with the Reformation in 1828. Sangamon County's first Christian Church was planted in 1820. The Little Grove Church, east of Paris, was planted in 1826, and both Mulkeytown, which today claims it is the oldest church in Illinois, and Spring Creek were established before 1830. The Armington (Hittle's Grove) Christian Church dates from 1829, moving from the Baptists to the Reformers. The churches grew in number and membership, and were soon one of the prominent communions in Illinois. As early as as 1839, the first state meeting had been held at Pittsfield (1962:125).

Tennessee

Probably the oldest church in Tennessee is the Post Oak Springs Christian Church organized in 1812. Kentucky Christians moved into Tennessee and with them they took their faith. There were many Baptist Churches in the state as well, and by the scores they embraced the views expressed in *The Christian Baptist* by Alexander Campbell. Six times was Mr. Campbell in Nashville, and his visits there won numbers of friends with the consequence that many Baptist Churches joined the Reformers' movement (1962:125). Leaders in the state were P. S. Fall, his brother-in-law, Tolbert Fanning and David Lipscomb. Fanning and Lipscomb stood in opposition to any kind of inter-church

294

organization or association (Wilburn 1969:144-145). Other churches from the period, are Buffaloe, Carter County, 1828; Concord in Sullivan County, 1833, in Washington County, both Boone's Creek and Union Church; and in Johnson County the Liberty Church, all from 1835. Evangelist of note was John Mulkey, who in his fifty-three years of ministry, preached ten thousand times and baptized as many believers. The first institution in the state, a female school, was founded by Mr. and Mrs. Tolbert Fanning at Franklin in 1837.

Michigan
Years before 1840, two or three men were likely preaching in southwestern Michigan.

The Christians of New England
At the time of the Georgetown-Lexington union in 1832, the Christian Churches of Elias Smith and Abner Jones in the New England States refused, almost unanimously, to share in the union movement. A reformer church was established in Boston in 1843 but traced its beginning to Alexander Campbell's visit to the Baptist Tremont Temple in Boston in 1836. Three Christian Churches in Massachusetts affiliated with The Restoration Movement and a church at Danbury, Connecticut, where Mr. Campbell preached in 1836 also joined the Reformers. Two churches in Vermont affiliated with the movement as the result of Mr. Campbell's visit, but they did not grow, and two congregations near Lubec, Maine, were the only churches coming into the Reformation from that state (Murch 1962:126).

The problem with the churches of the east was that they were inclined towards Unitarianism and Alexander

Campbell was fearful of their theological liberalism (*Millennial Harbinger* 1845:415-417; 1846:216-225; 388-394); (Freese 1852:176-177. Note also p. 39).

New York

The reforming church in New York City, dating from 1810, had its antecedents in Scotch Baptist relationships that went back to Scotland and Robert and James Alexander Haldane (Baxter 1874:46-53). The theology of the congregation predated the *Declaration and Address* and the *Sermon on the Law.* Leaders of the Restoration Movement were to come out of the New York church. The church at Throopsville was formed in the center of the state in 1830. North Lancaster was planted in 1833, and a church established by a Baptist minister with a number of his congregation, was excluded from the Baptist denomination for embracing the Campbell or heretical principle (Garrison and DeGroot 1948:266).

Pennsylvania

In Pennsylvania the Brush Run Church, established in 1811, two years following Alexander Campbell's arrival in America, was the first Reformed Church to be organized. "The three Marys," Mrs. Mary Ogle, Mrs. Mary Morrison, and Mrs. Mary Graft, overcoming the social restrictions of their day, accomplished a first among planters of Reformation Churches. Mary Ogle heard Alexander Campbell speak before the Redstone Association in 1813 as he enunciated his principles of reformation. At Somerset she and her two friends formed the "Female Society for the Use of the Gospel" in the year 1815. Baptist ministers did the

296

preaching, and a church was organized in 1817. The Redstone Association offered them fellowship though the three Marys burned the creed proposed to the church by the Association. In 1830 the Morrisons moved to Johnstown. Immediately Mary Morrison began to win converts, and a church was planted there. The city of Philadelphia gained its first church in 1832, and a congregation was planted in Howard the same year.

In 1832 there were five churches in Bradford County in favor of reform; Canton that claimed one hundred ten members, Smithfield with forty, Columbia with thirty-five. Troy with forty-one, Ridgeburg with about forty and a small church in Luzerne County with twenty members (*Millennial Harbinger* 1832:228f.).

(West) Virginia

West Virginia became a separate state in 1863. The story, through the period covered, belongs to Virginia. The O'Kelly and Christian Church provided the first of the Reformation pioneers in Virginia. In 1809 a Christian Church was established at Petersburg. One year earlier a congregation was established at Strasburg, later to be called Walnut Springs Church, which affiliated with the Reformation in 1835.

In 1815 the congregation at Wellsburg was formed with Alexander Campbell its minister, made up of members from Brush Run who had moved into the Wellsburg community. The home of Mr. Campbell at Bethany became the center of the reform movement for the following half century.

The year of 1830 is accepted as the date for the separation of the Baptists and Reformers. The years from 1823 to 1830 were filled with evidences of division and church separation. Garrison and DeGroot insist that "there is not a single instance of the Reformers putting Baptists out of the fold;" that separate existence of the Reformers was thrust upon them by the action of various Baptist Churches in withdrawing fellowship from the advocates of "Campbellism" (Garrison and DeGroot 1948:271).

Virginia

The Sycamore Church in Richmond, Virginia, came out of separaton of the Baptists and Reformers in 1832. In the same year the Tidewater churches sent out their first evangelist. Sixteen ministers and seven hundred members were present at the cooperation meeting at Acquintain in 1833. At a meeting in Richmond in the fall, twelve hundred members representing sixteen congregations were present, along with two generations of the Campbells (1948:273).

Maryland

The first church of the Reformers in Baltimore, Maryland, came out of the Haldane tradition known to the Campbells in Scotland, and was organized in 1831. Its antecedents go back to 1817 when a young preacher named Farquharson with principles unacceptable to the Baptists, started a separate congregation. Alexander Campbell visited Baltimore in 1833 and won many to the Reformers. After the Georgetown-Lexington, Kentucky, union in 1832, several New Light Christians affiliated with the movement as well (1948:328-329; Murch 1962:127).

North Carolina

Thomas Campbell preached the program of the Reformers in North Carolina in 1833. The population of the state was about seven hundred fifty thousand people, one

298

fourth of which were African slaves. Those professing membership in any church amounted to eight percent of the population. The Church at Edenton, through a man who had read the Campbell-McCalla debate, became the first to embrace an independent stand, followed by a number that rejected the Philadelphia Confession of Faith. A union meeting of Reformation Churches was organized in 1833.

South Carolina

In 1831 in Pendleton County, South Carolina, six disciples met, using the New Testament as their guide. At their first meeting, ten people were baptized for the remission of sins (*Millennial Harbinger* 1831:333). The first congregation of the Reformers was the Evergreen Church in Pendleton County. The second came in a more spectacular way. After reading *The Christian Baptist* in 1833, Dr. William R. Erwin asked for a letter of dismissal from the Kirkland Regular Baptist Church. Instead of the sought after letter, he and Mrs. Erwin (Julia C. Robert) and Mrs. Ulysses M. Robert were excommunicated. Deacon William Henry Robert, father of Mrs. Erwin and father-in-law of Mr. Ulysses M. Robert, acted as moderator (Garrison and DeGroot 1948:281).

Georgia

Immigrants settling in Oconee County, Georgia, in 1807, the year Thomas Campbell arrived in America from Ireland, planted a small church near Scull Shoals. The Church, sixteen miles from Athens, was called "Old Republican," for the brethren were followers of James O'Kelly. In 1822 the congregation was reorganized, adopting Bible Christian as its name. In 1795, the young Barton Warren Stone, not yet licensed to preach by the Presbyterian Church, was teaching at the Academy of Hope Hull near Washington. In 1842 the Old Republican Bible Christian Church reorganized according to the New Testament pattern. It chose for its name, the Antioch Christian Church, and is still worshiping in its third building on the original site. In 1838 Alexander Campbell visited Savannah where a New Testament Church had been planted in 1819 (Murch 1962:128-129).

Alabama

Alabama entered statehood in 1819. The following year a Free Will Baptist from Georgia, Cyrus White, came into Alabama with a James O'Kelly man and began preaching. About the same time, two followers of Barton Warren Stone entered the state just south of the Tennessee border. Those associated with the Reformation came in at the same time. One of the strongest congregations near Florence, was Republican after the influence of James O'Kelly, planted in 1829. Though not possible today to locate many of the churches, there is knowledge of an annual meeting of the Christian Conference at Antioch, Jackson County, in 1827, with twenty-one preachers and three hundred members present (Garrison and DeGroot 1948:290).

Mississippi

A Baptist preacher and medical doctor came into Mississippi in 1828 with a plea for Christian unity based upon apostolic writing. Three Baptist Churches responded within a year. A correspondent from Yazoo wrote to the editor of the *Harbinger* in 1832 that he was informed that five Baptist Churches had declared themselves in favor of the

Reformation (*Millennial Harbinger* 1832:472). In the same year the *Harbinger* reported a congregation of disciples near Grand Gulf, and of churches in Hines and Wilkerson Counties that were progressing rapidly (1832:570). A church was planted in Holmes County in 1833 (1835:374).

Missouri

Among settlers from Kentucky that migrated to Missouri, about the time that the territory became a state in 1821, were a number of Christians of the Stone movement. When they settled, they planted churches. Likely the first church in the state was Salt Creek, organized in 1817, near Franklin in Howard County. It was washed away with the town by the river before 1830. After the flood, newly planted churches were reported by the score (Murch 1962:129-130). The building for the church of McBride was dedicated in 1817. Other churches started before statehood were Dover, Antioch, Fulton, Red Top, Bear Creek, Richland, and Mount Pleasant.

One of the pioneers in Missouri was a converted O'Kelly Methodist who planted the first church in Springfield in 1834 (Garrison and DeGroot 1948:310). Other planted congregations in central, northeastern and other areas of the state. Reflecting the fellowship among the several movements was the uniting of a Christian Church and a reforming Baptist Church in 1835 to form the church at Fayette (1948:311).

Arkansas

The first church in Arkansas, located at Little Rock, has an unbroken history from 1824 when it was founded as a Baptist Church. A Kentucky preacher began worshiping with the congregation in 1832 and led the church to renounce their creed, rules of decorum and name, taking only Jesus as their king (Murch 1962:130).

Iowa

The Blackhawk Indian War ended in the Wisconsin-Iowa-Minnesota area in 1832. After the treaty was signed, the first church of the Reformers was organized in Dubuque, Iowa. In July, 1836, a second church was planted north of Fort Madison. Pleasant Hill Church was organized in Washington County in 1836. However, Christian Church preachers were baptizing hundreds and planting numerous churches in Iowa as early as 1828 and before (*Christian Messenger* 1829:283; 1830:142), etc.

Texas

A Stonite preacher, Collen McKinney, from Kentucky, having accepted the principles of Barton Warren Stone before 1823, moved westward with a number of his family and settled in Bowie County, Texas, in 1831. In 1841-1842 a church was organized with sixteen members. These migrants moved on, but churches planted elsewhere were the result. The first church of the Reformers moved in a body from Alabama, through Mississippi and Tennessee, and arrived in Clarksville in early 1836. Dr. Mansel W. Matthews and Lynn D'Spain led the group, stopping each Lord's Day for worship and the Lord's Supper, as it moved by wagon and horseback ever westward. Their guide was Davy Crockett, who left them at Memphis as he galloped ahead with the Texas army volunteers (Murch 1962:131). Out of the Clarksville Church came the founders of Addran College, now Texas Christian University.

Before 1850 Reliable Reports Not in Existence

Accurate records of the growth of the Reformation prior to 1850 simply do not exist. In 1828, referring to the quarter century of growth among Christian Churches, Barton Warren Stone wrote, "The sect called Christians have risen from nothing to fifteen hundred congregations with a membership of one hundred fifty thousand" (Garrison and DeGroot 1948:325). The figures were a wild estimate and only had value in revealing that the Christian movements had their origins in a number of reformations — at least five that Stone was aware of; the Reformed Baptists and Christians, the Republican Methodists, the followers of the Haldanes and the Christian Churches of New England.

In the early years up to 1832, Alexander Campbell and the Reformers only gained a substantial membership with the separation from the Baptists. This gave the reformers from twelve to twenty thousand members and was virtually completed by 1832 when the union movement brought in most of the Christians from the west and a number from the east. If ten thousand were gained by the union, the approximate for the Reformers in 1832 could safely be twenty-two thousand. In that same year, Walter Scott, in a published table, claimed twenty-five thousand Christians, but he did not define them (*Evangelist* 1832:72). This is likely the most accurate estimate available up to that time.

Alexander Campbell wrote that during the preceding seven years, there had been unprecedented growth and that in 1833 ten thousand had joined the standard. He went on to say that probably at that time at least one hundred thousand were part of the movement (Garrison and DeGroot 1948:324). A change could be observed in *The Millennial Harbinger* for 1833 in contrast to earlier years of the *Harbinger* and *The Christian Baptist*. In 1833, one hundred twenty-one or more letters were published reporting on the growth of the churches. Reports of numerous churches planted and hundreds baptized were the order of the day. From 1833 onward, regular entries in *The Millennial Harbinger* carried news of the rapid expansion of The Restoration Movement.

In1836 there was published a table listing, Christians ". . . one thousand churches, three hundred ministers, thirty thousand members. Reformers or Campbellites have been computed at one hundred fifty thousand."

After 1832 and the union of the Campbell and Stone movements, Kentucky claimed more churches and members of the Reformers than any other state. No later than 1834, Barton Warren Stone was visited by a David Millard* at Georgetown, Kentucky. Millard reported large and fast-growing Christian Churches with talented ministers and that in four counties surrounding Georgetown, it was estimated that the Christian Churches had grown by two thousand in nine months (*Christian Paladium* 1841:266). This estimate is significant as it comes from a man who was unsympathetic with the direction Barton Warren Stone and many of his churches had taken in joining the Campbell movement. Barton Warren Stone, John T. Johnson, and John Smith, all principals in the recent union movement, through their preaching continued to win multitudes numbering in thousands each year.

One must not deprecate the impetus of the union nor the truth propounded nor the growth due to the persuasiveness

---

* Prominent leader of Christian Connection Churches; served as Chairman of, the Committee that founded Antioch College, Yellow Springs, Ohio, 1852.

of evangelists such as Barton Warren Stone, John T. Johnson, John Secrest, Raccoon John Smith, Walter Scott, and others. The rapid expansion of the united Christian or Disciples of Christ Churches was due to the above factors, and historians have been correct in pointing this out. But there was another factor.

In late spring and early summer of 1830, there began another awakening in the United States, so effective that Lyman Beecher (as quoted by the evangelist Charles G. Finney) described it as "the greatest work, of God, and the greatest revival of religion, that the world has ever seen, in so short a time." One hundred thousand were reported as having connected themselves with churches, the result of that revival, accomplished in a single year, 1830-1831.

There is only slight reference to the Awakening of 1830-1842 in the writings of church historians, but a chapter in a recent volume by J. Edwin Orr details the movement among Congregationalists, Presbyterians, Baptists, Methodists, and other denominations. Finney won a thousand converts in Rochester, New York, a city with a population of ten thousand, though the general movement did not begin with his ministry late in 1830, but at least six months earlier (Orr 1975:132-141).

The earlier Awakening, which began in Britian and was manifested in the United States after 1792, cresting in New England five years later, evidenced little extravagance or fanaticism in the New England and Middle Atlantic states, report after report emphasizing that it was neither noisy, convulsive, extravagant, nor fanatical, but rational, deep and profound (Orr 1975:53-58). It was otherwise on the western and southern frontiers where the people were rough and illiterate, and the movement was marked by prostrations, outcries, trembling, jerking, dancing for joy, and other exuberant 'exercises' (1975:59-70). Apparently, exuberance continued on the frontier and provoked distrust of revival in the mind of Alexander Campbell.

The Awakening of 1830, however, was reported as deep and calm. The cities and colleges were the scenes of deepest movement, and the circumstances in the south and west, marked by extravagance in the early 1800's were the same. The Presbyterian General Assembly of 1831 reported that the movement, in general, was "still, solemn, and in some cases overwhelming," (Narrative of the State of Religion, 1832), but

> There were no extravagances reported, nor any in the awakenings anywhere in Kentucky, Tennessee or camp-meeting country. Rather there were reports of a strange stillness in the trans-Appalachian country, in which sinners wept and trembled under conviction of sin (Orr 1975:135).

It was not only the Restoration evangelists who were adding multitudes to their fellowships. In two years, the Methodists doubled in membership from a total of 580,098 to 1,171,356 (Methodist Episcopal Statistics). The same story was told about the Baptists, while the Presbyterians more than trebled their annual increase. The Restoratation gains, following the union of 1832, were only part of a general harvest in all the churches of the United States.

Chapter Thirteen

THE AMAZING RECEPTIVITY BETWEEN
1832 AND 1860

The Christian Messenger, edited by Barton Warren Stone, in February of 1841 carried a note from Mr. J. Creath, Jr. of Monticello, Lewis County, Missouri, dated January 20th.

> Dear Brother Stone: My poor afflicted wife lies in her bed beside me not able to set up, or do anything for me and her children. She declines fast. It is consumption. I go out preaching a few days sometimes, and I feel when I return I shall find her a corpse.
>
> On the ninth and tenth instant we held a two days meeting in this county, 30 miles northwest of Monticello, on the North Fabius River, and organized a Christian Church consisting of 17 members. It is named Antioch.
>
> Last Lord's Day at Houston, in Marion County, two young gentlemen confessed the Lord. Signed: J. Creath Jr.

The three best known journals of the Restoration Movement published at this time, were already acquainted with Mr. J. Creath, Jr.

On June 24th, 1841, Mr. Creath, recounted, writing from Monticello, Lewis County:

> Since the beginning of this month, with the aid of brethren Hatchell, Ballinger and Thomas, we have received 90 persons in this part of Missouri. We received between 75 and 80 at two meetings in Shelbyville, in Shelby County (*The Christian Messenger* 1841:392).

The announcement of the death of Mrs. Creath came, as expected. An obituary found in the August, 1841, extra edition of the *Messenger* announced:

> Died, at her residence, in Monticello, Lewis County, Missouri, July 16, 1841, of pulmonary and hereditary consumption, sister Susan Creath, the wife of brother Jacob Creath, Jr., age 32 years. She died a Christian, with a hope full of immortality. She had labored more than three years under the disease that finished her earthly career. Few persons suffered more than she did during this period (1841:430).

The next entry relating to Mr. Creath was a report from Mr. William Brown from Jacksonville, Illinois, dated November 25th, 1841.

> During my visit in Missouri, we had some interesting meetings. One at Monticello, 16 additions, one at Houston 22, one at Palmyra 73, and one at New London 1. We had brother Creath to help us (1841:31).

Nothing so illustrates the spirit of the times nor the commitment of the leaders as does this insight into the life of Jacob Creath, Jr. He typified the human factor in the growth of the church through the second third of the nineteenth century.

The Sources of Information

Any effort to determine growth of the churches of the Restoration Movement between 1832 and 1860 must depend upon information contained in the three most prominent journals* of the Movement, *The Christian Messenger*,

---

* *The Millennial Harbinger* for 1835 listed seven journals then being published by Restoration Movement editors: *The Christian Mesenger*, *The Evangelist*, *The Apostolic Advocate*, *The Gospel Advocate*, *The Primitive Christian*, *The Christian Investigator*, and *The Millennial Harbinger*, with three new periodicals proposed for 1836: *The Christian Preacher*, *The Christian Reformer* and *The Disciple*. Only *The Harbinger*, *The Evangelist* and *The Christian Messenger* stood the test of time (1835:618).

1826-1837, 1839-1845, edited by Barton Warren Stone, *The Evangelist*, 1832-1844, edited by Walter Scott, and *The Millennial Harbinger*, 1830-1864, edited by Alexander Campbell.

The Outcome of Union Between the Stone and Campbell Movements

When union came between "Christian" Churches and the followers of Mr. Campbell, in Georgetown, Lexington, Paris and other places in Kentucky, he was disturbed, though he neither encouraged nor opposed the action taken. He did strongly emphasize the necessity for propounding

> the ancient gospel and the ancient order of things in the words and sentences found in the apostolic writings — to abandon all traditions and usages not found in the Record, and to make no human terms of communion (*Millennial Harbinger* 1832:195).

Union was a fact regardless of Mr. Campbell's ambivalence towards it, and others accepted it with greater enthusiasm. Like wild fire it spread. In April, 1832, a brother M. N. Matthews wrote from Tennessee:

> Those who are called, by way of reproach, Cambellites, and the Christians, are friendly. We are united in spirit, and generally in form. We preach, pray, sing, and commune together. We join in all social acts of worship together — unitedly labor to reform the world. Opinions are mutually held as private property. We have nothing to do with speculative theories, but the plain truth of God (*The Christian Messenger* 1832:157-158).

From Brother B. Jones of Richmond, Virginia, in May, 1932, came the following information:

I am exceedingly rejoiced to know that those Christians that plead for reformation, are so nearly, as I hope, come to a real union. The news is hailed with joy amongst us reformers . . . (1832:220).

From Tennessee came the word, "It affords us much satisfaction to hear of Christians uniting upon the Word of God, laying aside creeds and party names." From Missouri, "The brethren here, just 100 in number, have taken the name Christian only, and have no other creed than the Bible" (1832:220).

In a letter from Jesse Marity of Madison, Iowa, written in September, 1832 was the announcement:

We had the pleasure of beholding three large congregations resolved to practice the New Testament institutions in primitive order. They take the name Christian, and exclude every other name; they take the New Testament and exclude all other governments; they meet and break bread on every first day, and as the Lord has prospered them, so each one casts into the treasury when they come together (1832:300).

Barton Warren Stone wrote from Jacksonville, Illinois in August, 1832:

In Jacksonville we witnessed a happy union of two societies, Christians and Reformers, in one body or church . . . In Jersey Prairie about fifty of these two societies would unite on the same foundation the next Lord's day following. In Carrolton the same union was to take place at the same time (1832:347).

Brother Thomas G. Meredity of Louisa City, Virginia, wrote in January of 1833:

We are much pleased to hear of the union of the Disciples and Christians in the west, and indulge the hope that the

310

'reformation' may be still gaining ground in that part of the country. In this part of the country, prejudices and prepossessions are giving away rapidly before the mighty efficacy of truth, and churches of Christians are springing up in rapid succession, holding the Bible as the only rule of faith and practice (1833:57).

The *Evangelist*, founded and edited by Walter Scott, did not begin until January, 1832. Scott was aware of the union of the Reformers and the Christians. In May Mr. Scott carried an article in The *Evangelist* entitled, "Union of the Disciples and Christians," written by Raccoon John Smith. Smith concluded the piece by saying:

> As we do desire above all things to know the whole truth and to practice it; and as we think that the best of us either as individuals or as congregations, not fully reformed by reforming, we hope that the editors of reforming periodicals, brothers Campbell, Scott, etc., if they see this in the *Messenger*, will notice it in their journals with such remarks of commendation or correction as they may think proper; we make this request because circumstances we think, actually require it (1832:110).

In March of 1832, editor Walter Scott carried in *The Evangelist* a note from Barton Warren Stone. "Our union is attended with happy consequences, and our meetings crowned with success" (1832:71).

With union having started in Georgetown and Lexington, through the efforts of Barton Warren Stone, it seems obvious that *The Christian Messenger* would carry the continuing news of the progress of union, and it did. With the *Evangelist* and the *Harbinger*, with Scott and Campbell noting the progressing union, that union was a fact.

The Year-by-Year Amazing Growth of the Churches Following Union

The Christian Messenger, *The Evangelist* and *The Millennial Harbinger*, with their editors, were agreed on the unprecedented growth of the churches* of the Restoration Movement after 1832. A review is still exciting today, a century and a half later.

Paucity of reports regarding the progress of growth among the churches of the Campbell movement is noticeable in *The Millennial Harbinger* for the years of 1830 and 1831. This began to change by 1832, and by 1833 and following, "The Progress of Reform" was a monthly feature in that journal.

The Year of 1832

Several entires in 1832 *Harbinger* demand attention. From New York, "I would inform you that notwithstanding the united exertions of all the clergy of all denominations, the light of divine truth is making progress in the different sections of this country" (*Millennial Harbinger* 1832:141). In May, 1832, a letter from brother J. Frisbie of Monticello, Kentucky reported that the "infant society recently organized in that place now amounts to more than fifty disciples" (1832:411). G. W. Elley, from Nicholasville, Kentucky, reporting in June, noted that at "Clear Creek . . . fifteen were immersed." "At Nicholsville . . . eight persons were immersed." Near "Lexington . . . immersed eight";

---

*Prior to 1832 the churches following Mr. Campbell were called the Reformers or Disciples. After the union of the two streams in 1832, the name, "Christian Church" became increasingly popular with the name, "Church of Christ" also favored.

At the Republican Meeting House, eight miles from Nicholas-ville, at a meeting of many disciples, say five hundred, and a number of public brethren, with many citizens, twenty-one were immersed. Great love and harmony prevailed at this meeting, and the fruits of the Holy Spirit were very manifest among the disciples (1832:411).

From J. T. Johnson, in June, 1832, "Including the adjacent counties, within the last four weeks there have been im-mersed about one hundred and thirty persons. "Also in June, from David S. Burnet at "Mayslick . . . 12 persons were immersed"; on Red Oak in Brown County, Ohio, "twenty-three gladly were immersed"; at "Our meeting at Spencer Meeting House . . . there were twenty-two con-versions" (1832:412-413).

The progress of union did not move smoothly in some areas. Mr. Campbell nonetheless endorsed union and soon deprecated those that hindered its momentum. In the August, 1832, *Millennial Harbinger* Extra, editor Campbell commented both on the opposition to union and the satis-factory growth of the churches.

Mr. Ball has been endeavoring to have the brethren of another of his churches at Deep Run to cast out the re-formers. He has been trying to divide that church, and then no doubt, blame the reformers for it, and say, 'Mark them who cause divisions, and avoid them.' . . .

One of Mr. Clopton's men, at the last meeting of the Meherrin Association, made an unsuccessful attempt to have the reformers cast out . . .

Considerable additions to the churches in Virginia by new conversions; but much is doing in reconciling old disciples to the Christian institution in its primitive simplicity — in organizing churches and setting things in order (1832:413).

313

The September, 1832 *Harbinger* reported a total of 154 baptisms. The editor observed that many correspondents communicated in general terms how the churches were growing and the Reformation was progressing, but they omitted the details (1832:471-473).

A brother Aylett Rains wrote a letter to Mr. Campbell, dated September 4, 1832. This communication was published in full.

> I have recently returned from a tour of four weeks through several counties in the state of Ohio; within which time we received the good confession from forty-three persons, and immersed forty-one. Since last winter, about forty persons have been added to many congregations in Kentucky. Without doubt, there will be many more conversions this year, than were last year; and if I do not very much mistake, this work of gospel conversion will go on, in one increasing ratio, until the kingdom of the clergy will be shaken from its foundations, and the whole earth filled with the glory of the Lord (1832:513).

The same issue of the *Harbinger* carried a letter from William Hayden. His judgment was similar to that of Aylett Rains.

> It appears from the reports, which from personal knowledge, I know to be correct, that the apostolic gospel and order of things are gradually and regularly gaining influence among us (1832:514).

The November *Harbinger* reported approximately nine hundred immersed. In December one hundred and forty accessions were noted, and Mr. Campbell saw fit to note also the progress of reform as reported in *The Christian Messenger* for November. Approximately 375 additions to the churches were recorded. A note from the senior editor, Barton Warren Stone, of the *Messenger* made the observation:

> We can safely say, that the ancient gospel is prevailing beyond the most sanguine anticipation. The ears of thousands are open to hear; and, like the Corinthians, many, by hearing, believe and are baptized (*Millennial Harbinger* 1832:569-572, 607-611).

The Evangelist, edited by Walter Scott, was also quick to publish news of the growth of the church. From Canfield, Ohio, came the assurance, "The brethren who travel proclaim the word with as much success now as at any time since you labored among us" (1832:47). From Richmond, Virginia came the encouraging word, "The cause of Reformation is progressing in this place notwithstanding the great efforts made to put it down" (1832:119).

Communication from the Western Reserve in Ohio brought the news:

> I have been at a great many large meetings which I thought could not be exceeded for love and affection, but such a one as this I never before witnessed; and, though none of the great spirits of the Reformation were present, yet was the meeting as numerously attended as any that ever preceded it. It was supposed that 2,500 were present, chiefly disciples; thirty-five were immersed, and on the last and great day of the feast, William Hayden stood in the water until he immersed eighteen . . .

> Brother William Hayden informs us per letter that upwards of 400 have been converted on the above ground during last year (1832:239).

> From David S. Burnet at Maysville, Kentucky came the report, "In my two last visits to Mayslick and vicinity, I

immersed nineteen persons, making in all 144, at our meeting in three months, besides many others by those cooperating with me occasionally" (1832:239).

Evangelist John C. Ashley, writing from Portsmouth, Ohio, commented:

> Never did such emotions of mingled joy and sorrow arise in my bosom, as at a three days' meeting in Adams county, thirty-nine miles from this place, from which I had just returned, to see a large congregation melted to tears . . . not by enthusiastic appeals to passions, but by the impulse of Apostolic doctrine. To see backsliders return . . . to see persons confessing the Lord, declaring themselves the chief of sinners . . . to see children coming forward to confess the Lord, and renounce the prince and power of the air . . . to see parents and grandparents rejoicing over the tender age thus devoted to the Lord . . . to see husbands and wives buried into the Savior's death . . . to hear the admonitions and exhortations of fathers to their disobedient children . . . the lamentations of wives over their disobedient husbands, presented a scene to me altogether overwhelming. I can truly say, my cup ran o'er: Twenty-three here confessed the name of the Lord (1832:263).

From June through December, the pages of *The Christian Messenger*, edited by Barton Warren Stone, reported over eight hundred accessions to the churches through faith and obedience, and these were but a percentage of the real growth of the churches. Examples taken from the *Evangelist* and the *Harbinger* confirm that thousands were brought to Christian faith in the year of 1832.

The Year of 1833
For 1833, *The Christian Messenger* carried the news that over thirty-five hundred were added to the churches.

A letter from J. T. Powell of Felicity, Ohio expressed the spirit of that year:

> Opposed as the truth is, its march is glorious . . . for the last seven months, I have never witnessed in all my life, such signaled victory on the Lord's side; our meetings are crowded; often more than our houses will contain; and many of those promise submission to the King of saints, by professing to take his yoke upon them; and thus learn of him that they may find rest to their souls (1833:189).

In the same year, *The Evangelist* reported accessions totaling approximately two thousand. *The Millennial Harbinger* reported well over thirty-nine hundred.

Indicative of the excitement was a letter from George W. Elley, written at Nicholasville, Kentucky, August 13, 1833.

> The cause of reformation is rapidly progressing here and elsewhere in Kentucky. Since the first of June brother Morton and myself have immersed about seventy-five persons; brother Thomas Smith, about forty in the adjoining county; brother John Smith, about three hundred in the neighborhood of Mount Sterling; besides many others who have been immersed by other brethren around him. Brethren Stone, J. T. Johnson, and J. Creath, Jr., have immersed in Georgetown, Scott County, about three hundred and fifty, or more; besides others immersed by other brethren. So far as I am able to learn, I would say, there have been no less than one thousand persons immersed during the last two months in a few counties around us (1833:474-475).

From Louisville, Kentucky, a letter from John R. McCall, dated September 4, 1833 said in part:

> I have witnessed the good confession of upwards of three hundred, who are now, so far as they have come under my

317

notice since their obedience to the gospel, walking in the truth . . . Those who have proclaimed the gospel have introduced a number into the kingdom of Jesus, which would probably swell the whole number to about six hundred in the district of country where I have labored as an evangelist (1833:617).

The Year of 1834

As one scans the letters published in the journals of 1834, expressions of discouragement are often noted. O. C. Steele of Richmond, Kentucky wrote on June 9, 1834:

I regret that I have no good news to communicate in reference to the advancement of truth and piety among the congregations of this county. Not one of them worships God according to the word of truth (1834:379).

B. F. Hall, from Georgetown, Kentucky, wrote on August 4, 1834,

The churches in this country do not advance in the cause of reform as fast as I should like to see them. Several of the teaching brethren are not hearty in what we believe to be the ancient order of the church. There are but few churches that meet every first day to keep the ordinances. They are too much in the monthly system (1834:472).

Reporting from Paris, Tennessee on October 13th, 1834, John R. Howard noted:

The reformation is progressing slowly in this part of the Western Country. At our union, or camp meeting, at Crooked Creek, Carroll county, three only were immersed . . . (1834:604).

There was still considerable optimism among many of the preaching brethren. On the 10th of November, 1834, brother Gill W. Watts wrote from Wattsborough, Virginia:

Reformation has prospered beyond our most sanguine expectation for the last eight months. Hundreds have come in, and the prospect is still good. Though the opposition is great, we hope we shall conquer through the word of the Lord, if we persevere (1834:607).

Campbell reminded his readers that reports published under the caption, "The Progress of Reform," were only a small percentage of all the correspondence he received monthly relating to the churches, but compared to 1833, the growth of the churches had diminished considerably in 1834. *The Millennial Harbinger* reported approximately twenty-three hundred immersions in 1834. *The Christian Messenger* reported approximately thirteen hundred, and *The Evangelist* reported about three hundred and fifty.

The Year of 1835

1835 was little better than 1834. *The Christian Messenger* reported approximately fifteen hundred added through the year. *The Evangelist* noted few over eight hundred, and *The Millennial Harbinger* recounted about eighteen hundred immersions.

Significantly, Campbell omitted "The Progress of Reform" in six of thirteen (there was an August Extra) editions of *The Millennial Harbinger* for 1835. While it is presumptuous to draw detailed conclusions from this fact, there are indications that the movement was facing serious problems.

The "Christian" stream, recently united with the "Reformer" stream, was confronted with disturbing repercussions from Christians of the east. The February, 1835, edition of *The Christian Messenger* carried a letter from J. V. Himes of Boston, Massachusetts, dated January 16, 1835 that contained questions related to the recent union.

Have the Christians given up the old ground, or, that on which they first came out in doctrine, and practice, thirty years ago? Are they now amalgamated with the Reformers, or Disciples, so as to make of both parties one body, or do the Christians retain a distinct standing, and adhere to the name, and the divine unity, and so forth as formerly? Or have the Reformers united with the Christians, in part, or fully? (*The Christian Messenger* 1835:41-42).

Mr. Stone gave a detailed reply adequately summarized in his introduction:

The ground on which we then stood, was the Bible alone, as the only rule of our faith, and practice. This ground we yet occupy, to the exclusion of all creeds of human mold, and device, as authoritative (1835:41-42).

The problem troubled Mr. Stone. Again he wrote:

From several sources I have taken up the idea, that the Christians of the east have believed, and do yet believe, that the Christians of the west have abandoned their former ground of profession, and have joined the Campbellites, or Reformers, so called (1835:107-110).

By June, 1835 there were indications that many "Christians" were withdrawing from the leadership of Barton Warren Stone following the union of the Christians and Reformers. In that month, Mr. Stone wrote:

Many of my old patrons have done me a serious injury. I solicited them long before the commencement of Volume IX, that they would notify me in due time, if they discontinued. If this were not done by them, I should still consider them as subscribers, and send them the Messenger. I have continued to send to them, and not till four or five numbers were sent, have I received any information of their discontinuance. Hundreds have treated me thus (1835:144).

320

The dissension grieved the editor. In July he wrote again.

> I have lamented, and do lament the state of some of our old brethren a little to the east . . . who have become so very warm and zealous in their opposition to what they call Campbellism (1835:226-227).

Problems troubling the young brotherhood were also obvious in *The Millennial Harbinger*. Moses Martin wrote to the editor of the *Harbinger* from Washington County, Indiana in February, 1835:

> There are a few of us in this place, professing to be reformers after the apostolic mould, as expressly exhibited in the New Testament; but I fear we scarcely deserve the name . . . (*Millennial Harbinger* 1835:277).

Mr. Campbell, after a visit to Louisville, Kentucky, in April, 1835, observed:

> Hindrances have been thrown in the way of the weekly meetings of the brethren, that the growth has been rather downward than upward, and progress rather backward than forward. Other unpropitious circumstances have much retarded the progress of the cause in this city (1835:331).

William Hayden wrote from Streetsborough, Ohio in July: "We are going on slowly, I think, in every respect." Barton Warren Stone wrote to Mr. Campbell in August:

> Everything flourishes here but religion — this is very sickly, and almost sick unto death. 'Like people, like priest.' The preachers have almost left the field and only preach when it suits their convenience (1835:477).

In the December issue of the *Harbinger*, Robert Richardson contributed a piece entitled, "Reminiscences of 1835." Part of what he wrote gives explanation to some of the tension among the churches.

But the bee has its sting and the rose its thorn, and while we rejoice in the influence of the press we must not forget that whatever has ability to benefit has equal power to injure, and that the press may be so poorly managed and its influence so misdirected that it will displease where it should delight, and wound where it should defend. That this has, in some measure, been the case with some of our periodicals during the past year, is unhappily true. A great degree of carelessness has been betrayed, unbecoming expressions admitted, unjust charges made, and unscriptural questions — subjects of debate and strife have been too often substituted for those things which promote peace on earth and good will among men (1835:618).

The Year of 1836

Through 1836 *The Millennial Harbinger* included "The Progress of Reform" every month but one. The additions by faith and obedience were down again and lower than in 1835. Letters to the editor reported approximately seventeen hundred immersions for the year, and *The Christian Messenger* less than three hundred.

Alexander Campbell suggested one possible reason why numbers continued to diminish.

The brethren are too remiss in forwarding accounts of the progress of the gospel in their respective vicinities. We know that many of them, though glad to hear of the triumphs of truth in other quarters, are scrupulous of the propriety of announcing the progress of light in their own communities. They think of the sin of David in numbering Israel as some speak of it, or they do not think it for other reasons pertinent to report the increase of disciples. Such sqeamish Christians were not those in Judea, Samaria, and among the Gentiles who first believed in Jesus. The inspired and

322

divinely authenticated history of the church frequently names the multitudes, the thousands, the myriads, and the individuals too, that turned to the Lord. It is most exhilarating to hear of the success of the truth, and as we receive pleasure and encouragement from the communications of others, we ought, in payment of those debts, when we have good news, to communicate them (1836:184).

The Year of 1837

Approximately eleven hundred additions to the churches were reported in the *Harbinger* in 1837. Granting there were more accessions than indicated above, yet there was a drop in growth, and it was obvious to many. At the same time, there were expressions of optimism. A. S. Hayden observed:

There is a spirit manifested by most of the disciples now, much more salutary in its effects on community than what we have so often seen. I think the fruits of the Spirit, love, joy, peace, long-suffering, gentleness, fidelity, are abounding more. This is a happy improvement: may all the saints abound therein more and more! (1837:239).

And yet B. Allen wrote out of Jefferson County, Kentucky three months later:

There are but few, very few congregations, that, on their personal, relative, and congregational order, have come up to the standard of the New Testament (1837:429).

Later in the year, N. J. Mitchell forwarded a letter to the editor of the *Harbinger* from Howard, Centre County, Pennsylvania. He offered the opinion that

Since the spring of 1832, more than three hundred persons have been immersed for remission within the bounds of a very small portion of this country. Some have apostatized through the influence of the tyrant Habit (1837:475).

The Year of 1838

The picture changed in a most extraordinary way in 1838, and cause for optimism was obvious from the beginning of the year. Mr. Campbell, in January introduced the section, "News From the Churches," with the happy comment:

> We have much, very much good news from the churches. I could wish to have laid it all before our readers in extenso, but it would fill a whole number to give all the incidents and details, with the many excellent remarks accompanying (1838:44).

In April, the editor commented on the advance of the Movement. He seems to suggest, however, a factor that has, since then, become a major flaw in the outreach of Christian Churches. Her leaders, for the most part, have ignored the cities.

> We are happy to learn that the good cause we plead is steadily advancing. It is gaining a little in the cities of New York, Philadelphia, Baltimore, and Richmond, and the Western cities generally; but in the country it advances much more rapidly. We flatter ourselves that it is about to spread more extensively in the South. Still the brethren have it in their power instrumentally to send it throughout the land much more speedily and successfully (1838:192).

In June, Mr. Campbell once more expressed his joy over the accelerating growth throughout the brotherhood.

> There is much good news from the churches. It seems as though the primitive zeal and the triumphs of ancient times

324

were returning in these last days. The power of the truth is about being displayed in the state of Indiana and Illinois, may we hope, as it is in Kentucky (1838:282-283).

The best indication of a change for the good was the increase in the numbers added to the churches. Five thousand eight hundred and thirty-six accessions were revealed through the pages of the *Harbinger* and twenty-three hundred and sixty-five were reported in the *Evangelist*. The latter journal numbered many of the additions found in the *Harbinger*, but both journals reflected a spirit of optimism so far as the future was concerned.

The Year of 1839

1839 was also a good year. *The Millennial Harbinger* contained the news of fifty-one hundred and fifty added; only a percentage of those actually won. A few over five hundred were noted in *The Evangelist*. While pleased with the labors of many of the preaching brethren, Alexander Campbell was disturbed with the lack of concern evidenced by others.

> I have much to reason and remonstrate with some of our preaching brethren that are now lying in dry dock, sails furled, and the worms preying upon the hull. Put to sea, brethren, or your ship will perish with the dry rot (1839: 264).

By 1839, a problem lying below the surface and that several of the brethren had raised, demanded critical attention. Hundreds of churches were being planted and thousands were being added through primary obedience, and there were no pastors and preachers to care for these congregations. Mr. Campbell was aware of this difficulty.

The cry for help is universal. Brethren that have truly given themselves away to the Lord, his cause, and people, are kept posting up and down, as field marshals in the heat of battle, until their energies are gone in a few years. Churches are not set in order. Evangelists convert, but do not generally set things in order. Helps in the church, shepherds over the flocks, under the Chief Shepherd, as well as evangelists, are wanting. The people pray for laborers in the vineyard. But it seems to me they must still farther be awakened; and their wants be farther liberalized, and heavenly things must more effectually eclipse the earthly, before the word of the Lord will advance as it ought to do (1839:427).

A handicap for all men desiring to give their full time to the preaching ministry was the lack of any means of support. Mr. Campbell, with his affluent means, travelled and preached at his own expense, but few could do as he did, and the problem was often referred to. To this, Mr. Campbell also addressed himself.

Has not the Lord ordained that they who preach the gospel should live by the gospel? Will any one deny this decree, or say it must not now be obeyed. Awake, brethren, awake! Read Paul our Apostle, I Cor. 9th chapter; and when you pray that the word of the Lord may run and be glorified, do not muzzle the preacher nor tie him to the plough (1839: 472).

By 1839, some evidence of the organization of churches within given states was apparent. In Indiana one hundred and fifteen churches were reported (1839:356) with approximately fifteen thousand members, with one hundred qualified laboring evangelists, and approximately one hundred and fifty teaching bishops (1839:551).

T. M. Allen from Boone County, noted that in November of 1839, Missouri could boast of thirty churches with a communicant membership of one thousand eight hundred and forty-seven (*The Evangelist* 1839:264).

In the above year, the *Harbinger* noted that:

> There are in the United States about two hundred thousand (professors of the Ancient Gospel) who distinguish themselves from other denominations of professing Christians by the above scriptural name (*Millennial Harbinger* 1839: 165).

The Millennial Harbinger reported over fifty-eight hundred added to the churches in 1840. *The Evangelist* reported five hundred and seventy-nine, and the *Christian Messenger* tabulated six hundred and one. There was some duplication in figures between the *Evangelist*, the *Messenger*, and the *Harbinger*, but 1840 was a good year for the Restoration Movement.

The Year of 1840

A number of developments indicated continued outreach of the churches. An example was the expressed desire of the churches of Indiana to have their own state paper.

> We have no paper to meet the calumnies with which the cause of reformation and of restoration of primitive Christianity, to which we are attached, is often assailed. Such a paper, by some of us, has long been considered a desideratum. We want a weekly or semi-monthly sheet, to be issued from some central point, which shall be taken by every congregation (1840:277).

There was a growing brotherhood among the churches in given states. J. T. Johnson, in May, 1840, wrote from

327

Georgetown, Kentucky, commenting on the recent state meeting at Harrodsburg.

> It was very partially attended. It is confidently believed that not more than one third of our strength was reported. The returns gave 10,000 members. I feel assured from my own knowledge and the information received from others, that our numbers would fall very little, if any, short of 30,000 (1840:335).

Alexander Campbell, after attending the meetings of the Western Reserve churches in Warren and Euclid, Ohio, reported in October, 1840:

> During the last year very large additions have been made to many churches. From a number of detailed statements we concluded that the number of disciples on the Reserve has nearly, or altogether, doubled during the last year (1840:478).

There were in November of 1840, in Illinois, seventy-five churches with three thousand, seven hundred and seventy-three communicant members (*The Christian Messenger* 1940:105-107).

Walter Scott of *The Evangelist*, inserted an interesting piece in the March, 1840 issue of that journal.

> There has been a very great religious excitement in Cincinnati. The Methodists have received, it is reported, about 700 converts; our brethren about 200; Mr. Lynd's church, 150; and the New School Presbyterians from 60-100. The preachers who have been in successive attendance in Sycamore Street meeting house are brothers Challen, Burnet, Jameson, Thompson, New, Ricketts, and Moss, and at present brother New again. The meeting still continues and promises good things (*The Evangelist* 1840:72).

The Year of 1841

1841 was the finest year in the growth of churches from the beginning of the movement through that year. With sixty-eight hundred additions reported in *The Millennial Harbinger*, twenty-six hundred numbered in *The Evangelist* and fifteen hundred recorded through *The Christian Messenger*, only a small percentage of those won during the year, one is led to acknowledge that the real growth was little short of phenomenal.

Alexander Campbell observed in the January, 1941, *Christian Messenger* that "Since our last, upwards of sixteen hundred additions have been reported to us, to say nothing of those reported to other periodicals. We thank God and take courage (*The Christian Messenger* 1841:173).

The Millennial Harbinger for November, 1841, gave an account of the churches in Missouri. There were at least fifty-eight churches throughout the state with five thousand communicant members, and the churches reported, through the year, sixteen hundred additions. For the first time the churches chose two of their finest preachers to serve as evangelists for the state.

The Year of 1842

Reports from *The Christian Messenger* reflect the cause for the continued growth of the churches in that year.

From the February *Messenger* came the news that:

> The religion of Jesus is prospering in this country. Since June last, at the meetings I have attended, there have been added to the Lord and introduced into his kingdom, three hundred and twenty-four (*The Christian Messenger* 1842:128).

Walter Scott reported fifty immersed at one meeting at Minerva, Mason county, Kentucky. Brother Crihfield

329

reported fifty-two additions in Lexington; forty of them by immersion. Five were immersed at Mount Iberd, Kentucky; ten in Jefferson County, Indiana. Brother Rice at Owingsville, Kentucky, added twenty-five. Brother Short at Warsaw and New Liberty added twelve; brothers Short and Thompson, at Coffee Creek, sixty-eight. At Winchester, Kentucky, seventy were added to the church; fifty-five at Mount Sterling, twenty-four at Macedonia, chiefly by brother Kendrick. Brother Girt and Dunn immersed in Tennessee last summer about one hundred and fifty, reclaiming many that had become lukewarm, and organized several congregations. Brother William A. Howard of Lewiston, Illinois, wrote on March 1, that the Otter Creek church had eighty members. Brother H. Thomas of Florida, Missouri, reported that he had just closed a meeting resulting in thirty-two additions. Brother T. M. Allen reported on February 9, twelve additions at Fayette, Missouri. John T. Johnson reported from New Castle, Kentucky, forty-eight additions (*The Christian Messenger* 1842:191).

From Morgan County, Illinois, as reported in July, 1842, at Princeton, thirty-five added, at Franklin, about eighty in a few days, at Apple Creek and Sandy, sixty, and at Lick Creek in Sangamon County, 9 (1842:288). On July 17th, Walter Bowles of DeWitt County, Illinois reported that in the previous seven weeks two hundred and twenty-seven accessions had been won. In a letter written in June to *The Christian Messenger*, Carroll Kendrick of Kentucky reported two hundred and eighty-one additions (1842:288).

Other evidences of interest for the cause were revealed in various ways. At the Cooperation meeting for Athens and Morgan Counties in Virginia, a sum of three hundred and ninety-seven dollars was raised to underwrite the labors of two evangelists, "to ride in this district so long as said amount will pay them" (*Millennial Harbinger* 1842: 188).

A report of the churches south of the Green River, in Kentucky, revealed that as of August 13, 1842, fifty-one congregations, many organized within the previous four years, had enjoyed six hundred and nine additions through the past twelve months (1842:478).

Evangelist Elly, serving the Christian Churches for Warren, Simpson and Logan counties of Kentucky, recounted his labors in association with J. T. Johnson, H. T. Anderson and H. C. Rice in a letter published in the October, 1842, *Harbinger.*

> There have been added within the range of my operations up to the 13th June past, one hundred and one, making the total number of one hundred sixty-nine.
>
> The third Lord's Day in June last I commenced a series of meetings . . . embracing a period of seven weeks, and resulting in one hundred and eighty-four additions to the churches; and up to this time at Pleasant Hill Meeting, thirty-six additions more have been gained; making the total number of additions since the first of September last, three hundred and eighty-nine; and two hundred and twenty during the past seven weeks (1842:479).

The Millennial Harbinger revealed nine thousand, four hundred and fifty additions; *The Christian Messenger*, three thousand, nine hundred and eighty-five additions, and *The Evangelist*, nine hundred and seventy-seven additions for the year of 1842. There were many more than that.

While additions totaled only ten thousand, one hundred and ninety-five from reports in the *Harbinger* and *Messenger* for 1843, considerably lower than for 1842, yet, there were

331

evidences of greater activity, more careful planning and systematized organization of the work, than ever before. An example was the reports from associations of churches from various states.

The churches of Boone and neighboring counties in Missouri met in annual meeting at Bear Creek on the 21st of October, 1842, and forwarded statistics pertaining to the state of the churches at that time. There were thirty-eight congregations with a communicant membership of three thousand forty-three. Eight hundred and fifty-two additions were reported by twenty-nine churches. Seven new churches were established during the year (1843:92).

Later in 1843, on June 1, reports of the state meeting for Missouri were forwarded to the editor,

> Brother Campbell: Yesterday, our state meeting closed, after an interesting interview and very pleasant meeting which commenced on Friday, the 26th. Seventy-eight congregations were heard from, having five thousand, one hundred and sixty-six members; and to which there have been added since our last meeting two thousand, eight hundred and sixty-four members. Forty-two congregations reported to the last state meeting, were not heard from at this: their number then was two thousand two hundred and seventeen, which, added to the above number, would make seven thousand nine hundred and eighty-three members; but as large additions have been made in some of them, and there are other churches not heard from, I am certain that our number in Missouri is not less than ten thousand (1843:376).

Indicative of healthy growth in Illinois was the news from Pittsfield, Pike county, that "there have been about two hundred additions to the good cause in the bounds of this country, within the last three months" (1843:356).

A similar note from the Annual Cooperation for Smith-field, Ohio, was also found in the news of the churches of the *Harbinger* for October, 1843. Twenty-one churches reported sixteen hundred and twenty-seven members, with four hundred and eighty-five additions over the previous year (1843:476).

In a short piece in the *Christian Messenger* for September, 1843, twenty-three churches were listed in Iowa territory as of August, 1842, having a membership of one thousand and twenty-three members (*The Christian Messenger* 1843: 157-158).

Men giving their time to evangelism reported outstanding success. J. M. Mathis of Gossport, Indiana, wrote that from March through November he "had the pleasure of seeing about six hundred submit to our glorious King" (1842:30). In the February, 1843, *Harbinger* J. T. Johnson wrote, "I have closed my labors for the present year, and have reported to the churches, composing the cooperation in this country, five hundred and eighty-two additons" (*Millennial Harbinger* 1843:88). A note from W. M. Brown of Jacksonville, Illinois, announced that he had immersed within a few weeks four hundred and fifty persons (1843:91).

From Kentucky, W. P. Clark reported on December 24, 1842, that:

> during his last trip of three months there were two hundred and six additions, and during the year of 1842, within the bounds of his labors, in the counties of Marion, Green, Adair, Russel, and Cumberland, in Kentucky, seven hundred and eight persons were added to the army of the faithful (1843: 142).

In January of 1843 J. P. Robison from Bedford, Ohio, wrote that "Within three weeks, in Cuyahoga County, some two hundred have yielded in obedience to the faith of Prophets and Apostles." From J. J. Harvey came the news that "Two hundred and seventy-five have, within six weeks, been immersed on the profession of their faith in the Messiah" (1842:142).

The Year of 1844

A few more than three thousand were reported through the pages of the *Harbinger* in 1844 with the *Messenger* adding less than two thousand. The multiple accessions so noticeable in 1842 and to a degee in 1843 were, with exceptions, absent in 1844. The report of a large number won came from J. P. Robison of Bedford, Ohio, and it referred to 1843 rather than 1844.

> I have just closed my first year's evangelical labors, in which I have devoted my whole time. I have seen added to the saved over seven hundred (1844:142).

News of a great number of accessions came from Joseph Baker of Ross County, Ohio and it was dated March 4, 1844.

> There has been a great increase in the church since last June, without any intermission. The additions are every week, so that within twenty miles, there have been four hundred and fifty added. We have attended to baptizing every few days all winter. We also learn that more than two hundred have joined a small distance south of us — one hundred and fifty east of us — and one hundred and fifty northeast, all within forty miles, making about nine hundred, and our prospects are as good as ever (*The Christian Messenger* 1844:376).

From the state meeting at Fayette, Howard County, Missouri, May 17th, 1844, came news regarding the strength of the churches in that state.

Eighty-one churches were listed with five thousand, five hundred and forty-three members and reporting one thousand two hundred and eighty-two added since last May. There are fifty-five churches hitherto reported to our state meetings that were not heard from at this; they had when heard from, two thousand nine hundred and eighty-one members, which added to the above list, would make eight thousand, five hundred and twenty-four members and one hundred and thirty-six churches; but as there have been many new churches planted, and large additions to some others (if not to most of them), the number of the churches and members in the state would be much larger, if we could hear from them all (1844:95).

A note in the November issue of the *Harbinger* indicated the strength of the Movement in Kentucky by the end of 1844.

A week or two ago we put down the number of members of the Church of Christ in Kentucky, at forty thousand; but having conversed with brother S. M. Scott, who has been collecting our numbers in a portion of the state, we have no hesitation in saying, from the information he has collected, that we number fifty thousand in this state (*Millennial Harbinger* 1844:525).

Significant to the development of the churches was the move by the state brotherhoods of both Virginia and Indiana towards state-wide structure, the object, to establish closer cooperation in promoting the cause (1844:525-528).

The Year of 1845
By 1845 the *Harbinger* was the principal journal among the Christian Churches. Walter Scott's *Evangelist* had

335

ceased publication in 1844 and, following Barton Warren Stone's death in '44, *The Christian Messenger* ceased publication in early 1845.

The reports found in the *Harbinger* were incomplete. However, a study of the statistics provides an accurate barometer of the growth of the churches, and the rate of growth had dropped in 1845. A total of three thousand, eight hundred and ninety-eight accessions were noted.

Intimation of the problems facing the churches may be found in a note from William Hayden from Chagrin Falls, Ohio. He wrote, "I have been again on a tour among some of the churches in New York; but political strife, in addition to other things, has carnalized many minds" (1845:46).

The churches continued to be concerned about organization. Mr. Campbell wrote in February, 1845:

Much has been written, a great deal said, and little done, on the whole subject of Christian organization. But there is a growing interest in the subject manifested, and there is a growing need felt for a more scriptural and efficient organization and cooperation (1845:59).

Slavery was of major concern in 1845. Almost ten per cent of *The Millennial Harbinger* for that year was given to a discussion of that subject. Mr. Campbell was opposed to its practice, and in the war, now imminent, while there were numerous Christian Churches on both sides of the issue, they did not divide over the matter. The issue, however caused considerable tension among the churches.

Masonry also found its way into the pages of the *Harbinger* for 1845. Brethren took sides, and the question created problems.

The most encouraging news of the year had to do with the Missouri state meeting held at Columbia in mid-October. Alexander Campbell was there.

> One hundred and fifty-four churches were heard from, having eleven thousand, seven hundred and fifteen members, with seventeen hundred and forty additions during the past year; forty-two churches reported to our meeting in 1844, were not heard from at this meeting; they had last year thirteen hundred and forty-two members, which, added to the above, would make thirteen thousand and fifty-seven members, and one hundred and ninety-six churches in the state. That, however, is but a partial account, as there are many churches in the state from which no intelligence has been received; neither was there any thing like a full report of the additions made since the last state meeting. It is generally believed, if we could hear from all the congregations in the state, there would be considerably upwards of fifteen thousand members (1845:569).

The Year of 1846

News of the annual meeting in Trumbull County, Ohio, in October, 1846, gave evidence of the strength of the Restoration Movement on the Western Reserve. It was

> The largest assembly ever seen on the Western Reserve on a Lord's day. It has been variously estimated from ten to fifteen thousand persons (1846:600).

The small number of accessions to the churches for 1846 reported in the *Harbinger* was only one thousand seven hundred and twenty-one, indicating, in spite of the cheering reports from Ohio, that the churches were confronted with difficulties.

The Year of 1847 and 1848

Fifteen hundred and forty accessions were reported in the 1847 *Millennial Harbinger*. The number more than doubled in 1848 to thirty-nine hundred and thirty-seven. A footnote in the July, 1848 *Harbinger* gave an estimate of thirty-five thousand communicant members in that year for the churches of Illinois and Missouri.

The Year of 1849

Forty-one hundred and fifty-four additions were noted in 1849, and there was growing interest in promoting means of more efficient cooperation. Twice during the year Alexander Campbell stressed the need for a convention. In July he wrote:

> We all seem to see the necessity of such a meeting, and doubtless a great majority of the brotherhood are anxious to have it; but there is difficulty in taking the initiative (1849:418).

Again in August Mr. Campbell said,

> I am of the opinion that a convention, or general meeting, of the churches of the Reformation is a very great desideratum. Nay, I will say further, that it is all important to the cause of reformation . . . The purposes of such a primary convention are already indicated by the general demand for a more efficient and Scriptural organization — for a more general and efficient cooperation in the Bible cause, in the missionary cause, in the education cause (1849:476).

A program was formulated, and the convention of Christian Churches met in Cincinnati, October 24th, 1849. W. K. Pendleton provided a report of the conclave.

> We met, not for the purpose of enacting ecclesiastic laws, nor to interfere with the true and scriptural independence of the churches, but to consult about the best ways for giving efficiency to our power, and to devise such methods of cooperation, in the great work of converting and sanctifying the world, as our combined counsels, under the guidance of Providence, might suggest and approve (1849:690).

One decision of significance had to do with the formation of the American Christian Missionary Society. Mr. Campbell was its first president.

The Years of 1850 and 1851

1850, through monthly reports forwarded to the editors of the *Harbinger*, reflected an increase in numbers reported over the previous year. Out of churches now found from coast to coast and from Canada to Mexico, six thousand and fifty-nine accessions were listed. 1850 was a good year. 1851 revealed seven thousand eight hundred and forty-one additions. If, as the editor of *The Millennial Harbinger* insisted, numbers recounted represented but a percentage of the total growth of the churches of the brotherhood, and there is little cause for doubt that the editor was right, then the Restoration Movement was expanding at a healthy rate.

The Year of 1852

Letters to the *Harbinger* reported thirty-eight hundred and sixty-four accessions in 1852. A note from brother Walsh from North Carolina, dated June 16th, 1852 carried the following interesting information.

> We number here in eastern North Carolina, near three thousand members, many of whom are highly intelligent and zealous . . . (1852:537).

339

The Years of 1853, 1854, 1855 and 1856

Four thousand three hundred and forty-one accessions were noted in 1853, five thousand one hundred and eighty-five in 1854, six thousand one hundred and twenty-two in 1855 and two thousand one hundred and five in 1856.

From 1832 through 1860, the combined journals accounted for approximately one hundred and fifty-four thousand added to the churches in twenty-nine years. If this figure represents but half the total added, which is reasonable, then there were over three hundred thousand accessions between 1832 and 1860.

Alexander Campbell in 1833 estimated that there were already one hundred thousand members of the Reformed Movement (Garrison and DeGroot 1948:325). The above figures, added to Campbell's estimate, provide for more than four hundred thousand by 1860, not considering losses by death.

To estimate membership figures by the end of 1860, it is important to recognize that death was constantly depleting the membership of the churches. On the basis of a sixty year life span, reasonable for mid-nineteenth century Americans who had reached adulthood, sixteen and two thirds percent of the membership of the movement would be expected to die every decade. In three decades, fifty percent of the above four hundred thousand would have died, leaving approximately two hundred thousand for the membership of the movement at the end of 1860, which compares favorably with the one hundred ninety-two thousand, three hundred twenty-three given by Garrison and DeGroot (1948:328-329).

One can only marvel at the receptivity of the American people through these years.

Chapter Fourteen

THE GREAT REVIVAL OF 1858-1859

Two additional issues must be resolved. The first has to do with the growth of the churches through 1860, reviewed in Chapter Thirteen. The second has to do with the impact of the 1858-1859 revival upon the churches of the Restoration Movement.

Though the founders of the movement were influenced directly and indirectly by the awakenings of the 18th and early 19th centuries, yet historians have said little about the impact of subsequent revivals that swept across America and the world. The 1858-1859 revival provides a classic case study.

At best Alexander Campbell entertained a strong ambivalence towards the revivals of his day, and his continuing criticism, coupled with like expressions from other leaders of the movement provide ample explanation for the lack of endorsement, in any way, of popular revivals of the time.

The significant world-wide revival of 1858-1859, that blessed so greatly American Christianity, was as far as possible, minimized by Restoration leaders and publications.

The World-Wide Revival of 1858-1859

First evidences of the spiritual awakening in North America became apparent in the fall of 1857. Success in revival and evangelism was noted in Presbyterian and Anglican churches in Hamilton, Ontario, Canada in November where "from three to four hundred souls" were converted in a few days time (Orr 1965:101). Confessions multiplied to approximately forty-five per day, the revival spreading throughout the community and subsequently down to the states where it swept across the nation.

In December of 1857, the Presbyterians of Western Pennsylvania called a convention at Pittsburgh to consider "the necessity of a general revival of religion," in Presbyterian and other churches as well (1965:102).

Two hundred ministers and numerous laymen attended, and time was spent in prayer. A plan was made to call all believers to prayer, which was extended to all the churches on the first Sunday of 1858. God blessed, and a similar convention was called in Cincinnati for May which, when it was convened, became a gigantic prayer meeting.

That the revival began in Presbyterian Churches from which Alexander Campbell differed so sharply is reason for his dismissing it as unimportant. The Conservative Baptists today do not rejoice over evidence of spiritual vitality in the American Baptists from whom they departed thirty-five years ago!

In late September of 1857, a weekly prayer meeting started in a downtown Reformed Church in New York City, that in the first week in October began to meet daily. To that gathering came "merchants, mechanics, clerks, strangers and business men" (1965:103) who came together to "call upon God amid the perplexities incident to their respective avocations."

A financial crash with its consequent panic occurred in August of 1857, having much to do with starting this "most unusual revival in the history of religious awakenings in America," (Sweet 1973:310) in the financial center of New York City. Twenty daily prayer meetings were soon gathering across the city, and the movement soon spread to Boston and Philadelphia, and eventually to every town and city of consequence in the north.

Evangelical ministers from Congregational, Methodist and Presbyterian denominations were leading in the movement

— again ample reason for not mentioning it in the *Millennial Harbinger.*

Each day preaching services were held in downtown theatres, next to prominent business houses. At Burton's Theatre, every corner from the orchestra pit to the last balcony was filled at least one half hour before services were to begin. Soon the entrances were packed and the streets were crowded with pedestrians and carriages so that the excitement was overwhelming. On the 20th of March the famous preacher, Henry Ward Beecher, led in the devotions at Burton's with three thousand in attendance as reported by the *New York Times* (Orr 1965:106).

By the month of May, 1858, it was estimated that there had been 50,000 converts in New York City since the revival began, causing it to sweep across New England, to flood the cities and states of the Ohio River Valley, and to thunder across the newly populated Western States, washing the whole of the United States with the blessing of God.

No part of the nation escaped this outpouring. It began in the great cities, but it spread to the towns, the villages, hamlets and rural areas. It bathed the land, moving all classes of people, regardless of their circumstances. Orr says that "a divine influence seemed to pervade the land, and men's hearts were strangely warmed by a power that was outpoured in unusual ways" (1965:109). The numbers of converted men and women soon reached an estimated 50,000 per week for all churches combined across the nation.

Not only was the United States gloriously moved. Beginning in 1859, Ulster in Northern Ireland was blessed, with approximately 10% of Wales and Scotland also professing faith in Jesus Christ. In England the Awakening continued for a number of years, touching a number of European countries as well.

343

Similar phenomenal reports of Awakenings came from as far afield as South Africa and India, and from other countries also.

In the United States and in the United Kingdom, at least one million converts were reported. Beyond this, existing evangelistic institutions and missionary organizations were revived and strengthened, and new structures for the propagation of the gospel were created. The Bible Societies enjoyed growth and outreach never known before (Orr 1973:xii-xiii).

The Restoration Movement in the Context of the 1858-1859 Awakening

The Reformation, ultimately called the Restoration Movement, came into existence during the second Great Awakening, and became a substantial movement only in the early 1830's through the union of the followers of Alexander Campbell and many of the followers of Barton Warren Stone. The 1858-1859 Awakening, therefore, was the first in the life of the Restoration after it became a strong fellowship of hundreds of churches with many thousands of members in numerous states.

The Restoration Movement was still very young — less than thirty years* — at the time of the 1858-1859 Awakening.

---

*The author is fully aware that most Restoration Movement historians date the beginings of the movement from September 7th, 1809, the time of the publication of Thomas Campbell's famous Declaration and Address (Garrison 1809:8). However, it was not until 1811 that Thomas and Alexander Campbell established their first church and as late as 1827 they had planted only two, one of which disbanded in that year (Richardson 1868 v.2:167).

There are those, too, who date the beginnings of the movement from 1801, Barton Warren Stone and Cane Ridge. To the author it seems most reasonable to date the beginnings from the union of Stone "Christian" Churches and the Campbell Reformation Churches in 1831-1832. Obviously, some will differ (Williams 1904:361-375).

The work by states had yet to be organized, and few, if any, state papers had been published. A number of journals, beginning with the *Christian Baptist*, 1823-1830, and succeeded by *The Millennial Harbinger*, 1830-1864, both edited by Alexander Campbell; *The Christian Messenger*, 1826-1837, 1839-1845, edited by Barton Warren Stone, and *The Evangelist*, 1832-1844, edited by Walter Scott, had been published. Other lesser publications of shorter duration flourished for a time, but by 1858-1859 *The Millennial Harbinger* was the universally accepted journal among the Churches of Christ/Christian Churches. Any documentation concerning the 1858-1859 revival must therefore come from the *Harbinger.*

The Millennial Harbinger the Primary Source of Information

One has little difficulty in understanding the reasons for playing down the impact of the mid-century awakenings in the pages of *The Millennial Harbinger*, in spite of the massive amount of publicity given to the revivals in other religious and secular journals of the day (Orr 1965:108).

The secular press itself became the promoter of revival. Drawing attention to the part the newspapers played, a writer of the day observed:

> The Press, which speaks in the ears of millions, is taken possession of by the Spirit, willing or unwilling, to proclaim His wonders and go everywhere preaching the Word in its most impressive, its living forms and examples . . . a new thing and, under God a mighty thing in the religious world . . . The barest statement in figures . . . is more eloquent

of divine love than the voice of an apostle (Conant, *Narrative of Remarkable Conversions*, p. 394; as quoted by Orr 1974:35).

The Presbyterian Magazine for May, 1858, expressed its amazement at the favorable response of the press as follows:

Since the first settlement of our country, no religious movement has attracted more attention than the present. As might be expected, the religious press has chronicled numerous incidents connected with this work. But, what has seldom occurred before, the secular newspapers have also appropriated a portion of their columns almost daily, for two or three months, in giving detailed notices of prayer meetings in our large cities and various other particulars concerning the movement (Orr 1974:34).

Few were the critics of the revivals. *The Boston Courier* for April 5th, 1858 quoted the Unitarian, Theodore Parker, thus:

In this city, in March, 1858, in a meeting house, on a Saturday afternoon, we find honest and respectable men and women met together for prayer and conference; most exciting speeches are made; exciting stories are told; fanatical prayers are put up; a part of the assembly seems beside themselves and out of their minds; they say, 'The Lord is in Chicago and great revival is going on there; the Lord is in Boston and He has poured out His Spirit here' (Orr 1974:37).

A remarkable comparison between churches of the Restoration and churches of denominations encouraging the revivals can be seen in the number of members added through faith and obedience within Restoration churches. How the churches grew! In this growth, the contributors and editors of *The Millennial Harbinger* rejoiced and praised

346

God, with Alexander Campbell commenting upon the fast-expanding brotherhood with as much enthusiasm as any of the editors.

Growth Among the Denominations

The Gothic church in Brooklyn reported seventy-five conversions in a local awakening in January. During the same month, a thorough revival moved the Hudson River town of Yonkers, when nearly ninety conversions occurred. Over in new Jersey towns, unusual awakenings were beginning, and throughout the whole country was increasing an expectancy of a downpour of divine blessing (Orr 1965:104).

Dr. J. Edwin Orr has described in detail the growth of the churches in 1858: of "eight thousand people converted in Methodist meetings in one week"; "of seventeen thousand conversions reported . . . by Baptist leaders in three weeks"; of "96,216 people . . . converted to God in the few months passed"; the number of conversions reported soon reached the total of fifty thousand weekly, a figure borne out by church statistics showing an average of ten thousand additions to church membership a week for a period of two years" (Orr 1965:109). WIlliam Warren Sweet recorded that "the final total ingathering of new members into the churches throughout the country as the direct result of the revival was more than 1,000,000" (Sweet 1973:311).

Comparable Statistics From Restoration Movement Churches

The editors of *The Millennial Harbinger* did not intimate that the growth of the churches of the Restoration Movement was in any way influenced by the Awakenings, but

The Millennial Harbinger announced with pride that the growth of Restoration or Christian Churches in the year of 1858 was nothing less than explosive.

Circumstances among Restoration Movement churches were not unlike those described by Orr among the Methodists, Presbyterians, Baptists and others.

"Brother Allen Wright, and L. B. Wilkes have recently held a meeting in Petis County, Missouri, where there were 100 additions" *(Millennial Harbinger* 1857:599): "Trenton, 16 additions; Lindley, 35; Middlebury 10, Linnaeus 15, Chillicothe, 18; Richmond, 10; Louisville, 9; making 171 accessions to the army of the faithful" (1857:660).

In February of 1858 A. S. Hayden reported a total of 401 additions in Northeastern Ohio (1858:172-174). From Texas, S. B. Giles, near Austin, reported "200 additions over the past six months" (1858:237-238). From Missouri Allen Wright reported from Lexington 40 additions, from Salt River church, 39 additions, from Canton 80 additions and from Louisiana, 70 additions (1858:238).

A note in the May, 1858, issue of the *Harbinger* reveals that the editors of the journal were fully aware that something unusual was occurring.

> In adding up the reports made to us of the success attending the labors of the brethren in the ministry, we are pleased to see that for the months of March and April, up to this date, April 2nd, one thousand nine hundred and twenty-six immersions have been reported to us. Of course, this has been accomplished by comparatively a very small portion of our ministry, and in a few months (1858:300).

Alexander Campbell could not ignore the phenomenon so obvious in so many of the denominations and of the

Restoration Movement alike. In June, 1858 he wrote a significant piece on "The Revival in America."

> Those who sneer at this religious agitation forget that at the worst it is better than a mania for rotten banks, or for railway shares. Anything that takes away New York men from their dollar worship for an hour during the busiest part of the day must, incidentally, if not directly, do some good. Beyond this there is no doubt that some of the prayers and preachings they hear during the hour have in them much nobility of thought, and much of the spirit of true religion . . . We have from Ward Beecher and others some fine words that would do honor to a Wesley or a Whitefield.

> There are seasons of refreshment in the New as well as in the Old world. We are blessed with one of these at Bethany College. During a few days past over twenty, mostly students, have been buried in Baptism, and have enlisted for life in the service of the Divine Redeemer. We have reason to hope that the harvest is not yet ended, but that others will participate in the greatest of all blessings in having their names registered in the Book of Life everlasting. A. C. (Alexander Campbell) (1858:346-347).

Mr. Campbell's "seasons of refreshment" not only affected Bethany College. A letter from D. S. Burnet written while he was in Leavenworth City, Kansas Territory, and dated June 10, 1858, reported 83 additions in twelve days at Hannibal, Missouri and since then 120 added in Fayette, Lexington, Richmond, Liberty, Independence and Kansas City (1858:413-414).

The July, 1858 *Millennial Harbinger* also quoted an article from the Paris, Missouri, *Mercury*. It reported that in a protracted meeting that was commenced in the Christian Church by elder D. S. Burnet:

349

Seventy-five of our citizens, many of them just in the morning of life and entering upon the duties of manhood, accepted the terms of the gospel and enrolled themselves as soldiers of the cross and followers of the lamb . . . On Thursday last, a scene occurred, the like of which was never before witnessed here — the baptizing of some fifty or more persons at the same time. On Monday morning a large number were baptized, in the presence of one of the largest assemblages that ever convened here on a like occasion. Elder Burnet preached a series of some twenty-one discourses, (two per day) and was listened to throughout, by enthusiastically large and attentive audiences — There were large crowds daily in attendance. Some of the remotest parts of the county were represented, and at the close of the meeting there seemed to be as great an eagerness to hear him as in the commencement (1858:418-419).

From Kansas City on June 7th, 1858, Mr. D. S. Burnet reported an excitement over spiritual things that equalled in intensity, if not in numbers, the "religious agitation" of the New York City money men commented upon by Alexander Campbell.

For a week past all business had been suspended, by common consent during the forenoon services — Every store and shop was closed . . . I have spoken five times here to large audiences, which have tested the capacity of the two largest houses in the city. Yesterday no house here would hold half the people (1858:419-420).

Again in the October issue of the *Harbinger*, Mr. Campbell wrote:

The cause we plead had not been more successfully pled for many years, so far as we are posted, than during the present year. From our exchanges, we observe its continuous progress and success. Some five hundred additions by immersion are reported during the last month . . . A. C. (1858:594).

Note that Campbell credited the extraordinary growth observed in the previous month, not to the revival or general awakening, but "to the cause we plead." This comes close to the heart of the reason for the complete lack of recognition among Christian Church historians of the tremendous 1858-1859 revival.

Through the close of 1858 and into the year of 1859, continuing news of extraordinary growth of the churches was reported. These paragraphs but touch the highlights. From Missouri, T. N. Allen reported; at Glasgow, 1 addition; at Smithville, 159 additons; at Berry, 17 additions; at Miami, 20 additions; at Huntsville, 5 additions; at Middlegrove, 44 additions; at Millersburg, 2 additions; at Antioch, 4 additions; at Salem Church, 27 additions (1858:656).

From Kentucky, John Allen Gano reported, 150 additions in a period of six weeks at Carlisle and Sharpsburg; at New Castle 44 additions. From A. E. Myers in Virginia, about 150 additions in Belle Aire, Barnesville and Beeler's Station (1858:657-658). From Texas Henry Thomas reported 28 additions at Lyons and 70 additions at DeWitt, Goliad, Lavacca, Caldwell and Fayette, and C. Kendrick from Salado, Belle Air County, reported 200 additions to the good cause (1858:718).

Brother Chester Bullard, reporting from Virginia recounted 73 added at Christianburg (1859:58). D. S. Burnet reported 76 additions at Platte City, Missouri in two visits (1859:116). Robert R. Rice from Owen County, Indiana reported, "There has been in this past year 400 additions

351

to the cause of our Master" (1859:118). C. LeVan reporting from Minnesota wrote of 77 additions (1859:179).

Apprehension felt by leaders of the Restoration Movement may be found in an article written by Robert Richardson entitled, "Converting Influence."

> We deprecate, therefore, the adoption of any theory upon this subject, and desire only to urge the claims of the gospel, as, at least, the only revealed instrumentality through which the Spirit of God accomplishes the conversion of the sinner. What influences he may exert in and of the gospel, and in what particular manner the heart is 'opened' for reception, we regard as questions entirely subordinate, and as matters of opinion about which men may differ, without any just cause or occasion of dissension. R. R. (1859:230-231).

In the above article, Richardson emphasized his conviction, and that of the editors of the *Millennial Harbinger*, that it would be unfortunate if an impression with regard to this matter were to gather momentum which would either diminish the effectiveness of the word of God, or represent the Heavenly Father as nothing more than an inactive observer of the progress of the gospel.

> The Spirit of God is not to be separated from the word; neither is the word to be separated from the Spirit, in the great work of man's salvation. The former view opens the door to wild enthusiasm and every species of delusion; while the latter leads to a cold, abstract, undevotional philosophy, under whose influence true heartfelt religion declines and perishes. That men are regenerated by the incorruptible seed of the word, and sanctified through the truth, the Scripture distinctly affirms; as it does, also that it is 'the Spirit that quickeneth, and that Christians are

352

God's workmanship, created in Christ Jesus unto good works.' It should be sufficient for all reverently to believe these revealed truths, without presuming to theorize and dogmatize in regard to the particular mode in which either the word or the Spirit accomplishes the Divine purpose. R. R. (1859:231).

The leaders of the Restoration Movement could do no other, however, than relate the growth of the churches to the infectious spirit of the Awakening affecting the denominational churches. Their expressed ambivalence towards the revivals continuing to be reported in the religious journals indicates the connection they saw between the Awakenings and that phenomenal growth.

"Ambivalence" is not quite the right word. Theologically they held that the revival was the expression of the "cause we plead," of the pure, primitive gospel we announce, of the effectiveness of New Testament religion as preached by the apostles, unencumbered with accretions, man-made creeds, and the paraphernalia of the denominations. It is easy to say now that they might better have rejoiced that the general awakening was in essence that primitive gospel and operated in all kinds of denominational trappings. Hindsight is so much more effective than present sight.

Numerous reports in the pages of the *Harbinger* establish the above conclusion. For example, brother R. M. Bishop of Cincinnati, Ohio, in reporting a "meeting" in that city resulting in ninety additions, recounted that brother Hopson of Palmyra, Missouri, the evangelist:

Having preached a discourse during the meeting upon the 'three-fold influence of the Spirit' which was much misrepresented by some of the press of the city, he was urged to repeat it; and that those wishing to hear might be accommodated, we secured the use of Smith and Nixon's hall (the largest in the city) which holds about 2,500 persons. It was filled to over-flowing; and from 1,000 to 1,500 persons had to leave for want of room. This meeting has been the means of giving us a hearing and position in this community that we never had before (1859:235).

Restoration leaders also saw the connection between the revival in the British Isles and the revival in America. The October, 1859 *Harbinger* carried news of the revival in Scotland.

We give the following from the *National Intelligencer*, extracted by that paper from the *London Beacon*, which the editor states, 'was read at the 5 o'clock Union Prayer meeting, in Washington City, on Friday afternoon, July 22nd — after which the whole congregation rose and joined in the Doxology, Praise God from whom all blessings flow.' To the honor of Scotland the news of the American Revival was received with implicit confidence and unfeigned joy by the ministers and members of the Scottish churches, and a union prayer meeting was established in Aberdeen (1859:571).

Again, an informative piece on *The Revival in Ireland* was found in the *Harbinger* for November of 1859. It was copied from the British *Millennial Harbinger* for August. The description is familiar.

It must not be thought of as confined to one town, nor to one country. Communications from some thirty places are now before us, and its range is widening. The following statement which relates to Belfast is, in substance, made in regard to various towns and villages. . . .

The influence of the revival is now almost without limit. All ranks, and classes, and creeds, have been reached by it

in this town and its vicinity; and hundreds have so completely changed, that it may be truly said of them – 'Old
things are passed away; behold, all things have become
new.' Entire streets which were known to be the most disorderly portions of town, in which nothing was to be heard
but quarrelling, cursing, and blaspheming, especially on
Saturday nights, have been so throughly changed, that last
Saturday night, there was scarcely a house in them in which
prayer and praise had not taken the place of drunkeness and
disorderly conduct. In some of these streets every house
had its penitent, or penitents. Those engaged in this work
of calling upon penitents have not had far to go from house
to house; for scarcely had they got out of one residence
when they were earnestly entreated to enter another in the
immediate vicinity, as a son or a daughter, a father or a
mother, had been brought to repentance. In some instances
the mental agony was evidently most intense (1859:626-627).

Comments of the editor of the British *Millennial Harbinger* upon the information out of Ireland must be noted.
However reluctant they were to reveal it, it expresses accurately the feeling of the leaders of the American Restoration
Movement regarding the whole matter of the Awakenings.

The British editor affirmed that although all those phenomenal things recounted in his article could be accounted
for, they could not be justified by apostolic example, and
this because of two deviations. While the Acts of the Apostles provided numerous records of conversion, of individuals, family groups, and even thousands in one day, not
one example of an awakened sinner could be found, with
access to the disciples of the Lord so that he could ask the
question, "What must I do to be saved?" having to wait
so much as half a day to enjoy the blessing of forgiveness
that many modern awakened ones agonize for, for days.

The first deviation, according to the editor was from the manner in which the apostles addressed unconverted sinners. The second was a deviation from the answer given by the apostles to convinced men and women who were anxious to be saved. It is true that the apostles carefully underscored the dangers in which the sinner stood, and they deliberately emphasized the danger to bring conviction and repentance, but at the same time they focused upon the mercy and love of God to create hope as the forerunner of the certainty of forgiveness. This did not at all bring an end to weeping, but the tears of fear were soon transformed to tears of gratitude and joy. With the apostles, as quickly as belief in the truths of the gospel had brought sorrow because of sin, they were at once prepared to say, "Repent and be baptized every one of you, for the remission of sins." With them, repentance was a change of mind with regard to God and His Son Jesus Christ. At one and the same time it was a change of mind with regard to sin, and it was for the penitent sinner a determination

> to live to him who died that they might live — and every sinner thus changed or begotten of God, was called upon without delay to 'arise and be baptized, and wash away thy sins, calling upon the name of the Lord.' They saw the Lord standing ready to seal their pardon by baptism — they 'went down into the water' — they 'went on their way rejoicing.' There were no singing parties standing over prostrate sinners — no praying men, relieving one another that constant prayer might be offered over the seeking soul — no calling upon God for the assurance 'just now' — all this is modern — deviation — the result of departing from apostolic example (1859:630-631).

356

Alexander Campbell and the editors of the American *Millennial Harbinger* were in reasonable agreement with the above, or the piece would not have been reprinted.

A significant article from the pen of W. K. Pendleton, one of the editors of *The Millennial Harbinger*, entitled "Our Progress and Prospects," reveals dramatically the dimensions of growth among churches of the Restoration in the year of 1859. Mr. Pendleton would have been reluctant, however, to relate this expansion of the movement to the American Awakening, then at its zenith.

> The year has been one of great activity among the disciples. Never has the gospel been proclaimed with more earnestness or its power more joyfully manifested in the conversion of souls. From every part of the wide union the story of its triumphs is sent up to us, and we feel fully warranted in saying, that during the last twelve months not less than thirty or forty thousand converts have been enlisted under the banner of the cross. Hundreds of churches have been planted and organized, in districts where, hitherto, we have scarcely had a name, and their influence and power are steadily increasing and constantly exerted to the further extension of the principles of pure, primitive, apostolic Christianity, both in faith and practice (1859:706-707).

Mr. Campbell, with the news of the 1858-1859 revival capturing the attention of Christian people everywhere, continued to be apprehensive about the Awakenings. His growing ambivalence is obvious in an article entitled, "Effusions of the Holy Spirit" found in the 1860 *Harbinger*.

> We rarely receive a mail of the religious press—whether Calvinistic or Arminian; Presbyterian, old school, or new school; Congregational or Independent; Methodist Episcopal, or Methodist Protestant; Baptist or Pedo Baptist;

in some of whose periodicals we do not at frequent intervals, read of remarkable 'effusions,' or outpourings of the Holy Spirit; 'great revivals,' 'large accessions,' 'glorious triumphs' won, and large additions made to their respective communities! These too, are proclaimed, and regarded by multitudes, as tokens, special tokens from heaven in divine attestation both of the call and mission of the preacher; and of course, of the doctrine, the gospel, or the theory which he may have promulgated. These converts, too, are frequently and publically presented and alleged as visible seals and pledges of the ministry, and of the divine call of the prominent actor, or actors, on such felicitous occasions (1860:189).

Mr. Campbell saw the revivals condoning an unbiblical freedom in leading the sinner to Christian faith, in opposition to the teaching of Scripture as exemplified in Ephesians 4:4-6, "There is one body, and one Spirit, even as ye are called in one hope of your calling; one Lord, one faith, one baptism, one God and Father of all, who is above all, and in you all." He insisted that there was no latitudinarianism in any Holy Spirit inspired passage of Scripture, but that quite to the contrary, "The laws of Grace are . . . consistent with themselves."

It was the conviction of Mr. Campbell, as he lived in the midst of the 1858-1859 revivals, still going on in 1860, that

the 'revivals of religion' — 'the outpourings of the Holy Spirit' in the reported conversions of our times, are not only never once found in the Old Testament or in the New, but are in sober reason and reflection, reprobate and delusive in the superlative degree. Religion has never died, and therefore it cannot revive. Men may revive — sin may revive — the heart may revive, and righteousness may revive, but religion can never revive in a heart in which it never existed.

358

'A pure language,' is indispensable to a pure religion, to a pure faith. So deposes the Holy Spirit. It is absolutely indispensable — and therefore we plead for it. During the Babylonian captivity, the children of Israel lost a pure speech. They afterward spoke in the language of Ashdod. So deposes Nehemiah, Chapter 13, 23. The Jews in their capitivity, intermarried with the daughters of Ashdod, Ammon and Moab. Hence, their children spoke half in the language of Ashdod and half in the language of Canaan. A. C. (1860:193).

One is compelled to affirm, regardless of preconceptions once held, and in spite of previous apprehensions over the revivals, for theological reasons or due to the writings of Campbell and others, that churches of The Movement experienced the same extraordinary results as did many of the denominational churches through those pehnomenal years. One is also compelled to reflect that the churches of The Restoration Movement lost a great opportunity when, instead of saying that the revivals were *not* New Testament practice and therefore suspect, they ought to have declared that such revival was essential New Testament practice and therefore to be greatly encouraged and duplicated.

The judgment of the British editor concerning the spiritual authenticity of the 1859 revival in Ireland must be accepted for the American revival as well. He affirmed that:

We believe that a few earnest, Christ-loving Christians well instructed in the apostolic method, that is, acquainted with God's plan, could at this time do a great work in the north of Ireland. The awakening is of the Holy Spirit — give to God the glory! The misdirecting and its results are of man, and as the Bible is in his hand, let him have the shame (1859:631).

Chapter Fifteen

THE RESTORATION MOVEMENT: PRODUCT OF THE AWAKENINGS

Alexander Campbell a Product of the Awakenings

Any effort to show that the Awakenings of the eighteenth and nineteenth centuries impinged upon the fathers of the Restoration Movement must take into consideration the thinking of Alexander Campbell, and he had critical views regarding the revivals of his day.

That his early life was influenced by the division within his own Presbyterian Church, by the independency observed in a number of congregations in Ireland and Scotland and by such men as John Glas, Robert Sandeman, the Haldane brothers, James and Robert, by the celebrated Rowland Hill, and by Greville Ewing, among others, these men products of the Great Awakenings, are factors readily admitted. In a real sense Alexander Campbell was a product, directly and indirectly, of the Great Awakenings.

Campbell's Preaching Not Accompanied by Bodily Exercises and Fanaticism

Mr. Campbell arrived in America in 1809. The Second Great Awakening, which began in Britain in 1791, spreading quickly to Europe and America, was in full bloom in the United States, particularly in Kentucky and Tennessee. Barton Warren Stone described certain "bodily agitations or exercises" which took place in revivals he attended in the early nineteenth century, such as "the falling exercise, the jerks, the dancing exercise, the barking exercise, the laughing and singing exercise, etc." (Rogers 1847:39).

360

Archibald McLean, writing one century later, in referring to these various exercises and Alexander Campbell's attitude toward them, was undoubtedly correct in writing,

> When Mr. Campbell preached, these bodily agitations were conspicuously absent. There were no swoonings or trances or roarings, no running against the wall, no beating themselves against the ground or tearing it up with their hands, no screamings or ravings or other evidence of mental derangement. The effect was perhaps as great, but it was different (McLean 1908:24-25).

That Mr. Campbell preached to large audiences and great numbers of people is well known. His preaching, however, was without passionate emotionalism. It was so presented as to appeal to one's logic and reason as he built his arguments, point by point, from the word of Scripture. The results obtained from his preaching, however, were, in many respects, not unlike those of the revivalist preachers:

> . . . many of those that heard gave themselves then and there to the Lord. Others resolved to mend their ways and their doings. Others, still, went home to search the Scriptures to see whether the things they heard were true (1908:25).

Ambivalence Towards Revivalism

Mr. Campbell, at best, entertained a strong ambivalence towards the popular revivalism of his day. He was attracted by powerful evangelistic preaching, one of the features in times of revival. This led him to join with men like J. Merrill, John Secrest and Joseph Gaston, all associated with Barton Warren Stone and the "Christian party," and eleven other preachers in choosing Walter Scott to be evangelist of the

Mahoning Association in northeastern Ohio in 1827. Merrill, Secrest and Gaston were revivalists and they were most successful "making many converts among the people" (Richardson 1868:Vol. II,175); and Alexander Campbell knew it. He hoped for similar results through the preaching of Mr. Scott. He had to envision some parallel between the preaching of Scott on the one hand and Merrill, Secrest and Gaston on the other.

In the above expectations Campbell was not disappointed. Numerous churches embraced what Walter Scott called the New Testament view of conversion. In the first year, Scott baptized hundreds of penitent believers.

It was at this point that Campbell's ambivalence became apparent. If he was attracted by evangelistic preaching, he was turned away by the fanaticism of revivalistic preaching about which he was well aware, and word of Walter Scott's success in Ohio soon reached him. Rumor had it that Scott was preaching some new heresy, and because Campbell was already suspicious, he feared, as J. D. Murch discreetly wrote, that Scott's enthusiasm "might have carried him beyond the bounds of prudence" (Murch 1962:102). Alexander Campbell sent his father to examine the work. Any question of impropriety in preaching or practice was eliminated when Thomas Campbell saw the consequences of Scott's labor. Alexander Campbell's real fear was that Walter Scott, in his enthusiasm, was being carried away by the Cane-Ridge Meeting kind of revivalism so popular at that time.

The above transpired in the year of 1827 and the spring of 1828. In the year of 1827, Mr. Campbell addressed himself to the subject of revivals following reports of the same during the previous year in and around Boston.

> Some rumors and some symptoms exhibited not a hundred miles from Boston, within the last year, indicated that a revival was got up by some distinguished preacher or preachers . . . It seals the mission of a man to be the instrument of, or the great actor in a revival . . . When we see a revival got up by two men, about the same time, in different parts of the country, who are opposing each other, and one saying to the other, See how the Lord is blessing us: — ("but look how he has blessed and is still blessing us!") I say, when such is the fact, (as it is at this very time in some places to my knowledge,) revivals are divested of those miraculous powers which otherwise they would possess, and are incapable of being made seals of attestations to the mission of any of our textuaries (*Christian Baptist* 1827:403-404).

One can comprehend Mr. Campbell's understanding of revival; that it is not "got up" by men, and that true revival possesses divine manifestations of miraculous power. In other words; Mr. Campbell believed that true revival came only from God.

Alexander Campbell was not opposed to "real and genuine revivals of religion." Said he,

> I am fully convinced that there are real and genuine revivals of religion at different times and places, and that much good has resulted from them; . . . (1827:404).

Campbell's enthusiasm for the appointment of Walter Scott as evangelist of the Mahoning Association in this same year of 1827 was in full harmony with his views on "real and genuine revivals of religion."

Mr. Campbell was, however, dramatically opposed to "mock" revivals. He wrote further, "But there are so many mock revivals, that any doctrine can be proved to be true by them, and any preacher can be proved to be sent by God by them, if a revival under his labors, or attendance on his doctrine, will be admitted as evidence" (1827:404).

Continuing, Campbell said,

> I therefore judge of no doctrine or cause by the revivals that attend it. If I did, I cannot tell whether I should be a Cumberland Presbyterian, a Congregationalist, a common Presbyterian, a Baptist, of the Gillite, Fullerite — of the creed, or anti-creed school; whether I should be of the "Christian Church" or of the "Church of Christ," — a Methodist, a Calvinist, a Unitarian, or a Trinitarian; for they all, this year, have abounded in revivals. What says the Savior and his apostles, what say the law and the testimony, therefore, must turn the beam or decide the point with me (1827:404).

Fear of Union with the Revivalists

Mr. Campbell's apprehension concerning the popular revivals of religion of his day can be seen in his reluctance to encourage the union between his followers and those of Barton Warren Stone.

Mr. Stone had written in the *Christian Messenger* in 1831:

> The question is going the round of society, and is often proposed to us, Why are not you and the Reformed Baptists one people? or, Why are you not united? We have uniformly answered; In spirit we are united, and that no reason existed on our side to prevent the union in form. It is well known to those brethren, and to the world, that we have always, from the beginning, declared our willingness, and desire to be united with the whole family of God on earth, irrespective of the diversity of opinion among them. The Reformed Baptists have received the doctrine taught by us many years ago . . . (*Millennial Harbinger* 1831:385).

In the same issue of the *Harbinger*, Mr. Campbell answered Mr. Stone:

> For our part, we might be honored much by a union and public, with a society so large and so respectable as the Christian denomination; but if our union with them, though so advantageous to us, would merge "the ancient gospel and ancient order of things," in the long vexed question of simple anti-trinitarianism, anti-creedism, or anti-sectarianism, I should be ashamed of myself in the presence of him whose "Well done, good and faithful servant" is worth the universe to me. We all could have had honorable alliances with honorable sectaries, many years since, had this been our object (1831:391).

Concluding the article quoted above, Campbell wrote, "Indeed I think the question of union and cooperation is one which deserves the attention of all those who believe the ancient gospel and desire to see the ancient order of things restored" (1831:396).

Alexander Campbell's reluctance to unite with the followers of Stone came in part a result of his apprehension over the Christians' revivalistic practices. His response to the announcement that the Christians and Disciples had united in Georgetown and Lexington, Kentucky (*Millennial Harbinger* 1832:191) left the implication that the Christians of Kentucky gave more importance to oratory and declamation (a mark of much revival preaching) than they did to Jesus Christ and His apostles.

> But until the Christians have more love to Jesus Christ and more veneration for His apostles, than for fine oratory, or the warmth of a fervid and boisterous declaimer . . . it will be in vain to profess reformation or a love for the union of Christians upon New Testament premises (1832:194).

Apprehension Over the Christian Name

Mr. Campbell was also apprehensive over the name "Christian" itself. He granted that it was a name we can legitimately assume, but he added that some have taken it as a name only. In 1830 he wrote,

> Suppose, for example, that these reforming Baptists, who contend for the ancient gospel and the ancient order of things, should assume to be called Christians, how would they be distinguished from those who are called Christians, who neither immerse for the remission of sins, show forth the Lord's death weekly, nor keep the imitations, manners and customs of those called 'Christians first at Antioch?' (*Millennial Harbinger* 1830:372-373).

Mr. Campbell here alluded to the Christians of New England, and his fear was that if the reforming Baptists (associated with Campbell) were to unite with the Christians of Kentucky and were to embrace the name "Christian," they would, by that action be associated with the Christians of New England, who entertained enthusiastic views and continuing participation in popular revivals.

Thinking of the New England Christians, and this also applied to the Kentucky Christians, was best expressed by Abner Jones (1772-1841), one of the pioneers of the New England movement.

> Nearly every Christian Church in New England are (sic) the fruits (sic) of special revivals. Among all our faithful and successful preachers, where is one, who is not the fruit of some revival. Portland, Portsmouth, and many neighboring churches; Haverhill, Salem, Boston, New Bedford, and many flourishing churches in that region are all and every one of them the fruits of revivals. When we no longer have revivals, we no longer have prosperity (*Christian Palladium* 1837:375).

366

Because of his apprehension over revivalism and because those in Kentucky and those in New England, advocates of revival, wore the name "Christian," Mr. Campbell advocated the name, "disciples of Christ."

> But if anyone shall suppose that the term 'Christian' denotes a Unitarian, or Trinitarian, in its appropriated sense, we shall choose the older name, 'disciple,' and recommend to all the brotherhood to be called not 'Christians,' but 'the disciples of Christ' (*Millennial Harbinger* 1830:373).

Use of Term, Revival

When John T. Johnson of Georgetown, Kentucky, affiliated with the Reformers, Mr. Campbell captioned the announcement in the *Millennial Harbinger*, "Revival in Georgetown, Kentucky." However, before concluding the articles, he felt compelled to defend his use of the word revival.

> In calling this 'a revival,' I speak in some sense after the manner of men. The 'revival of literature,' and the 'revival of religion' are phrases specifically the same; and, when used in this acception, may be harmless. Literature had been dead and buried for ages before the Reformation. It was then resuscitated. In reference to Georgetown, Kentucky, since the crusade against reform commenced, the above incidents deserve to be called a revival. If it were not a great license of speech, I would say that the doings of the antireformers in that place since the conception and birth of the 'Literary Register and Baptist Chronicle,' have been a revival of irreligion. The recent occurrences in that place are like a refreshing shower in a long drought upon a parched soil. My prayer is that the good work begun in that place may progress until the works of the man of sin be consumed, and until all who are determined for eternal

life shall obey the gospel, and stand erect in the liberty with which Christ has made his people free. The Lord's freemen are free indeed (1831:180).

Aversion to Emotionalism

Mr. Campbell had a strong aversion towards emotionalism. When Sydney Rigdon rejected what Campbell referred to as the "Ancient Gospel," for Mormonism, Campbell commented,

> His instability I was induced to ascribe to a peculiar mental and corporeal malady, to which he has been subject for some years. Fits of melancholy succeeded by fits of enthusiasm accompanied by some kind of nervous spasms and swoonings which he has, since his defection, interpreted into the agency of the Holy Spirit, or the recovery of spiritual gifts, produced a versatility in his genius and deportment which has been increasing for some time (1831:100).

In the same year of 1831, the editor of the *Harbinger* published news of a Rochester, New York, revival in which he emphasizes again his distaste for such proceedings. His concluding comment regarding that occasion described the gathering as "deeds of violence against reason, revelation and the Holy Spirit" (West 1954:170).

> We must occasionally notice the fanaticism of this age on the subject of mystic impulses; for, in our humble opinion the constant proclamation of 'the Holy Spirit' of the schoolmen and all its influences, is the greatest delusion of this our age, and one of the most prolific causes of the infidelity, immorality, and irreligion of our contemporaries (*Millennial Harbinger* 1831:215).

In Alexander Campbell's understanding of the New Testament, no man could be converted by the internal workings of the Holy Spirit on his mind, and unregenerate men could not be suitable candidates for the Holy Spirit (West 1954:170).

Mr. Campbell wrote,

> But in the rage for sectarian proselytism, 'the Holy Ghost' is an admirable contrivance. Every qualm of conscience, every new motion of the heart, every strange feeling or thrill — all doubts, fears, despondencies, horrors, remorse, etc., are the work of this Holy Ghost. The Holy Spirit is equivalent to the spirit of holiness, and its fruits are goodness, gentleness, purity, peace, joy, etc. But not so the fruits of this evangelical Holy Ghost. To it is ascribed all the anguish, horror of conscience, lamentations and grief, which precede that calm called regeneration, so often witnessed in our greatest revivals (*Millennial Harbinger* 1831:212).

Mr. Campbell's Problem

Alexander Campbell's problem was scriptural, but it encompassed a metaphysical difficulty as well. It was his conviction that there was physical and moral power — power of two kinds. With physical power men put matter into motion, but they use motives and arguments to activate minds. Campbell contended that God reaches the minds of men with argument and motive as well (West 1954:171). But, he emphasized that revivals which give emphasis to physical exercises are not addressed to man's reason and logic.

> We have two sorts of power, physical and moral. By the former we operate upon matter — by the latter on the mind. To put matter into motion we use physical power . . . to put minds into motion we use arguments or motives addressed to the reason and nature of man (*Millennial Harbinger* 1831:293).

It was not because of their physical power that Mr. Campbell gave importance to the tongue and pen. Rather, it was because they could activate the mind. "The tongue of the orator and the pen of the writer, though small instruments in the world; because they are to the mind as the arms are to the body — they are the instruments of moral power" (1831:294). However, MR. Campbell was aware of misusing the tongue and was highly critical of those orators then popular in the revivals.

> Oratory is now the rage of Protestant Christendom. The good orator is the good divine, and men will be more at pains and labor to gratify this Athenian itch, than to keep the commandments of him who redeemed them by his own blood (1832:194).

In 1840 the editor of the *Harbinger* wrote a rather long article on religious excitement.

> What then shall we think of that religion which is the mere offspring of excited feeling — of sympathy with tones, and attitudes, and gestures — of the noise, and tumults, and shoutings of enthusiasm — of the machinery of the mourning bench, the anxious seat, the boisterous interlocutory prayers, intercessions, and exhortations to "get religion on the spot" etc., with which all are conversant who frequent revival meetings in seasons of great excitement (1840:167).

Revivals were "animal and imaginative" and when the revival was over, the "animal powers" would invariably cool, leaving the convert as cold and as dark within as before the revival, with "no fire in the soul — no light, nor knowledge, nor faith resting upon the rock of ages" (1840: 168). He contended that such revivals resulted in "apostacies, backslidings and public scandals," and it was his judgment that "those who have observed with the greatest accuracy the history of revivals and the consequences upon society, have doubted whether, upon the whole and in the long run, they are not a real disadvantage to the cause of true and vital religion" (1840:168).

Mr. Campbell recounted that a shrewd lawyer of his acquaintance, within one hundred miles of Wellsburg, Virginia, over ten or twelve years, kept a record of all revivals in the Methodist Church of a particular village. Accounting for all converts made during that time in a community of 800 to 1,000 people, he discovered that the totals of all reported converted exceeded the whole adult population of the town, and yet from that time to the day of Mr. Campbell's article in the *Harbinger*, never had that Methodist Church numbered as many as one hundred communicants (1840:168).

The best that can be noted with regard to Campbell's evaluation of revivals is found in his summary of his own feelings.

> While I believe that some good is done by such meetings and efforts, I have always believed that a great deal more was lost than gained by them; and constant observation has confirmed the verdict of former years (1840:168).

Campbell Favored Protracted Meetings

Mr. Campbell was favorably disposed to what he called "Protracted meetings."

> To fix the mind for a long time on the subject of religion, to abandon the business, and care, and perplexity, and pleasures of this life for some days in succession, and to turn all our thoughts to religious truth, to things unseen and eternal, is, in my judgment, sound wisdom and discretion. But on such occasions the people must be fed with the bread and water of life — with the word of God — with the gospel facts — revelations, precepts and promises, and

371

not with dreams, anecdotes, fictions, ballads, and unmeaning vociferations. No effort ought ever to be made to raise the feelings, the affections, or the passions beyond the understanding and the faith of the hearers (1840:168).

Campbell's View That Religious Excitement and Revivals Are Not Divine but Human

It was his judgment that:

The machinery of modern revivals is not divine, but human. It is certainly divisive. They are undoubtedly deceived who repose the slightest confidence in it. The spirit of the crusades is in it — the spirit of fanaticism is in it — the spirit of delusion is in it. The Spirit of God is not in it, else he was not in the Apostles; for he taught them no such schemes — no such means of catching men. This is a bait which was never put by Christ's fishermen on the evangelical hook. 'To the law and to the testimony; if they speak not according to this, there is no light in them.' So I believe and so I teach (1840:170).

Late in his life Alexander Campbell addressed himself again to the subject of revival.

A death of religion must always imply an antecedent life of religion; for nothing that never died has ever revived. Therefore a revival of religion of any sort, Jewish, Pagan, Mahometan or Christian is simply absurd; for not one of them has died. Is it not an axiomatic truth that nothing can revive that has never died? Therefore a revival of religion in any person that has never possessed it, is simply and obviously absurd (1862:351).

W. K. Pendleton's View

In 1853 an article recounting the Cane Ridge and other revivals of about 1801 and written by George A. Baxter,

Principal of the Washington Academy, appeared in the *Harbinger*, with a response by W. K. Pendleton, then co-editor with Alexander Campbell. Baxter described in great detail the nervous wonders, the jerks, barkings, fallings, etc. so common with the Kentucky revivals of that time, and he was a witness to these things.

Mr. Pendleton gives his "opinion" regarding those events that transpired more than a half century earlier.

> Simply that it was a peculiar form of nervous disease, that was both epidemic and contagious. It came suddenly, as the destruction and the pestilence, both at noonday and in darkness — seized upon all classes and conditions, good and bad, old and young, male and female, bond and free, saint and sinner; affected them all with the same characteristic symptoms of bodily derangement — tarried for a season and then disappeared. Its effect on the mind, so far as it was peculiar, was simply excitement. No new truths were communicated, — no old errors corrected — nor miraculous utterances given; but simply an excitement, despondent or hopeful, gloomy or joyful, clear or confused, according to the convictions of the mind at the time of the attack, and influence of circumstances during its continuance (1853:677).

Comparison of Campbell, Jonathan Edwards and George Whitefield

The above detailed examination of the views of Alexander Campbell concerning revival reveals that the major criticism focused on the bodily exercises and fanaticism often associated with revivals. In this regard, the advocates of the Reformation did not stand alone. The problem was grievous in the ministries of both Jonathan Edwards and

George Whitefield, so prominent in the Great Awakening of the early eighteenth century.

Jonathan Edwards was for twenty-three years minister at Northampton, Massachusetts, experiencing two times of revival: the first in 1735, and the second with George Whitefield, in 1740. The question,

> What is the nature of true religion? or, What are the distinguishing marks of that holiness, which is acceptable in the sight of God? . . . had become . . . a subject of warm and extended controversy. The advocates of revivals in religions, had too generally been accustomed to attach to the mere circumstances of conversion — to the time, place, manner, and means, in and by which it was supposed to be effected — and importance, no where given them in the Scriptures; as well as to conclude, that all affections which were high in degree, and accompanied with great apparent zeal and ardour, were of course gracious in their nature; while their apposers insisted, that true religion did not consist at all in the affections, but wholly in the external conduct. The latter class attributed the uncommon attention to religion, which they could not deny had existed for four years in New England, to artificial excitement merely; while the former saw nothing in it, or in the measures taken to promote it, to condemn, but everything to approve. Mr. Edwards, in his views of the subject, differed materially from both classes. As he knew from his own experience, that sin and the saving grace of God might dwell in the same heart; so he had learned, both from observation and testimony, that much false religion might prevail during a powerful revival of true religion, and that at such a time, multitudes of hypocrites might spring up among real Christians (*The Works of Jonathan Edwards* 1976:Vol. I,xxxii).

One of the disturbing problems that faced George Whitefield in his ministry in the American colonies in 1740 "lay

in the danger that fanaticism might creep into the work"
(Dallimore 1971:Vol. I,565). In New York, Whitefield had
become acquainted with a prominent Long Island minister,
the Reverend James Davenport, and from this man the
danger came. As a young man, Davenport had studied
at Yale, and he had a brilliant mind. So hard did he apply
himself to his studies that he suffered a nervous breakdown.
In spite of this, he went on to graduate and afterward
distinguished himself among his fellow ministers for his
learning, zeal and piety. He was an advocate and vigorous
participant in revivals and was stimulated by the excitement accompanying them, so much so that he engaged
in an itinerant ministry over a vast area. The effects of
his breakdown continued so that some months after Mr.
Whitefield returned to Britain in 1742, he nearly became
insane. On one occasion, he preached for twenty-four
hours, sadly discrediting the whole revival movement
(1971:Vol. I,566).

Under the preaching of James Davenport there were
frequent outcryings, and he did nothing to discourage
them. Consequently, the effort to stimulate emotional
outbursts during the services, a practice common among
some of the people, was at least tolerated by Mr. Davenport.
This was the circumstance when George Whitefield made a
return visit to New York and northern New Jersey.

None of this fanaticism had accompanied Whitefield in
New England, but as soon as he came to where Davenport
had been, it began to occur.

> Of his first service in New York he says, "Two or three cried
> out," and of his second, "crying, weeping and wailing were
> to be heard in every corner; men's hearts failing them for
> fear and many were to be seen falling into the arms of their
> friends" (1971:Vol. I,567).

As Whitefield came to Backenridge, similar events occurred. John Cross, minister at that place, had encouraged these outbursts, and as Mr. Whitefield preached, they happened again. He recounted,

> When I came to Backenridge, I found Mr. Davenport had been preaching to the congregation . . . It consisted of about three thousand people. I had not discoursed long, when, in every part of the congregation, someone or other began to cry out, and almost all were melted to tears (*George Whitefield Journals* 1765:487).

The circumstances were similar at Fagg's Manor and Nottingham. There, too, the people "had learned to seek the outcryings and faintings."
Dallimore observes that

> In witnessing these outbursts Whitefield was again confronted with the question as to where the work of the Spirit of God ended and where human imitation began — . . . He desired to see hearts broken under the hammer blows of the Word of God, and it was to his liking to report, as he did at New York, 'there was a great and gracious melting down among the people both times, but no crying out.' But he sought to prevent the displays of mere emotionalism, for example, at Backinridge; there he stopped preaching on account of the outcrying, prayed for the affected persons, sang a hymn and therewith closed the service. And likewise at Philadelphia was such a universal commotion in the congregation that he broke off prayer after sermon sooner than otherwise he would have done (Dallimore 1971:Vol. I.567-568).

Though they were three-quarters of a century apart, there were parallels between Whitefield, universally recognized product of the First Great Awakening, and Alexander

376

Campbell, a product of the Second Great Awakening. Both men were confronted with the same problem; and it was biblical: Where did the work of the Spirit of God end, and where did human imitation begin?

Mr. Campbell was a witness to similar bodily manifestations that were so upsetting to Edwards and Whitefield. On October 7, 1825, he attended the meeting of the Dover Association. Of that gathering he wrote,

> I had sat down from a calm and deliberate address on the first principles of the Gospel . . . It was equal to Wesleyan Methodism in its palmiest days. What a shaking there was in the camp! What a hugging of men with men! What weeping of females! What screaming of negroes! I thought I had got into a Methodist camp meeting and began to apprehend that it would find its way into the preacher's tent. I looked around and saw the muscles begin to work, in grotesque forms, in the cheeks of even Bishop Semple. It spread throughout our whole camp, with the exception, perhaps of Elder Broadus and myself . . . I could not hear one word, or appreciate one idea, as the worthy parent of what I saw and heard in the great congregation. I confess it awakened more painful than pleasurable associations, because indicating a condition of the pulpit, and of the public taste, that depressed my spirit, and saddened my heart with many a painful association and anticipation as likely to arise from my new association (*Millennial Harbinger* 1855:130).

A Question of Import for People
of the Restoration Movement

It seems clear that while they were an outcome of the Awakenings, it is not correct to equate the revivals of Jonathan Edwards, George Whitefield, John Wesley, Barton

Warren Stone and others with the Awakenings themselves. Not all the revivals were accompanied by bodily exercises and fanatic outbursts of emotion. George Whitefield preferred it that way. Nor were the great revivals of the Haldane brothers, Greville Ewing and Rowland Hill. The Awakenings were of far greater import and outreach than the mere fanatical outbursts and bodily exercises of the Cane Ridge or any other of the revival meetings.

This necessary distinction between revival and awakening was noted in the British *Millennial Harbinger* for August of 1859.

> 'Revival' is the word in use, but to say the 'great revival of religion,' seems to be using words not most fit to express what is intended. 'The Awakening' would better represent the movement, and better accord with the language of Scripture, 'awake thou that sleepest, and arise from the dead, and Christ shall give thee light' (Eph. 5:14). There has been, and there is still going on, in the North of Ireland, a great awakening of sinners to a sense of their danger and need of pardon and of Christ (1859:626).

The Word and the Holy Spirit

Early in 1855 Jeremiah Jeter, a Baptist preacher from Richmond, Virginia, published a book which he entitled *Campbellism Examined.* Jeter wrote,

> Mr. Campbell maintains, or did maintain, that all converting power of the Holy Spirit is in the arguments or motives which he presents to the mind in the written word. On this point I take issue with him. I maintain that there is an influence of the Spirit, internal, mighty, and efficacious, differing from moral suasion, but ordinarily exerted through the inspired word, in the conversion of sinners.

Whether this influence shall be called moral, from the effect which it produces, physical, from the energy which is put forth in it; or spiritual, from the nature of the agent who exerts it, I have no wish to decide. It is for the reality and importance of this influence, not for its name, that I contend (Jeter 1858:125).

Mr. Campbell quotes the above paragraph of Mr. Jeter and responds to his attack. The crux of the controversy between Jeter and Campbell was over the work of the Holy Spirit and centered on the question of regeneration.

Campbell answered Jeter, "He states what I did maintain or do now maintain," that all of the converting power of the Holy Spirit is effected through the revealed Word. Jeter argued that there is an influence of the Holy Spirit "internal, mighty and efficacious, differing from moral suasion, but ordinarily exerted through the inspired word in the conversion of sinners." Jeter said, "ordinarily!" Campbell asserted that "always" the influence of the Spirit was exerted through the inspired word.

A major difference between Campbell and Jeter centered on Jeter's statement, "He that made, can certainly renew the spirit of man, with means, or without them, as he pleases" (1858:127). Mr. Campbell took exception to this statement. He did not deny that God was able to work. This was not the issue. Because God is God he can do whatever he wills. The question that Campbell put to Jeter was, "On the evidence of the Scriptures, is there any record of the salvation of any man, woman or child without using means of any kind?"

Mr. Campbell said,

I will charge myself and credit Mr. Jeter for proof, even one proof, of the proposition that 'God works without means'

379

in creation, providence or redemption! Moses forgot to name any of those things which God created without means!! But my friend Mr. Jeter is the man to set him right, or, at least, to fill up that chasm in his account of creation!!

Again Mr. Campbell said,

We only ask one case in the Bible without it! Produce it, and then we have settled one of the greatest points in modern piebald Christianity (1855:144).

Campbell quoted Paul, "by faith we understand that the worlds were framed by the word of God" (Heb. 11:3) and declared that this statement of the Apostle was fatal to the speculations of Mr. Jeter.

If God did not, for reasons good and valid, create anything without his word, or without means, what shall we say of the wisdom or the presumption of the affirmation, that 'God who made man without means can renew him without means' (1855:133).

It was the understanding of Mr. Campbell that regeneration is a process and not a final act with regard to the salvation of a man. Campbell held that first the seed is sown in the heart, that the seed germinates and growth follows with new life eventuating with the new birth. The Holy Spirit both creates and quickens. In both instances it is the Word of God that is used to restore to a more perfect state the soul that was lost in sin.

Campbell held that the Spirit and the Word are the powers of the Heavenly Father working to bring about the salvation of the lost. The human responses are in hearing and believing. The Holy Spirit only has the opportunity to work when the Word has entered the heart. Campbell was convinced that men are not the authors of their own salvation. He knew that facts, or testimony or evidence alone was not sufficient to turn the hearts of the lost to the Father. He believed that men were convicted of sin and converted by the Holy Spirit, through the facts, the testimony, the evidence and the grace and truth of God made evident through Jesus Christ.

Mr. Campbell affirmed that the Spirit does illumine, sanctify and comfort Christians, as the Church has taught through all its history. "That there is a new creation, and frequently a recreation, a renewal, or, in a figure, a 'regeneration,' is conceded by all evangelical Christians" (1855: 189). This re-creation or renewal came through the Word of God through the work of the Spirit, but this did not mean that the Word and the Spirit were identical.

Jeremiah Jeter asserted that Alexander Campbell believed that "When the Spirit has presented all his arguments, he has spent all his power" (Jeter 1858:131). According to Mr. Campbell, the Holy Spirit uses the word to teach, to correct, to inspire and give direction to those who make up the body of Christ. It is the word that must impact upon the heart and mind of man, before the fruits of the Spirit can appear.

Revivalism was a phenomenon with which Alexander Campbell was well acquainted. He had been exposed to the camp-meeting type revival in 1825 at the Dover Association in Virginia (*Millennial Harbinger* 1855:130). The revivalism of the early nineteenth century emphasized the power of the Holy Spirit. Focus upon the Spirit rather than a focus upon Jesus Christ was, in the judgment of

Mr. Campbell, the characteristic of the revival movements. To a degree, this was the reason for the lack of enthusiasm of Mr. Campbell for the revivals. In his discussion of Jeter's book he is critical of revivalism. There was "more heat than life . . . there was much said of the Spirit, something to the Spirit, but little of Christ." There was more preaching "about the Spirit than about the Saviour, and more about getting religion, than living it" (1855:131). Campbell's concern was to be faithful to the teaching of Scripture on the cognitive and ethical impact of the work of the Holy Spirit in restoring men to the Heavenly Father. He did not deny the import of emotional response. It was indispensable to the love of God. Those heart-felt feelings, however, must be grounded in the revealed word, sincerely embraced, and must be anchored to an unchangeable commitment.

Impact of the Great Awakenings on the Restoration Movement

Recognition is given by Robert Richardson, biographer of Alexander Campbell, by Mr. Campbell, and by other scholars as well, to the most noteworthy personalities associated with the Great Awakenings.

Benjamin Grosvenor had strong influence on Samuel Davies, Davies influenced Rice Haggard and Haggard influenced Barton Warren Stone, so that adherents of the Restoration Movement are content to be known only as "Christians" and their churches simply as "Christian Churches."

The *Harbinger* for 1836, in an article entitled "Elder Jones and the Baptist Apostacy," revealed much regarding the uniqueness of the teachings of John Glas:

Mr. John Glas had . . . imbibed the principles of independency, or the congregational plan of church government,
which led him to give up his ministry in the Church of Scotland, and by the publication of his valuable treatise, titled,
The Testimony of the King of Martyrs, concerning his
kingdom, he poured a flood of light throughout the regions
of Caledonia, the effects of which soon became manifest
(1836:123).

Mr. Campbell acknowledged his debt to Archibald
McLean who had borrowed liberally from John Glas and
others (1835:304). Regarding the nature of faith he agreed
with Sandeman, McLean and Fuller (Longan 1889:67). In
the debate generated by Robert Sandeman in his *Letters to
Theron and Aspasio,* Campbell was convinced that Sandeman handled himself as a giant among dwarfs (*Christian
Baptist* 1825:228).

Robert Richardson, having in mind the Haldane brothers,
spoke of the great movement of which they were a part
"as the first phase of that religious reformation which he
(Alexander Campbell) subsequently carried out . . . to its
ultimate issues" (Richardson 1868:Vol. I,149). Campbell
himself acknowledged the influences of the Haldanes as
"the first streaks of light — the first dawning of the day"
that helped him formulate his own understanding of the
Bible (*Millennial Harbinger* 1843:173-177; 201-204). J. D.
Murch noted that the Haldane brothers emphasized "the
authenticity and inspiration of the Holy Scripture," and
he also recorded the decision of the Haldanes in rejecting
extra-congregational church government, that Christ was
the sole head of the church and that the government of
each congregation should be vested in a plurality of elders.

He observed the importance of the Haldanes having abandoned infant baptism and their decision that only immersion of believers was supported by Scriptures, and he recounted that they introduced the keeping of the Lord's Supper each Lord's Day (Murch 1962:17). W. E. Garrison concluded that chief among the causes of Alexander Campbell's dissatisfaction with the Seceder Presbyterians were the influences of Robert and James Haldane and Greville Ewing (Garrison 1931:80, 84).

In several issues of the *Millennial Harbinger* the views of John Wesley with regard to baptism were favorably acknowledged (1830, Extra:50, 1834:601; 1841:140).

Timothy Dwight, "the greatest name in America," was quoted in detail by Alexander Campbell with regards to the preposition "into" as it applied to baptism.

> All persons are baptized, not in, but into the name of the Father and of the Son, and of the Holy Spirit; that is, they are in this ordinance publically and solemnly introduced into the family, and entitled in a peculiar manner to the name of God (1831:239).

A commendable article on the famous preacher, Rowland Hill, "one of the most popular men of his day," who "drew the people toward him by an irresistable charm" was published in the *Millennial Harbinger* (1863:328-332).

The sermon of Bishop James Madison, preached before the Protestant Episcopal Church in Virginia in 1786, was also quoted in detail by Mr. Campbell in the *Christian Baptist*. Of that sermon Campbell wrote, "I have not met in any one extract so many of the sentiments advanced in this work; nor have I seen so unexceptional an exposition of my 'peculiar views' from any pen . . ." (*Christian Baptist* 1829:578).

The above by no means exhausts the list of those recognized great men who are associated with the Great Awakenings, but it does serve to establish that the founders of the Restoration Movement were acutely aware, not only of the men, but also of what they taught. The movement was undeniably influenced by them and the spiritual ferment they generated in both the First and Second Great Awakenings.

Appendix I

The Christian Mesenger, Vol. V., No. 7, July, 1831, entitled *Revivals of Religion* by Barton Warren Stone in pages 164-167.

Revivals of Religion, this term I use for want of a better. It fully expresses my understanding of the subject; and so commonly is it used to express the same idea, that it needs no definition. Philologists may object to the propriety of the term; but philology must sometimes yield to general use. While I hear daily of the great revivals in many parts of the east, my mind with a mournful pleasure reverts to the great revival of the west 30 years ago, and which continued for several years, and spread far and wide. To give a full history of it would be impossible. Often I have gazed with inexpressible emotions at the gathering crowds hurrying to the place of worship. All clothed with solemnity — many wetting their paths with tears — and thousands anxious to find the way of life — many sunk under the burden of sin, and little groups around pointing to them the hope of Israel, and uniting their solemn prayers for their salvation. Many praising God alone for delivering grace, and cheerfully uniting with the church of God. Thousands silently hanging on the lips of the preacher, who in the warm, loving spirit of his Lord, was ministering to them the word of reconciliation. I then saw, and yet acknowledge some imperfection, some eccentricities or aberrations from what I thought right, among the vast multitudes assembled. But I remembered they were but men, and that I could not reasonably expect to find perfection in such multitudes of imperfect beings. The good so far exceeded the evil, the latter almost disappeared. I saw the religion of Jesus more clearly exhibited in the lives of Christians then, than I had ever seen before or since to the same extent. The preachers were revived. I saw them filled with the Holy Spirit of their Lord addressing the multitudes, not in iceberg style, nor according to the studied rules of rhetoric and oratory; but in the language and spirit of heaven. Impressed with the worth of souls — of unconverted souls, exposed to everlasting punishment — feeling their awful responsibility to God; and feeling the force of divine truth, and the power of religion, in their own souls, they spoke with earnestness, as dying men to dying men. They regarded not the censure, nor the hard speeches of opposers — they might be called enthusiasts and represented as mad, and beside themselves. — This did not move them, unless to pity, to tears and prayers for their opposers. Through many difficulties, they labored night and day, privately and publicly, from house to house, from neighborhood to neighborhood, preaching the word of salvation to all, not for filthy lucre, but of a ready mind; they labored to save souls, and to establish them in the faith and hope of the gospel, — they, feeling the spirit of love, peace and union, endeavored to promote and culti-vate these essentials of religion, wherever they could.

I saw the congregations revived. The saints of every name mingling together, and together offering their sacri-fices of prayer and praise in the fire of love to their common Father and Redeemer, and together surrounding the table of their Lord. How affecting! to see parents then weeping over their unconverted children, and praying fervently for them — to see brothers and sisters engaged in the same work for their brothers and sisters — neighbor for neighbor — friends for their friends and enemies. All, old and young, even small children engaged in the same work, not only at the place of worship, but at home and abroad. Religion was their great work, and employed and filled up their happy months and years. Out of the abundance of their hearts they spoke often one to another on the subject of religion; controverted notions were not the themes of their conversation, but the soul-cheering doctrine of heaven, and its divine effects, as experienced by themselves and others. Here was unity indeed—not in opinions, but in spirit.

I saw sinners everywhere, of every age and sex, rich and poor, bond and free, old and young, weeping, praying, and converting to God—I saw enemies become friends, and sweetly united in the bonds of love—I saw brotherly kindness, meekness, gentleness, obedience, all the divine graces, growing and abounding among the saints of God. The Bible was read with intense desire to find the truth. This, this I call a revival. This I call the work of God.

Philosophers, dogmatists, and formalists, who were for measuring religion according to their own rule, were generally opposers of this revival. Their opposition appeared portentous of evil, but past harmlessly over as a threatening, empty cloud. The great obstruction to this revival was the spirit of sectarianism, which like a restless demon, infected and destroyed the glorious work, wherever it came. Never can this spirit, and the spirit of Christ amalgamate. As much opposed as darkness and light—as fire and water are they.

Shall we oppose revivals because we discover in them much enthusiasm, mismanagement, and unscriptural means employed by those engaged in them? If we do, we may also oppose every good, not perfect, or to which is attached any imperfection. The imperfection should be opposed, but in the meekness and gentleness of Christ; but great care should be taken that while rooting out the tares, we do not root out the wheat.

388

Shall we oppose a revival, because we think the conductors of it are ignorant of what we may deem the most important doctrine of the gospel? If this be our privilege, it is also the privilege of all; every party will reject of course every revival not their own. If genuine religion be the fruit of such revivals, we dare not reject without incurring the divine displeasure.

I have read in an eastern paper of the character of the revivals in one section of that country. It states that Christians of all denominations lovingly united in worship, even in the breaking of bread at the Lord's table. In such a work I will rejoice. Yet I have my fears that the demon of partyism will trek and destroy it. Yet Christianity will prevail so far as to have enlisted under her banners many, who cannot and will not be drawn into the vortex of sectarianism, and who will remain free, and preach reformation to the sects in bondage.

Some reject revivals because they think we should always be revived. Will such reject religion, because they do not always feel that they love God with all their heart, and their neighbors as themselves? In other words, because they are not perfect. Do they always feel the same divine affections in the same degree? Have they always the same vivid perceptions of truth? Have they always the same fervid engagedness in the cause of God? If not, why object to revivals! The frames of devotion cannot be confined; they will break forth, as in Jeremiah's case; and their efforts are mighty in families, neighborhoods, and congregations, in destroying the kingdom of darkness, and in building up Zion. "Oh Lord! Let thy priests be clothed with salvation; and let thy saints shout for joy." Psalms 132:9.

Signed the Editor.

Appendix II

The Christian Messenger, Vol. VII, No. 7, July, 1833, pages 210-212, an article by Barton Warren Stone on *Revivals.*

We have seen many things called revivals — great revivals. We have seen congregations greatly excited — many crying aloud for mercy, and many praising God for delivering grace. We have seen this state of things continue but a short time, and then disappear for years. We have seen many of these converts soon dwindle, sicken and die, and become more hardened against the fear of God, than they were before — many of them becoming infidels, by thinking that all professors of religion are like themselves deluded by strong passion and imagination. Others of them cling to the church, held there, not by delight in God, his service, or his people, but from other reasons than such as are approved of God. Others, and lamentable to tell, the fewest number by far, manifest by their holy walk and conversation, that they are truly pious and accepted of God. All must acknowledge that some good results from such revivals; but all must acknowledge that great evil also rose out of them. Those, who under strong affections, believed they were born of God, and who made a public confession of faith, and fell from it, are of all people in the most pitiable situation, seldom do they ever after embrace religion — these by their example, discourage others, and fill their minds with prejudices against religion.

After a lapse of a few years, these scenes pass off forgotten, then another similar revival takes place, and similar events succeed — such revivals are periodical — once in a few years; but of an evanescent nature; like a flash of lightning. Indeed, the people are taught by public teachers, not to expect their continuance — by experience and observation they have found them to be of short duration.

The general sentiment has been that these revivals depend on the sovereign will of God, who at certain seasons pours out of his spirit on the people as the angel at certain times troubled the waters in the pool of Bethesda. This sentiment we think of dangerous tendency. It teaches that the means ordained for salvation are not always on the same efficacy — of no efficacy at all, till God by special, almighty power, makes them so. "The gospel is the power of God unto salvation to everyone that believeth." I ask, — is it the power of God to save the obedient believer today? Is it invariably his power every day to the believer! None will deny it. Now should I be taught that the gospel loses its power to save me, though I believe and obey it, until God by some nondescript operation makes it powerful to this effect, should I not view this means inadequate to the end, and wait in death for this operation? Should I not be disposed to neglect the means, believing they cannot benefit me, till they are made more powerful by the power of God? Should I reasonably feel guilty that I am carnal, lifeless, and dead, believing that the means ordained by God were able to meliorate my condition? This faith, and the legitimate fruit of it, appear evidently the reason, why true revivals of religion are so rare, or rather why they do not always continue.

Dare we say, that God does not will, and therefore does not continue revivals without ceasing? Dare we think that God is more willing at one time than at another to grant his favors, or give his Holy Spirit? Dare we impute the long, lifeless intervals between revivals to God's pleasure or will it should be so? Dare we impute to him the bondage, carnality and death experienced by his professed people —

and justify these people in this state, because he willed it should be so? But few, if any, would be thus daring.

When in heart we believe and obey the gospel, God gives us his holy, quickening spirit; he gives us salvation, and eternal life — in this spirit we feel a tender concern for sinners, and are led to plead with them, and pray for them. They see our good works, and from conviction are led to glorify God — they see the light of Zion, and flow to it — they see the union of Christians, and are by this means led to believing Jesus unto salvation and eternal life. God has ordained that the unbelieving world are to be saved by the means of this truth, shining in his church on earth. Signed B. W. Stone, Editor

Bibliography

ABBOT, B. A.
   1924 *The Disciples, An Interpretation.* St. Louis, The
      Bethany Press.

ANDREW, Edward Deming.
   1963 *The People Called Shakers.* New York, Dover
      Publications.

ANONYMOUS.
   1908 *Summary of the Customs of the Churches of Christ
      as Found in the New Testament.* Edinburgh, George
      Watterson and Sons.

ASBURY, Francis.
   1953 *The Journal and Letters of Francis Asbury,* ed. J.
      Manning Potts. Nashville, Abingdon.

BALLINGER, John.
   1925 *The National Library of Wales. A Bibliography
      of Robert Owen, the Socialist, 1771-1858.* London,
      Humphrey Milford.

BARRETT, J. Pressley.
   1908 *The Centennial of Religious Journalism.* Dayton,
      O., Christian Publishing Association.

BAXTER, William.
   1874 *Life of Elder Walter Scott.* Cincinnati, Bosworth,
      Chase and Hall.

BISHOP, Robert H.
   1824 *An Outline of the History of the Church in the
      State of Kentucky.* Lexington, Thomas T. Skillman.

BLAKEMORE, W. B.
   1963 The Challenge of Christian Unity. St. Louis, Beth-
      any Press.

BOST, George H.
   1942 *Samuel Davies.* (Unpublished Ph.D dissertation),
      Chicago, University of Chicago.

BROWN, John.
1852 *Remarks on Certain Statements by Alexander Haldane, Esq. in his Memoirs of Robert Haldane of Airthrey, and his Brother, James A. Haldane.* Edinburgh, William Oliphant and Sons.

BROWN, John Thomas.
1904 *Churches of Christ: A Historical Bibliographical and Pictorial History of the Churches of Christ in the United States, Australia, England and Canada.* Louisville, J. P. Morton and Company.

BUCKLEY, J. M.
1903 *A History of Methodists in the United States.* New York, Charles Scribner Sons.

BURNET, D. S.
1840 *Christian Age and Protestant Unionist.* Cincinnati, O.

BURNETT, John Franklin.
1921 *The Origin and Principles of the Christians.* Dayton, Christian Publishing Association.

BURR, Nelson R.
1961 *A Critical Bibliography of Religion in America.* Vol. 4, Princeton, Princeton University Press.

CAMERON, Richard M.
1961 Methodism and Society, Vol. 1, New York, Abingdon Press.

CAMPBELL, Alexander.
1823- *The Christian Baptist,* Bethany, Bethany College
1829 Press.

CAMPBELL, Alexander.
1823- *The Christian Baptist,* D. S. Burnet edition. St.
1829 Louis, Christian Publishing Company.

CAMPBELL, Alexander.
 The Millennial Harbinger, published monthly from 1831 through 1870. Bethany, Va.

CAMPBELL. A. and RICE, N. L.
 1844 *A Debate Between Rev. A. Campbell and Rev. N. L. Rice on the Action, Subject, Design and Administrator of Christian Baptism; Also on the Character of Spiritual Influence in Conversion and Sanctification, and on the Expediency and Tendency of Ecclesiastic Creeds as Terms of Union and Communion.* Lexington, Ky., A. T. Skillman and Sons.

CAMPBELL, Alexander.
 1861 Memoirs of Elder Thomas Campbell: Together with a Brief Memoir of Mrs. Jane Campbell. Cincinnati, H. S. Bosworth.

CAMPBELL, Alexander.
 1861 *Popular Lectures and Addresses.* Bethany, Va., Bethany College Press.

CAMPBELL, Alexander.
 1866 *The Christian System, in Reference to the Union of Christians, and a Restoration of Primitive Christianity.* Cincinnati, H. S. Bosworth.

CAMPBELL, John P.
 1805 *Strictures on Two Letters, Published by Barton W. Stone, entitled Atonement.* Lexington, Daniel Bradford.

CAMPBELL, John P.
 1811 The Pelagian Detected; or, A Review of Mr. Craighead's Letters, Addressed to the Public and the Author. Lexington, Thomas Skillman.

CAMPBELL, John P.
1812 *A Portrait of the Times, or, the Church's Duty.* Lexington, Thomas Skillman.

CAMPBELL, Selina H.
c.1882 *Home LIfe and Reminiscenses of Alexander Campbell.* St. Louis, John Burns, Publ.

CARUTHERS, E. W.
1842 *A Sketch of the Life and Character of the Reverend David Caldwell, D. D.* Greensborough, N. C., Swaim and Sherwood.

CAUBLE, Commodore Wesley.
1930 *Disciples of Christ in India.* Indianapolis, Meigs Publishing Company.

CHRISTIAN, John T.
1926 *A History of the Baptists of the United States.* Nashville, Sunday School Board of the Southern Baptist Convention.

CLARK, Thomas D.
1972 *Pleasant Hill in the Civil War.* Lexington, Pleasant Hill Press.

CLELAND, Thomas.
1822 *Letters to Barton W. Stone, Containing a Vindication Principally of the Doctrines of the Trinity, the Divinity and Atonement of the Savior, Against His Recent Attack, in the Second Edition of His Address.* Lexington, Thomas Skillman.

CLELAND, Thomas.
1825 *Unitarianism Unmasked; Its Anti-Christian Features Displayed; Its Infidel Tendency Exhibited; and Its Foundation Shewn to be Untenable; in a*

Reply to Mr. Barton W. Stone's Letters to the Reverend Dr. Blythe. Lexington, Thomas Skillman.

COOK, Richard B.
1886 *The Story of the Baptists.* New York, Willey Bros. & Company.

COREY, Stephen J.
1953 *Fifty Years of Attack and Controversy.* St. Louis, Christian Board of Publication.

COX, F. A.
1836 *The Baptists in America. New York.*

CRAIGHEAD, T. B.
1809 *Sermon on Regeneration, With an Apology and an Address to the Sinod of Kentucky: Together with an Appendix.* Lexington, William W. Worsley.

CRAMBLET, Wilbur H.
1971 The Christian Church in West Virginia. St. Louis, Bethany Press.

DALLIMORE, Arnold.
1971 *George Whitefield, the Life and Times of the Great Evangelist of the Eighteenth Century Revival.* Vol. 1, London, The Banner of Truth Trust.

DAVENPORT, F. M.
1905 *Primitive Traits in Religious Revivals.* New York, Macmillan.

DAVIDSON, Robert.
1847 *History of the Presbyterian Church in the State of Kentucky.* New York, Robert Carter.

DAVIES, Samuel.
1828 *Sermons on Important Subjects by the Late Reverend and Pious Samuel Davies, A.M., Some Time President of the College of New Jersey. To Which*

are Prefixed Memoirs and Character of the Author: And Two Sermons on Occasion of His Death, by the Rev. Drs. Gibbons and Finley. Fourth American Edition, Containing all Author's Sermons Ever Published. Vol. 1, New York, J. and J. Harper.

DAVIES, Rupert O.
   1863 *Methodism.* Middlesex, Penguin Books Ltd.

DAVIS, M. M.
   1913 *The Restoration Movements of the Nineteenth Century.* Cincinnati, The Standard Publishing Company.

DAVIS, M. M.
   1915 *How the Disciples Began and Grew.* Cincinnati, The Standard Publishing Company.

DE GROOT, Alfred Thomas, and DOWLING, Enos E.
   1933 *The Literature of the Disciples of Christ.* Advance Indiana, Hustler Print.

DE GROOT, Alfred T.
   1960 *The Restoration Principle.* St. Louis, The Bethany Press.

DE GROOT, Alfred Thomas.
   1965 *Disciple Thought: A History.* Fort Worth, Texas, Texas Christian University.

DOWLING, Enos E.
   1964 *The Restoration Movement.* Cincinnati, The Standard Publishing Company.

EDWARDS, Jonathan.
   1954 *The Works of Jonathan Edwards, v. 1 and 2.* Edinburgh, The Banner of Truth Trust.

FERRIER, Robert.
  1856 *Index to the Second Edition of Mr. John Glas's Works*. Perth, James Morison, Jun.
FORD, Harold W.
  1952 *A History of the Restoration Plea*. Oklahoma City, Semco Color Press.
FORSTER, Ada L.
  1953 *A History of the Christian Church and Church of Christ in Minnesota*. St. Louis, Christian Board of Publication.
FORTUNE, Alonzo Willard.
  1932 *The Disciples in Kentucky*. Lexington, The Convention of the Christian Churches in Kentucky.
FREESE, J. R.
  1852 *A History and Advocacy of the Christian Church*. Christian General Book Concern, Philadelphia.
GARRETT, Leroy
  1981 *The Stone-Campbell Movement, An Anecdotal History of Three Churches*. Joplin, Missouri, College Press Publishing Company.
GARRISON, J. H.
  1891 *The Old Faith Restated*. St. Louis, Christian Publishing Company.
GARRISON, J. H.
  1901 *The Reformation of the Nineteenth Century*. St. Louis, Christian Publishing Company.
GARRISON, J. H.
  1909 *The Story of a Century*. St. Louis, Christian Publishing Company.
GARRISON, Winfred E.
  1931 *Religion Follows the Frontier: A History of the Disciples of Christ*. New York, Harper and Brothers.

GARRISON, Winfred E.
1945 *An American Religious Movement.* St. Luis, Bethany Press.

GARRISON, Winfred E. and DE GROOT, Alfred T.
1948 *The Disciples of Christ, A History.* St. Louis, Christian Board of Publication.

GARRISON, Winfred E.
1964 Variations on a Theme. St. Louis, Bethany Press.

GATES, Errett.
1904 *The Early Relation and Separation of Baptist and Disciples.* Chicago, The Christian Century.

GATES, Errett.
1905 *The Story of the Churches: The Disciples of Christ.* New York, The Baker and Taylor Company.

GATES, Robert William.
1964 Samuel Davies to Barton W. Stone: A Study of Antecedents. Unpublished Thesis, Lexington, Ky., The College of the Bible.

GIBSON, Marywebb.
1942 *Shakerism in Kentucky Founded in America by Ann Lee.* Cynthiana, Kentucky, The Hobson Press.

(No author given)
1813 *An Account of the Life and Character of Mr. John Glass.* Edinburgh, D. Schaw and Son.

GLAS, John.
1728 *A Narrative of the Rise and Progress of the Controversy About the National Covenants.* Edinburgh, New College Library.

1730 The Speech of Mr. John Glas Before the Commission of the General Assembly, March 11, 1730. Edinburgh, James Davidson & Co. New College Library.

400

GLAS, John.
1730 *Remarks Upon the Memorial of the Synod of Angus Against Mr. Glas and the Sentence of the Commission Deposing Him From the Ministry.* Edinburgh, Mr. James Davidson & Co.

GLAS, John.
1743 *A Treatise on the Lord's Supper.* Edinburgh, J. Cochran and Company.

GLAS, John.
1743 *A View of the New Communion Office, Printed at London in 1718, Together with Some Thoughts Occasioned by Reading Mr. Johnson's Unbloody Sacrifice and Alter Unveiled.* Edinburgh, J. Cochran and Company.

GLAS, John.
1777 *The Testimony of the King of Martyrs Concerning His Kingdom; Jo. 18:36-37 Explained, and Illustrated in Scripture Light.* Edinburgh, William Coke.

GLAS, John.
1782 *The Works of Mr. John Glass, In Five Volumes.* Perth, R. Morrison & Sons.

GLAS, John.
1801 *Remarks on the Subject of Modern Religious Divisions in a Letter by a Later Minister of the Church of Scotland.* Edinburgh, H. Ingles.

GLAS, John and SANDEMAN, Robert.
1865 *Supplementary Volume of Letters and Other Documents.* Perth, Morison and Duncan: Robert Peat.

GLAS, John.
1887 *A Plea for Pure and Undefiled Religion.* Edinburgh, George Waterson and Sons, Printers.

GOODNIGHT, Cloyd, and STEVENSON, Dwight E.
  1949 *A Biography of Robert Richardson.* St. Louis, Christian Board of Publication.

GRAFTON, Thomas W.
  1899 *Men of Yesterday: A Series of Character Sketches of Prominent Men Among the Disciples of Christ.* St. Louis, The Christian Publishing Company.

GREENE, Nancy Lewis.
  1930 *Ye Olde Shaker Bells.* Lexington, Transylvania Printing Company.

GROSVENOR, Benjamin.
  1728 *An Essay on the Christian Name, its Origin, Import, Obligation, and Preference to all Party Names.* London, John Clark and Richard Clark.

HAGGARD, Rice, with a Preface by John W. Neth, Jr.
  1954 *An Address to the Different Religious Societies, on the Sacred Import of the Christian Name.* Nashville, The Disciples of Christ Historical Society.

HAILEY, Homer.
  1945 *Attitudes and Consequences in the Restoration Movement.* Los Angeles, Old Paths Book Club.

HALDANE, Alexander.
  1855 *The Lives of Robert Haldane of Airthey and of His Brother, James Alexander Haldane.* Edinbrugh, W. F. Kennedy.

HALDANE, J. A.
  1809 *Reasons of a Change of Sentiment and Practice on the Subject of Baptism.* Edinburgh, J. Ritchie.

HALDANE, J. A.
  1829 *Refutation of the Heretical Doctrine Promulgated by the Rev. Edward Irving Respecting the Person*

and Atonement of the Lord Jesus Christ. Edinburgh, William Oliphant.

HALDANE, J. A.
1843 *The Crown of Righteousness, The Substance of a Sermon Preached in the Tabernacle, on the Sabbath, 25th December, 1842.* Edinburgh, Thorton and Collie.

HALDANE, J. A.
1848 *An Exposition of the Epistle to the Galatians Showing That the Present Diversions among Christians Originate in Binding the Ordinances of the old and new Covenants.* Edinburgh, William Whyte.

HALDANE, J. A.
1860 *Notes Intended for the Exposition of the Epistle to the Hebrews.* London, James Nisbet and Co.

HALDANE, J. A.
1862 *The Doctrine of the Atonement with Strictures on Recent Publications.* (3rd ed.) Edinburgh, William P. Kennedy.

HALDANE, J. A.
n.d. *To the Church Assembling for Worship in the Tabernacle.* Edinburgh, New College Library.

HALDANE, J. A.
n.d. *The Atonement.* Edinburgh, New College Library.

HALDANE, J. A.
n.d. *The Voluntary Question, Political, Not Religious.* A Letter to the Rev. Dr. John Brown. Edinburgh, William Whyte and Company.

HALDANE, J. A.

1878 *Four Treatises on the Following Subjects: (1) Mystery of Redemption, (2) Prayer of Moses, (3) Doctrine and Duty of Self Examination, (4) On the Faith of the Gospel. To which is added The Revelation of God's Righteousness.* London, George Milton.

(No author given).

n.d. Biography of Eminent Christians. Robert and James Haldane. London, The Religious Tract Society.

HALDANE, Robert.

1800 *An Address to the Public Concerning Political Opinions and Plans Lately Adopted to Promote Religion in Scotland.* Edinburgh, J. Ritchie.

HALDANE, Robert.

1809 Remarks on a Late Publication by Mr. Greville Ewing, Entitled, Facts and Documents. Edinburgh. New College Library.

HALDANE, Robert.

1809 Letter to Mr. Ewing, Respecting the Tabernacle at Glasgow. Edinburgh, New College Library.

HALDANE, Robert.

1812 Hypocracy Detected; In a Letter to the Late Firm of Haldane (Robert), Ewing (Greville) and Co. With a Preface Containing the Narrative of Mr. James Reid, a Missionary Sent by These Gentlemen to Upper Canada. Aberdeen. New College Library.

HALDANE, Robert.

1816 *The Evidence and Authority of Divine Revelation.* (2 v.) Edinburgh, New College Library.

HALDANE, Robert.

1824 *Letter from Robert Haldane, Esq. to M. J. J. Cheneviere, Pastor and Professor of Divinity at Geneva.*

Edinburgh, William Oliphant.

HALDANE, Robert.

1825 Review of the Conduct of the Directors of the British and Foreign Bible Society, Relative to the Apocrypha, and to Their Administration on the Continent. With an Answer to the Rev. C. Simeon, and Observations on the Cambridge Remarks. Edinburgh, New College Library.

HALDANE, Robert.

1827 *Authenticity and Inspiration of the Holy Scriptures Considered; In Opposition to the Erroneous Opinions that are Circulated on the Subject.* Edinburgh, John Lindsay and Company.

HALDANE, Robert.

1828 Exposure of the Rev. Henry Grey's Personal Misrepresentation, Doctrinal Heresies and Important Misstatements, Respecting the Bible Society, as Contained in the Letters of Anglicans. Edinburgh, New College Library.

HALDANE, Robert.

1828 *Exposure of the Edinburgh Corresponding Board.* Edinburgh, New College Library.

HALDANE, Robert.

1828 *Answer to the Rev. Grey's Reply to Mr. Haldane's Exposure of His Personal Misrepresentations, Doctrinal Heresies and Important Misstatements Respecting the Bible Society as Contained in the Letters of Anglicanus.* Edinburgh, William Whyte and Co.

HALDANE, Robert.

1829 A Letter to the Editor of the Edinburgh Christian

Instructor; Containing Strictures on Warburton, Lardner, Paley, Campbell and MacKnight. Edinburgh. In New College Library.

HALDANE, Robert.

1829 *Review of the Sixteenth Annual Report of the Glasgow Auxiliary Bible Society.* Edinburgh. Found in New College Library.

HALDANE, Robert.

1830 View of the Report of the Glasgow Bible Society. Edinburgh. In New College Library.

HALDANE, Robert.

1830 Review of the Speeches of Drs. Dick and Wardlow at the Last Meeting of the Glasgow Bible Society. Edinburgh, New College Library.

HALDANE, Robert.

1832 The Books of the Old Testament and New Testament Proved to be Cannonical, and Their Verbal Inspiration Maintained and Established, with an Account of the Introduction and Character of the Apocrypha. Edinburgh, New College Library.

HALDANE, Robert.

1832 *Review of the Rev. John Scott's Apology for the Proceedings of the Committee of the British and Foreign Bible Society, in which the Object of a Bible Society, and the Duty of Prayer, and the Exclusion of Socinians are Considered.* Edinburgh, William Whyte and Co.

HALDANE, Robert.

1833 Letter to the Lord Bishop of Salisbury, Occasioned by the Pamphlet Addressed to His Lordship by the Rev. S. C. Wild "On the Bible Society Question in its Principle and Detail." Edinburgh, New College Library.

HALDANE, Robert.
1833 Mr. John Joseph Gurney's Defence of Union with Socinians in the British and Foreign Bible Society, and of the Omission of Prayer by that Society, Proved to be Untenable. Edinburgh, New College Library.

HALDANE, Robert.
1836 Letter to the Rev. Dr. Morison, Editor of The Evangelical Magazine, Respecting the commentary of Professor Stuart, On the Epistle of Romans. London. Edinburgh, New College Library.

HALDANE, Robert.
1838 For the Consideration of the Ministers of the Church of Scotland. Remarks on Dr. Tholuck's Exposition of St. Paul's Epistle to the Romans, Translated by one of Themselves. Edinburgh, New College Library.

HALDANE, Robert.
1838 Further Considerations for the Ministers of the Church of Scotland. Occasioned by the Rev. Mr. Menzies Apology for Dr. Tholuck's Perversions of the Word of God, and His Attack on Some of the Most Important Scriptural Doctrines. Edinburgh. In New College Library.

HALDANE, Robert.
1839 *The Evidence And Authority of Divine Revelation, Being a View of the Testimony of the Law and of the Prophets, to the Messiah with the Subsequent Testimonies.* (3rd ed.) (2 v.) London, Hamilton Adams, and Co.

HALDANE, Robert.
1845 *The Books of the Old and New Testaments Proved to be Canonical, and Their Verbal Inspiration*

Maintained and Established; With an Account of the Introduction and Character of the Apocrypha. (5th ed.) Edinburgh, William Whyte and Co.

HALDANE, Robert.
1960 *Exposition of the Epistle to the Romans.* London, The Banner of Truth Trust.

HALEY, J. J.
1914 *Makers and Molders of the Reformation Movement.* St. Louis, Christian Board of Publication.

HALL, Colby D.
1953 *Texas Disciples.* Fort Worth, Texas Christian University Press.

HALL, Colby D.
1957 *Rice Haggard, the American Evangelist Who Revived the Name Christian.* Fort Worth, T.C.U. Press.

HALL, Colby D.
1954 Article entitled, "Barton W. Stone and the Name 'Christian.'" St. Louis, MO., The Christian Board of Publication.

HANNA, William Herbert.
1935 *Thomas Campbell, Seceder and Christian Union Advocate.* Cincinnati, Standard Publishing.

HARMON, M. F.
1929 *A History of the Christian Churches in Mississippi.* Louisville, KY., Connors & Ridsdale.

HARRELL, David Edwin.
1966 *Quest for a Christian America.* Nashville, The Disciples of Christ Historical Society.

HAYDEN, A. S.
1875 *Early History of the Disciples in the Western Reserve, Ohio.* Cincinnati, Chase & Hall, Publishers.

HAYDEN, Roger, (ed.)
  1974 *The Records of a Church of Christ in Bristol, 1640-1687*. Gateshead, Northumberland Press, Ltd.

HAYNES, Nathaniel S.
  1915 *History of the Disciples of Christ in Illinois*. Cincinnati, The Standard Publishing Company.

HAYS, George P.
  1892 *Presbyterians*. New York, J. A. Hill.

HODGE, Frederick Arthur.
  1905 *The Plea of the Pioneers in Virginia*. Richmond, Everett Waddey Company.

HORNSBY, John T.
  1936 *John Glas: A Study in the Origins, Development, And Influence of the Glasite Movement*. An unpublished doctoral dissertation, Edinburgh, The University of Edinburgh.

HUDSON, John Allen.
  1948 *The Church in Great Britain*. Rosemead, CA., The Old Paths Book Club.

HUMBERT, Royal.
  1961 *Compend of Alexander Campbell's Theology*. St. Louis, Bethany Press.

HUMBLE, Bill J.
  1952 *Campbell and Controversy*. Rosemead, CA., Old Paths Book Club.

HUTTON, Daniel M.
  1936 *Old Shakertown and the Shakers, a Brief History of Rise of the United Society of Believers in Christ's Second Coming, the Establishment of the Pleasant Hill Colony, Their Beliefs, Customs and Pathetic End*. Harrodsburg, KY., Harrodsburg Herald Press.

HYDE, A. B.
1888 *Methodism.* Springfield, Mass.

JENNINGS, Obadiah.
1832 *Debate on Campbellism; Held in Nashville, Tennessee, in Which the Principles of Alexander Campbell Are Confuted, And His Conduct Examined.* Pittsburg, D. and M. Maclean.

JENNINGS, Walter Wilson.
1919 *Origin and Early History of the Disciples of Christ.* Cincinnati, The Standard Publishing Company.

JETER, Jeremiah B.
1858 *Campbellism Examined.* New York, Sheldon, Blakeman and Co.

JONES, A. B., *et. al.*
1879 A Symposium on the Holy Spirit. St. Louis, John Burns Publ.

KNIGHT, Edgar Wallace.
1922 *Public Education in the South.* New York, Ginn & Company.

KNIGHT, Edgar Wallace.
1922 *Public School Education in North Carolina.* New York, Houghton Mifflin.

KONKLE, Burton Alva.
1922 *John Motley Morehead and the Development of North Carolina.* Philadelphia, William J. Campbell.

LANDIS, Robert W.
1844 *Rabbah Taken: or the Theological System of Rev. Alexander Campbell, Examined and Refuted.* Cincinnati, William H. Moore and Co.

410

LARD, Moses E.
1955 *A Review of Rev. J. B. Jeter's Book Entitled Camp-bellism Examined.* Rosemead, CA., Reproduced by the Old Paths Book Club.

LATOURETTE, Kenneth Scott
1964 *A History of Christianity.* New York, Harper and Row.

LATOURETTE, Kenneth Scott.
1971 *A History of the Expansion of Christianity; Vol. 3, Three Centuries of Advance.* Grand Rapids, Zondervan.

LATOURETTE, Kenneth Scott.
1971 *A History of the Expansion of Christianity; Vol. 4, The Great Century: Europe and United States.* Grand Rapids, Zondervan.

LLOYD-JONES, D. Martyn.
n.d. "Sandemanianism," found in "Profitable for Doctrine and Reproof" from The Evangelical Magazine, Providence House, 3 Speke Road, Battersea, S. W. 11.

LLOYD-JONES, D Martyn.
1972 *Exposition of Chapter 6, The New Man. Romans.* London, The Banner of Trust.

LLOYD-JONES D. M.
n.d. Article entitled "Summing Up," from the pamphlet, "Press Towards the Mark," from The Evangelical Magazine. Chiswick, W 4, 22 Grove Park Road.

LONGAN, George W.
1889 *Origin of the Disciples of Christ.* St. Louis, Christian Publishing Company.

MAC LEOD, John.
1943 *Scottish Theology in Relation to Church History*

Since the Reformation. Edinburgh, Free Church of
Scotland.

MAC CLENNY, W. E.

1950 *The Life of James O'Kelly, and the Early History
of the Christian Church in the South.* Indianapolis,
Religious Book Service.

MADISON, James.

1786 *A Sermon Preached Before the Convention of the
Protestant Episcopal Church in the State of Virginia.*
Richmond, VA., Thomas Nicholson.

MARSHALL, Robert, and THOMPSON, John.

1811 *A Brief Historical Account of the New Light
Church.* Cincinnati, J. Carpenter and Co.

MATTHES, James M.

1859 *Works of Elder B. W. Stone.* Cincinnati, Moore,
Wistach, Keys, and Co.

MCCALLA, W. L.

1828 *A Discussion of Christian Baptism as to its Subject, its Mode, its History, and its Effects Upon
Civil and Religous Society. In opposition to the
Views of Alexander Campbell, as Expressed in a
Seven Day's Debate with the Author, at Washington, KY., October, 1823, and His Spurious Publication of That Debate and of a Previous One of
Two Days with the Rev. John Walker of Ohio,
and in Opposition to the Views of the Celebrated
Mr. Robinson, and Other Baptist Authors.* (Vol.
1) Philadelphia, George M'Laughlin.

MCCALLA, W. L., and CAMPBELL, Alexander.

1842 *A Public Debate on Christian Baptism.* London,
Simpkin and Marshall, Stationers' Hall Court.

MC ALLISTER, Lester G.
  1954 *Thomas Campbell: Man of the Book.* St. Louis, Bethany Press.

MC ALLISTER, Lester G., and TUCKER, William E.
  1975 *Journey in Faith.* St. Louis, Bethany Press.

MC GAVRAN, Donald A.
  1970 *Understanding Church Growth.* Grand Rapids, Eerdmans.

MC GREADY, James.
  1831 *The Posthumous Works of James McGready.* Compiled by James Smith, Louisville, W. W. Worsley.

MC KERROW, John.
  1854 *History of the Secession Church.* Edinburgh and London, A. Fullerton and Co.

MC LEAN, Archibald.
  c. 1908 *Alexander Campbell as a Preacher.* New York, Fleming H. Revell Co.

MC LEAN, Archibald.
  1909 *Disciples of Christ: One Hundredth Anniversary.* Cincinnati, American Christian Missionary Society.

MC LEAN, Ralph.
  1975 *Directory of the Ministry, A Yearbook of Christian Churches and Churches of Christ.* Springfield, IL.

M'NEMAR, Richard.
  1808 *The Kentucky Revival, or a Short History of the Late Extraordinary Out-Pouring of the Spirit of God, in the Western States of America, Agreeably to Scripture — Promises, and Prophecies Concerning the Latter Day: With a Brief Account of the*

413

Entrance and Progress of What the World Call Shakerism, Among the Subjects of the Late Revival in Ohio and Kentucky. Cincinnati, Art Guild Reprints.

M'NEMAR, Richard.
  1846 *The Kentucky Revival, or a Short History of the Late Extraordinary Out-Pouring of the Spirit of God, in the Western States of America, Agreeably to Scripture — Promises, and Prophecies Concerning the Latter Day: With a Brief Account of the Entrance and Progress of What the World Call Shakerism, Among the Subjects of the Late Revival in Ohio and Kentucky.* New York, Edward O. Jenkins.

MERRIAM - WEBSTER.
  1965 *Webster's New Collegiate Dictionary.* Springfield, Mass., G. & C. Merriam Co.

MITCHELL, Nathan J.
  1877 *Reminiscences and Incidents in the Life and Travels of a Pioneer Preacher of the "Ancient" Gospel; With a Few Characteristic Discourses.* Cincinnati, Chase & Hall. Publishers.

MOORE, William Thomas.
  1909 *A Comprehensive History of the Disciples of Christ.* New York, Fleming H. Revell Company.

MORRELL, Milo True.
  1912 *A History of the Christian Denomination in America.* Dayton, Ohio, The Christian Publishing Company.

MOSELEY, J. Edward.
  1954 *Disciples of Christ in Georgia.* St. Louis, Bethany Press.

MURCH, James DeForest.
1962 *Christians Only.* Cincinnati, Standard Publishing.

NANCE, Elwood C.
1941 *Florida Christians.* Winter Park, Fla., The College Press.

NEAL, Julia.
1947 *By Their Fruits. The Story of Shakerism in South Union, Kentucky.* Chapel Hill, The University of North Carolina Press.

NEILL, Stephen.
1966 *A History of Christian Missions.* Baltimore, Penguin.

NETH, John W. Jr.
1951 *An Introduction to George Forrester.* (Unpublished Masters' Thesis, Butler University), Indianapolis, Ind.

NETH, John W.
1967 *Walter Scott Speaks.* Milligan College, Tenn., Emmanuel School of Religion.

NEWMAN, A. H.
1900 *American Church History. A History of the Baptist Churches in the United States.* New York, Charles Scribner's Sons.

NORTON, Herman A.
1971 *Tennessee Christians.* Nashville, Reed and Company.

NORWOOD, Frederick A.
1974 *The Story of American Methodism.* Nashville, Abingdon.

NYGAARD, Norman E.
1962 *Bishop on Horseback.* Grand Rapids, Zondervan.

OGILVIE, J. N.
   1897 *The Presbyterian Churches.* New York, Fleming
        H. Revell.

OLMSTEAD, Clifton E.
   1960 *History of Religion in the United States.* Engle-
        wood Cliffs, N. J., Prentice Hall.

ORR, J. Edwin.
   1965 *The Light of the Nations.* Grand Rapids, Eerdmans.

ORR, J. Edwin.
   1970 *Evangelical Awakenings in India.* New Delhi,
        Masihi Sahitya Sanatha.

ORR, J. Edwin
   1973 *The Flaming Tongue.* Chicago, Moody Press.

ORR, J. Edwin
   1974 *The Fervent Prayer.* Chicago, Moody Press.

ORR, J. Edwin.
   1975a *The Eager Feet, Evangelical Awakenings 1790-
        1830.* Chicago, Moody Press.

ORR, J. Edwin.
   1975b Paper entitled *"Definition and Discussion,"* pre-
        pared for Oxford, England Reading and Research;
        summer, 1975.

OWEN, Robert.
   1818 *A New View of Society: Or Essays on the Forma-
        tion of the Human Character Preparatory to the
        Development of a Plan for Gradually Ameliorating
        the Condition of Mankind.* London, Longman,
        Hurst, Rees, Orme and Brown.

OWEN, Robert.
   1825 *An Address Delivered to the Inhabitants of New*

Lanark, on the First of January, 1816, at the Opening of the Institution Established for the Formation of Character. (From the 4th London Edition, Cincinnati, S. J. Browne).

OWEN, Robert.
1841 *A Development of the Principles and Plans on Which to Establish Self-Supporting Home Colonies as a Most Secure and Profitable Investment for Capital, and an Effectual Means Permanently to Remove the Causes of Ignorance, Poverty and Crime; and Most Materially to Benefit all Classes of Society; By Giving a Right Applicatoin to the Now Greatly Misdirected Powers of the Human Faculties, and of Physical and Moral Science.* London, The Home Colonization Society.

OWEN, Robert, and CAMPBELL, Alexander.
1852 *The Evidences of Christianity; A Debate.* Cincinnati, Jethro Jackson.

PATILLO, Henry.
1788 *Sermons, Etc.,* Wilmington, James Adams.

PETERS, George L.
1937 *The Disciples of Christ in Missouri.* Canton, The Centennial Commission.

PHILLIPS, William.
1860 *Campbellism Exposed; or Strictures on the Peculiar Tenents of Alexander Campbell.* Cincinnati, Swormstedt & Poe.

PLUMLEY, Gardiner Spring.
1874 *The Presbyterian Church Throughout the World.* New York, DeWitt C. Lent and Co.

417

POWER, Frederick D.
   1898 *Sketches of Our Pioneers.* New York, Fleming H. Revell Company.

PURVIANCE, David.
   1848 *The Biography of Elder David Purviance Written by Himself.* Compiled by Levi Purviance, Dayton, B. F. and G. W. Ells.

QUALBEN, Lars P.
   1942 *A History of the Christian Church.* New York, Thomas Nelson and Sons.

REED, R. C.
   1905 *History of the Presbyterian Churches of the World.* Philadelphia, Westminster.

RICHARDSON, Robert.
   1868 *Memoirs of Alexander Campbell. 2 Vol.* Philadelphia, J. B. Lippincott & Co.

RODEFER, C. M., Chair.
   1928 *Survey of Service.* St. Louis, Christian Board of Publication.

ROGERS, William.
   1847 *The Cane Ridge Meeting House.* Cincinnati, The Standard Publishing Company.

ROGERS, John.
   1861 *The Biography of Elder J. T. Johnson.* Cincinnati, (Published by the Author).

ROSS, Bob L.
   1973 *Campbellism: Its History and Heresies.* Pasadena, Texas, Pilgrim Publ.

ROWE, John F.
   1894 *A History of Reformatory Movements.* Cincinnati, John F. Rowe.

SANDEMAN, Robert.
   1763 *An Essay on Preaching. Lately Wrote in Answer
        to the Request of a Young Minister.* Edinburgh,
        A. Donaldson, Murray and Cochran.

SANDEMAN, Robert.
   1819 Letter from Mr. Robert Sandeman to Mrs. Jeffrey
        in England. Edinburgh, J. Schaw.

SCHUTTENHELM, Ernest W.
   1942 *Inventory of the Church Archives of Wisconsin;
        Disciples of Christ.* Madison, Wis., The Wisconsin
        Historical Records Survey.

SCOTT, Walter
   1836 *The Gospel Restored, A Discourse of the True
        Gospel of Jesus Christ.* Cincinnati, O. H. Donagle.

SCOTT, Walter.
   n.d. *The Messiahship or Great Demonstration, Written
        for the Union of Christians on Christian Principles,
        as Plead for in the Current Reformation.* Kansas
        City, Reproduced by the Old Paths Book Club.

SCOTT, Walter.
   1852 *To Themelion, The Union of Christians on Chris-
        tian Principles.* Cincinnati, C. A. Morgan and Co.

SHAW, Henry K.
   1952 *Buckeye Disciples: A History of the Disciples
        of Christ in Ohio.* St. Louis, Christian Board of
        Publication.

SHEPHERD, J. W.
   1929 *The Church, The Falling Away, and the Restora-
        tion.* Cincinnati, F. L. Rowe, Publisher.

419

SHORT, Howard E.
1951 *Doctrine and Thought of the Disciples of Christ.* St. Louis, Christian Board of Publication.

SMITH, Benjamin Lyon.
1930 *Alexander Campbell.* St. Louis, Bethany.

SMITH, Elias
1840 *The Life, Conversion, Preaching, Travels and Sufferings of Elias Smith.* Boston, Sold by himself.

SMITH, Fred W.
1964 Article entitled, "Earliest American Expression of Restoration." Cincinnati, Ohio, *The Restoration Herald.*

SMITH, James.
1835 *History of the Christian Church, Including a History of the Cumberland Presbyterian Church.*

SPENCER, Claude Elbert.
1946 *An Author Catalogue of Disciples of Christ and Related Religious Groups.* Canton, MO., Disciples of Christ Historical Society.

SPENCER, J. H.
1886 *A History of the Kentucky Baptists.* (2 v.) Cincinnati, Spencer.

STEVENS, Abel.
1878 *The History of the Religious Movement of the Eighteenth Century, called Methodism.* (3 vol.) London, Wesleyan Conference Office.

STEVENSON, Dwight E.
1946 *Walter Scott, Voice of the Golden Oracle.* St. Louis, Christian Board of Publication.

STONE, Barton W., and Presbytery of Springfield.
1804 *An Apology for Renouncing the Jurisdiction of the Synod of Kentucky.* Lexington, Joseph Charless.

STONE, Barton W.
1805 *Atonement, the Substance of Two Letters Written to a Friend.* Lexington, Joseph Charless.

STONE, Barton W.
1805 *A Reply to John P. Campbell's Strictures on Atonement.* Lexington, Joseph Charless.

STONE, Barton W.
1821 *An Address To The Christian Churches.* Lexington, I. T. Cavins and Co.

STONE, Barton Warren.
1847 *The Biography of Eld. Barton Warren Stone, Written by Himself: With Additions and Reflections by Elder John Rogers.* Cincinnati, J. A. and U. P. James.

STONE, Barton W.
1859 *Works of Elder B. W. Stone.* Compiled by James Madison Mathes, Cincinnati, Moore, Wilstack, Keys.

STREATOR, A. L.
1885 *The Disciples of Christ in Montana.* St. Paul, Minn., The Pioneer Press Company.

STRICKLAND, A. B.
1934 *The Great American Revival.* Cincinnati.

SWEET, William Warren.
1931 *Religion on the American Frontier; The Baptists.* New York, Henry Holt & Co.

SWEET, William Warren.
1936 *Religion on the American Frontier; The Presbyterians.* New York, Harper and Bros.

SWEET, William Warren.
1939 *Religion on the American Frontier; the Congregationalists.* Chicago, University of Chicago Press.

SWEET, William Warren.
1947 *Religion on the American Frontier; The Methodists.* Chicago, University of Chicago Press.

SWEET, William Warren.
1952 *Religion in the Development of American Culture: 1765-1840.* New York, Charles Scribner's Sons.

SWEET, William W.
1973 *The Story of Religion in America.* Grand Rapids, Baker.

THOMAS, David.
1802 *The Observer Trying the Great Reformation in this State, and Proving it to Have Been Originally a Work of Divine Power. With A Survey of Several Objections to the Contrary, as Being Chiefly Comprised of Mr. Renkin's Review of the Noted Revival, Lately Published.* Lexington, John Bradford.

THOMPSON, Robert Ellis.
1895 *The American Church History Series: A History of the Presbyterian Churches in the United States.* (vol. 6) New York, The Christian Literature Co.

TIPPLE, Ezra S.
1916 *Francis Asbury: The Prophet of the Long Road.* New York, The Methodist Book Concern.

TORBET, Robert G.
1950 *A History of the Baptists.* Philadelphia, The Judson Press.

TOWNSEND, W. J., WORKMAN, H. B., and EAYRS, George.
  1909 *A History of Methodism.* (2 v.) London, Hodder and Stoughton.
TYLER, Alice Felt.
  1962 *Freedom's Ferment.* New York, Harper Torchbooks, Harper & Row.
TYLER, B. B., THOMAS, A. C., THOMAS, R. H., BERGER, D., SPRENG, S. P., and JACKSON, Samuel Macauley.
  1894 *American Church History: A History of the Disciples of Christ, The Society of Friends, The United Brethren in Christ and the Evangelical Association.* New York, The Christian Literature Co.
VEDDER, Henry C.
  1897 *A Short History of the Baptists.* Philadelphia, American Baptist Publication Society.
WALKER, Dean E.
  1935 *Adventuring For Christian Unity.* Birmingham, Eng., The Berean Press.
WALKER, Granville T.
  c.1954 *Preaching In the Thought of Alexander Campbell.* St. Louis, Bethany Press.
WALKER, John, and CAMPBELL, Alexander.
  1822 *Debate on Christian Baptism.* Pittsburgh, Eichbaum and Johnston.
WALKER, Williston.
  1947 *A History of the Christian Church.* New York, Charles Scribner and Sons.
WARE, Charles Crossfield.
  1927 *North Carolina Disciples of Christ.* St. Louis, Christian Board of Publication.

WARE, Charles Crossfield.
   1932 *Barton Warren Stone, Pathfinder of Christian Union.* St. Louis, Bethany Press.

WARE, Charles Crossfield.
   1954 Article entitled, "Critical Notes on the Newly Discovered Rice Haggard Pamphlet." Vol. 14, Nov. 1954. Nashville, Tenn., Disciples of Christ Historical Society.

WARE, Charles Crossfield.
   1967 *South Carolina Disciples of Christ: A History.* Charleston, S. C., Christian Churches of South Carolina.

WATKINS, W. T.
   1937 *Out of Aldersgate.* Nashville, Board of Missions, Methodist Episcopal Church.

WATTERS, A. C.
   1948 *History of the British Churches of Christ.* Birmingham, The Berean Press.

WELLS, Joseph William.
   1947 *History of Cumberland County, Kentucky.* Louisville, Standard Printing Company.

WELSHIMER, P. H.
   1935 *Concerning the Disciples.* Cincinnati, The Standard Publishing Company.

WERTENBAKER, Thomas Jefferson.
   1942 *The Old South.* New York, Scribner.

WEST, Earl Irvin.
   1950 *The Search for the Ancient Order.* Indianapolis, Religious Book Service.

WEST, William Garrett
1954 *Barton Warren Stone: Early American Advocate of Christian Unity.* Nashville, The Disciples of Christ Historical Society.

WHITEFIELD, George.
1965 *George Whitefield's Journals.* London, Banner of Truth.

WHITLEY, Oliver Read
1959 *The Trumpet Call of Reformation.* St. Louis, The Bethany Press.

WHITSITT, William H.
1891 *Origin of the Disciples of Christ.* Louisville Baptist Book Concern.

WILBURN, James R.
1969 *The Hazard of the Die: Tolbert Fanning and the Restoration Movement.* Austin, Texas, Sweet Publishing Company.

WILLIAMS, John Augustus.
1904 *Life of Elder John Smith with Some Account of the Rise and Progress of the Current Reformation.* Cincinnati, Standard Publishing Company.

YOUNG, Charles A.
1904 *Historical Documents Advocating Christian Union.* Chicago, The Christian Century Company.

YOUNG, M. Norval.
1949 *A History of Colleges Established and Controlled by Members of the Churches of Christ.* Kansas City, MO., The Old Paths Book CLub.

PERIODICALS

Christian Baptists, Buffalo and Bethany, VA, 1823-1830.

Christian Baptist, Seven Volumes in One. Revised by D. S. Burnet, Cincinnati, Bosworth, 1867.

The Christian Evangelist, St. Louis, 1881-.

The Christian Messenger, Georgetown, KY., Jacksonville, IL. 1826-37, 1839-45.

The Christian Paladium, Albany, New York.

Christian Preacher. 1836 - (Editors, D. S. Burnet with J. T. Johnson). (On microfilm) 1840.

The Christian Standard, Cincinnati, 1886-.

The Cincinnati Advertizer, 1829, Cincinnati, Ohio.

The Daily Cincinnati Gazette, 1829, Cincinnati, Ohio.

Discipliana, Nashville, (Published quarterly), 1940-.

The Evangelical Inquirer, Dayton, 1830.

The Evangelist, Cincinnati, Carthage, and Pittsburgh. 1832-1844.

The Kentucky Gazette, The Weekly Magazine Newspaper. 1843, Lexington, KY.

The Liberty Hall and Cincinnati Gazette, 1837, Cincinnati, Ohio.

Millennial Harbinger, Bethany, VA and Bethany, WV, 1830-1864 (continued to 1870 under Pendleton, Loos, et al).

The Pittsburg Murcury, Vol. 8, Jan. 1820.

The Restoration Herald, Cincinnati, Ohio, 1925.

CORRESPONDENCE

An Explication of That Proposition Contained in Mr. 1728 Glas's Answers to the Synod's Queries, A Congregation or Church of Jesus Christ, With its Presbytery, is in its Discipline Subject to no Jurisdiction Under Heaven. Edinburgh, New College Library.

A Continuation of Mr. Glas's Narrative Containing a True
1729 State of the Process Against Him, as it is in the
Extracts to be Laid Before the Assembly in May,
1729. Edinburgh, New College Library.

Reflections on an Epistolary Correspondence Between
1759 S. P. and R. S.. London, J. Ward at the King's
Arms, in Cornhill.

A Friend of the Ancient Protestant Doctrine. A Short
1769 View of, and Inquiry into the Glasite and New
Independent Scheme of Doctrine. Edinburgh, New
College Library.

An Epistolary Correspondence Between S. P. and R. S.
1809 (Samuel Pike and Robert Sandeman) Relating to
the Letters on Theron and Aspasio. Edinburgh,
D. Shaw and Son, Lawnmarket.

ANNUAL MINUTES

Minutes of the Redstone Baptist Association.
1804-Copy in the library of Lincoln Christian College,
1836 Lincoln, Illinois.

Index

McKinney, Collen: 302.
McLean, Archibald: 55, 135, 137, 158-159, 361, 383.
McNemar, Richard: 57-60, 64, 68-69, 79-80, 93-94.
Meachem, John: 68.
Meigs County, Ohio: 70.
Mennonite Church, The: 13, 18.
Meredity, Thomas G.: 310.
Merrill, J.: 240, 361-362.
Methodist Episcopal Church, The: 8-9, 13, 18, 20, 22-25, 29, 32, 43.
Miles, Barzillia H.: 289.
Millard, David: 304.
Millennial Harbinger, The: 214, 269, 280-281, 291, 300-301, 303-304, 308-309, 311-314, 316-317, 319, 321-323, 325, 327, 329, 333-339, 343, 345-350, 352-355, 357, 365, 367-368, 370-371, 373, 382, 384.
Mitchell, N. J.: 323.
Moore, W. T.: 55.
Moravian Church, The: 13, 18, 94.
Mormonism: 368.
Morris, David W.: 289.
Morrison, Mrs. Mary: 296-297.
Morton, William: 284.
Mulkey, John: 295.
Munro, Andrew: 109.
Murch, James DeForest: 5-6, 37, 48, 56-57, 71, 113, 195, 250, 362, 383.
Myers, A. E.: 351.

N

Name Christian, The: 72-77, 87, 92, 94, 98, 366.
Name Christian and the Name Disciples of Christ, The: 367.
Name, Disciples of Christ, The: 92.
National Intelligencer, The: 354.
Neth, John: 77.
New Brunswick Presbytery, The: 85-86.

New England Christian Churches, The: 36, 64.
New Lanark Mills: 254.
New Light Presbyterians, The: 24.
New York Times, The: 343.
Norvell, John: 76.

O

Observations on Church Government: 78.
Ogle, Mrs. Mary: 296.
O'Kelly, James: 1, 7, 28-33, 36-37, 41-42, 44, 65-66, 73, 75-76, 80, 82, 253, 274, 299-300.
Orange Presbytery, The: 42.
Orr, J. Edwin: 3-5, 20-21, 50, 182, 250, 305, 343, 347-348.
Osborne, Jacob: 240.
Owen, Robert: 254-263, 269.
Oxford University: 133.

P

Paine, Thomas: 14, 19.
Palmer, Henry D.: 289.
Paraner, E.: 287.
Patillo, Henry: 40, 42-44, 56, 61, 81-82, 87.
Pendleton, W. K.: 338, 372-373.
Philadelphia Confession of Faith: 299.
Pittsylvania County, Virginia: 37.
Port Tobacco, Maryland: 37.
Powell, J. T.: 317.
Preble County, Ohio: 70.
Presbyterian Churches, The: 9, 11, 20, 22, 61, 94.
Presbyterian Churches Become Christian Churches: 66.
Presbyterian Confession, The: 61.
Presbyterian Magazine, The: 346.
Presbytery of Dundee, The: 137, 145, 148.
Primitive Christian, The: 308.
Princeton University: 17, 86, 94.

Max Ward Randall
A Biographical Sketch

Max Ward Randall was born in 1917 at Readstown, Wisconsin where he attended grade and high school and where he was baptized into Jesus Christ. At the Minnesota Bible College he met and married Gladys Waller. He received his Bachelor of Arts degree in 1939.

In 1940 Max and Gladys began further studies at The Cincinnati Bible Seminary, where Gladys earned her Bachelor of Arts degree and where in 1942 and 1943 Max earned his M.A. and M. Div. degrees.

Before going to the missions field, the Randalls ministered to three congregations: at Lamberton, Minnesota; Waynesville, Ohio; and Redwood Falls, Minnesota.

In 1945 Mr. Randall shared with Dr. George Calvin Campbell, Tibbs and Mark Maxey in founding the College of the Scriptures in Louisville, Kentucky. In 1947 he and Mrs. Randall, with their family, decided to go to South Africa, but it was more than three years before they were allowed to enter. In the meantime, Mr. Randall served one year as Academic Dean of the College of the Scriptures.

The Randalls arrived in South Africa in late 1950, and for ten years Max served as the Superintendent of the South African Church of Christ Mission. Other missionaries soon joined the work, and the mission has grown throughout the years. In 1955, while giving oversight to the mission, Max assumed the responsibility for ministering to the European (White) Polo Road Church of Christ in Capetown, where he served for five years. Twelve men and women from Polo Road entered the ministry during that period, several of whom are still active in the Lord's service.

When Max and Gladys went to South Africa, they took an airplane with them. Max used his Stinson in new field survey, opening many new fields in Southern Rhodesia, and opening the door and getting firmly under way the first missions work of the American churches in Northern Rhodesia (now Zambia).

In 1963 Max shared in opening the country of Ghana for the Christian Church mission. In 1967 he travelled around the world sharing in the opening of Indonesia in the South Pacific.

In 1968 he did surveys in Malawi, where we now have a rapidly growing field. Max was back in the South Pacific in 1970 where he found additional opportunities for missions expansion in New Guinea that, in 1977, opened for the American Christian Churches. In 1971 he and Mrs. Randall toured Europe, spending six weeks with the churches in Poland, and found exciting new opportunities in Spain. In 1972 he returned to Africa to conduct additional surveys. In 1973 he and his wife travelled through the South Pacific, spending six weeks in New Zealand.

In the summer of 1974 Mr. and Mrs. Randall were official participants in the International Congress on World Evangelization in Lausanne, Switzerland. On the same trip they visited Spain once again and were also in Ireland and England. Also since 1974, Mr. Randall along with others, has been working to send American ministers to both Australia and New Zealand. In the summer of 1974 Max shared in a seminar on revival at Oxford University, and in the summer of 1975 he and Mrs. Randall were invited to return to Oxford University and Max presented a paper on the impact of revival within the Restoration Movement.

In 1966 Max was invited to become Professor of Missions at Lincoln Christian College and Seminary in Lincoln, Illinois. After earning an additional Master of Arts degree (in Missiology) at Fuller Theological Seminary in Pasadena, California, under Dr. Donald A. McGavran, he became a full-time professor at LCC where he still serves.

In 1964 the Minnesota Bible College conferred upon Mr. Randall the honorary Doctor of Divinity degree.

During the 1975-1976 academic year, Mr. Randall completed all resident requirements for his Doctor of Missiology degree at Fuller Theological Seminary. He completed his dissertation and received his Doctor's degree in 1979. Dr. Randall also does considerable writing, most of it on a missionary theme for a number of religious journals; and he is the author of several books, and he has shared in writing two other volumes. One, and likely two, significant new volumes from his pen will be published in 1983 and 1984.

During the Christmas holiday of 1976-1977, Mr. and Mrs. Randall travelled to Bangladesh to investigate the possibilities for opening a new missions field in that country. On that same journey, they spent time in Calcutta with a tribal brother from Northeast India, encouraging him in an exciting, fast growing new work in the Manipur district that continues to accelerate with hundreds of churches and thousands of members.

The Randalls travelled around the world in the summer of 1979, visiting many fields Mr. Randall has shared in opening, and in the summer of 1981 they were back in Australia once again.

Max Ward Randall is listed in *Who's Who in Religion* from 1975 to the present.

441

The Randalls have six children, three sons and three daughters, and sixteen grandchildren. Their three sons are ministers in Western Australia. Two of their three daughters are married to Bible College professors at the Cincinnati Bible College in Cincinnati, Ohio, and the third daughter, a fine Christian, is the manager of a prosperous travel agency, also in Cincinnati.

Mr. Randall, now retired, has been a popular speaker in churches, colleges and conferences all across America and in many parts of the world.